PEN

THE LIFE OF

BY P

THE LIFE OF
WILLIAM HAZLITT

BY

P. P. HOWE

WITH AN INTRODUCTION BY

FRANK SWINNERTON

A man in himself is always the
same, though he may not always
appear to be so.

Eloquence o the British Senate

PENGUIN BOOKS
IN ASSOCIATION WITH
HAMISH HAMILTON

FIRST PUBLISHED 1922
PUBLISHED IN PENGUIN BOOKS 1949

MADE AND PRINTED IN GREAT BRITAIN
FOR PENGUIN BOOKS LTD, HARMONDSWORTH, MIDDLESEX
BY HAZELL, WATSON AND VINEY, LTD
AYLESBURY AND LONDON

CONTENTS

INTRODUCTION

I

THE author of this book, Percival Presland Howe, was my closest friend for more than forty years. I met him first in 1901, when he attended University College School; and I can still see him as he was at that time, a reserved, handsome schoolboy, fair and quiet, with fine, rather heavy-lidded grey eyes and a ready smile. He used to come into the Bedford Street showroom of J. M. Dent & Co., publishers of the Temple Classics, where his brother Garfield and I worked, and spend a few minutes each morning with the new books before going on to Gower Street. He was then fourteen; I was sixteen; his brother was eighteen or nineteen. We were all three dabblers in amateur journalism, eager readers, and as different as possible in temperament and upbringing. I, although the son of refined and gifted parents, was untaught, very poor, the younger of only two children, and fatherless; the Howes belonged to a large, cultured, middle-class family, of which the father, a religious and most remarkable man, had his own business as a ship-broker, and to strong Liberalism and wide sympathy for all good causes added a love of letters and a real passion for the work of Blake and Browning.

Owing much, also, to their mother, and having one well-loved sister, the Howes were chiefly a family of boys. Arthur, the eldest, was already in his father's business, which he now controls; Garfield, my kind introducer to the family, was then and has been all his life devoted to book-publishing; P. P., the third son, averse from City life, planned to use his pen. Younger than he, Charles, a very talented artist, and Arnold, a quick, delightful boy of great business promise, were killed in the First World War, while Harold and Eric, who fought in and survived the War, have both achieved distinction, the one as headmaster for the last twenty years of Keswick School, the

7

other as a leading psychiatrist, E. Graham Howe. I had never before encountered such a large family or, I must say, such an intelligent family; and the freely expressed mutual candours of the brothers, which were in strong contrast to the more subtle comedy of my own small home, were impressive. P. P., I think, was the shyest member of the family.

In the next few years he, Garfield, and I went together with catholic but severe taste to the galleries of most of the London theatres. We also frequented various halls where we could hear Shaw, Chesterton, and Belloc lecture and debate; and at the week-ends we walked about the nearer countryside of Kent discussing whatever we had read and thought since our last meeting. Serious argument was sustained by Garfield, with myself as light skirmisher and coat-trailer; P. P. laughed a good deal and bided his time. His speciality was history, of which he knew much more than his companions. His brother's was a highly dogmatic rationalism which he called 'common sense' or 'mother wit.' I had no speciality, but an effervescent loquaciousness. So we made a happy, good-tempered trio; and P. P.'s silences were so far from empty that, when he presently felt able to engage in our debates, he showed that he had well learned the strengths and weaknesses of his adversaries. What he said was always witty and usually sagacious; he was listened to.

When he left school, and had confirmed his dislike of the City, he found a sub-editorial job in the publishing firm of Eveleigh Nash, more particularly in connection with the then recently launched *Nash's Magazine*. And at Nash's he met Martin Secker, a reader for the firm, who in 1910 started his own publishing business with a small cash capital and a genius for discovering young authors destined to become famous. The theatre was then having one of its periods of vigour. Shaw, Barrie, Galsworthy, and Granville Barker were in their heyday; Ibsen, Hauptmann, and Sudermann glowed in the West End; theatrical 'production' (chiefly by Granville Barker) had arrived; and P. P., writing regular criticism for a minor weekly Socialist periodical, contributed to Secker's earliest list a small, well-reviewed book about the Barker-Frohman Repertory Theatre of 1910 which made him, at the age of twenty-four, an accepted critic. He was not as dazzling as Montague, or as scathingly 'modern' as Gilbert Cannan; but his quiet, youthful knowledge of history, politics, and economics added exactitude to a graceful talent and were an augury of the future. His was not a creative mind; but he was sensitive, receptive, and honest, capable of such close application that he was born to be a scholar.

Both as boy and man, P. P. was in manner indolent and charming, full of a laughing humour of which the astringent quality was robbed of dryness by cordial, almost boyish fun. He was ironic rather than ebullient. But that was a part of his nature. He strolled; he did not run. Nobody ever played lawn tennis with more masterly languor, or used so many matches to relight a pipe that was always going out, or drawled more attractively to cover, perhaps, some lack of confidence in himself. The drawl was accentuated when he was not wholly at ease; it was least when he was absolutely confident of understanding. At such times he would become so allusive, such a dealer in ellipsis, that I sometimes wondered what he was talking about. I never cared to ask, so amusing were the allusiveness and the ellipses on their own account, and so flattering to the hearer; but in any case they entirely conquered his apparent slowness, which was a sign of disturbance, and were irresistible. He and I could and sometimes did talk all night, in peace and war; I abominably profuse, he alert, wary, quietly laughing, and without haste. He was a perfect companion. In a lifetime of exceptional friendships, I have never liked any man better.

P. P. followed *The Repertory Theatre* (1910) with a study of Synge in which enthusiasm led him to reproduce almost too exactly the rhythms and idioms of his subject. This book, however, forecast the authoritative work of later days, because it showed – for all who could read portents – a very young man's already-formed ability to give himself entirely to intensive study and interpretation. It was published in 1912, when he was twenty-six, and so was a small pamphlet recommending that books should be showered less wantonly upon the world than they are. The pamphlet – amusingly so in view of Hazlitt's famous attacks on the author of *An Essay on the Principle of Population* – was called *Malthus and the Publishing Trade*. In the year after were collected the essays P. P. had written about Pinero, Wilde, Barrie, Galsworthy, Hankin, and others under the title *Dramatic Portraits*, a book which demonstrated much increased maturity and pungency of judgement. This was the year of his happy marriage and removal to a small house on the Downs near Lewes, where he lived and read and wrote, first a short essay on *Criticism* (1914) and then, along with reviewing for *The Globe* and dramatic criticism for *The Outlook*, which took him to town once a week, a study of Bernard Shaw which I fear gave little pleasure to the Master, who, in an article, complained of 'Pretentious Pigmies'. It was at this time that P. P. first determined to write the life of Hazlitt.

But the War of 1914–18 stopped all his literary activity. It meant a long period of service in France, which was in every way so distasteful to P. P. that he afterwards spoke of himself as having been only half alive during the whole of it. He lost Charles, the artist brother who was probably his best companion and whom he missed for the rest of his life. He hated the blood and filth of the Western Front, and would never speak of it. And when the War was over he was desperate to get back to civilian life and to the work of his heart. But how was that to be managed? Fortunately his old friendship with Martin Secker produced an unexpected bonanza; for Secker, meaning, perhaps only a ruse of kindness, offered to apply for P. P.'s release as his partner. That was sensational news to P. P., who could have wished for nothing better. He pressed it; what had been half-serious was seen to be ideal; and the two were associated in business until circumstances produced catastrophe some time before the beginning of the Second World War.

There, then, was P. P., established in No. 5 John Street in

conditions which assured him of an income; and there, too, he could count upon all the time he needed for research, and a publisher for the biography when it was finished. He settled in Battersea, took over from me the post of dramatic critic for *Truth,* and was armed at all points for the last struggle with ambition. It answered every hope. He was happy, busy, and engrossed. Indeed, as I write, I remember those days with laughter; for P. P. gave himself completely to Hazlitt. We heard about Hazlitt at every meal. At every meeting, brief or long, there was no topic we could speak of on which Hazlitt had not already said the wisest word or made the most amusing quip. On current politics, criticism, wit, and character, Hazlitt had been prophetic. To me, who knew the range and felicity of that great writer, this was a credible and enchanting miracle; but to Secker, whose retrospective enthusiasm went no farther than the eighteen eighties, and who, of course, heard much more of Hazlitt than I did, Hazlitt seemed positively to dominate John Street as a monstrous invisible presence. Now I must not be misunderstood; P. P. was never ridiculous; he was never a bore. Nor was he wrong. Hazlitt is a writer who deals in first principles; and, as Wordsworth and Southey found to their great irritation, a writer who deals in first principles cannot be ignored. Moreover, P. P. was word perfect in the principles.

He lived in spirit with Hazlitt. The proof is to be found in this book. It is to be found in the precise and wonderful annotation of Hazlitt's text in the great Centenary Edition of his works which P. P. later edited. And if any reader will compare other men's biographies of Hazlitt and editing of Hazlitt with those of P. P., he will be filled with admiring gratitude to this modest scholar, who was so free from display or pedantry that he never obtruded his own personality, but sought only to record and elucidate for the benefit of those less learned than himself everything that might vex or perplex novice and expert alike. The result, whether offered in this biography or in the Centenary Edition, was obtained by years of devotion to Hazlitt's writing, endless research among Hazlitt's contemporaries and those earlier authors whom Hazlitt quoted with tenacious but inexact memory. No explorer less loving than P. P. could have done this work.

It brought him new friends, among whom I should put first the fine and wise Mrs Arnold Glover. And it did not prevent him from keeping a firm secondary eye upon contemporary literature, about which, as Secker's partner, it was his business to know. Then and afterwards, when he worked at the Bodley Head or in happy co-operation with Hamish Hamilton, by whom this new edition of the Life of Hazlitt is intended as a lasting tribute, he maintained close contact with living authors of all types. No detail of book production was alien to him. He was so much the publisher that, although he forgot nothing about them, he ceased in time to speak much of Hazlitt or the theatre. Instead, he took a detached, non-controversial view of the literary battlefield, lived in great happiness with his wife and four children at the elder boy's farm on the London side of Guildford; and during the Second World War travelled backwards and forwards between Horsley and London, deputizing for Hamish Hamilton (who was away on War service), fire-watching in London or the country, and despite every strain preserving a really beautiful equanimity.

But he was tired. Abstractedness began to show in his manner. Though his character was unchanged, he was a little more obviously grateful to those upon whose affectionate understanding he could rely. Moreover, as he began to be very ill, he was disquieted by his illness. What I had always thought a natural and endearing gift for extolling his own circumstances gave way to a slightly questioning optimism. The illness was diagnosed and treated. He did not get better. At last he was taken to hospital for 'observation'; an operation was performed on the lung; for many weeks he lay in bed, cheerful and seemingly unperturbed in spite of the candidly discussed gravity of his state; and I, at least thought the cure made progress. But that was not so. On the day of his death, although he had been in great pain, he talked as happily as ever, smoked his old pipe with relish, slept, and passed smiling from life on 19 March 1944, four months short of his fifty-eighth birthday.

II

What of the author to whom P. P. gave those years of his life? While Hazlitt lived he was libelled as 'pimpled', when in fact he was pale and clear-skinned. He was called 'miscreant', 'treacherous', a gin-drinker, a physical coward, a misanthrope, envious, jealous, gloomy, and a failure. After his death, when his books were out of print and the personal rancours of the Lake Poets were half forgotten, Stevenson thought of writing his life, but gave up the project after reading and being disgusted by *Liber Amoris*. Even when, in the fulness of time, he was made the subject of a volume in the English Men of Letters Series, Augustus Birrell perpetuated the animosities, and left Hazlitt stained by scandal and traduced by misinterpretation. Is the more favourable view of his character which is held today, largely as a result of P. P.'s labour, any more to be relied on than the old hatred?

I think it is. We have other testimonies, and we can assess the value of the men who spoke harshly of one from whom they had suffered criticism. We know what Hazlitt said of himself. We also live in an age which, whatever its follies, does not shudder at conduct until it has been examined by the light of Nature. We may still waste energy enough upon dislike of our own literary rivals; but when somebody has been dead for a hundred years we feel a toleration for him. His politics do not enrage us, because his politics belong to the past ; his personality is not irksome, because it has become a clinical case ; his most outrageous disclosures, which if they were made about some living men would produce a fury of retaliation, are to us no more than amusing sidelights upon the defunct famous. What Hazlitt said of Wordsworth, Coleridge, and Southey has been largely confirmed by the movement of taste; what he said of Haydon and Leigh Hunt shows, not malignity, as was said, but the forbearance of compassion; and as for his love of the French Revolution, his hatred of the Bourbons, and his fury against the attempted absolutism of George the Third, we have parallels today for them all which no Victorian could have imagined.

The first thing to be remembered is the date of Hazlitt's birth. In April 1778 Chatham and Dr Johnson were both still alive. Charles James Fox was only twenty-nine, and Pitt not yet nineteen; the American War of Independence was at its height. And Hazlitt's father, a Unitarian minister of Ulster descent cared so vehemently for the cause of the revolting Colonies that he went at last among them, taking his family with him. His American sermons, which our five-year-old William heard, sitting in the pulpit, were only a part of the family enthusiasm for Liberty. How could William have been anything, in such conditions, but a revolutionary or a reactionary? He was a Revolutionary, a 'Reformer'. And a Reformer, he said, 'is necessarily and naturally a Marplot ... First, he does not very well know what he would be at. Secondly, if he did, he does not care very much about it. Thirdly, he is governed habitually by a spirit of contradiction, and is always wise beyond what is practicable. He is a bad tool to work with; a part of a machine that never fits its place ; he cannot be trained to discipline, for he follows his own idle humours, or drilled into an obedience to orders: for the first principle of his mind is the supremacy of conscience and the independent right of private judgement.' When Hazlitt was eleven, the Bastille fell. 'For my part, I set out in life with the French Revolution.' That was not true. He set off with the history of Ireland in his bones, and with his father's zealous detestation of monarchy as his first lesson.

Nor was this the only lesson taught by the elder Hazlitt. Another was, 'You must fixedly resolve never, through any possible motives, to do anything which you believe to be wrong'. And, 'If we only think justly we shall always easily foil all the advocates of tyranny'. William was the youngest child of this family, the most active, lively, and happiest of boys', 'one of the most entertaining and prepossessing children ever seen', the favourite of his father and sister, an ardent lover of Nature; but already possessed of what he called 'that unfortunate attachment to a set of abstract phrases, such as *liberty, truth, justice, humanity, honour,* which are continually abused by knaves, and misunderstood by fools'. The attachment began at an early age; it lasted all his life. Few men can have changed their convictions as little as he. 'If', he said, ' "to be wise were to be obstinate," I might set up for as great a philosopher as the best of them; for some of my conclusions are as fixed and as incorrigible as need be ... I remember once saying to Mr Northcote, a great while ago, that I did not seem to have altered any of my ideas since I was sixteen years old. "Why then," said he, "you are no wiser now than you were then." '

In reality, his ideas were set much earlier than he knew. Having accepted his father's until he was twelve, he was sent away from home for a time, into an uncongenial atmosphere, and from then until he was twenty he studied until his brain and temper were both overwrought, and irreparable harm was done to a nature which was at bottom that of an artist, excitable, emotional, and idealistic. He became lonely; he had no friend; books, and a racking of immature brains for solutions to the problems of metaphysics, were his only resource. 'I did arrive at some very satisfactory and potent conclusions; nor will I go so far, however ungrateful the subject might seem, as to exclaim with Marlowe's Faustus – "Would I had never seen Wittenberg, never read book" – that is, never studied such authors as Hartley, Hume, Berkeley, etc.'; but he was 'entangled in the briars and thorns of subtle distinctions', and 'made a toil of pleasure'. No wonder his first work, in which he sought upon intellectual grounds to attribute to others his own boyish modesty and disinterestedness (combating the detestable materialism of Hobbes), was so turgid! It seems to me to be heavy with exhaustion.

Then the study ceased. Hazlitt was not to become a Unitarian minister. He turned to a craft suggested by his brother's example; and decided to paint. But that brought him into contact with other people, for which his years of brooding overstrained had unfitted him. He made his first, fatally perceived bad impressions upon these people, some of whom were cruel to the hobbledehoy. Crabb Robinson, meeting him then, says: 'His bashfulness, want of words, slovenliness of dress, etc., made him sometimes the object of ridicule ... He was excessively shy, especially in the company of young ladies, who on their part were very apt to make fun of him. The prettiest girl of our party ... used to drive him mad by teasing him.' She used to drive him mad: she probably saw that he was half in love with her. You can see how much he was affected from a later story of Lamb's, who reported taking him to a house where there were two young girls. 'The very head and sum of the girls was two young girls – they neither laughed nor sneered nor giggled nor whispered – but they were young girls – and he sat and frowned blacker and blacker, indignant that there should be such a thing as Youth and Beauty, till he tore me away before supper in perfect misery, and owned he could not bear young girl.' It was not that he could not bear them; it was that he was susceptible to them. His true loves were both young girls; the girl for whom, in the Lakes, he nearly earned a ducking was young, and treacherous. It was not surprising that he should be in misery at the memory of so much sexual torment.

But indeed, that awkwardness in demeanour which Crabb Robinson noted was to remain with him until the end. 'His manner', wrote Coleridge, four years later than Robinson, 'are so in no singularly repulsive; brow-hanging, shoe-contemplative, strange ... He is, I verily believe, kindly natured; ... but he is jealous, gloomy, and of an irritable pride.' It was no better than this in 1818; for Patmore, who met him then for the first time, describes 'a pale anatomy of a man, sitting uneasily, half on half off a chair, with his legs tucked awkwardly under with the rail, his hands folded listlessly on his knees, his head drooping on one side, and one of his elbows leaning (not resting) on the edge of the table ... as if in fear of its having no right to be there.' 'His eyes', says Patmore again, 'were not good.... There was a furtive and at times a sinister look about them, as they glanced suspiciously from under their overhanging brows, that conveyed a very unpleasant impression to those who did not know him. And they were seldom directed frankly and fairly towards you ... Hazlitt entered a room as if he had been brought to it in custody ; he shuffled sidelong to the nearest chair, sat himself down upon one corner of it, dropped his hat and his eyes upon the floor ... and seemed to resign himself to his fate.'

Nor was his manner better than his bearing. 'From habitual shyness,' said Coleridge, 'and the outside and bearskin, at least, of misanthropy, he is strangely confused and dark in his conversation.' 'I was dumb, inarticulate, helpless,' explains Hazlitt; 'my soul ... dark, obscure, with longings infinite and unsatisfied; my heart, shut up in the prison-house of this rude clay, has never found, nor will it ever find, a heart to speak to.' 'I declare to God I never seem to know,' says Leigh Hunt, 'whether he is pleased or displeased, cordial or uncordial – indeed, his manners are never cordial – and he has a way with him, when first introduced to you, and ever afterwards, as if he said, "I have no faith in anything, especially your advances; don't you flatter yourself you have any road to my credulity : we have nothing in common between us".'

Hazlitt, of course, had his reply to all this. When bidding 'a Farewell to Essay-Writing' he protests : 'Mr Hunt ... is puzzled to reconcile the shyness of my pretensions with the inveteracy and sturdiness of my principles. I should have thought they were nearly the same thing. Both from disposition and habit, I can *assume* nothing in word, look, or manner. I cannot steal a march upon public opinion in any way. My standing upright, speaking loud, entering a room gracefully, proves nothing; therefore I neglect these ordinary means of recommending myself to the good graces and admiration of strangers (and as it appears, even of philosophers and friends). Why ? Because I ...

... absorbed in other studies and pursuits. Suppose this absorption to be extreme, and even morbid ... is it not rather an
argument (together with a want of animal spirits) why I should
... myself, and perhaps acquire a nervous and uneasy
... All the same, in a letter to Leigh Hunt, he exclaimed:
I ... to know why everybody has such a dislike to me'.

I ... inclined to think that only two men really disliked
Hazlitt, and they disliked him because he disconcerted them.
He could not forget that they, in the days of his obscurity, had
been as ardent for the French Revolution as himself, and as
much against the Royal Prerogative. He constantly reminded
them of that ardour, and contrasted it with present enjoyment
of office under Government, and present praise of the Sovereign's
Fortune or rebuke to the unruly rabble. They, on their part,
could not ignore Hazlitt, as they would have wished to do,
because he was too able to be ignored. They therefore hated
him. As far as I am able to remember, all the evil report of
Hazlitt was circulated by Wordsworth. Wordsworth demanded
that Haydon should have nothing to do with Hazlitt. Wordsworth told shocking tales of him to Crabb Robinson, which
Robinson was at pains to hide in his ridiculous shorthand.
Wordsworth called him 'miscreant' and '—' (whatever that
unprinted word may be), 'the most perverse and malevolent
creature that ill-luck has ever thrown in my way'. And Crabb
Robinson, a worshipper of Wordsworth, decides in future to
cut Hazlitt, not because of any personal quarrel, not on grounds
of character or contempt, but because Hazlitt has referred once
again in the *Examiner* to Wordsworth's change of opinions.
Wordsworth thus repaid the scorn of a man of unchanging
principles with moral slander; because he did not care to be
reminded of political apostasy, he tried to ruin Hazlitt's moral
reputation. Robinson merely took the line of a partisan.

As for the second of the two who disliked Hazlitt, that also
was a critical matter. It would ill have become Southey, who
was a bitter critic of other men's work, to resent ridicule of his
own again; but Southey as a young man had been an extreme

idealist, and his vehement early works were not allowed by the Hunts to be suppressed or by Hazlitt to be forgotten. His indignation was real; and, like other literary men, he read into candour all the hints provided by his own self-doubting. Every word deriding themselves was attributed by Wordsworth and Southey to Hazlitt. Even when he praised Wordsworth (I do not think he praised Southey), they missed the praise and saw only what they called the abuse.

They, like the highbrows of today, were in a curious position of fame with the few and neglect by the many. Prestige was essential to them ; they lived, uneasily, in a state of sensitive, arrogant, and exclusive egotism. But Hazlitt, a benevolent egotist, had no patience with exclusiveness. 'We hate comparisons or the *exclusive* in matters of taste,' he said; 'and reject, abjure, and renounce all decisions and systems of criticism founded upon them.... What do these moot points and hair-breadth differences prove? Surely, not that there is some one thing in the world which we have found out to be good, and that mankind are fools for admiring anything else, but that there is an endless variety of excellence.' And, when he wrote of poetry, he said : 'I would speak of the living poets as I have spoken of the dead (for I think highly of many of them) ; but I cannot speak of them with the same reverence, because I do not feel it.' If only he had felt it, or if only he had winked at their changed views, Wordsworth and Southey could have loved him. But reverence was what they wanted; and he spoke out terribly in the manner of the child in *The Emperor's New Clothes*. Moreover, he could remember and repeat what he had read twenty years earlier, even though it had never been printed. He was dangerous. He must be evil. They hated him. The third of the trio, Coleridge, did not hate him. He might accuse Hazlitt of plagiary; but with grand ineffectual genius he respected a fellow metaphysician.

Apart, then, from Wordsworth and Southey, Hazlitt was wrong in thinking himself disliked. On the contrary, he was liked as well as he allowed himself to be liked. 'Literary men are act attached,' he said, speaking for himself, 'to the persons of their friends, but to their minds. They look upon them in the same light as on the books in their library, and read them till they are tired ... and as the same remarks or the same *bon mots* come to be often repeated, or others so like them, that we are no longer surprised into admiration, we begin to relax in the frequency of our visits and the heartiness of our welcome.' With such a guest it cannot have been easy to deal; yet Leigh Hunt said, 'I have a sort of irrepressible love for Hazlitt.' Haydon said, referring to Talfourd, 'We talked of Hazlitt, and agreed that we felt inclined to overlook in him everything treacherous, mean, contemptible, from the apparent candour of his nature.' 'I like Hazlitt, in spite of all: everybody must.' And Lamb, a better witness than any other, replying to Southey in print, said: 'I stood well with him for fifteen years (the proudest of my life), and have ever spoken my full mind of him to some of whom his panegyric must naturally be least tasteful ... Protesting against much that he has written, and some things which he chooses to do; judging him by his conversation which I enjoyed so long, and relished so deeply; or by his books, in those places where no clouding passion intervenes – I should belie my own conscience, if I said less, than that I think W. H. to be, in his natural and healthy state, one of the wisest and finest spirits breathing. So far from being ashamed of that intimacy which was betwixt us, it is my boast that I was able for so many years to have preserved it entire; and I think I shall go to my grave without finding, or expecting to find, such another companion.'

III

What of Hazlitt's work, which fills twenty large volumes, and covers the vast field of human nature, politics, literary history, metaphysics, art, and the drama? Why did he abandon painting, which gave him the purest of all pleasures? Why did he never attempt, apart from a doggerel verse, the poetry for which the early passion for the countryside and the heat and vigour of his imagination would seem to have fitted him? The obvious answer, given by himself, is that he wanted invention; Haydon said he was idle and easily discouraged, and, in painting, bitterly conscious of failure ; Coleridge that he was thinking, observant, and original, but incapable of doing anything unless the objects were actually before him. I think diffidence, however caused, was the real problem. In all those early years he had no happy rival to emulate ; though well aware of his own brains and his own talents, he had no measure for them but his father's clerical mind. But while forced and painful thought may have marred his genius as well as his self-confidence, he was the greater critic for that determined settling of his own principles beforehand. One has only to read the first chapter of *Lectures on the English Comic Writers* to see a proof of this. He might be sometimes hurried or laboured or perfunctory, as is excusable in one who writes for the Press or in haste (the second volume of *Table-Talk,* consisting of eleven essays, took Hazlitt little more than a month to produce). He might be, as Leigh Hunt accused him of being, capricious, or, as Lamb said, sometimes clouded by passion ; he might be guilty, as Coleridge alleged, of round and round imitations of Lamb;[1] but he was never bogus. He said what he thought; he was incapable of saying anything else. 'He concealed nothing ... He brought it all out, good, bad or indifferent: it was his nature.' But, in criticism, he had first well pondered the general principles of what he wrote about.

This love of principles causes him to strike superficial readers as a little heavy, and persistent readers as repetitive. He is on

1. What Coleridge had in mind was such a pair of passages as this: 'But his [Pope's] compliments are divine; they are equal in value to a house or an estate', *Lectures on the English Poets,* 1818, and the original, in *Persons one would wish to have Seen* : 'I thought', said A——, turning short round upon L——, 'that you of the Lake School did not like Pope.' 'Not like Pope!... I can read him over and over for ever!... Not his Satires, but his friendly Epistles and his compliments.' – 'Compliments! I did not know he ever made any.' 'The finest,' said L——, 'that were ever paid by the wit of man. Each of them is worth an estate for life – nay, is an immortality.'

he whole less breath-taking than Coleridge and less uniformly felicitous than Lamb. Otherwise he has in his own age no rivals in the art of grasping a period and distinguishing between the excellences of individual minds and talents. I think it is desirable to recall a second time the fact that Johnson only finished his *Lives of the Poets* in 1781, three years after Hazlitt's birth. Hazlitt himself was a man of the eighteenth century. It was with the literature of the eighteenth century that he was really familiar. If you add to that literature the names and work of Hobbes and Shakespeare, you have the basis for all his literary information, and, of course, the basis upon which all the judgement of his maturer reading was built. This was equally true of Lamb and Coleridge, from which two authors he derived, and acknowledged that he derived, in the one case a discovery of the Elizabethans, and in the other a profound liberation of thought and language. The late William Macdonald drew attention to the slow development of Lamb's wider knowledge of literature; and the same slowness can be found in Hazlitt. It is only when he shows enthusiasm for 'the imagination' and for 'gusto' that he salutes the new romantic movement and the aeration of critical standards. Then his love of truth, and his joy in poetry, are hampered only by the difficulty of obtaining the work of poets neglected in the eighteenth century. Hence the brevity of his remarks on such writers as Marvell and Donne, and the limitations of his remarks upon poetic theory. He, like Lamb, was a pioneer: he brought to whatever he read a delight in discovery which causes the modern sophisticated reader, who must neither feel nor express unmitigated enthusiasm, slight embarrassment. But the embarrassment is out of place. It passes with experience of Hazlitt's range and wisdom, and appreciation of the quality of his 'perfectly simple character'. 'He is', said Crabb Robinson, 'too proud and high-minded to lie'; and that pride, which is interchangeable in Hazlitt with humility, forbids him to deny ignorance or to hide his pleasure or his imperfect sympathy. He loved imaginative literature, and described it with zest.

In his critical writing, but still more markedly in the essays with which Stevenson established so friendly a link, Hazlitt used what he called a familiar style, a style in which he thought aloud. It was the natural medium for one who had been dumb, and he found it in time to make a reputation which will never die. His manner lies halfway between the irresistible antique of Lamb and the twitter of Leigh Hunt. It never quite attains the poignancy of Lamb; but otherwise, in its genre, it is unequalled. 'It is not easy to write a familiar style,' Hazlitt confesses. 'There is nothing that requires more precision, and, if I may say so, purity of expression.' That is true, and his triumph is, therefore, the greater. He is never undignified, and never at a loss. The essays have just that air of good talk, good monologue, which slips thought into our minds as if unawares and leaves us in possession of half the writer's riches. He tells of his first walk with Coleridge (and anticipates Carlyle's discovery that Coleridge could never decide which side of the path best suited him); he describes a great fight. He discusses mind and motive, living and walking by one's self, coffee-house politicians, or the character of Rousseau; and if he is never as simple as Montaigne, he does, over a thousand pages, clearly paint his own portrait and reveal his own mind and heart. It is a strong mind, as the dialogue on Self-love and Benevolence profoundly shows, and a heart that is less open than some other hearts; but the candour of the revelation is perfect.

I cannot end this preface without referring directly to one book of Hazlitt's which has for years been among my truest favourites, the *Conversations of James Northcote*. This book, the imaginative rather than the literal report of talks in Northcote's studio, comes nearer to Hazlitt himself than any other. One need not – although that would be a fascinating task – distinguish too precisely between the speakers, and decide if it is true, as was said when it appeared, that 'all the ill-nature in the book is Northcote's, and all, or almost all, the talent, Hazlitt's'; but as a portrait, a recalling of talk and the contrast between two centuries, and a footnote to critical theory, it is superb. I think if Hazlitt had written nothing else, the *Conversations of North-*

...e would give him immortality with those who love letters. ...t, so fertile, so active, and so inexhaustible was this idler, who ... by the fire, he said, eight or ten hours a day, often, his friends ...ure us unshaven and with the breakfast-things still unre-...ved gloomy and misanthropical, malignant, clouded with ...sion and the rest of it, the *Conversations of Northcote* repres-...t only a detail in the body of his work, and have not even ...standing with modern critics of that tragic piece of futility, ...r *moris*.

FRANK SWINNERTON

PREFACE TO FIRST EDITION

THIS book is an attempt to present in clear outline, and with reasonable attention to detail, a narrative of what has been termed the 'rather imperfectly known life' of a great English man of letters. In seeking to render it a little less imperfectly known I have not spared any pains, and I have not, I believe, sought to evade any difficulties. Since a good deal which has hitherto been believed of Hazlitt has proved itself to be not altogether worthy of credence, and since a good deal more is told in these pages for the first time, I have thought it better not to recast the narrative in my own words, but to present it as far as possible in those of the various witnesses. If this method has drawbacks, of which I am conscious, it will be found also, I hope, to have certain advantages, not the least of which is that everything which appears in this book bears its own authority, good or less good, on its face. In a life the groundwork of which had already been fixed this would not be a matter of so much importance, but a life of Hazlitt is still, after a hundred years, in the nature of a pioneer work. It is so, at least, that I have regarded it.

My acknowledgements for sympathy and encouragement are many, and are due first of all to Miss G. H. C. Hazlitt, great-grand-daughter of my subject, who by freely and generously throwing open to me all the works of her father, the late Mr William Carew Hazlitt, in which the rights are held by herself, has rendered me assistance with which I could not possibly have dispensed. Owing to the bequest to the British Museum of the whole of the late Mr Hazlitt's materials which have remained in this country, I have been able to check his conclusions at nearly every point, and in one or two instances to put right errors into which I find he has unwittingly fallen. With the sanction of the Trustees of Dr Williams' Library I have made my copy of Crabb Robinson's evidence direct from the diaries and letters in their charge, and to Mr E. V. Lucas I am grateful for permission to make my Lamb quotations from his text. For reply to inquiries, involving research on my behalf in varying degrees, I am indebted, among others, to Professor Ernest Weekley. of Nottingham University; to the Public Librarians of Liverpool and Taunton; and to the Secretary of the Royal Academy My collaborator in the matter of the illustrations has been Mr J. H. Allchin, of the Maidstone Museum, to whom, and to whose Committee, I tender my thanks.

cannot conclude this note without an acknowledgement of the value of the work done in the same field by the late A. R. Waller and the late Arnold Glover, editors of the Collected Works, and that of M. Jules Douady, author of the best Hazlitt biography and of the French 'Life'. While I have accepted none of the conclusions of these writers without first going over the ground for myself, I have at many points been conscious of the assistance their labours have rendered me.

P. P. H.

CHAPTER I

BEGINNINGS

(1778-95)

*

For my part, I set out in life with the French Revolution.
On the Feeling of Immortality in Youth.

I

THE name Hazlitt, though not a common one, has a well-recorded history, and we need not go so far afield for it as has sometimes been suggested. Belonging to that largest class of surnames which are local in origin, its earliest occurrence, in the thirteenth century, is in the form de Heselenheved, denoting residence in the Yorkshire hamlet of that name, now Hazlehead Bridge, near Penistone. In the fifteenth century the name becomes Hesilheved and in the sixteenth Haslehead, which is contracted into Haslett or Hazlitt in accordance with a practice of which Aikett (Scotch, *aik,* oak), Birkett (north country, *birk,* birch), Bromet (broom), are kindred examples. It happens that the records of the name here traced confine themselves to Yorkshire and Cumberland, but that there were also Hasletts and Hazlitts who were Scotch (the etymological origin of their name remaining the same) we receive assurance from the existing place-names of Hazlehead, Aberdeen, and Hesselhead, Ayrshire. From Scotland, no doubt, rather than from northern England, the name was carried to Ulster, where we find it established early in the seventeenth century. The proposed Dutch origin of the name (Haesluyt) may, in the opinion of Professor Ernest Weekley, be finally disposed of.

By the opening of the eighteenth century a branch of the family had removed from Ulster to the south, and in 1737 William, the eldest son of John and Margaret Hazlitt, was born in the village of Shronell, County Tipperary. Leaving his father's farm, 'a poor Irish lad', at the age of eighteen to prepare himself for the Presbyterian ministry, the elder Hazlitt graduated at Glasgow University, joined the Unitarians, and was appointed to the ministry of Wisbeach in Cambridgeshire. Here, in his twenty-ninth year, he married Grace Loftus, nine years his junior and the daughter of an ironmonger in the market-place. A move was made to Marshfield near Bath, and in 1770 to Maidstone. At Maidstone during ten years the Rev. William Hazlitt enjoyed the respect of a wider circle than his congregation: he was the friend and correspondent of Doctors Priestley and Price, and an acquaintance during his English residence of Benjamin Franklin. On 10 April 1778, his fourth child William was born, who is the subject of these pages. A son John was aged eleven at this date, a daughter Margaret seven: it is to a narrative written late in life by the latter and based on her father's journals that we owe our earliest biographical particulars. The visitor to Maidstone will find the Unitarian chapel in Bullock Lane, between Earl Street and the High Street, still standing as it was in Hazlitt's father's time; the dwelling-house in Rose Yard adjacent, where Hazlitt was born, has long since disappeared.

If we seek for a reason for the excellent minister's leaving Maidstone when his son William was eighteen months old, we find it in his open advocacy, during a crisis in the war, of the cause of American independence. A move was made back to Ireland where at Bandon, county Cork, there was a Unitarian congregation. Hard by, at Kinsale, were the American prisoners, and these the Rev. William Hazlitt befriended. The war was not yet over, but with the surrender at Yorktown it was drawing to its close. 'The feud between Whigs and Tories', notes Margaret Hazlitt, 'ran high, and my father, who never disguised his sentiments, gave great offence by his freedom in

writing and speaking at a time when the unbridled licence of
the army (who took liberties in Ireland that they dared not do
at home) made it dangerous to offend the haughty officers, who
seemed to think wearing a sword entitled them to domineer
over their fellow-subjects.' America (whither a number of their
name had already proceeded) was the land of liberty to this
little family. When Hazlitt's father, the excellent Unitarian
minister, embarked the whole group of them at Cork, on 3
April 1783, and proceeded with handsome testimonials to seek
the friendship and the suffrages of his Majesty's late rebels,
the boy was a week short of his fifth birthday and the
great republic six months short of its acknowledged independence.

Hazlitt in America, from his sixth to his ninth year, need not
very long detain us. The pictures given us by Margaret Hazlitt[1]
are charming, but they are pictures of scenes and events which
Hazlitt himself in after life did not remember. In all his works,
built upon personal recollection as they are, the only reference
to his stay in America is to the taste of the barberries picked on
the hills, where they had lain beneath a winter's snow. The
hills were those about Weymouth and Upper Dorchester, at
which places, after a short stay in New York and a longer one
in Philadelphia, the family successively resided. In Boston the
Rev. William Hazlitt founded the first Unitarian church; and
in his numerous journeys about this countryside his younger
son accompanied him and sat in the pulpit while his father
preached. 'How often have we stood', writes his sister, 'at the
window, looking at my father as he went up this road with
William in his nankeen dress, marching by his side, like one
that could never be tired.' The road is that from Dorchester
to Boston. But the opportunity for permanent settlement, for
which the minister had hoped, did not present itself; and at the
end of three years he returned to England.

The nine months during which the family stayed behind in

1. In extracts, in the late Mr W. C. Hazlitt's *Four Generations of a
Literary Family* (1897). The narrative in its entirety has not been published.

Worcester was a period in which, after a late start at learning, the boy Hazlitt 'nearly killed himself' (the phrase is his sister's) by excessive application to his Latin grammar. The tuition was that of his brother John, who for his part was already assisting the family by painting the portraits of American citizens. The inenesy with which Hazlitt applied himself to this earliest of his studies is the key to the first of our letters.

Hazlitt to his Father

12 of Nov. [1786]

My dear Papa, – I shall never forget that we came to america. If we had not came to america, we should not have been away from one and other, though now it can not be helped I think for my part that it would have been a great deal better if the white people had not found it out. Let the others have it to themselves, for it was made for them. I have got a little of my grammar; sometimes I get three pages and sometimes but one. I do not sifer any at all. Mamma Peggy and Jacky are all very well, and I am to. – I still remain your most affectionate son.

WILLIAM HAZLITT.

No sooner had the Rev. William Hazlitt returned, says his daughter, than two openings occurred in the ministry of the nature for which he had been waiting, and either of which he would have accepted. It is to such a slight chance we owe it that William Hazlitt grew up to be a figure in English letters and not an American – if, indeed, he would in other circumstances have grown up to be a figure in letters at all.

II

The father had obtained a settlement at Wem, in Shropshire, but before the removal of the family thither, after their arrival in August 1787, a few weeks were spent in London, at the then salubrious suburb of Walworth, for the benefit of the mother's

health after the voyage. It was in the pleasure gardens there,
somewhat curiously, that the boy's conscious memory began, as
readers of the essays on *Why Distant Objects Please,* written
thirty-five years afterwards, will remember: 'I see the beds of
larkspur with purple eyes; tall hollyoaks, red and yellow; the
broad sunflowers, caked in gold, with bees buzzing round
them; wildernesses of pinks, and hot-glowing pionies; poppies
run to seed; the sugared lily, and faint mignionette, all ranged
in order, and as thick as they can grow; the box-tree borders;
the gravel-walks, the painted alcove, the confectionery, the
clotted cream: I think I see them now with sparkling looks; or
have they vanished while I have been writing this description
of them? No matter; they will return again when I least think
of them. All that I have observed since, of flowers and plants,
and grass-plots, and of suburb delights, seems, to me, borrowed
from "that first garden of my innocence" – to be slips and
scions stolen from that bed of memory.'

The removal to Wem was made towards the end of the year,
and John Hazlitt, now aged twenty-one, was left in London
to study under Sir Joshua Reynolds, to move in the Godwin
circle,[1] and to live by his gift as a painter of miniatures. We
shall best acquaint ourselves with the progress made by his
younger brother from the letter which follows.

Hazlitt to his Brother

> Wem, Saturday morning.
> [March 1788]

Dear Brother, – I received your letter this morning. We
were all glad to hear that you were well, and that you have so
much business to do. We cannot be happy without being
employed. I want you to tell me whether you go to the
Academy or not, and what pictures you intend for the exhi-

1. An association between the Godwin and Loftus families, as Margaret Hazlitt informs us, had been formed at Wisbeach, in the ministry
of which place the father of William Godwin was a predecessor of the
Rev. William Hazlitt.

bition. Tell the exhibitioners to finish the exhibition soon, that you may come and see us. You must send your picture to us directly. You want to know what I do. I am a busybody, and do many silly things: I drew eyes and noses till about a fortnight ago. I have drawn a little boy since, a man's face, and a little boy's front face, taken from a bust. Next Monday I shall begin to read Ovid's Metamorphoses and Eutropius. I shall like to know all the Latin and Greek I can. I want to learn how to measure the stars. I shall not, I suppose, paint the worse for knowing everything else. I begun to cypher a fortnight after Christmas, and shall go into the rule of three next week. I can teach a boy of sixteen already who was cyphering eight months before me; is he not a great dunce? I shall go through the whole cyphering book this summer, and then I am to learn Euclid. We go to school at nine every morning. Three boys begin with reading the Bible. Then I and two others show our exercises. We then read the [Enfield's] Speaker. Then we all set about our lessons, and those who are first ready say first. At eleven we write and cypher. In the afternoon we stand for places at spelling, and I am almost always first. We also read, and do a great deal of business besides. I can say no more about the boys here: some are so sulky they wont play; others are quarrelsome because they cannot learn, and are only fit for fighting like stupid dogs and cats. I can jump four yards at a running jump, and two at a standing jump. I intend to try you at this when you come down. We are not all well, for poor Peggy has a great cold ... Write soon again. I wish I could see all those paintings that you see, and that Peggy had a good prize. I don't want your old clothes. I shall go to dancing this month. This is all I can say. I am your affectionate brother,

WILLIAM HAZLITT.

The impression we gain from this letter is confirmed for us by Margaret Hazlitt in one of the latest of her notes: 'He was at this time the most active, lively, and happiest of boys; his time, divided between his studies and his childish sports, passed smoothly on. Beloved by all for his amiable temper and manners, pleasing above his years. The delight and pride of his own family.' The child, in a word, who looks out from his brother's miniature portrait.

There are other hints for a picture of the boy's life at this period. In the essay already quoted we may go on to read: 'If I have pleasure in a flower-garden, I have in a kitchen-garden too, and for the same reason. If I see a row of cabbage-plants or of peas or beans coming up, I immediately think of those which I used so carefully to water of an evening at W[e]m, when my day's tasks were done, and of the pain with which I saw them droop and hang down their leaves in the morning sun. Again, I never see a child's kite in the air but it seems to pull at my heart. It is to me "a thing of life". I feel the twinge at my elbow, the flutter and palpitation with which I used to let go the string of my own, as it rose in the air and towered among the clouds.' Again: 'When I was a boy, I lived within sight of a range of lofty hills, whose blue tops blending with the setting sun had often tempted my longing eyes and wandering feet. At last I put my project in execution, and on a nearer approach, instead of glimmering air woven into fantastic shapes, found them huge lumpish heaps of discoloured earth.'

In 1789, when Hazlitt was nearly eleven, the Estates General were summoned and the French Revolution began. The Bastille fell, his father's friend Dr Price preached a celebrated sermon, the Doctor was answered by the even more justly celebrated 'reflections' of Burke. These were great events, certain to re-echo in the quiet of the Shropshire presbytery. Each of them at the time, however, meant less to the boy than his first visit to Liverpool.

This came about in 1790, and was due to the interest shown in him by a Mrs Tracy, the wife of a West India merchant. The period of his residence is documented by a group of letters, which we shall draw upon here in the degree in which they

seemed likely to afford us guidance for the future. The first is
to his father. 'I now sit down', we read, 'to spend a little time
in an employment, the productions of which I know will give
you pleasure, though I know that every minute that I am
employed in doing anything which will be advantageous to
me will give you pleasure. Happy indeed, unspeakably happy,
are those people who, when at the point of death, are able to
say, with a satisfaction which none but themselves can have
any idea of : "I have done with this world, I shall now have no
more of its temptations to struggle with, and praise be to God
I have overcome them; now no more sorrow, now no more
grief, but happiness for evermore!" ' We may here take a few
more lines in this dutiful strain for granted. 'After I had sealed
up my last letter to you, George asked me if I were glad the
Test Act was not repealed. I told him, No. Then he asked me
why, and I told him because I thought that all the people who
are the inhabitants of a country, of whatsoever sect or denomina-
tion, should have the same rights with others. But, says he,
then they would try to get their religion established, or something to that purpose. -- Well, what if it should be so? -- He
said that the Church religion was an old one. Well, said I,
Popery is older than that. -- But then, said he, the Church
religion is better than Popery. -- And the Presbyterian is better
than that, said I. I told him I thought so for certain reasons,
not because I went to Chapel. But at last, when I had overpowered him with my arguments, he said he wished he understood it as well as I did, for I was too high learned for him. I
then went to the concert.' The letter contains also strictures
upon a certain 'unhospitable English prim "lady", if such she
may be called. She asked us, as if she were afraid we would
accept it, if we would stay to tea. And at the other English
person's, for I am sure she belongs to no other country than to
England, I got such a surfeit of their ceremonial unsociality,
that I could not help wishing myself in America. I had rather
people would tell one to go out of the house than ask one to
stay, and, at the same time, be trembling all over, for fear one

should take a slice of meat, or a dish of tea, with them. Such as these require an Horace or a Shakespeare to describe them. I have not yet learned the gamut perfectly, but I would have done it if I could. I spent a very agreeable day yesterday, as I read 160 pages of Priestley, and heard two good sermons.'

To this letter we are fortunate in possessing the Rev. William Hazlitt's reply: 'On Wednesday evening we had your letter, which was finished on the preceding Monday. The piety displayed in the first part of it was a great refreshment to me. Continue to cherish those thoughts which then occupied your mind, continue to be virtuous, and you will finally be that happy being whom you describe, and to this purpose you have nothing more to do than to pursue that conduct, which will always yield you the highest pleasures even in this present life. But he who once gives way to any known vice, in the very instant hazards his total depravity and total ruin. You must, therefore, fixedly resolve never, through any possible motives, to do anything which you believe to be wrong. This will be only resolving never to be miserable, and this I rejoicingly expect will be the unwavering resolution of my William. Your conversation upon the Test Act did you honour. If we only think justly we shall always easily foil all the advocates of tyranny. The inhospitable ladies whom you mention were, perhaps, treated by you with too great severity. We know not how people may be circumstanced at a particular moment, whose disposition is generally friendly. They may then happen to pass under a cloud, which unfits them for social intercourse. We must see them more than once or twice to be able to form a tolerable judgement of their characters. There are but few, like Mrs Tracy, who can always appear what they really are. I do not say, however, that the English ladies whom you mentioned are not exactly as you described them. I only wish to caution you against forming too hasty a judgement of characters, who can seldom be known at a single interview. I wish you, if you can, to become master of the gamut whilst you are there. I am glad that you have made so great a progress in

French.' The father's letter goes on to give news of America, and of one Boston friend, a Mr Booth, in particular. 'He says, concerning you, "I read Billy's letter to Fanny, and she was delighted with it. She sends her love to him; but Fanny has lost the recollection of her little playfellow. The letter does Billy much credit. He has uncommon powers of mind, and if nothing happens to prevent his receiving a liberal education, he must make a great man."' This Boston friend, Mr Booth, deserves remembrance for his early confidence in Hazlitt's powers of mind.

We need not concern ourselves with further evidences of his piety, nor with the continued progress of his education. We may note, however, that he has been to Church, 'the first time I ever was in one, and I do not care if I should never go into one again. ... The Clergyman, after he had gabbled over half a dozen prayers, began his sermon, the text of which was as follows: Zachariah, 3rd chapter, 2nd verse, latter part – "Is not this a brand plucked out of the fire?" If a person had come in five minutes after he began, he would have thought that he had taken his text out of Joshua. In short, his sermon had neither head nor tail. I was sorry that so much time should be thrown away upon nonsense.' He has been, he tells his mother, to dinner at a certain gentleman's. 'He is a very rich man, but – The man who is a well-wisher to slavery, is always a slave himself. The King, who wishes to enslave all mankind, is a slave to ambition. The man who wishes to enslave all mankind for his king, is himself a slave to his king.... Be sure to tell me if I may sell my old Buckles.' Again: 'They were pressing on Saturday evening. The world is not quite perfect yet; nor will it ever be so whilst such practices are reckoned lawful. – P.S. I like my Balls very well, and have also received the money.'

At Liverpool he saw his first play, and wrote his first dramatic criticism. 'The play was "Love in Many Masks", and the farce, "No Song, no Supper". It was very entertaining, and was performed by some of the best players in London, as for instance, Kemble, Suett, Dignum, the famous singer, Mrs. Williams,

Miss Hagley, Miss Romanzini, and others. Suett, who acted in the character of Ned Blunt, was enough to make any one laugh, though he stood still; and Kemble acted admirably as an officer. Mr Dignum sang beautifully, and Miss Hagley acted the country-girl with much exactness.'

With his return from Liverpool, the youth of Hazlitt passes behind a curtain – a curtain which is lifted for a moment in the following year for the display of what his son terms his 'first literary production'. This took the form of a letter to the *Shrewsbury Chronicle,* in protest against the treatment accorded to Joseph Priestley at the hands of the mob of Birmingham, on the occasion of the second anniversary of the Fall of the Bastille. We need not have that document of the father's Wil- liam here, but may take instead a small piece of evidence which has not hitherto been reproduced.

We find it, in the British Museum, in some unpublished 'Biographical Notices' prepared by the Rev. Joseph Hunter of Bath, who became intimate with the Hazlitt family after their removal from Wem to that city many years later. Having, as he said, 'some particular friends here who were members of Mr Hazlitt's congregation at Wem,' he put down such par- ticulars regarding the youth of the younger and more distin- guished son as he gained from the lips of 'a lady not at all given to embellishing':

He was one of the most entertaining and prepossessing children ever seen; and so he continued till he was about nine [*sic*] years old. It happened that a lady from Liverpool came to spend some time at Wem. She was wonderfully taken with this child, and she invited him to spend some little time with her at Liverpool. To Liverpool he went. But he soon found that he was not made so much of there as he had been at Wem. The lady went out visiting, leaving him at home by himself: and, in short, the child of nine years old thought himself slighted: he became sullen: and this sullenness con- tinued ever after, and formed the predominant feature in his character during the remainder of his schoolboy days. He now showed his talent for satire, mimicry, and caricature. By the time he was twelve or thirteen, he would not attend the devotions of the family. He would not go to chapel. He would shut himself up from the rest of the family: be seen by no one during the day: but at night he would ramble forth no one knew where: and in the moonlight nights he used to scamper about the fields, like, as my informant says, any wild thing.

The correction is subsequently added, on the authority of the *Literary Remains,* that the visit to Liverpool took place at the age of twelve; and the account so amended may no doubt be accepted as having a certain limited objective value. Other hints will occur that at about this time the boy (in the phrase of his father for the ladies of Liverpool) 'passed under a cloud, which unfitted him for social intercourse'.

What the young Hazlitt was doing with his days, of course, was making those first intensive efforts at reading which we may allow him more fully to describe in the next chapter. As to his abstentions from his father's chapel, that these were not complete we may gather from his own evidence. 'When I was about fourteen,' he says, '(as long ago as the year 1792), in consequence of a dispute, one day after meeting, between my my father and an old lady of the congregation, respecting the repeal of the Corporation and Test Acts and the limits of religious tolerance, I set about forming in my head (the first time I ever attempted to think) the following system of political rights and general jurisprudence.' This was the *Project for a New Theory of Civil and Criminal Legislation,* which, persevered with at college, and then set aside, was returned to by Hazlitt in the last years of his life. It was, in its earliest form, the rock on which the career his father had planned for him was destined to split; the 'circumstance', as he himself says, 'that decided the fate of my future life; or rather, I would say it was from an original bias or craving to be satisfied of the

reason of things, that I seized hold of this accidental opportunity to indulge in its uneasy and unconscious determination'.

When, having attained his fifteenth birthday, he departed
for the Unitarian New College at Hackney, he bore the draft
of this essay with him.

III

Hazlitt's first residence in London, at Hackney College – of
which Dr Priestley, from the death of Dr Price in 1791 to his
own enforced departure for America in 1794, was the presiding
influence – and at the house of his newly-married brother John
in Long Acre, comprised years that were critical in the history
of the French Revolution and of its repercussion in England.
In 1791 Burke had been answered by Paine's *Rights of Man* and
Mackintosh's *Vindiciæ Gallicæ*; in 1792 Mary Wollstonecraft's
Rights of Women appeared, followed in 1793 by William
Godwin's *Political Justice.* This last was the year in which
war was declared upon the Revolution abroad and its sym-
pathisers at home. In 1794 Thomas Holcroft, Horne Tooke,
Thomas Hardy, John Thelwall and others were brought to
trial on the charge of high treason, and acquitted amid excitement. Undisturbed by events, but not uninfluenced by them,
the young Hazlitt got on with his education. It is without surprise that we find in the letters which form our sole guide
through this period a minimum of external allusion.

We come at once to the first of these, of date 6 October 1793.
'Dear Father,' we read, 'I recd. your very kind letter yesterday
evening. With respect to my past behaviour, I have often said,
and I now assure you, that it did not proceed from any real
disaffection, but merely from the nervous disorders to which,
you well know, I was so much subject. This was really the
case, however improbable it may appear. Nothing particular
occurred from the time I wrote last till the Saturday following.
On the Wednesday before, C[urrie] had given me a thesis. As
it was not a subject suited to my genius, and from other causes,
I had not written anything on it; so that I was [not] pleased to

hear his bell on Saturday morning, which was the time for showing our themes. When I came to him, he asked me whether I
had prepared my theme. I told him I had not. You should have
a very good reason indeed, sir, says he, for neglecting it. Why
really, sir, says I, I could not write it. Did you never write anything, then? says he. Yes, sir, I said, I have written some things.
Very well, then, go along and write your theme immediately,
said he. I accordingly went away, but did not make much progress in my theme an hour after, when his bell rang for another
lecture. My eyes were much swollen, and I assumed as sullen a
countenance as I could, intimating that he had not treated me
well. After the lecture, as I was going away, he called me back,
and asked me very mildly if I had never written anything. I answered, I had written several things. On which he desired me to
let him see one of my compositions, if I had no objection. I immediately took him my essay on laws,[1] and gave it to him. When
he had read it, he asked me a few questions on the subject, which
I answered very satisfactorily, I believe. Well, sir, says he, I wish
you'd write some more such things as this. Why, sir, said I, I
intended to write several things, which I had planned, but that
I could not write any of them in a week, or two or three weeks.
What did you intend to write, says he. Among other things I
told him that I intended to inlarge and improve the essay he
had been reading. Aye, says he, I wish you would. Well! I will
do it then, sir, said I. Do so, said he; take your own time now;
I shall not ask you for it; only write it as soon as you can, for I
shall often be thinking of it, and very desirous of it. This he
repeated once or twice. On this I wished him a good morning,
and came away, very well pleased with the reception I had met.'

1. 'Mr Currie, my old tutor of Hackney, may still have the rough
draft of this speculation, which I gave him with tears in my eyes, and
which he good-naturedly accepted in lieu of the customary *themes*, and
as a proof that I was no idler, but that my inability to produce a line on
the ordinary school topics arose from my being involved in more difficult
and abstruse matters.' – *Project for a New Theory of Civil and Criminal
Legislation* (1828). The task of the biographer of Hazlitt is so far simpli-
fied that he does hold together in this way.

After this, we have small need of the letters which follow; but we may glance at them, as we did at those written from Liverpool, for the sake of the guidance they contain.[1] The one which we take to come next carries forward the narrative. 'I recd. your letter safely on Monday,' we read. 'On the preceding Saturday, I finished the introduction to my essay on the political state of man, and showed [it] to Currie. He seemed very well pleased with it, and desired me to proceed with my essay as quickly as I could. After a few definitions, I give the following sketch of my plan. "In treating on the political state of man, I shall first endeavour to represent his natural political relations, and to deduce from these his natural political duties, and his artificial political relations, and to deduce from these his artificial duties, and his artificial rights." This I think an excellent plan. I wish I could recite it to my own satisfaction. I hope, however, to do it tolerably by Christmas. I have already got the greatest part of the ideas necessary, though in a crude and undigested state; so that my principal business will [be] to correct and arrange them. But this will be a terrible labour, and I shall rejoice most heartily when I have finished it. Currie seemed much pleased with some of my translations this week. I passed the Ass's bridge very safely, and very solitarily, on Friday.' The essay on laws, it will be seen, has very speedily been followed by a project more ambitious.

The next letter evidently followed closely upon the foregoing one : 'I was very much pleased you liked the plan of my essay. You need not fear for the execution of it, as I am sensible that, after I have made it as perfect as I can, it will have many imperfections, yet I know that I can finish in a manner equal to the introduction. I have made some progress since I wrote last. The essay on laws will make a part of it. I will here give you an account of my studies, &c.' The account follows, and at the end of a very well-spent, representative day we find : 'From half

1. The remaining letters are without date, and I do not find it possible to observe the sequence in which they are presented by the late Mr W. C. Hazlitt. – (*The Hazlitts*, 1911.)

past nine till eleven, reading David Hartley.' By way of compensation : 'I like Hebrew very well, the mathematics very much. They are very much suited to my genius.'

We have no reason to doubt, and every reason to believe, that the superstructure placed at Hackney upon the foundations of Hazlitt's education as laid by his father was a sound one. But essays on the political state of man were hardly what the boy had been sent to college for, and the excellent minister, hoping against hope for a successor in his second son, may very well have been excused for thinking so. That the former's misgivings, hitherto held at arm's length with some ingenuity, now became explicit, and based themselves on the dangers of over-study, we receive some evidence in the letter which follows : 'I was sorry to hear from your two last letters that you wish me to discontinue my essay, as I am very desirous of finishing it, and as I think it almost necessary to do so. For I have already completed the two first prop. and the third I have planned and shall be able to finish in a very short time; the fourth prop., which will be the last, will consist only of a few lines. The first section you know I have done for some time; and the first, second, and fourth propositions are exactly similar to the first, second, and fourth of the second section, so that I have little else to do than alter a few words. The third will consist principally of observations on government, laws, &c., most of which will be the same with what I have written before in my essay on laws. My chief reason for wishing to continue my observations is, that, by having a particular system of politics I shall be better able to judge of the truth or falsehood of any prevarication which I hear, or read, and of the justice, or the contrary, of any political transactions. Moreover, by comparing my own system with those of others, and with particular facts, I shall have it in my power to correct and improve it continually. But I can have neither of these advantages unless I have some standard by which to judge of, and of which to judge by, any ideas, or proceedings which I may meet with. Besides, so far is my studying this subject from making me gloomy or low-spirited, that I am never so perfectly easy as when I am, or have been, studying it. With respect to theories, I really think them rather disserviceable than otherwise. I should not be able to make a good oration from my essay. It is too abstruse and exact for that purpose. I shall endeavour to write one on Providence, which will, I think, be a very good subject.' This letter concludes: 'I hope my mother and P. are quite well before this time. I long to see you. I wish they could come too. I am, dear father, your aff. son, W. HAZLITT. I forgot to tell you that Currie has not returned me the first part of my essay.'

We are at the end of our letters, with a single exception, and they have taken us no further than Hazlitt's first year at Hackney College. With a visit from his father imminent, the small drama withdraws itself into the shades. We have seen enough, however, to have little difficulty in making out the rest. Even without the information which his son gives us, we might know that Hazlitt was speaking with his own case in mind in *My First Acquaintance with Poets,* where, of his father, he says: 'It was his mother's proudest wish to see her son a Dissenting Minister. So if we look back to past generations (as far as eye can reach) we see the same hopes, fears, wishes, followed by the same disappointments, throbbing in the human heart; and so we may see them (if we look forward) rising up for ever, and disappearing like vapourish bubbles, in the human breast!'

In the *Literary Remains* of 1836 (at which date both John and Margaret Hazlitt were living) Hazlitt's son wrote: 'The profession destined for my father was that of the Dissenting Ministry, but to this at a very early period he manifested an extreme distaste. This, in spite of persuasion and remonstrance, deepened with his years and became at length insurmountable. My grandfather, who with a natural subtlety of apprehension, observed the point at which prejudice outgrew all power of reasoning, at length consented to give up all further idea of his favourite project, and my father accordingly left College, and returned home in the year 1795.' We can only take this statement as we find it: nevertheless, it would appear probable

that Hazlitt's residence in London was for three and not for
two years.

It is, at all events, to the moment immediately preceding his
return that we should suppose our remaining letter to belong:

Hazlitt to his Father

Sunday, Oct. 23rd. [1796][1]

My dear Father, – I write, not so much because I have anything particular to communicate, as because I know that you,
and my mother, and Peggy will be glad to hear from me. I
know well the pleasure with which you will recognize the
characters of my hand, characters calling back to mind with
strong impression the idea of the person by whom they were
traced, & in vivid & thick succession, all the ready associations
clinging to that idea & impatience with which you will receive
any news which I can give you of myself. I know these things:
& I feel them. Amidst that repeated disappointment, & that
long dejection, which have served to overcast & to throw into
deep obscurity some of the best years of my life, years which
the idle & illusive dreams of boyish expectation had presented
glittering & gay & prosperous decked out in all the fairness
and all the brightness of colouring, & crowded with fantastic
forms of numerous hues of ever-varying pleasure, – amidst
much dissatisfaction and much sorrow, the reflection that
there are one or two persons in the world who are not quite
indifferent towards me, nor altogether unanxious for my
welfare, is that which is, perhaps, the most 'soothing to my
wounded spirit.'

Monday.

We have just received your letter. With respect to that part
of it which concerns my brother's business, I have information to give you of one new 7 guinea picture. As to my essay,
it goes on or rather it moves backwards & forwards; however

1. It is possible, of course, that he did return to Wem in 1795, and
that this letter was written during a visit to his brother in the following
year which is not otherwise documented.

it does not stand still. I have been chiefly employed hitherto in rendering my knowledge of my subject as clear & intimate as I could, & in arrangement of my plan. I have done little else. I have proceeded some way in a delineation of the system, which founds the propriety of virtue on its coincidence with the pursuit of private interest, & of the imperfections inseparable from its scheme. I have written in all about half a dozen pages of shorthand, & have composed one or two good passages, together with a number of scraps & fragments, some to make their appearance at the head of my essay, some to be affixed to the tail, some to be inserted in the middle, & some not at all. I know not whether I can augur certainly of ultimate success. I write more easily than I did. I hope for good. I have ventured to look at high things. I have toiled long and painfully to attain to some stand of eminence. It were hard to be thrown back from the mid-way of the steep to the lowest humiliation. I must conclude. You will not fail to give my love, & all our loves, to my mother & Peggy. ... Farewell. I am your affectionate son,

W. HAZLITT.

If we ask what had happened to produce the particular tone of this letter, the answer is to be found in the single word, overstudy. From 'reading David Hartley' for the purposes of his schoolboy essay, he had taken the plunge with his customary intensity into the sea of metaphysics. Hume, Berkeley, and Hobbes he had read for their own sakes; from Hobbes he had come back to Hartley, and started off again on a course of the French Encyclopædists. It was while reading the *Système de la Nature* of D'Holbach, he tells us, that he made a 'discovery', and conceived the desire of writing his own *Essay on the Principles of Human Action,* which essay, and no earlier one, is clearly the subject of the letter we have just read. He tried, and failed, and his failure is not surprising. The boy who had 'nearly killed himself' in America by the severity of his application to Latin Grammar was now rendering himself ill in

London by wrestling with intellectual problems too big for him. For his father's profession of the ministry he had no vocation. Leaving his brother's circle in which he was too young at present to feel any reassuring foothold, leaving his youthful essay in metaphysics uncompleted, he went back home to Wem. The first chapter in his life was over.

Twenty-seven years afterwards, writing an essay *On the Conduct of Life* for his own son aged twelve he said : 'I applied too close to my studies, soon after I was of your age, and hurt myself irreparably by it.'[1]

1. In the British Museum, among the Leigh Hunt MSS., are the original notes (unfortunately not complete) from which Hazlitt's son proposed to compile the biographical introduction to the *Literary Remains*. We there read : 'Enters a student early at Hackney College – school acquaintance – breaking up of the establishment in consequence of all the pupils (ill probationers for the ministry) turning Deists'. I have not succeeded in finding this interesting consequence of the French Revolution in England confirmed in independent evidence. The immediately following entry (also not conveyed to the text) is 'Overstudy'.

CHAPTER II

READING

(1796–8)

*

The greatest pleasure in life is that of reading, while we are young.
Whether Genius is Conscious of Its Powers.

I

HE came back to Wem and resumed his reading for pleasure.
We say resumed, because that reading had been begun long
before.

His earliest reading had been done in his father's library. We
may take here his portrait of his father, and of that library, from
My First Acquaintance with Poets:

After being tossed about from congregation to congregation
in the heats of the Unitarian controversy, and squabbles about
the American war, he had been relegated to an obscure
village, where he was to spend the last thirty years of his life,
far from the only converse that he loved, the talk about dis-
puted texts of Scripture, and the cause of civil and religious
liberty. Here he passed his days, repining but resigned, in the
study of the Bible, and the perusal of the Commentators –
huge folios, not easily got through, one of which would outlast
a winter! Why did he pore on these from morn to night (with
the exception of a walk in the fields or a turn in the garden to
gather broccoli-plants of his own rearing, with no small degree of pride and pleasure)? Here were 'no figures nor no
fantasies' – neither poetry nor philosophy – nothing to dazzle,

nothing to excite modern curiosity; but to his lack-lustre eyes there appeared, within the pages of the ponderous, unwieldy, neglected tomes, the sacred name of JEHOVAH in Hebrew capitals: pressed down by the weight of the style, worn to the last fading thinness of the understanding, there were glimpses, glimmering notions of the patriarchal wanderings, with palm-trees hovering in the horizon, and processions of camels at the distance of three thousand years; there was Moses with the Burning Bush, the number of the Twelve Tribes, types, shadows, glosses on the law and the prophets; there were discussions (dull enough) on the age of Methuselah, a mighty speculation! there were outlines, rude guesses at the shape of Noah's Ark and of the riches of Solomon's Temple; questions as to the date of the creation, predictions of the end of all things; the great lapses of time, the strange mutations of the globe were unfolded with the voluminous leaf, as it turned over; and though the soul might slumber with an hieroglyphic veil of inscrutable mysteries drawn over it, yet it was in a slumber ill-exchanged for all the sharpened realities of sense, wit, fancy or reason. My father's life was comparatively a dream; but it was a dream of infinity and eternity, of death, the resurrection, and a judgement to come!

In this library the boy brooded and browsed, turning over the pages, occasionally tackling a volume. Here he awoke to the superior charms of the humane essayists. Of Steele he says, in the *English Comic Writers*: 'I owe this acknowledgement to a writer who has so often put me in good humour with myself, and everything about me, when few things else could, and when the tomes of casuistry and ecclesiastical history, with which the little duodecimo volumes of the Tatler were overwhelmed and surrounded, in the only library to which I had access when a boy, had tried their tranquillising effects upon me in vain'.

We have come, we may think, to the period subsequent to the Liverpool visit. The Rev. William Hazlitt had been in youth a lover of the English novelists, but he had not perhaps thought their works worthy of possession. This deficiency was now corrected, and Cooke's Edition (1792) we are able to date. We may listen to Hazlitt on them, in *On Reading Old Books*:

Tom Jones, I remember, was the first work that broke the spell. It came down in numbers once a fortnight, in Cooke's pocket-edition, embellished with cuts. I had hitherto read only in school-books, and a tiresome ecclesiastical history (with the exception of Mrs Radcliffe's *Romance of the Forest*): but this had a different relish with it, – 'sweet in the mouth', though not 'bitter in the belly'. It smacked of the world I lived in, and in which I was to live – and shewed me groups, 'gay creatures', not 'of the element' but of the earth; not 'living in the clouds', but travelling the same road that I did; some that had passed on before me, and others that might soon overtake me. My heart had palpitated at the thoughts of a boarding-school ball, or gala-day at Midsummer or Christmas: but the world I had found out in Cooke's edition of the British Novelists was to me a dance through life, a perpetual gala-day. The sixpenny numbers of this work regularly contrived to leave off just in the middle of a sentence, and in the nick of a story, where Tom Jones discovers Square behind the blanket; or where Parson Adams, in the inextricable confusion of events, very undesignedly gets to bed to Mrs Slipslop ... With what eagerness I used to look forward to the next number, and open the prints! Ah! never again shall I feel the enthusiastic delight with which I gazed at the figures, and anticipated the story and adventures of Major Bath and Commodore Trunnion, of Trim and my Uncle Toby, of Don Quixote and Sancho and Dapple, of Gil Blas and Dame Lorenza Sephora, of Laura and the fair Lucretia, whose lips open and shut like buds of roses. To what nameless ideas did they give rise – with what airy delights I filled up the outlines, as I hung in silence over the page!

There is small reason to ask what the boy was doing with his days when the neighbours saw him only upon his nocturnal excursions. 'I knew "Tom Jones" by heart, and was deep in "Peregrine Pickle". I was intimately acquainted with all the heroes and heroines of Richardson's romances, and could turn from the one to the other as I pleased. I could con over that single passage in "Pamela" about her "lumpish heart", and never have done admiring the skill of the author and the truth of nature.' Sterne, Fielding, Smollett, Richardson, Cervantes, Le Sage, the Periodical Essayists -- such we make the tale of his reading to the age of fifteen.

Then there came, in London, the metaphysical studies, 'into which I launched shortly after with great ardour, so as to make a toil of a pleasure'. Nevertheless, he adds in the same essay, 'I did arrive at some very satisfactory and potent conclusions; nor will I go so far, however ungrateful the subject might seem, as to exclaim with Marlowe's Faustus -- "Would I had never seen Wittenberg, never read book" -- that is, never studied such authors as Hartley, Hume, Berkeley &c.' To the English he added the French philosophers, Condorcet, D'Holbach, Helvetius, and as a result of doing so, as we have seen, embarked unsuccessfully, and almost disastrously, upon his own first serious effort in writing.

To the period of his London residence had belonged one personal influence, and one only that we know of. Joseph Fawcett, who lives in Hazlitt's pages as the perfect reader and 'the friend of my early youth', is otherwise, we must admit, a figure of a good deal of obscurity to us. The school friend of Godwin, and from an early age Unitarian minister of Walthamstow, he combined with that office from 1785 the Sunday evening lectureship at the Old Jewry meeting-house, where he attracted, as we read in contemporary evidence, 'the largest and most genteel audience that ever assembled in a dissenting place of worship' -- an audience which included Mrs Siddons in the height of her fame.[1] It was here that the young Wordsworth, passing

1. *Gentleman's Magazine*, February 1804. Such is the obscurity into which an excellent man may fall, that no record is preserved (*Dict. Nat.*

through London on his way to France, sat at the feet of the
celebrated man and responded to his advocacy of the first principles of the Revolution. That Fawcett himself had a firsthand
acquaintance with events across the Channel we may learn
from the preface to his *Poems*: he was present at the Federa-
tion Festival of 1792 and composed an ode on the occasion.
Early in the war he resigned from the ministry. He did not
attain to the eminence of Priestley, who was driven from this
country to seek refuge in America, nor to that of Price, who
had enjoyed the honour of attack by Burke, but published his
principal poem, *The Art of War* (1795), and retired to Edge-
grove near Watford, where he tilled the soil and enjoyed good
literature until his premature death. 'It was here,' says Hazlitt
in a note to the *Life of Holcroft* of 1810, 'that I first became
acquainted with him, and passed some of the pleasantest days
of my life. He was the friend of my early youth. He was the first
person of literary eminence whom I had then known; and the
conversations I had with him on subjects of taste and philosophy
(for his taste was as refined as his powers of reasoning were
profound and subtle) gave me a delight such as I can never feel
again. The writings of Sterne, Fielding, Cervantes, Richardson,
Rousseau, Godwin, Goethe, etc., were the usual subjects of our
discourse, and the pleasure I had had in reading these authors
seemed more than doubled. Of all the persons I have ever
known he was the most perfectly free from every taint of
jealousy or narrowness. Never did a mean or sinister motive
come near his heart. He was one of the most enthusiastic
admirers of the French Revolution, and I believe that the disappointment of the hopes he had cherished of the freedom and

Biog.) of the date of Fawcett's birth; but as Godwin's contemporary he
would be Hazlitt's senior by about twenty years. His works are: *Sermons
Delivered at the Evening Lecture at the Old Jewry,* 1795; *The Art of
War,* 1795; *Poems,* 1798; *War Elegies,* 1801. The poetical works are
all directed against the institution of war, and Fawcett, it is clear to us,
was what the modern world has agreed to call a pacifist. Hazlitt may be
found quoting the opening lines of the *Art of War* as late as 1827, in
his essay *On the Feeling of Immortality in Youth.*

happiness of mankind preyed upon his mind, and hastened his death.' Fawcett's death was not until 1804, and long before that date we shall find Hazlitt once more in his company.

He came back to Wem, and here for two years he has no history, save the history of his reading. It was, no doubt, on his parents' part a time during which his health was being indulged. Spenser he read 'with a sort of voluptuous indolence,' and Chaucer he liked even better. He read Pope and Dryden and Goldsmith and Collins and the comic dramatists of the Restoration. We do not hear of Milton yet, nor yet, apparently, of Shakespeare. From time to time his uncompleted essay was taken out, without seriously troubling him. We learn of his influences from the essay on *Whether Genius is Conscious of Its Powers*:

> My three favourite writers about the time I speak of were Burke, Junius and Rousseau. I was never weary of admiring and wondering at the felicities of the style, the turns of expression, the refinements of thought and sentiment: I laid the book down to find out the secret of so much strength and beauty, and took it up again to read on and admire. So I passed whole days, months, and I may add years; and I have only this to say now, that as my life began, so I could wish that it may end.

One or two particulars we are able to add to this account.

His first meeting with Burke, he tells us, was in 1796, in some excerpts from the *Letter to a Noble Lord* which he read in a newspaper; and he became a convert to their style on the instant. 'I said to myself, "This is true eloquence: this is a man pouring out his mind on paper".' That, as we have seen and as we shall see again, was what he himself was not as yet able to do. 'All other styles seemed to me pedantic and impertinent. Dr Johnson's was walking on stilts; and even Junius's (who was at that time a favourite with me) with all his terseness, shrunk up into little antithetic points and well-trimmed sentences. But Burke's style was forked and playful as the lightning, crested like the serpent. He delivered plain things on a plain ground; but when he rose, there was no end of his flights and circumgyrations.' That Hazlitt learned from his study of Junius something about epigram, and from his study of Burke to deliver plain things on a plain ground, and to soar when soaring was suitable, would not, I think, be unreasonable contentions.

We come to Rousseau. 'Nothing could exceed the gravity, the solemnity', we read, 'with which I carried home and read the Dedication to the Social Contract, with some other pieces of the same author, which I picked up at a stall in a coarse leathern cover.' This we should suppose to have been in London. But he followed the *Contrat Social* with the *Confessions,* and the *Confessions* with *La Nouvelle Héloïse,* and these he read at Wem. 'We spent two whole years in reading these two works ... They were the happiest years of our life.'

Of Hazlitt reading Rousseau from his eighteenth to his twentieth year, we have a typical picture in the essay *On Novelty and Familiarity* :

I once sat on a sunny bank in a field in which the green blades of corn waved in the fitful northern breeze, and read the letter in the New Eloise in which St Preux describes the Pays de Vaud. I never felt what Shakespear calls my 'glassy essence', so much as then. My thoughts were pure and free. They took a tone from the objects before me, and from the simple manners of the inhabitants of mountain-scenery, so well described in the letter. The style gave me the same sensation as the drops of the morning dew before they are scorched by the sun; and I thought Julia did well to praise it. I wished I could have written such a letter. That wish, enhanced by my admiration of genius and the feeling of the objects around me, was accompanied with more pleasure than if I had written fifty such letters, or had gained all the reputation of its immortal author! Of all the pictures, prints, or drawings I ever saw, none ever gave me such satisfaction as the

rude etchings at the top of Rousseau's Confessions. There is
a necromantic spell in the outlines. Imagination is a witch.
It is not even said anywhere that such is the case, but I have
got it in my head that the rude sketches of old-fashioned
houses, stone-walls, and stumps of trees represented the
scenes at Annecy and Vevey, where he who relished all more
sharply than others, and by his own intense aspirations after
good had nearly delivered mankind from the yoke of evil,
first drew the breath of hope. Here love's golden rigol bound
his brow, and here fell from it. It was the partition-wall between life and death to him, and all beyond it was a desert! ...

'And bade the lovely scenes at distance hail.'

I used to apply this line to the distant range of hills in a paltry
landscape, which however had a tender vernal tone and a
dewy freshness. I could look at them till my eyes filled with
tears, and my heart dissolved in faintness. Why do I recall the
circumstance after a lapse of years with so much interest?
Because I felt it then. Those feeble outlines were linked in my
mind to the purest, fondest yearnings after good, that dim,
airy space contained my little all of hope, buoyed up by charming fears; the delight with which I dwelt upon it, enhanced by
my ignorance of what was in store for me, was free from
mortal grossness, familiarity or disappointment, and I drank
pleasure out of the bosom of the silent hills and gleaming
vallies as from a cup filled to the brim with love-philtres and
poisonous sweetness by the sorceress. Fancy!

He read Rousseau, and quoted Collins. He read Rousseau, and
even while he felt his 'glassy essence', was conscious that
Chaucer could do things which Rousseau could not do. He held
himself 'heart-whole' in the cause of the French Revolution,
and yet was willing to make tardy discovery of the beauties
in Burke's *Reflections* upon that event. He discovered Milton,
'I remember as long ago as the year 1798, going to a neigh-

bouring town (Shrewsbury, where Farquhar has laid the plot of his Recruiting Officer) and bringing home with me, "at one proud swoop", a copy of Milton's Paradise Lost, and another of Burke's Reflections on the French Revolution _. I was set up for one while.'

It is by stages such as these that he conducts us – or gives us the hints, rather scattered in many places, by which we may follow his progress if we choose – to his twentieth birthday. For that we may turn to *On Going a Journey*:

It was on the tenth of April 1798, and I sat down to a volume of the New Eloise, at the inn at Llangollen, over a bottle of sherry and a cold chicken. The letter I chose was that in which St Preux describes his feelings as he first caught a glimpse from the heights of the Jura of the Pays de Vaud, which I had brought with me as a *bonne bouche* to crown the evening with. It was my birthday, and I had for the first time come from a place in the neighbourhood to visit this delightful spot. The road to Llangollen turns off between Chirk and Wrexham; and on passing a certain point, you come all at once upon the valley, which opens like an amphitheatre, broad, barren hills rising in majestic state on either side, with 'green upland swells that echo to the bleat of flocks' below, and the river Dee babbling over its stony bed in the midst of them. The valley at this time 'glittered green with sunny showers', and a budding ash-tree dipped its tender branches in the chiding stream. How proud, how glad I was to walk along the high road that overlooks the delicious prospect, repeating the lines which I have just quoted from Mr Coleridge's poems.

Hazlitt, on his twentieth birthday, was still reading Rousseau, but he was quoting Coleridge's 'Ode on the Departing Year'. In the answer to the question how he came to be doing this lies the key not only to the passage but to an understanding of much in his life.

II

When Hazlitt, at the age of fifteen, entered Hackney College, Wordsworth, aged twenty-three, had already left Cambridge and been two years in France, Coleridge, aged twenty-one, was midway in his career at the same university, and Southey, two years younger, was at Oxford. For each of these young men, closely resembling himself in station, the five years from 1793 held experiences very different from those we have seen them hold for Hazlitt. Nor was their superiority in years the only factor in this difference. Wordsworth, flying towards the heart of the Revolution upon as strong a pinion as he afterwards flew away from it, immersed himself in its affairs at first in Paris and later in London. The degree of this immersion Professor Harper, following M. Legouis, has only recently made clear. Wordsworth was, what Hazlitt with more intimate opportunities never was, a disciple of Godwin. 'He met', in the words of his biographer, 'the passion of the hour with his own deep inward passion. He conquered love of country with love of mankind. He rebuked with a reasoned hatred of war the elemental instincts of a people in arms. For six years his tenacious and inwardly energetic nature held fast to his own religion. Well for him was it that prudence bade him keep to himself his perilous thoughts.' It was his prudence as well as his passion that took Wordsworth to nature. Receiving a legacy from a friend which, if small, was sufficient, he withdrew at the end of 1795 with his sister Dorothy to Racedown in Dorsetshire. A little earlier he had first met Coleridge in London.

In neither Coleridge nor Southey, who had met in 1794, was prudence at this or any other date a distinguishing characteristic, and it thus happens that the early career of each is lacking in that dignity from which Wordsworth's is never separable. If Southey, aided by his fellow-undergraduate George Burnett and in facile submission to the influences of the moment, invented Pantisocracy, it was Coleridge no doubt who named it. Unfortunately for Coleridge, the project of ideal residence on

the banks of the Susquehannah postulated feminine companionship, in the speedy and suitable provision of which he was no
match for his friend's superior practical abilities. When the
proposition of marriage presented itself singly – the funds required for Pantisocracy following less freely upon the joint
literary efforts of the friends than the wives upon the single
efforts of Southey – Coleridge fled from Bristol to London, to his
old schoolfellow Charles Lamb; from whom Southey, in whom
a passion for the principles of the Revolution had resulted in
no loosening of the moral fibres, retrieved him. The point which
we seize is that each of these young men, in a fashion more
public than Wordsworth's, had deeply committed himself. The
revolutionary dramas of Southey may fail to arouse in us any
longer an emotion of interest; but it is to the *Conciones ad
Populum* and *Watchman* of Coleridge (in which he had not
kept to himself his perilous thoughts), that we turn to this day
if we wish to learn in unmistakable prose how the young and
ardent of that generation regarded 'a causeless war against a
patriot people'.

Southey, after marrying his friend, began to draw away from
him, while Coleridge and Wordsworth drew closer together.
In July 1797, while on a visit to the cottage at Nether Stowey
in Somersetshire in which the former had settled, the latter
found a mansion, Alfoxden, available on exceptional terms, and
entered on a year's tenancy. Hence, as all the world knows,
sprang *Lyrical Ballads*. Both poets – Wordsworth now twenty-
eight, Coleridge twenty-six – were as yet unchanged in their
political views, the one the author in this year of 'The Ruined
Cottage', the other of that 'Ode on the Departing Year', which
we found Hazlitt reading. Coleridge, in addition, was a Unitarian in religion. He was sufficient of a Unitarian, at least,
to have gone about the country a good deal preaching to the
adherents of that sect with acceptance; with the result that in
December 1797 he received an invitation to submit himself as
successor to Mr Rowe of Shrewsbury. It remains to be added
that the emolument attaching to the office was £150 per annum,

and that in alleviation of neuralgia Coleridge had in the previous year resorted to laudanum. 'The Ancient Mariner' was written, and 'Christabel' – begun.

III

My First Acquaintance with Poets begins at the point at which our interpolated narrative has left off. In the belief that, however accessible to reference, it is more convenient to have the text before us, we shall make large excerpts from that essay here.

'My father,' says Hazlitt, 'lived ten miles from Shrewsbury, and was in the habit of exchanging visits with Mr Rowe, and with Mr Jenkins of Whitchurch (nine miles farther on), according to the custom of Dissenting ministers in each other's neighbourhood ... Coleridge had agreed to come over and see my father, according to the courtesy of the country, as Mr Rowe's probable successor; but in the meantime, I had gone to hear him preach the Sunday after his arrival. A poet and a philosopher getting up into a Unitarian pulpit to preach the gospel, was a romance in these degenerate days, a sort of revival of the primitive spirit of Christianity, which was not to be resisted.

'It was in January 1798, that I rose one morning before daylight, to hear this celebrated person[1] preach. Never, the longest day I have to live, shall I have such another walk as this cold, raw, comfortless one, in the winter of the year 1798. *Il y a des impressions qui ni le tems ni les circonstances peuvent effacer. Dusse-je vivre des siècles entiers, le doux tems de ma jeunesse ne peut renaître pour moi, ni s'effacer jamais dans ma mémoire.* When I got there, the organ was playing the 100th Psalm, and when it was done, Mr Coleridge rose and gave out his text, "And he went up into the mountain to pray, HIMSELF, ALONE". As he gave out this text, his voice "rose like a steam of rich distilled perfumes", and when he came to the last

---

1. 'Celebrated', of course, in other than a personal circle, not so much in 1798 as in 1817, the year in which Hazlitt was writing this passage. The completed essay was not written until 1823.

two words, which he pronounced loud, deep, and distinct, it seemed to me, who was then young, as if the sounds had echoed from the bottom of the human heart, and as if that prayer might have floated in solemn silence through the universe. The idea of St John came into my mind, "of one crying in the wilderness, who had his loins girt about, and whose food was locusts and wild honey". The preacher then launched into his subject, like an eagle dallying with the wind. The sermon was upon peace and war; upon church and state – not their alliance but their separation – on the spirit of the world and the spirit of Christianity, not as the same, but as opposed to one another. He talked of those who had "inscribed the cross of Christ on banners dripping with human gore". He made a poetical and pastoral excursion – and to show the fatal effects of war, drew a striking contrast between the simple shepherd-boy, driving his team afield, or sitting under the hawthorn, piping to his flock, "as though he should never be old", and the same poor country lad, crimped, kidnapped, brought into town, made drunk at an alehouse, turned into a wretched drummer-boy, with his hair sticking on end with powder and pomatum, a long cue at his back, and tricked out in the loathsome finery of the profession of blood :

"*Such were the notes our once-lov'd poet sung.*"

'And for myself, I could not have been more delighted if I had heard the music of the spheres. Poetry and Philosophy had met together. Truth and Genius had embraced, under the eye and with the sanction of Religion. This was even beyond my hopes. I returned home well satisfied. The sun that was still labouring pale and wan through the sky, obscured by thick mists, seemed an emblem of the *good cause*; and the cold dank drops of dew that hung half melted on the beard of the thistle had something genial and refreshing in them; for there was a spirit of hope and youth in all nature, that turned everything into good.'

So much for the young Hazlitt's pilgrimage to hear the

young Coleridge. Coleridge's visit to the Hazlitts follows.

'No two individuals were ever more unlike than were the host and his guest. A poet was to my father a sort of nondescript; yet whatever added grace to the Unitarian cause was to him welcome. He could hardly have been more surprised or pleased, if our visitor had worn wings. Indeed, his thoughts had wings, and as the silken sounds rustled round our little wainscoted parlour, my father threw back his spectacles over his forehead, his white hairs mixing with its sanguine hue; and a smile of delight beamed across his rugged, cordial face, to think that Truth had found a new ally in Fancy! Besides, Coleridge seemed to take considerable notice of me, and that of itself was enough. He talked very familiarly, but agreeably, and glanced over a variety of subjects. At dinner-time he grew more animated, and dilated in a very edifying manner on Mary Wollstonecraft and Mackintosh. The last, he said, he considered (on my father's speaking of his Vindiciæ Gallicæ as a capital performance) as a clever, scholastic man – a master of the topics – or, as the ready warehouseman of letters, who knew exactly where to lay his hand on what he wanted, though the goods were not his own. He thought him no match for Burke, either in style or matter. Burke was a metaphysician, Mackintosh a mere logician. Burke was an orator, (almost a poet) who reasoned in figures, because he had an eye for nature; Mackintosh, on the other hand, was a rhetorician, who had only an eye to common-places. On this I ventured to say that I had always entertained a great opinion of Burke, and that (as far as I could find) the speaking of him with contempt might be made the test of a vulgar democratical mind. This was the first observation I ever made to Coleridge, and he said it was a very just and striking one. I remember the leg of Welsh mutton and the turnips on the table that day had the finest flavour imaginable. Coleridge added that Mackintosh and Tom Wedgwood (of whom, however, he spoke highly) had expressed a very indifferent opinion of his friend Mr Wordsworth, on which he remarked to them – "He strides on so far before you, that he

dwindles in the distance!" Godwin had once boasted to him
of having carried on an argument with Mackintosh for three
hours with dubious success; Coleridge told him – "If there had
been a man of genius in the room, he would have settled the
question in five minutes". He asked me if I had ever seen Mary
Wollstonecraft, and I said, I had once for a few moments, and
that she seemed to me to turn off Godwin's objections to something she advanced with quite a playful, easy air. He replied,
that "this was only one instance of the ascendancy which people
of imagination exercised over those of mere intellect." He did
not rate Godwin very high (this was caprice or prejudice, real
or affected) but he had a great idea of Mrs Wollstonecraft's
powers of conversation, none at all of her talent for book-
making. We talked a little about Holcroft. He had been asked
if he was not much struck *with* him, and he said, he thought
himself in more danger of being struck *by* him. I complained
that he would not let me get on at all, for he required a definition of every the commonest word, exclaiming, "What do you
mean by a *sensation*, sir? What do you mean by an *idea*?" This,
Coleridge said, was barricading the road to truth; – it was
setting up a turnpike-gate at every step we took. I forget a
great number of things, many more than I remember; but the
day passed off pleasantly, and the next morning Mr Coleridge
was to return to Shrewsbury. When I came down to breakfast,
I found that he had just received a letter from his friend T.
Wedgwood, making him an offer of £150 a-year if he chose to
wave his present pursuit, and devote himself entirely to the
study of poetry and philosophy.[1] Coleridge seemed to make up
his mind to close with this proposal in the act of tying on one
of his shoes. It threw an additional damp on his departure. It

1. For the letter Coleridge received see Mrs Sandford's *T. Poole and
his Friends* (I. 259). Josiah and Thomas Wedgwood, aged at this date
thirty and twenty-seven, respectively, were the sons of the original potter
of Etruria, and were 'possessed of a considerable superfluity of fortune'
which they were 'earnestly desirous to convert into a fund of benevolence'.
They had been introduced to Coleridge by Thomas Poole of Nether Stowey
in the previous year.

took the wayward enthusiast quite from us to cast him into Deva's winding vales, or by the shores of old romance. Instead of living at ten miles distance, of being the pastor of a Dissenting congregation at Shrewsbury, he was henceforth to inhabit the Hill of Parnassus, to be a Shepherd on the Delectable Mountains. Alas! I knew not the way thither, and felt very little gratitude for Mr Wedgwood's bounty. I was presently relieved from this dilemma; for Mr Coleridge, asking for a pen and ink, and going to a table to write something on a bit of card, advanced towards me with undulating step, and giving me the precious document, said that that was his address, *Mr Coleridge, Nether-Stowey, Somersetshire*; and that he should be glad to see me there in a few weeks' time, and, if I chose, would come half-way to meet me. I was not less surprised than the shepherd-boy (this simile is to be found in Cassandra) when he sees a thunder-bolt fall close at his feet. I stammered out my acknowledgments and acceptance of this offer (I thought Mr Wedgwood's annuity a trifle to it) as well as I could; and this mighty business being settled, the poet-preacher took leave, and I accompanied him six miles on the road. It was a fine morning in the middle of winter, and he talked the whole way. The scholar in Chaucer is described as going

> *"Sounding on his way."*

So Coleridge went on his. In digressing, in dilating, in passing from subject to subject, he appeared to me to float in air, to slide on ice. He told me in confidence (going along) that he should have preached two sermons before he accepted the situation at Shrewsbury, one on Infant Baptism, the other on the Lord's Supper, shewing that he could not administer either, which would have effectually disqualified him for the object in view. I observed that he continually crossed me on the way by shifting from one side of the foot-path to the other. This struck me as an odd movement, but I did not at that time connect it with any instability of purpose or involuntary change of principle, as I have done since. He seemed unable to keep on in a straight line ...

'On my way back, I had a sound in my ears, it was the voice of Fancy: I had a light before me, it was the face of Poetry ... I had an uneasy, pleasurable sensation all the time, till I was to visit him. During these months the chill breath of winter gave me a welcoming; the vernal air was balm and inspiration to me. The golden sunsets, the silver star of evening, lighted me on my way to new hopes and prospects. *I was to visit Coleridge in the spring.* This circumstance was never absent from my thoughts, and mingled with all my feelings. I wrote to him at the time proposed, and received an answer postponing my intended visit for a week or two, but very cordially urging me to complete my promise then.[1] This delay did not damp, but rather increased my ardour. In the meantime I went to Llangollen Vale, by way of initiating myself in the mysteries of natural scenery; and I must say I was enchanted with it. I had been reading Coleridge's description of England in his fine Ode on the Departing Year, and I applied it, *con amore,* to the objects before me. That valley was to me (in a manner) the cradle of a new existence. ...'

The reason is now clear to us why Hazlitt, on his twentieth birthday, in the valley of the Dee, was reading Rousseau and

1. The postponement of the visit, apparently first planned to take place in late April or early May, may be variously accounted for. From the 10th to the 18th of April Coleridge was at Ottery St Mary visiting his relatives. (Harper, *Wordsworth,* I. 342.) In the same month Mr Campbell is disposed to place the retirement to 'a lonely farm-house between Porlock and Lynton', and the production of *Kubla Khan.* (*Coleridge,* p. 88.) Sime time in May, Cottle spent a week at Alfoxden, arranging for the publication of *Lyrical Ballads.* On the 14th, Coleridge's second son Berkeley was born. Two days later, Coleridge accompanied the Wordsworths on a trip through Bridgwater to Cheddar, and on the 22nd was at Cross, from which place he writes to a friend in Bristol that Wordsworth will return by way of that city (Harper, I. 345; Coleridge, *Letters,* I. 246). There is a variety of incident here, not unusual in the lives of these poets at this date. It is from this visit to Bristol, no doubt, that Wordsworth in the essay makes his return; while Hazlitt's arrival at Stowey, to which Coleridge and Dorothy Wordsworth had returned direct, may be dated with some certainty at the last days of May.

quoting Coleridge. He returned home from his solitary walking tour, and immediately afterwards set out for Somersetshire.

IV

His way lay through Shrewsbury, Worcester, Upton, Tewkesbury, Gloucester, Bristol, and Bridgwater, – a distance of one-hundred-and-fifty, or one-hundred-and-sixty, miles. We learn from the essay we are quoting that he did not hurry; we learn from other essays of adventures by the way – a metaphysical 'discovery' at Witham-Common (imparted to Coleridge on the sands at Lynton), an encounter with a strolling player in the valley of the Severn, half a night spent at Tewkesbury in reading the inn's copy of *Paul and Virginia,* two days (by which he found himself in advance of his time) at Bridgwater over Miss Burney's recently published *Camilla.*

'I arrived, and was well received. The country about Nether-Stowey is beautiful, green and hilly, and near the sea-shore ... In the afternoon Coleridge took me over to All-Foxden, a romantic old family-mansion of the St Aubins, where Wordsworth lived. It was then in the possession of a friend of the poet's, who gave him the free use of it.[1] Somehow that period (the time just after the French Revolution) was not a time when *nothing was given for nothing.* The mind opened, and a softness might be perceived coming over the heart of individuals, beneath "the scales that fence" our self-interest. Wordsworth

1. 'A mistake. I rented the house and had no personal knowledge of the trustees of its owner, then a minor' – Wordsworth's manuscript note, added to this passage as quoted in Barron Field's unprinted memoir of the poet. Wordsworth's biographers have in general been angry with Hazlitt regarding this passage, and Professor Harper finds in it 'the venom of his rancour'. The facts, of course, about Alfoxden are that Wordsworth took the house furnished for one year at a rental of £23 free of rates and taxes from the tenant of the St Albyns. But if for Alfoxden, Wordsworth's immediately preceding residence Racedown is substituted, the pretty evident origin of Hazlitt's mistaken impression is discovered. Racedown *was* lent to Wordsworth, rent free and furnished, as Professor Harper demonstrates, by the Pinneys of Bristol, who were friends of the poet and of his and their then political opinions.

himself was from home, but his sister kept house, and set before us a frugal repast; and we had free access to her brother's poems, the Lyrical Ballads, which were still in manuscript, or in the form of *Sibylline Leaves*. I dipped into a few of these with great satisfaction, and with the faith of a novice. I slept that night in an old room with blue hangings, and covered with the round-faced family portraits of the age of George I and II, and from the wooded declivity of the adjoining park that overlooked my window, at the dawn of day, could

"hear the loud stag speak" ...

'The next day Wordsworth arrived from Bristol at Coleridge's cottage. I think I see him now. He answered in some degree to his friend's description of him, but was more gaunt and Don Quixote-like. He was quaintly dressed (according to the *costume* of that unconstrained period) in a brown fustian jacket, and striped pantaloons. There was something of a roll, a lounge in his gait, not unlike his own Peter Bell. There was a severe worn pressure of thought about his temples, a fire in his eye (as if he saw something in objects more than the outward appearance), an intense high narrow forehead, a Roman nose, cheeks furrowed by strong purpose and feeling, and a convulsive inclination to laughter about the mouth, a good deal at variance with the solemn, stately expression of the rest of his face. ... He sat down and talked very naturally and freely, with a mixture of clear gushing accents in his voice, a deep guttural intonation, and a strong tincture of the northern *burr*, like the crust on wine. He instantly began to make havoc of the half of a Cheshire cheese on the table, and said triumphantly that "his marriage with experience had not been so unproductive as Mr Southey's in teaching him a knowledge of the good things of this life" ...

'We went over to All-Foxden again the day following, and Wordsworth read us the story of Peter Bell in the open air; and the comment made upon it by his face and voice was very different from that of some later critics! Whatever might be thought of the poem, "his face was as a book where men might read strange matters", and he announced the fate of his hero in prophetic tones. ... Returning that same evening, I got into a metaphysical argument with Wordsworth, while Coleridge was explaining the different notes of the nightingale to his sister, in which we neither of us succeeded in making ourselves perfectly clear and intelligible. Thus I passed three weeks at Nether Stowey and in the neighbourhood, generally devoting the afternoons to a delightful chat in an arbour made of bark by the poet's friend Tom Poole, sitting under two fine elm-trees, and listening to the bees humming round us, while we quaffed our *flip*.' That the elm-trees were lime-trees, and the bower that in which Coleridge's friend Charles Lamb had sat an exact year before, we may suppose.

But the narrative moves forward. 'It was agreed, among other things, that we should make a jaunt down the Bristol Channel, as far as Lynton. We set off together on foot, Coleridge, John Chester, and I. This Chester was a native of Nether Stowey, one of those who were attracted to Coleridge's discourse as flies are to honey, or bees in swarming-time to the sound of a brass pan. He "followed in the chase, like a dog who hunts, not like one that made up the cry". He had on a brown cloth coat, boots, and corduroy breeches, was low in stature, bow-legged, had a drag in his walk like a drover, which he assisted by a hazel switch, and kept on a sort of trot by the side of Coleridge, like a running footman by a state coach, that he might not lose a syllable or sound that fell from Coleridge's lips. He told me his private opinion, that Coleridge was a wonderful man. He scarcely opened his lips, much less offered an opinion the whole way: yet of the three, had I to choose during that journey, I would be John Chester. He afterwards followed Coleridge into Germany, where the Kantean philosophers were puzzled how to bring him under any of their categories. ... We passed Dunster on our right, a small town between the brow of a hill and the sea. I remember eyeing it wistfully as it lay below us: con-

trasted with the woody scene around, it looked as clear, as pure,
as *embrowned* and ideal as any landscape I have seen since, of
Gaspar Poussin's or Domenichino's. We had a long day's march
– (our feet kept time to the echoes of Coleridge's tongue)[1] –
through Minehead and by the Blue Anchor, and on to Lynton,
which we did not reach till near midnight, and where we had
some difficulty in making a lodgment. We however knocked
the people of the house up at last, and we were repaid for our
apprehensions and fatigue by some excellent rashers of fried
bacon and eggs. The view in coming along had been splendid.
We walked for miles and miles on dark brown heaths overlooking the Channel, with the Welsh hills beyond, and at times descended into little sheltered valleys close by the seaside, with a
smuggler's face scowling by us, and then had to ascend conical
hills with a path winding up through a coppice to a barren top,
like a monk's shaven crown, from one of which I pointed out to
Coleridge's notice the bare masts of a vessel on the very edge of
the horizon and within the red-orbed disk of the setting sun,
like his own spectre-ship in the Ancient Mariner. At Lynton the
character of the sea-coast becomes more marked and rugged.
There is a place called the *Valley of Rocks* (I suspect this was
only the poetical name for it) bedded among precipices overhanging the sea, with rocky caverns beneath, into which the
waves dash, and where the sea-gull for ever wheels its screaming
flight. On the tops of these are huge stones thrown transverse,
as if an earthquake had tossed them there, and behind these is a
fretwork of perpendicular rocks, something like the Giant's
Causeway. A thunder-storm came on while we were at the inn,
and Coleridge was running out bare-headed to enjoy the com-
motion of the elements in the Valley of Rocks, but as if in spite,

1. 'He could go on in the most delightful explanatory way over hill
and dale, a summer's day, and convert a landscape into a didactic poem
or a Pindaric ode. "He talked far above singing." If I could so clothe my
ideas in sounding and flowing words, I might perhaps wish to have some
one with me to admire the swelling theme; or I could be more content,
were it possible for me still to hear his echoing voice in the woods of
All-Foxden.' – *On Going a Journey* (1821).

the clouds only muttered a few angry sounds, and let fall a few
refreshing drops. Coleridge told me that he and Wordsworth
were to have made this place the scene of a prose-tale, which was
to have been in the manner of, but far superior to, the [Gess-
ner's] Death of Abel, but they had relinquished the design. In
the morning of the second day, we breakfasted luxuriously in an
old-fashioned parlour, on tea, toast, eggs, and honey, in the very
sight of the bee-hives from which it had been taken, and a
garden full of thyme and wild flowers that had produced it. On
this occasion Coleridge spoke of Virgil's Georgics, but not well.
I do not think he had much feeling for the classical or elegant.
It was in this room that we found a little worn-out copy of the
Seasons, lying in a window-seat, on which Coleridge exclaimed,
"*That* is true fame!" He said Thomson was a great poet, rather
than a good one; his style was as meretricious as his thoughts
were natural. He spoke of Cowper as the best modern poet. He
said the Lyrical Ballads were an experiment about to be tried
by him and Wordsworth, to see how far the public taste would
endure poetry written in a more natural and simple style than
had hitherto been attempted; totally discarding the artifices of
poetical diction, and making use only of such words as had
probably been common in the most ordinary language since the
days of Henry II. Some comparison was introduced between
Shakespear and Milton. He said "he hardly knew which to
prefer. Shakespear appeared to him a mere stripling in the art;
he was as tall and as strong, with infinitely more activity than
Milton, but he never appeared to have come to man's estate; or
if he had, he would not have been a man, but a monster." He
spoke with contempt of Gray, and with intolerance of Pope. ...
He liked Richardson, but not Fielding; nor could I get him to
enter into the merits of Caleb Williams. ... We loitered on the
"ribbed sea-sands", in such talk as this, a whole morning, and I
recollect met with a curious sea-weed, of which John Chester
told us the country name! A fisherman gave Coleridge an account of a boy who had been drowned the day before, and that
they had tried to save him at the risk of their own lives. He said,

"He did not know how it was that they ventured; but, Sir, we have a *nature* towards one another." This expression, Coleridge remarked to me, was a fine illustration of that theory of disinterestedness which I (in common with Butler) had adopted. I broached to him an argument of mine to prove that *likeness* was not mere association of ideas. I said that the mark in the sand put one in mind of a man's foot, not because it was part of a former impression of a man's foot (for it was quite new) but because it was like the shape of a man's foot. He assented to the justness of this distinction (which I have explained at length elsewhere, for the benefit of the curious)[1] and John Chester listened; not from any interest in the subject, but because he was astonished that I should be able to suggest any thing to Coleridge that he did not already know. We returned on the third morning, and Coleridge remarked the silent cottage-smoke curling up the valleys where, a few evenings before, we had seen the lights gleaming through the dark.

'In a day or two after we arrived at Stowey, we set out, I on my return home, and he for Germany. It was a Sunday morning, and he was to preach that day for Dr Toulmin of Taunton. I asked him if he had prepared anything for the occasion? He said he had not even thought of the text, but should as soon as we parted. I did not go to hear him – this was a fault – but we met in the evening at Bridgwater. The next day we had a long day's walk to Bristol, and sat down, I recollect, by a well-side on the road, to cool ourselves and satisfy our thirst, when Coleridge repeated to me some descriptive lines from his tragedy of Remorse ... I saw no more of him for a year or two.'

As though in confirmation of all the foregoing, we have a short note, which Mr W. C. Hazlitt prints, but is puzzled to allocate. We can allocate it with certainty, to the Sunday morning in late June on which the young Hazlitt said good-bye to Nether Stowey. 'My dear Father,' he says, 'I have just time to let you know that I shall set out on my way home this evening.

1. In 'Remarks on the Systems of Hartley and Helvetius,' attached to the *Essay on the Principles of Human Action* (1805).

Mr Coleridge is gone to Taunton to preach for Dr Toulmin. He is to meet me at Bridgwater, and we shall proceed from thence to Bristol tomorrow morning. You may expect to see me on Saturday, or perhaps not till the next day. I received your letter on Friday. Farewell. W. H.' We may know from this that six or seven days was the time he allowed himself for his not inconsiderable pedestrian journey.

V

He came back from his acquaintance with poets, not to try to write poetry, but to take out, 'for the twentieth time', his own uncompleted essay. 'I got new pens and paper, determined to make clear work of it, wrote a few meagre sentences in the style of a mathematical demonstration, stopped half-way down the second page; and, after trying in vain to pump up any words, images, notions, apprehensions, facts, or observations, from that gulf of abstraction in which I had plunged myself for four or five years preceding, gave up the attempt as labour in vain, and shed tears of helpless despondency on the blank, unfinished paper.' But the time had arrived at which he must do something. If he could not write what he wanted to write, he must be a painter.

CHAPTER III

PAINTING

(1799–1802)

*

Till I was twenty I thought there was nothing in the world but books,
when I began to paint I found there were two things, both difficult to
do and worth doing ; and I concluded from that time there might be fifty.

Conversations of Northcote.

I

WE left Hazlitt at Wem in Shropshire in the summer of 1798,
and we pick him up again at Bury St Edmunds in Suffolk in
the following winter and spring.

John Hazlitt, whose progress in his own branch of his profession had been rapid, spent a portion of each year in seeking the
patronage of the outlying centres of political and religious non-
conformity. Such a centre, in the closing years of the eighteenth
century, was Bury. Hither had recently retired Thomas Clarkson, the liberationist, temporarily worn out at the age of forty
by his efforts on behalf of the West African Negro. His wife was
Catherine, daughter of William Buck of the town. Friends of
the Clarksons, of the Bucks, and of Capel Lofft, constitutional
lawyer and political reformer, were the Robinsons, a family
engaged in trade in Bury, whose youngest son Henry Crabb was
now serving his apprenticeship to the law in London, but was
continuing to spend his vacations with his family. On one of
these, late in 1798 or early in 1799, he first met Hazlitt. We may
gather the manner of it.

'There was living in the Abbey Gate Street,' he says, 'a tea
dealer of the name of Kitchener, whose wife was the sister of

three gentlemen of considerable property, Messrs John, Nathan and Samuel Robinson. They (the Kitcheners) had a son who about this time married Miss Crisp, a cousin of Mrs Clarkson, and a daughter, a remarkably pretty girl, but not at all interesting, nor to be compared in any respect favourably with my sister, except as to beauty – yet my brother Hab. became this year her accepted suitor, and an intimacy of course arose between the families. One of the necessary consequences of this connection was that my brother Hab. had to look out for a business. ... Miss K.'s uncles were consulted, and with Mr Sam Robinson an intimacy sprang up which lasted during S. Robinson's life. It was through Sam Robinson that we all became acquainted with the Hazlitts.' This is dated 1799, but another passage which states that the first acquaintance was with 'John Hazlitt, the miniaturist' bears the date 1798. What appears clear is that Samuel Robinson was one of John Hazlitt's London patrons, that he introduced him to the Bury circle early in 1798,[1] and that Hazlitt, who had come to town to study under his brother since we last saw him, accompanied the latter on a professional stay in the neighbourhood late in that year or early in the following one. Crabb Robinson says definitely: 'When I became acquainted with him at Bury, he was living with his elder brother, a miniature painter'. The acquaintance begun in Bury was continued both there and in London.

Crabb Robinson was not yet a diarist, and it is to some Reminiscences written very many years later (not until 1849) that we turn for the remainder of what he has to tell us at this date:

Another interesting acquaintance which commenced at this period was with William Hazlitt, a man who has left a deservedly high reputation as a critic, but who at the time I first knew him was struggling against a great difficulty of expres-

1. In the catalogue of the summer exhibition of 1798 at Somerset House, we find: 'J. Hazlitt.—A frame containing the portraits of Mr S. Robinson, Mrs S. Robinson, Mr J. Robinson, Miss Kitchener, Mr N. Robinson.'

sion, which rendered him by no means a great favourite in company. His bashfulness, want of words, slovenliness in dress, etc., made him the object of ridicule. It will be better perhaps if I confine myself at present to what he was at this the first period of our acquaintance. He was the younger brother of John Hazlitt, the miniature painter. His first design was to be a dissenting minister, and for that purpose he went to the Unitarian New College, Hackney, and he was one of the first students who left that college an avowed infidel. He was then striving to become a painter, and lived with his brother. The moment I saw him I saw he was an extraordinary man. He had few friends and was flattered by my attentions. He used frequently to breakfast with me, and I rendered him a great service by introducing him to Anthony Robinson, who procured him his first job by inducing Johnson to publish his first work, *The Eloquence of the British Senate* (sic). This he never forgot. Late in life, years after I had refused to speak to him, he said to Mary Lamb, 'Robinson cuts me, but I shall never cease to have a regard for him, for he was the first person who ever found out there was anything in me.' But I was alone of this opinion then. I recollect saying to my sister about this time, 'Whom do you suppose I hold to be the cleverest person I know?' – 'Capel Lofft, perhaps?' – 'No.' – 'Mrs Clarkson?' – 'Oh! no.' – 'Miss Maling?' – 'No.' – 'I give it up.' – 'William Hazlitt.' – 'Oh, you are joking. Why, we all take him to be a fool.' At this time he was excessively shy, and in company the girls always made game of him. He had a horror of the society of ladies, especially of smart and handsome and modest young women. The prettiest girl of our parties about this time was Miss Kitchener. She used to drive him mad by teasing him. I was under great obligations to Hazlitt as the director of my taste. It was he who first made me acquainted with the Lyrical Ballads and the poems generally of Wordsworth, Coleridge, Lamb and Southey, with whom he was through life afterwards so closely connected, whom he so ill-treated, and who became so important to me. Hazlitt was also like myself a great admirer of Godwin and Holcroft and also about this time became acquainted with them.

There is a good deal here which takes us forward. We may remark for the present that Crabb Robinson was three years older than Hazlitt, that his circle of town acquaintances was considerably larger, but that, while he had met Holcroft in the previous year, he had not yet met Godwin, in spite of every effort on his part. Among a plethora of Robinsons we are here introduced to Anthony of that name, sugar refiner and philanthropist, the author in this year, at the age of thirty-six, of *A View of the Causes and Consequences of English Wars,* a work courageously hostile to the foreign policy of Pitt. He was an intimate friend of the diarist's, but was not related to him; and, like Joseph Fawcett, had until recently been a Unitarian minister.

The first contemporary evidence of Crabb Robinson's new friendship we find in a letter of June, to his brother Thomas at Bury: 'As to my German expedition, in a few days I shall have formed some plan. Holcroft I am to call upon immediately. When anything is settled you shall be informed. Having so lately seen you, I have no wish to make a visit to Bury merely for the sake of appearances. ... It is nevertheless very likely that I shall come – if I do not you will I am sure attribute it to a proper cause and not to want of affection to you or my sister for whom my esteem and regard have long been on the increase. By the bye, I justify my shewing her letter to W. Hazlitt: First, Because it did her credit: Second, Because if it offended Mrs [John] H[azlitt] it was of no consequence, and Third, the letter contained nothing which could give offence and if it could W. H. agreed with the sentiment and was by no means disposed to report unfavourably.' In the disregard of 'appearances', we may find a hint of the good Godwinian Robinson was at this date. He adds: 'I have been greatly amused by hearing one of Mackintosh's lectures. It was on the British Constitution.'

The lectures of James (afterwards Sir James) Mackintosh,

'On the Law of Nature and Nations', form the next fixed point in our narrative. They were delivered, no less than thirty-nine in number, from February to June, in Lincoln's Inn Hall. Their text was simple: 'It is my intention to profess publicly and unequivocally that I abhor, abjure, and for ever renounce the French Revolution, with its sanguinary history, its abominable principles, and for ever execrable leaders'. Hazlitt, as we know from the *Spirit of the Age*, attended the course:

> The havoc was amazing, the desolation was complete. As to our visionary sceptics and Utopian philosophers, they stood no chance with our lecturer. ... Poor Godwin, who had come, in the *bonhommie* and candour of his nature to hear what new light had broken in upon his old friend, was obliged to quit the field, and slunk away after an exulting taunt thrown out at 'such fanciful chimeras as a golden mountain or a perfect man'. Mr Macintosh had something of the air, and much of the dexterity and self-possession, of a political and philosophical juggler; and an admiring audience gaped and greedily swallowed the gilded bait of sophistry prepared for their credulity and wonder. Those of us who attended day after day, and were accustomed to have all our previous notions confounded and struck out of our hands by some metaphysical legerdemain, were at some loss to know *whether two and two made four,* till we had heard the lecturer's opinion on that head.

Also an attendant at these lectures, as we know from the same source, was Hazlitt's friend Joseph Fawcett. We hear for the first time in connection with them of a young man named Stoddart, five years Hazlitt's senior, who put everything that the lecturer said down in a book, and who, after going all lengths in the one direction, was shortly to display an equal readiness to go all lengths in the other. These were the years of the *Anti-Jacobin,* and the ebbtide of political conversion was running strongly.

We come immediately to our next fixed point. It had been, as we have seen, Hazlitt's childish assumption that he would be a painter, like his brother (the talent, indeed, was in some measure common to the family). His father had had other plans for him, but these in their turn had been displaced. When the necessity to make a start in life could be deferred no longer, he had turned to his brother's profession for lack of another. This absence of enthusiasm at the start of the new career which had brought him to London we may find depicted in a passage in *On the Pleasure of Painting*. 'I remember,' he says, 'that one afternoon I was reading the Provoked Husband with the highest relish with a green woody landscape of Ruysdael or Hobbema just before me at which I looked off the book now and then, and wondered what there could be in that sort of work to satisfy or delight the mind – at the same time asking myself, as a speculative question, whether I should ever feel an interest in it like what I took in reading Vanbrugh or Cibber?' And of Coleridge at Lynton he asserts: 'He had no idea of pictures, and at this time I had as little as he'. But this ignorance and this indifference were within a few months of his start in painting all to be changed. In December 1798, an exhibition of old Italian masters, known as the Orleans Gallery from the circumstance that the bulk of the pictures had come from the collection of the Regent Orleans in Paris,[1] was placed on sale in Pall Mall, where it remained until the July following. Somewhat late in its course, as we should suppose, Hazlitt discovered it. From the moment he did so, he attended no more lectures from reformed Scottish advocates:

I was staggered when I saw the works there collected, and looked at them with wondering and with longing eyes. A mist passed away from my sight; the scales fell off. A new

1. Mr Birrell (*Hazlitt*, English Men of Letters, 1902), following Sir Edmund Gosse (*Conversations of Northcote*, 1894), places this gallery in Paris – an error which interferes somewhat seriously, of course, with his chronology.

> sense came upon me, a new heaven and a new earth stood
> before me. ... From that time I lived in a world of pictures.
> Battles, sieges, speeches in Parliament seemed mere idle noise
> and fury, 'signifying nothing', compared with these mighty
> works that spoke to me in the eternal silence of thought.

He had seen his first Titians, his first Raphaels. Henceforward
with the intensity with which he had formerly been a reader,
he was to be a painter and a student of painting.

Crabb Robinson, whose German expedition was delayed, took
a holiday tour into Wales in the autumn of this year, 'scattering
some Democracy' as he went. In the course of it he found himself in the neighbourhood of Wem. 'Having ordered a mutton
chop,' he writes to his friend John Dyer Collier, 'I sent a note to
William Hazlitt, whom you know by name. His brother came,
and after taking a glass of wine with me, he introduced me to
his father, a very respectable Socinian minister. We had a
pleasant evening, but it being a family party I left them after
tea and finding a stranger in my room, spent two hours most
luxuriously in bed reading Barry's Letter to the Dilettanti
Society.' Hazlitt, no doubt, read that pamphlet also, and viewed
with approval the painter's suggestion that part of the Orleans
Collection should be acquired for the nation. We do not know
where he was, but perhaps we should not be wrong if we pic-
tured him in this October in his brother's back painting-room,
or scouring the picture-galleries of the country.

In the following April, Crabb Robinson left England – the
second of our characters to go sounding on his way to Germany.

II

For two years – 1800 and 1801 – we are now left without guidance, save for that of the essays. The first of these to which we
may turn is *The Letter Bell* :

> I have sat and watched the decaying embers in a little back

painting-room (just as the wintry day declined), and brooded over the half-finished copy of a Rembrandt, or a landscape by Vangoyen, placing it where it might catch a dim gleam from the fire; while the Letter-Bell was the only sound that drew my thoughts to the world without, and reminded me that I had a task to perform in it. ... Perhaps there is no part of a painter's life (if we must tell 'the secrets of the prison house') in which he has more enjoyment of himself and his art, than that in which, after his work is over, and with furtive sidelong glances at what he has done, he is employed in washing his brushes and cleaning his pallet for the day. Afterwards, when he gets a servant in livery to do this for him, he may have other and more ostensible sources of satisfaction — greater splendour, wealth, or fame; but he will not be so wholly in his art, nor will his art have such a hold on him as when he was too poor to transfer its meanest drudgery to others — too humble to despise aught that had to do with the object of his glory and his pride, with that on which all his projects of ambition or pleasure were founded. ... I used sometimes to hurry through this part of my occupation, while the Letter-Bell (which was my dinner-bell) summoned me to the fraternal board, where youth and hope made

> '... *good digestion wait on appetite*
> *And health on both;*'

or oftener I put it off till after dinner, that I might loiter longer and with more luxurious indolence over it, and connect it with the thoughts of my next day's labours.

John Hazlitt, from 1799 to 1804, was resident at 12 Rathbone Place, and it was here that Hazlitt's earliest labours as a painter were performed.

His first picture, painted, says his son, 'in the neighbourhood of Manchester', is described for us in *On the Pleasure of Painting*:

The first head I ever tried to paint was an old woman with the upper part of the face shaded by her bonnet, and I certainly laboured it with great perseverance. It took me numberless sittings to do it. ... If art was long, I thought that life was so too at that moment. I got in the general effect the first day; and pleased and surprised enough I was at my success. The rest was a work of time – of weeks and months (if need were) of patient toil and careful finishing. I had seen an old head by Rembrandt at Burleigh House, and if I could produce a head at all like Rembrandt in a year, in my lifetime, it would be glory and felicity, and wealth and fame enough for me! ... I tried, and failed again and again; I strove harder, and succeeded as I thought. The wrinkles in Rembrandt were not hard lines; but broken and irregular. I saw the same appearance in nature, and strained every nerve to give it. If I could hit off this edgy appearance, and insert the reflected light in the furrows of old age in half a morning, I did not think I had lost a day. Beneath the shrivelled yellow parchment look of the skin, there was here and there a streak of the blood colour tinging the face; this I made a point of conveying, and did not cease to compare what I saw with what I did (with jealous lynx-eyed watchfulness) till I succeeded to the best of my ability and judgement. How many revisions were there! How many attempts to catch an expression which I had seen the day before! How often did we try to get the old position, and wait for the return of the same light! There was a puckering up of the lips, a cautious introversion of the eye under the shadow of the bonnet, indicative of the feebleness and suspicion of old age, which at last we managed, after many trials and some quarrels, to a tolerable nicety. The picture was never finished, and I might have gone on with it to the present hour.[1]

1. 'It is at present covered with a thick slough of oil and varnish (the perishable vehicle of the English school) like an envelope of goldbeater's skin, so as to be hardly visible.' – Hazlitt's note to this passage, written in 1820. His first picture, a century nearer invisibility, is now preserved in the Maidstone Museum.

'When I was young,' says Hazlitt, 'I spent a great deal of my time at Manchester and Liverpool.' We know his father's friends, and his own and his brother's patrons in these rising towns – Dr Shepherd, ten years his senior, Unitarian minister of Gateacre and a burgess of Liverpool; William Roscoe, Liberal banker and poet, acknowledged by Hazlitt many years later in conversation with Northcote 'a very excellent man, and a good patriot'; and a Mr Railton, father of a daughter with whose name that of Hazlitt has been associated. But of this matter, as of some others of a kindred nature, we shall admit, if we are candid, that we know nothing.

His visit to his mother's family at Peterborough, on the way to which he turned aside to view the *Pictures at Burleigh House,* may be found in the essay of that name. He is writing twenty years later, in a mood of retrospect which we shall better understand when we get to that date :

In this dreaming mood, dreaming of deathless works and deathless names, I went on to Peterborough. I had business there : I will not say what. ... Oh God! that I could but be for one day, one hour, nay but for an instant (to feel it in all the plentitude of unconscious bliss, and take one long, last lingering draught of that full brimming cup of thoughtless freedom), what I then was – that I might, as in a trance, a waking dream, hear the hoarse murmur of the bargemen, as the Minster tower appeared in the dim twilight, come up from the willowy stream, sounding low and underground like the voice of the bittern – that I might paint that field opposite the window where I lived, and feel that there was a green, dewy moisture in the tone, beyond my pencil's reach, but thus gaining almost a new sense, and watching the birth of new objects without me – that I might stroll down Peterborough bank (a winter's day) and see the fresh marshes stretching out in endless level perspective (as if Paul Potter had painted them), with the cattle, the windmills, and the red-tiled cottages, gleaming in the sun to the very verge of the horizon, and watch the fieldfares in innumerable flocks, gamboling in the air, and sporting in the sun, and racing before the clouds, making somersaults, and dazzling the eye by throwing themselves into a thousand figures and movements – that I might go, as then, a pilgrimage to the town [Wisbeach] where my mother was born, and visit the poor farmhouse where she was brought up, and lean upon the gate where she told me she used to stand when a child of ten years old and look at the setting sun! – I could do all this still; but with different feelings. ... I had at this time, simple as I seemed, many resources. I could in some sort 'play at bowls with the sun and moon'; or, at any rate, there was no question in metaphysics that I could not bandy to and fro, as one might play at cup-and-ball, for twenty, thirty, forty miles of the great North Road, and at it again, the next day, as fresh as ever.

We pass to his portrait of his father, painted at Wem:

To give one instance more, and then I will have done with this rambling discourse. One of my first attempts was a picture of my father, who was then in a green old age, with strong-marked features, and scarred with the small-pox. I drew it with a broad light crossing the face, looking down, with spectacles on, reading. ... The sketch promised well; and I set to work to finish it, determined to spare no time nor pains. My father was willing to sit as long as I pleased; for there is a natural desire in the mind of man to sit for one's picture, to be the object of continued attention, to have one's likeness multiplied; and besides his satisfaction in the picture, he had some pride in the artist, though he would have rather I should have written a sermon than painted like Rembrandt or like Raphael. Those winter days, with the gleams of sunshine coming through the chapel windows, and cheered by the notes of the robin red-breast (that 'ever in the haunch of winter sings') – as my afternoon's work drew to a close, were among the happiest of my life. When I gave the effect I intended to any part of the picture for which I had prepared my colours, when I imitated the roughness of the skin by a lucky stroke of the pencil, when I hit the clear pearly tone of a vein, when I gave the ruddy complexion of health, the blood circulating under the broad shadows of one side of the face, I thought my fortune was made; or rather it was already more than made, in my fancying that I might one day be able to say with Correggio, '*I also am a painter!*' It was an idle thought, a boy's conceit; but it did not make me less happy at the time. I used regularly to set my work in the chair to look at it through the long evenings; and many a time did I return to take leave of it before I could go to bed at night. I remember sending it with a throbbing heart to the Exhibition, and seeing it hung up there by the side of one of the Honourable Mr Skeffington.

Hazlitt's Portrait of his Father was in the Royal Academy Exhibition of 1802 at Somerset House.

He was much out of London in these years, but it is to London that we turn for our only independent witness of him. In 1793 a Mr Knowles, a schoolmaster of Cork and a cousin of Sheridan, came to settle in London, bringing with him his son, James Sheridan Knowles. Either by political affinity with John Hazlitt, or by some association dating from the Bandon days of which we know nothing, the families became acquainted. The boy was a prodigy, and in 1798, at the age of fourteen, achieved publication with a ballad. It would be shortly after this date that he came to know Hazlitt, and we hear about their acquaintance in the little known *Life of Sheridan Knowles*[1] by his son:

1. Twenty copies only were printed, of which one is in the British Museum. The portraits of 'Sheridan Knowles and his daughter, about 1820', mentioned by Mr W. C. Hazlitt, from 1867 onwards, would, no doubt, be those of Knowles and his sister Charlotte alluded to above. Confirmation of Hazlitt's rope-dancing ambitions at this date will be found in *The Indian Jugglers* (1820): 'It is a great many years since I saw Richer, the famous rope-dancer, perform at Sadler's Wells. He was matchless in his art, and added to his extraordinary skill exquisite ease,

He had then recently left the Unitarian College at Hackney, and was trying his hand at painting. He was a frequent visitor at my grandfather's house, and both my father and his sister Charlotte served him as subjects for his canvas. ... At other times the critic and his pupil would diversify their labours by improvising a tight-rope, and trying to dance upon it; an art which Hazlitt desired, or fancied he desired, to cultivate. Later on he introduced the 'Boy-poet', as he called him, to Charles Lamb, and to Coleridge. Better still, he took the trouble of listening to his compositions and criticizing them. The tutelage of such a mind was invaluable to a lad who, with a strong love for poetry, had as yet insight only into his own ideas. And it was the more valuable because Hazlitt knew how to encourage as well as when to blame. He had an endearing tenderness of heart towards those whom he loved, and this was just the quality, and the only quality, which could gain complete mastery over the young poet. There is something very pleasing in the picture of a young man of Hazlitt's vigorous mind and large acquaintance with literature, conscious of powers which would make him a master among men, taking pains with a boy six years his junior, when he himself was not well out of his teens, and endeavouring to enlarge his views, and correct his judgement. 'He loved me,' said my father, years afterwards, looking back to this time, 'taught me as a friend, endearingly praising and condemning, as he saw cause, every little poem which I wrote. There was ore in him, and rich, but his maturer friends were blind to it. I saw it. He was a man to whom I could have submitted my life.'

Sheridan Knowles became an ensign in the militia, a medical student, an actor, a schoolmaster, and finally a tragic dramatist, and unaffected natural grace. I was at that time employed in copying a half-length picture of Sir Joshua Reynolds; and it put me out of conceit with it. ... Is it then so easy an undertaking (comparatively) to dance on a tight-rope? Let any one who thinks so, get up and try.' Knowles named one of his children, who died in infancy, Hazlitt Macready Knowles.

and, although after 1808 meeting him less frequently, continued his devotion to Hazlitt until the latter's death.

III

'I had made some progress in painting,' says Hazlitt, 'when I went to the Louvre to study.' In May 1802 the Peace of Amiens opened the door. His plans to see the finest picture gallery in the world – the Louvre enriched by the Italian spoils of Napoleon – were made in two quarters, the studio of his brother's friend Northcote, the contemporary of Reynolds, and the parlour of his Liverpool patron Mr Railton. In October, when he was successful in joining the stream Paris-wards, it was with a commission from the latter gentleman for five copies from the old masters that he did so.

With Hazlitt in Paris, we are on firm ground again, for this is one of the periods illustrated by his own letters. We may treat them, as we did those written earlier from Liverpool and from Hackney, to a process of selection. He put up at the Hotel Coq Heron, near the Palais Royal. His letter of first impressions, to his father, is dated 16 October : 'I arrived here yesterday. ... Paris is very dirty and disagreeable, except along the river side. Here it is much more splendid than any part of London. The Louvre is one of the buildings which overlook it. I went there this morning as soon as I got my *card of security* from the police-office. I had some difficulty in getting admission to the Italian pictures, as the fellows who kept the doors make a trade of it, and I was condemned to the purgatory of the modern French gallery for some time.[1] At last some one gave me a hint of what was expected, and I passed through. ... Titian's best portraits I did not see, as they were put by to be copied. The landscapes are for the most part exquisite. I intend to copy two

1. The reader desirous of testing Hazlitt's characteristic accuracy of recollection cannot do better than compare these contemporary letters with the account given twenty years later in *On the Pleasure of Painting*. The Louvre of 1802 will be found also in the *Life of Napoleon*.

out of the five I am to do for Railton. I promised Northcote to copy Titian's portrait of Hippolito de Medici for him. He had a print of it lying on the floor one morning when I called on him, and was saying that it was one of the finest pictures in the whole world; on which I told him that it was now at the Louvre, and that if he would give me leave, I would copy it for him as well as I could. He said I should delight him if I would, and was evidently excessively pleased. Holcroft is in London. He gave me a letter to Mr Merrimee, the same painter to whom Freebairn's letter was. I call on him this afternoon, and he is to go with me in the morning to obtain permission for me to copy any pictures which I like, and to assist me in procuring paints, canvas, etc.' J. F. L. Mérimée, painter, was the father of Prosper, author of *Colomba*. Freebairn was Robert Freebairn, a pupil of Wilson, and an exhibitor of landscapes at the Academy from 1782 to his death in 1808. This was the 'friend', no doubt, with whom Hazlitt, as narrated in *On the Pleasure of Painting,* had 'conned over the catalogue before setting out'. The letter concludes: 'I hope my mother is quite easy, as I hope to do very well'.

Four days later there is progress to report: 'I have begun to copy one of Titian's portraits. ... I made a very complete sketch of the head in about three hours, and have been working upon it longer this morning; I hope to finish it this week. Tomorrow and Saturday I can do nothing to it; there are only four days in the week in which one is allowed to, or at least able to, do anything. Friday is allotted to sweeping the rooms, and Saturday and Sunday are usually visiting days. There are great numbers of people in the rooms (most of them English) every day, and I was afraid at first that this would confuse and hinder me; but I found on beginning to copy that I was too occupied in my work to attend much to, or to care at all about, what was passing around me; or if this had any effect upon me indirectly, it was to make me more attentive to what I was about, in order that I and my copy might not fall into contempt. I intend to occupy the vacant days of the week in making duplicates of the copies

which I do here, and in doing a picture of myself, in the same
view as that of the Hippolito de Medici.' The postscript is: 'I
saw Bonaparte'.

Three weeks later we learn: 'I generally go to the Museum
about half-past nine or ten o'clock, and continue there till half-
past three or four. Charles Fox was there two or three mornings.
He talked a great deal, and was full of admiration.' Fox at the
Louvre will be found in the *Eloquence of the British Senate,*
and again in the essay *On Writing and Speaking.* The letter
adds: 'I have not yet seen Bonaparte near'.

The letter of a fortnight later says: 'I have been working
upon the portrait of Titian's Mistress, as it is called, these two
last days. I intend to complete this the beginning of next week,
if possible. ... If I succeed in this, which I am pretty confident
of doing, I shall have done eight of my pictures in eight weeks,
from the time I came here. But as one of them contains two
whole figures, it may be reckoned equal to two; so that I shall
have gone on at the rate of a portrait in a fortnight. I shall,
therefore, have a month left to do the other two heads, which
will make up the whole number. I intend to give an hour a day
to copying a Holy Family, by Raphael, one of the most beautiful
things in the world. Of this, and The Death of Clorinda [by
Lodovic Lana], I shall probably be able to get prints taken in
London, as this is frequently done; as my copies certainly contain all that is wanted for a print, which has nothing to do with
colouring. I intend to write to [Anthony] Robinson about it. I
was introduced this morning to Mr Cosway who is here, doing
sketches of the pictures in the Louvre, by a Mr Pellegrini, whose
pictures John knows very well, and whom I have seen with Mr
Merrimee. If Railton chooses, I will do a copy of a most divine
landscape by Rubens for him; but it will take at least a fortnight
to do it, most probably three weeks.'

On 19 December further progress is reported: 'I got on in
such a rapid style, that an Englishman, who had a party with
him, came up and told me, in French, that I was doing very
well. Upon my answering him in English he seemed surprised,

and said, "Upon my word, sir, you get on with great spirit and
boldness: you do us great credit, I am sure". He afterwards
returned: and after asking how long I had been about it, said
he was the more satisfied with his judgement, as he did not
know I was a countryman. Another wanted to know if I taught
painting in oil. I told him I stood more in need of instruction
myself; that that sort of rapid sketching was what I did better
than anything else; and that, after the first hour or two I generally made my pictures worse and worse, the more pains I took
with them.'

It is a little difficult to see how Hazlitt in Paris can have had
time for anything besides his painting, nor is there a word of
anything else in his letters. He visited the theatre, however, saw
Talma, and formed pretty definite views upon what the French
could do in the matter of acting. Henceforward he concedes to
Paris the three glories of 'the Louvre, the Garden of the Thuil-
leries, and the Théâtre Français'. We know that he read Racine
(apparently with a tutor), and preferred Shakespeare. There is
mention of a Paris resident of his own age named Edwards,
who took him about, and whose acquaintance he was pleased
to renew on his second visit twenty-two years later. In addition
to Cosway, he met Southey's friend Richard Duppa; but the
difficulty in Paris during the Peace of Amiens was not so much
to make English acquaintances as to avoid them. In this, we
may imagine, Hazlitt was fairly successful, in spite of the fact
that he lived in the Louvre. 'Here, for four months together, I
strolled and studied, and daily heard the warning sound –
"*Quatre heures passées, il faut fermer, Citoyens*" (ah! why did
they ever change their style?)' ...

It is in *On the Pleasure of Painting* too that we read: 'Where
the treasure is, there the heart is also. It is now seventeen years
since I was studying in the Louvre (and I have long since given
up all thoughts of the art as a profession), but long after I returned, and even still, I sometimes dream of being there again
– of asking for the old pictures – and not finding them, or
finding them changed or faded from what they were, I cry

myself awake! What gentleman-amateur ever does this at such
a distance of time – that is, ever received pleasure or took interest enough in them to produce so lasting an impression?'
The answer is that no gentleman-amateur ever did. The Louvre
did not suffice to make Hazlitt a painter, but it helped to make
him a writer.

CHAPTER IV

PAINTING AND WRITING
(1803–7)

*

Industry alone can only produce mediocrity, but mediocrity in art is not worth the trouble of industry.

On Certain Inconsistencies of Sir Joshua Reynolds' Discourses.

I

HE came back from the Louvre to renew his acquaintance with Coleridge. In the years that had passed since their parting at Bristol, Hazlitt, as we have seen, had been much out of London, while Coleridge had been very little in it. Returning from Germany late in 1799, he had begun to write for the *Morning Post* – 'not then,' as Hazlitt afterwards observes, 'a very ministerial paper.' In March appeared his 'Character of Pitt', which we know the latter to have read, admired, and noted for future reference. But in April Coleridge was off to the Lakes, where Wordsworth was getting on with the new *Lyrical Ballads* without him. What Coleridge got on with it would be harder to say: with his schemes at this period, as Mr Dykes Campbell says, 'it is impossible to keep pace'. However, they all came to nothing. He was again in town for a few weeks at the end of 1801, when his portrait was painted by John Hazlitt; and not again until February 1803, when he remained until April. Our best account of him at this date is given in a letter of May from his friend Humphry Davy to Poole: 'When I did see him, it was generally in large companies, where he is the image of power and activity. His eloquence is unimpaired, perhaps it is

89

softer and stronger. His will is probably less than ever com-
mensurate with his ability. Brilliant images of greatness float
upon his mind; like the images of the morning clouds upon the
waters, their forms are changed by the motions of the waves,
they are agitated by every breeze, and modified by every sunbeam. He talked in the course of one hour of beginning three
works, and he recited the poem of Christabel unfinished, and as
I had heard it before. What talent does he not waste in forming
visions sublime, but unconnected with the real world!' So
Hazlitt found him, doubtless, on his return from France.

If we wish to appreciate, or to localize, the decline of
Coleridge's practical powers, we cannot do so more conveniently
than by a reference to the reprinted *Essays on His Own Times*
(1850). We may there read the 'Character of Pitt' of March 1800,
and may follow it immediately with the 'Letter to Fox' of
November 1802. Each of these articles was contributed by
Coleridge to the *Morning Post,* and some part of the difference
between them we may be disposed to attribute to the circumstance that the proprietor of that journal, Daniel Stuart – an ex-
member with his brother-in-law Mackintosh of the Society of
the Friends of the People – had acquired it in 1795 as a Whig
organ and had continued its policy of opposition to Pitt until
the retirement of that statesman in 1801 gave him an opportunity
to transfer his support to Addington. But not all the difference.
Considerations of changed political viewpoint altogether apart,
the first is a fine and searching piece of prose writing, the second
a commonplace diatribe. Between the periods of journalistic
activity represented by these two articles, in the winter of
1800–1, Coleridge, unknown to his friends, had fallen for the
first time decisively under the domination of opium.

II

In the month of the renewal of the war – that renewal which
Coleridge, in his own after opinion, by his latest writings in the
Morning Post had done much to bring about – Hazlitt set out

from Liverpool on his second visit to poets. Our evidence for
his arrival is contained in a letter from Coleridge to Godwin in
June:

> You know the high character and present scarcity of
> Search's *Light of Nature*. A friend of mine, every way cal-
> culated by his prior tact and studies for such a work, is will-
> ing to abridge and systematize that work from eight to two
> volumes, in the words of Paley 'to dispose into method, to
> collect into heads and articles, and to exhibit in more compact
> and tangible masses what, in that otherwise excellent per-
> formance, is spread over too much surface'. I would prefix
> to it an essay containing the whole substance of the first
> volume of Hartley, entirely defeated from all corpuscular
> hypotheses, with more illustrations. Likewise I will revise
> every sheet of the abridgement. I should think the character
> of the work, and the above quotation from so high an
> authority (with the present public I mean) as Paley, would
> ensure its success. If you will read, or transcribe and send this
> to Mr Phillips, or to any other publisher (Longman and Rees
> excepted) you would greatly oblige me – that is to say, my
> dear Godwin, you would essentially serve a young man of
> profound genius and original mind, who wishes to get his
> *Sabine* subsistence from the booksellers, while he is employ-
> ing the remainder of his time in nursing up his genius for the
> destiny which he believes to be appurtenant to it.

This letter, written to Godwin in reference to Hazlitt but in
evident obliviousness that they were known to one another, is
our best evidence that Coleridge's relations with his former
protégé during the past five years cannot have been intimate.[1]

1. They had met, no doubt, on the return of Coleridge from Germany;
and at much the same date Hazlitt had seen Wordsworth in London, and
had met Southey. Our authority for these statements is a couple of
passages in Hazlitt's political writing of 1816–17. The first is from *Illustrations of the Times Newspaper*: 'See, here comes one of them [the
poets] to answer for himself. It is the same person who in the year 1800

The sojourn of the twenty-five-year-old Hazlitt in the Lakes is a somewhat tangled skein, which we shall do our best to unravel. That it began in all amity is evident; and its principal business is known to us. This was the execution of two portraits, of Coleridge and his son Hartley, now seven years old, to the order of Coleridge's recently acquired patron, Sir George Howland Beaumont.

Hazlitt, no doubt, soon met Wordsworth, for communication between the two establishments was constant, in spite of the dozen miles between them. The Clarksons of Bury were temporarily at Eusemere, at the north end of Ullswater. Southey had not yet arrived at Keswick, but was expected. De Quincey did not pay his first visit to the Lakes until 1807, and so, other considerations apart, is not a good informant on relations existing between Hazlitt and Dorothy Wordsworth. Unfortunately, the latter's published Journal is silent over this period, except

was for making an example of the whole House of Commons (in spite of the humble petition and remonstrance of the writer of this article in favour of a small minority), for being the echoes of the King's speeches for carrying on the war against the French Revolution. What is that *thing* he has in his hand? It is not, nor it cannot be, a sonnet to the King, celebrating his "royal fortitude" in having brought that war to a successful close fourteen years after!' The second is from *The Courier and Wat Tyler,* when Coleridge, in defending the Laureate's changed opinions, had likened Hazlitt, Leigh Hunt, and Cobbett to the ass which found Apollo's lute after he had ascended to the seat of the Muses. Hazlitt said: 'Of the three persons that Mr Coleridge, by a most preposterous anachronism, has selected to compose his asinine auditory, Mr Hunt was at the time in question a boy at school, not a *stripling bard* of nineteen or nine and twenty, but a real school-boy, "declaiming on the patriotism of Brutus". As to Mr Cobbett, he would at that time, had they come in his way, with one kick of his hard hoofs, have made a terrible crash among "the green corn" of Mr Southey's Jacobin Pan's-pipe, and gone near to knock out the musician's brains into the bargain. The second person in this absurd trinity, who certainly thinks it "a robbery to be made equal to the other two", was the only hearer present at the rehearsal of Mr Southey's overtures to Liberty and Equality.' Obscure as are the relations of Hazlitt with the poets between 1798 and 1803, it is of importance to note that he had seen each of them for himself in their phase of equalitarian and republican enthusiasm, and was the best of authorities as to its duration.

for the Scotch tour, as it happened to be silent over the period
of their earlier acquaintance at Stowey.

One or two hints we have. The first is thrown into *My First
Acquaintance with Poets*.

> I once hinted to Wordsworth, as we were sailing in his boat
> on Grasmere Lake, that I thought he had borrowed the idea
> of his Poems on the Naming of Places from the local inscrip-
> tions of the same kind in Paul and Virginia. He did not own
> the obligation.

And we may turn to *The Spirit of the Age* for the personal
portrait with some confidence, since Hazlitt only met Wordsworth on one occasion afterwards:[1]

> Mr Wordsworth, in his person, is above the middle size,
> with marked features, and an air somewhat stately and
> Quixotic. He reminds one of some of Holbein's heads, grave,
> saturnine, with a slight indication of sly humour, kept under
> by the manners of the age or by the pretensions of the person.
> He has a peculiar sweetness in his smile, and great depth and
> manliness and a rugged harmony in the tones of his voice.
> His manner of reading his own poetry is particularly impos-
> ing; and in his favourite passages his eye beams with preter-
> natural lustre, and the meaning labours slowly up from his
> swelling breast. ... In company, even in a *tête-à-tête*, Mr
> Wordsworth is often silent, indolent, and reserved. If he is
> become verbose and oracular of late years, he was not so in
> his better days. He threw out a bold or an indifferent remark
> without either effort or pretension, and relapsed into musing
> again. He shone most (because he seemed most roused and

1. 'I cannot recollect that I ever saw him but once since the year 1803
or 1804, when he passed some time in this neighbourhood. He was then
practising portrait-painting with professional views. At his desire I sat
to him, but as he did not satisfy himself or my friends, the unfinished
work was destroyed.' Wordsworth to Hazlitt's son, 23 May 1834. The
one occasion, which we shall come to (p. 129), was at Lamb's in April
1808.

animated) in reciting his own poetry, or in talking about it. He sometimes gave striking views of his feelings and trains of association in composing certain passages; or if one did not always understand his distinctions, still there was no want of interest – there was a latent meaning worth inquiring into, like a vein of ore that one cannot exactly hit upon at the moment, but of which there are sure indications. His standard of poetry is high and severe, almost to exclusiveness. He admits of nothing below, scarcely of anything above himself. It is fine to hear him talk of the way in which certain subjects should have been treated by eminent poets, according to his notions of the art. ... Mr Wordsworth himself wrote a tragedy when he was young; and we have heard the following energetic lines quoted from it,[1] as put into the mouth of a person smit with remorse for some rash crime:

> *'Action is momentary,*
> *The motion of a muscle, this way or that;*
> *Suffering is long, obscure and infinite!'*

And finally (in *On the Character of the Country People*):

I remember our laughing a good deal at Wordsworth's old Molly, who had never heard of the French Revolution, ten years after it happened.

It was soon to be Hazlitt's charge against Wordsworth, not entirely without justification, that he himself wrote as though he had never heard of the French Revolution.

Early in August Sir George Beaumont visited Greta Hall.

1. By Wordsworth himself, at this time. Compare 'The Borderers' (ll. 1539–42), and Wordsworth's note to 'The White Doe of Rylstone' (1837), to which poem these hitherto unpublished lines were added as part of a dedicatory postscript: 'This and the five lines that follow, were either read or recited by me, more than thirty years since, to the late Mr Hazlitt, who quoted some expressions in them (imperfectly remembered) in a work of his published several years ago.' This is a good example of Hazlitt's characteristic powers of memory, by which, there is reason to believe, he made the bulk of the quotations throughout his works.

This was the occasion on which he first met Wordsworth and presented him with a piece of ground at Keswick in order that he might live nearer to Coleridge, a project which was destined to disappointment. That this was the occasion also of Hazlitt's only meeting with him, we have every reason to believe. We learn of it in an entry made by Crabb Robinson in his Diary, under date 4 March 1811: 'Hazlitt had once hopes of being patronized by Sir George Beaumont. Coleridge and he were dining with him, when C. began a furious attack on Junius. H. grew impatient at C.'s cant, and could not refrain from contradicting him. A warm and angry dispute arose. The next day C. called on H. and said, "I am come to show you how foolish it is for persons who respect each other to dispute warmly, for after all they will probably think the same". C. produced an interlined copy of Junius full of expressions of admiration, from which it appeared that C. himself really agreed with H. "But," added H. to me, "Sir G. Beaumont is a high tory, and was so offended with me, both for presuming to contradict and interrupt Coleridge and for being a great admirer of Junius, that in disgust he never saw me afterwards. And I lost the expectation of gaining a patron."' We may gain from this a hint of what does not surprise us – that before the first part of Hazlitt's stay in the Lakes was over causes of difference had presented themselves.

From 8 to 14 August, the poet Rogers was at Grasmere, and it is with his presence in the neighbourhood, or with that of the Clarksons, that we should associate another visitor, Richard ('Conversation') Sharp, the Liberal banker and intimate of the Wedgwood-Mackintosh circle. On 14 August the Wordsworths (William and Dorothy) set off with Coleridge on their tour into Scotland, while Hazlitt returned to his painting headquarters at Liverpool and Manchester.

The history of this tour is well known, and forms no part of our subject. It will be remembered that all went well for a fortnight, when Coleridge made up his mind to leave his companions and their gig, and to return on foot by himself. Mr

Campbell supposes that he 'had found the close companionship incompatible with that free indulgence in narcotics which had become to him a necessity of pleasurable or even tolerable existence'. At any rate, after walking hundreds of miles on his own account, he was back at Greta Hall on 15 September.

We come immediately to this letter:

Coleridge to Thomas Wedgwood
Greta Hall, Keswick.
September 16, 1803.

My dear Wedgwood,

I reached home on yesterday noon, and it was not a Post Day. William Hazlitt is a thinking, observant, original man, of great power as a Painter of Character-Portraits, and far more in the manner of the old Painters than any living Artist, but the objects must be *before* him; he has no imaginative memory. So much for his intellectuals. His manners are 99 in 100 singularly repulsive; brow-hanging, shoe-contemplative, strange. Sharp seemed to like him; but Sharp saw him only for half an hour, and that walking. He is, I verily believe, kindly-natured; is very fond of, attentive to, and patient with children; but he is jealous, gloomy, and of an irritable pride. With all this, there is much good in him. He is disinterested; an enthusiastic lover of the great men who have been before us; he says things that are his own, in a way of his own; and though from habitual shyness, and the outside and bearskin at least, of misanthropy, he is strangely confused and dark in his conversation, and delivers himself of almost all his conceptions with a Forceps, yet he says more than any man I ever knew (yourself only excepted) that is his own in a way of his own; and oftentimes when he has warmed his mind, and the synovial juice has come out and spread over his joints, he will gallop for half an hour together with real eloquence. He sends well-headed and well-feathered Thoughts straight forwards to the mark with a Twang of the Bowstring. If you could recommend him as a portrait-painter, I should be glad. To be your

Companion, he is, in my opinion, utterly unfit. His own
health is fitful.

I have written as I ought to do, to you most freely, *imo ex
corde*; you know me, both head and heart, and will make
what deductions your reasons will dictate to you. I can think
of no other person. What wonder. For the last years I have
been shy of all new acquaintance, &c.

And so on, in the Coleridgean manner to a patron. This letter
was in reply to one from Thomas Wedgwood, whose health
was giving cause for anxiety, asking for a companion on his
projected tour abroad. He had waited long for Coleridge; but
Coleridge, whose own pet project was just now for 'Teneriffe
or Gran Canaria', had made up his mind that he was not well
enough to go anywhere with another invalid. Wedgwood had
then tried the poet Campbell, but Campbell was getting
married. He now thought of trying Hazlitt (on the report, no
doubt, of Richard Sharp), and met with Coleridge's discourage-
ment. Thus vanished for Hazlitt, although perhaps unknown
to him, another chance of a patron.

One further passage from this letter is relevant to our subject:
'For 5 months past my mind has been strangely shut up. I will
not trouble you with the gloomy Tale of my Health. While I
am awake, by patience, employment, effort of mind, and walking, I can keep the fiend at arm's length, but the Night is my
Hell! sleep my tormenting Angel! Three nights out of four I
fall asleep struggling to lie awake; and my frequent night-
screams have almost made me a nuisance in my own House.'
Hazlitt could by this date probably have written of Coleridge
imo ex corde.

In the meantime (7 September) Southey had arrived, to enter
upon that residence at Greta Hall which lasted so much longer
than Coleridge's. On 1 October we have Coleridge writing to
Sir George Beaumont: 'Southey seems very happy at present.
His eyes plague him, but he is a hard taskmaster to them. He
is the most industrious man I know, or have ever known. His

present occupations are the recomposition of his "Madoc", an epic poem, and his great History of Portugal, of which he had written considerably more than a quarto volume. We have not heard of or from Hazlitt. He is at Manchester, we suppose, and has both portraits with him.' Before the end of the month, however, Hazlitt was back at Keswick. We know this from an entry in Coleridge's published notebook, *Anima Poetæ,* under date 26 October. 'A most unpleasant dispute', we read, 'with Wordsworth and Hazlitt. I spoke, I fear, too contemptuously; but they spoke so irreverently, so malignantly of the Divine Wisdom, that it overset me. Hazlitt, how easily raised to rage and hatred self-projected! but who shall find the force that can drag him up out of the depth into one expression of kindness, into the showing of one gleam of the light of love in his countenance.' We are a long way here from the 'young man of profound genius and original mind' of the letter to Godwin, and even some distance from the letter to Wedgwood; but it is fair to remember that Coleridge was writing in his little book in the middle of the night, and just after having had the thin end of an agument. That its other end should have been shared by Wordsworth and Hazlitt is something that is unique in our experience.

The latter had evidently returned for the purpose of putting some finishing touches to the portrait of Coleridge, and the following morning (27 October), with Wordsworth gone back to Grasmere and to his military exercises,[1] we find all apparent amity again. 'I sate for my picture – heard from Southey the Institution of the Jesuits, during which some interesting idea occurred to me, and has escaped. I made out, however, the whole business of the origin of evil satisfactorily to my own mind, and forced Hazlitt to confess that the metaphysical argument re-

---

1. 'They are sadly remiss at Keswick in putting themselves to trouble in defence of the country. ... At Grasmere, we have turned out almost to a man. We are to go to Ambleside on Sunday, to be mustered, and to put on, for the first time, our military apparel.' Wordsworth to Sir George Beaumont, 14 October 1803.

duced itself to this.' Since the metaphysical argument did not reduce itself to small bulk, we need not go into it; but may content ourselves with the picture – of Coleridge talking, Hazlitt painting, and Southey reading to the pair of them from his great History of Portugal.

We would give much for a continuation of such evidence, but this is denied to us. The next news we have of any kind is of Hazlitt's departure, and it comes six weeks later, on 14 December, in a letter from Southey to the painter, Richard Duppa. 'Hazlitt,' says Southey, 'whom you saw at Paris, has been here; a man of real genius. He has made a very fine picture of Coleridge for Sir George Beaumont, which is said to be in Titian's manner: he has also painted Wordsworth, but so dismally, though Wordsworth's face is his idea of physiognomical perfection, that one of his friends, on seeing it, exclaimed, "At the gallows – deeply affected by his deserved fate – yet determined to die like a man"; and if you saw the picture, you would admire the criticism.' We might think it probable that the Wordsworth was painted, or at least resumed, during these six weeks, after the Coleridge was completed; but what we should not think probable was that Hazlitt, when the above words were written, had just left the neighbourhood under circumstances of notoriety with which Southey not only could not fail to have been familiar, but in which he had even borne a principal hand. Nevertheless it appears that this is what we have to believe.

Undoubtedly before Hazlitt left the Lakes he indulged in an amatory escapade from the consequences of which he had to be extricated. Our misfortune is that we are allowed to hear nothing about it in immediately contemporary evidence; and when we do hear about it, after twelve years have elapsed, we find it hard to resist the impression that the enormity of the offence has grown proportionately with political differences. When Wordsworth, smarting under the sense that Hazlitt was no fit person to review his 'Excursion', felt impelled to tell Lamb all about it, Lamb replied (28 December 1814): 'The 'scapes of the great god Pan who appeared among your mountains some dozen years since and his narrow chance of being submerged by the swains, afforded me much pleasure. I can conceive the water nymphs pulling for him. He would be another Hylas. W. Hylas.' Shortly afterwards, in the heat of Waterloo year, Wordsworth told his version of the story to Crabb Robinson, who, more receptive than Lamb, put it all down in his diary:

15 June 1815 : – After breakfast, I called on Wordsworth for the first time at his lodgings. He was luckily at home, and I spent the forenoon with him walking. We talked about Hazlitt in consequence of a malignant attack on W. by him in Sunday's *Examiner*. [The reader will perhaps reserve his judgement as to the 'malignancy' of this attack.] W. that very day called on Hunt, who in a manly way asked whether W. had seen the paper of the morning, saying if he had he should consider his call as a higher honour. He disclaimed the article. The attack by H. was a note in which after honouring Milton for being a consistent patriot he sneered at W. as the author of 'paltry sonnets upon the Royal fortitude', and insinuated that he had left out the Female Vagrant, a poem describing the miseries of war sustained by the poor. This led to W.'s mentioning the cause of his coolness towards H. It appears that H. when at Keswick narrowly escaped being ducked by the populace and probably sent to prison for some gross attacks on women. [Here follow half a dozen words in the diarist's not infrequent shorthand, the key to which is lacking.] The populace were incensed against him and pursued him, but he escaped to W. who took him into his house at midnight, gave him clothes and money (from 3 to 5 pounds). Since that time W. though he never refused to meet W. [*sic*] when by accident they came together did not choose that with his knowledge he should be invited. In consequence Lamb never asked H. when he was in town, which probably provoked H. and which Lamb himself disapproved of. But L. who needs very little indulgence for himself is very in-

dulgent towards others, and rather reproaches W. for being inveterate against H.[1]

What Wordsworth told Lamb and Crabb Robinson he told others, who did not scruple to use against Hazlitt in his fortieth year the alleged excesses of his twenty-sixth. Perhaps the singular degree in which his second sojourn with poets was to afford him proof that while action is momentary the consequences which result from it may be long, obscure, and infinite, was the reason he remembered the lines from Wordsworth's 'Borderers'.

III

Before Hazlitt could become a writer it was necessary that he should fail in some degree to satisfy himself as a painter. This he had done at the Lakes. But on looking back on his painting career he was inclined, as we can see, to telescope it. 'When I was young,' he writes, very nearly at the end of his life (in *The English Students at Rome*), 'I made one or two studies of strong contrasts of light and shade in the manner of Rembrandt with

1. The above account, which the reader will scarcely need to be told is not a very sympathetic or temperate one, is probably placed in its truer proportions by Patmore, who makes it 'a story relating to Hazlitt's alleged treatment of some pretty village jilt, who, when he was on a visit to Wordsworth, had led him to believe she was not insensible to his attentions; and then, having induced him to "commit" himself to her in some ridiculous manner, turned round upon him, and made him the laughing-stock of the village.' (*My Friends and Acquaintance*, III. 141–2.) We have here an earlier version of the *Liber Amoris* story, which would not in its outline appear incredible to us. Hazlitt's 'conduct on this occasion' (i.e. his angry conduct) Patmore understood to have been 'the immediate cause of that breach between him and his friends (at least Wordsworth and Southey) which was never afterwards healed'. That the breach was *not* immediate, however, the letter of the latter to Duppa (above) would seem to show. Our only other published source of information is Gillman's *Life of Coleridge*, and our confidence in the Wordsworth version is not increased when we read (p. 276), as the principal ground of a charge of 'ingratitude' against Hazlitt, that 'his very life had been saved by *Coleridge and Mr Southey*'. What is clear to us, I think, is that in after years, when Hazlitt had begun to write against them, each of the poets was equally anxious to appear in the character of his benefactor.

great care and (as it was thought) with some success. But after I had once copied some of Titian's portraits in the Louvre, my ambition took a higher flight. Nothing would serve my turn but heads like Titian – Titian expressions, Titian complexions, Titian dresses; and as I could not find these where I was, after one or two abortive attempts to engraft Italian art on English nature, I flung away my pencil in disgust and despair. Otherwise I might have done as well as others, I dare say, but from a desire to do too well.' His disgust and despair came, and we shall see pretty clearly when they came; but they did not come yet, as his son suggests, nor did he fling away his pencil before taking up his pen. We shall now find him writing his own first work with the one, while he paints his new friend Charles Lamb, in a Titian dress, with the other.

He came back from the Lakes to resume his residence with his brother, who, continuing to prosper, had recently removed from Rathbone Place to 109 Great Russell Street. His first meeting with Lamb we are able to date. 'It was at Godwin's,' he says, in that tail to the *Acquaintance with Poets* into which he also brings Southey, 'that I first met him with Holcroft and Coleridge, where they were disputing fiercely which was the best – *Man as he was, or man as he is to be*. "Give me", says Lamb, "man as he is *not* to be." This saying was the beginning of a friendship between us, which I believe still [1823] continues.' Holcroft, Coleridge and Lamb might be brought together at Godwin's in the spring of the year previous (but not earlier); but in view of the letter from Coleridge to Godwin which we have read (p. 91) it does not seem probable that the meeting can have belonged to any other year than the present one. From the middle of February Coleridge was in London, sitting to Northcote for his portrait, and seeing much of both Lamb and Godwin. On 27 March he left London for Malta.

Charles Lamb, aged twenty-nine, was three years and six months older than Hazlitt, and some eight years older as an author. His *Poems* dated from 1796, and those which he had contributed with Charles Lloyd to the second edition of

Coleridge's from the year following. In 1798 he had written
Rosamund Gray, and in 1800 *John Woodvil*. With George
Burnett he had compiled *Specimens of English Prose Writers*,
and with James White concocted *Falstaff's Letters*. He had
done about four years' journalism, chiefly for the *Morning Post*;
had revised Godwin's tragedy of *Antonio*, but not saved it; and
was now about to write his successful children's books for that
philosopher turned bookseller. His curiously composite circle
of friends (considering their disparity) was already for the most
part assembled; and in addition he had well established himself,
by old association and his own continued sterling merit, in that
position in the respective counsels of Coleridge, Wordsworth
and Southey which he held all his life so remarkably. The first-
named of these, with the Clarksons, he had visited in the Lakes
just a year before Hazlitt. All the time he was, of course, that
Charles Lamb of the India House, whose salary, though small,
was assured and rising; and the very faithful guardian of his
sister Mary.

It is Mary Lamb, in October, who gives us our first news.
Writing to the forsaken Mrs. Coleridge, she says: 'William
Hazlitt is painting my brother's picture, which has brought us
acquainted with the whole family. I like William Hazlitt and his
sister very much indeed.' The whole family was that of John
Hazlitt, with whom Margaret would be spending an occasional
holiday. Hazlitt's portrait of Lamb now hangs in the National
Portrait Gallery.

In February of this year had died Joseph Fawcett, at his retreat in Hertfordshire. He cannot have lived to see completed
the essay which his protégé had failed to write at seventeen,
failed to write again at twenty, and now, as his exclusive absorption in painting was beginning to leave him, had at last
succeeded in writing.

IV

An Essay on the Principles of Human Action is a book by a
metaphysician for metaphysicians. The few words we say of it

here may concern themselves only with its relation to Hazlitt's
other works, and to his character. We have seen the trouble he
had in writing it, and we shall see in due course the respect with
which he looked back on it. This may have been due to the fact
that it was his own first book; but it was due at least equally to
the fact that it was his *own*. Nothing is more characteristic of
him than that, coming to town at a moment when the author
of *Political Justice* was at the height of his fame, he should not
have become a disciple of Godwin, but should have devoted
himself as we have seen, to an independent study of the writers
to whom Godwin in his turn was indebted. In two of these, the
English philosopher Hartley and the French philosopher Helvetius, he had detected a principle to which he offered an opposition which was instinctive. This principle was that of the natural
selfishness of the human mind – a principle which even the
unmetaphysical have at no time found difficulty in grasping.
Its most familiar expression is the statement that there is no
such thing as a disinterested action, since the assistance given
in relief of another's distress, for example, succeeds in relieving
distress in the donor's own mind, and in reality proceeds from
that motive and no other. The principle, here crudely suggested,
was as old in English philosophy as Hobbes, and had been
answered as long ago as Butler; but it had recently received
new, although lateral, support from the 'corpuscular hypotheses' of Hartley, and was the chief stock-in-trade of the fashionable Helvetius. Hazlitt, at the age of seventeen, was overpowered
by the desire to answer it again, and the metaphysical 'discovery'
he conceived himself to have made enabled him, as he thought,
to do so upon new ground. Into the nature and value of that
discovery, which he had nursed for eight years, without prejudice to his other activities, we need not here go: it is on record
in the essay for those who are interested.[1] We may content our-

1. And, much more simply, in the dialogue *Self-Love and Benevolence*,
of 1828. One of the persons in this dialogue is obviously Lamb, and there
is extreme interest in Hazlitt's picture of the manner in which the former
comported himself at a metaphysical discussion. It is from Lamb in this

selves with his conclusion: 'I naturally desire and pursue my own good (in whatever this consists) simply from my having an idea of it sufficiently warm and vivid to excite in me an emotion of interest, or passion; and I love and pursue the good of others, of a relation, of a friend, of a family, a community, or of mankind for just the same reason. ... The love of others has the same necessary foundation in the human mind as the love of ourselves.'

This conclusion, it may just be noted, was not arrived at in the void. Hazlitt's first written work was not a mere metaphysical exercise. By a sort of intellectual tact he had felt for and found a principle which was at the heart of the 'modern philosophy', and which its more superficial practitioners were ready, when expediency invited, to turn against the positions they had formerly held. It was thus that the Whig advocate Mackintosh had demolished Godwinism by an ingenious recourse to the Hartleian theory of the association of ideas. Now that the tide was setting hard against the hopes of 'general benevolence' founded in the French Revolution, what theory could be more useful than that which (in the youthful words of Hazlitt) 'founded the propriety of virtue in its coincidence with the pursuit of private interest'? Already the economists, led by Malthus, were arriving, and giving to this principle their separate scientific sanction. Hazlitt, however, had anchored himself fast to a 'truth of nature'(his definition of a justifiable prejudice)to which he had given metaphysical expression. He had achieved, and at last announced, his first 'incorrigible attachment to a general proposition'.

V

If we have seen little of him in 1804, we see little more in 1805. In this year his first book was published, by Joseph Johnson

dialogue that we learn, of the one fully characteristic passage in Hazlitt's first book, that 'Southey said at the time it was something between the manner of Milton's prose-works and Jeremy Taylor'. There is here, once again, no evidence of that boycott in the Lakes which was subsequently imposed.

(twelve months after its completion, as his son says, and on the recommendation of Anthony Robinson, as Crabb Robinson no doubt intended to inform us) and his last Academy picture exhibited. This was a 'Portrait of a Gentleman' who may, for anything that we know to the contrary, have been Lamb. Encouraged by his beginning in literature, he got on with the abridgement which he had proposed to Coleridge, and in which Coleridge had offered all kinds of assistance, two years before. But Coleridge was in Malta, with this and other promises, to himself and to others, in a state of indefinite suspension. With Coleridge in Malta, and at this date sending home numerous bulletins about him to her friends the Lambs, was a young woman named Sarah Stoddart, sister to that Stoddart of whom we have heard, who, his conversion from his early principles completely effected, had in 1803 gone out to Malta at a salary of fifteen hundred a year as King's Advocate of that island.

Behind Lamb's earliest letter to Hazlitt lies eighteen months of increasing friendship. We come to it on 10 November, at which date the latter had recently left London for Wem by way of the picture galleries of Oxford and Blenheim. Lamb says: 'I was very glad to hear from you, and to know that your journey was so *picturesque*. We miss you, as we foretold we should. One or two things have happened, which are beneath the dignity of epistolary communication, but which, seated about our fire at night, gesture and emphasis might have talked into some importance.' There is news of common friends – of Thomas Manning, of a little girl called Monkey, and particularly of Hume. Joseph Hume, of whom we seem to know little except that he was in the Victualling Office and was Lamb's friend, appears to have become in this summer even more Hazlitt's. 'I met Mrs Hume one day, and agreed to go on the Sunday to Tea, but rain prevented us, and the distance. I have been to apologise, and we are to dine there the first fine Sunday. Strange perverseness! I never went while you staid here, and now *I go to find you*! What other news is there, Mary? – What puns have I made in the last fortnight? You never remember them. You have no relish for the Comic. "O! tell Hazlitt not to forget to send the American Farmer. I dare say it isn't so good as he fancies, but a Book's a Book." ' Hector St John Crèvecœur's *Letters of an American Farmer* had been instrumental, according to Margaret Hazlitt, in taking the family to America; and as late as 1829 we may find Hazlitt praising it in his article on 'American Literature' in the *Edinburgh Review*. Lamb's letter concludes: 'Luck to Ned Search and the new art of colouring'.

Hazlitt, at Wem, was painting his father again, and for the first time a memory of painting is crossed by a political consideration:

> I think, but am not sure, that I finished this portrait (or another afterwards) on the same day that the news of the battle of Austerlitz came; I walked out in the afternoon, and, as I returned, saw the evening star set over a poor man's cottage with other thoughts than I shall ever have again.

The term during which 'battles, sieges, speeches in Parliament' had 'signified nothing' was drawing to its close. The news of Austerlitz arrived in England towards the middle of December, and in the packet bearing it returned Crabb Robinson from his six years in Germany.

VI

Lamb's first letter of 1806, of 15 January, has reference to the *Light of Nature*: 'Dear Hazlitt – Godwin went to Johnson's yesterday about your business. Johnson would not come down, or give any answer, but has promised to open the manuscript, and to give you an answer in one month. Godwin will punctually go again (Wednesday is his Johnson's open day) yesterday four weeks next: i.e. in one lunar month from this time. Till when Johnson positively declines giving any answer. I wish you joy on ending your Search. Mrs [John] H[azlitt] was naming something about a Life of Fawcett, to be by you undertaken; the great Fawcett, as she explain'd to Manning, when he ask'd

What Fawcett? He innocently thought *Fawcett the player*. But Fawcett the Divine is known to many people, albeit unknown to the Chinese Enquirer. I should think, if you liked it, and Johnson declined it, that Phillips is the man. ... You might dish up a Fawcettiad in 3 months, and ask 60 or 80 pounds for it.' Hazlitt did not dish up a Fawcettiad, but reserved his earliest commendation of his friend for the *Life of Holcroft* of four years later. The letter adds : 'As for news – We have Miss Stoddart in our house, she has been with us a fortnight, and will stay a week or so longer. She is one of the few people who are not in the way when they are with you. No tidings of Coleridge.'

It is from this point forward that the Charles-Lamb – Hazlitt correspondence becomes interthreaded with the Mary-Lamb – Sarah-Stoddart. To that young lady, who was no longer in her first youth, and who was in consequence much concerned with the problem of marriage, Miss Lamb had written good advice while still in Malta. 'Secrecy,' she had said, 'though you appear all frankness, is certainly a grand failing of yours; it is likewise your brother's, and, therefore, a family failing – by secrecy, I mean you both want the habit of telling each other at the moment every thing that happens – where you go – and what you do – the free communication of letters and opinions just as they arise, as Charles and I do – and which is, after all, the only groundwork of friendship.' Miss Stoddart, whose father, a retired naval officer of Salisbury, was dead, and whose mother had recently gone out of her mind without dying (whereupon property hung), had returned from Malta to live in a cottage in the Wiltshire village of Winterslow, and Miss Lamb was sorry for her. Immediately on leaving the Lambs, however, she began to console herself with new hopes of matrimony, and the first of these of which we hear concern a Mr White of the locality.

Johnson was called upon at his month's end. On 19 February Lamb writes : 'Godwin has just been here in his way from Johnson's. Johnson has had a fire in his house; this happened about five weeks ago; it was in the daytime, so it did not burn the house down, but did so much damage that the house

must come down to be repaired : his nephew that we met on
Hampstead Hill put it out : well, this fire has put him so back,
that he craves one more month before he gives you an answer.'
There is news of picture sales, and of John Hazlitt's pictures,
which, miniatures apart, were beginning to betray, in Lamb's
opinion, a regrettable tendency to go astray after *ignes fatui*.

March gives us two letters. The first : 'Your Mother, and Mr
White, is running continually in my head; and this *second
winter* makes me think how cold, damp, and forlorn your
solitary house will feel to you. I would your feet were perched
up again on our fender.' The second : 'Dear H. – I am a little
surprised at no letter from you. This day week to wit, Saturday,
the 8th of March, 1806, I booked off by the Wem coach, Bull
and Mouth Inn, directed to *you,* at the Rev. Mr Hazlitt's, Wem,
Shropshire, a parcel containing besides a book, &c., a rare print,
which I take to be a Titian; begging the said W. H. to acknowledge the receipt thereof; which he not having done, I conclude
the said parcel to be lying at the inn, and may be lost; for which
reason, lest you may be a Wales-hunting at this instant, I have
authorised any of your family, whosoever first gets this, to open
it, that so precious a parcel may not moulder away for want of
looking after. What do you in Shropshire when so many fine
pictures are a-going, a-going every day in London? ... And
there are you, perverting Nature in lying landscapes, filched
from old rusty Titians such as I can scrape up here to send you,
with an additament from Shropshire Nature thrown in to make
the whole look unnatural.' Lamb, at Angerstein's, we may
note, has seen Claudes and Titians 'that will cure you [Hazlitt]
of restless, fidgetty passions for a week after.'

There are other hints that Hazlitt, his earliest literary promise to himself performed, had turned with renewed interest
to painting; that he was, in a word, engaged in his 'one or two
abortive attempts to engraft Italian art on English nature'. But
he was painting now with only half his mind. The scene shifts
to London, and in June we have two letters. On the 2nd, Mary
Lamb informs Miss Stoddart : 'William Hazlitt, the brother

of him you know, is in town. I believe you have heard us say we like him? He came in good time, for the loss of Manning made Charles very dull, and he likes Hazlitt better than any body, except Manning.' On the 26th Charles writes to Wordsworth : 'W. Hazlitt is in town. I took him to see a very pretty girl professedly, where there were two young girls – the very head and sum of the Girlery was two young girls – they neither laughed nor sneered nor giggled nor whispered – but they were young girls – and he sat and frowned blacker and blacker, indignant that there should be such a thing as Youth and Beauty, till he tore me away before supper in perfect misery, and owned he could not bear young girls. They drove him mad. So I took him home to my old Nurse, where he recover'd perfect tranquillity. Independent of this, and as I am not a young girl myself, he is a great acquisition to us. He is, rather imprudently, I think, printing a political pamphlet on his own account, and will have to pay for the paper, &c. The first duty of an Author, I take it, is never to pay anything. But *non cuivis attigit adire Corinthum*. The Managers I thank my stars have settled that question for me.'

The Managers (of Drury Lane) had accepted Lamb's farce *Mr H*. Hazlitt, during his spring at Wem, had written *Free Thoughts on Public Affairs, or Advice to a Patriot; in a Letter Addressed to a Member of the Old Opposition*.

VII

We paused at Hazlitt's first published work, and we may pause at his second. His political pamphlet, written on the death of Pitt (January 23) and the accession of Fox to office in the ministry of All the Talents, addressed itself to the 'old' Opposition which had continued to follow the latter statesman from the Whig secession of 1794 to the Peace of Amiens, and in reduced numbers beyond it. Of that event we may find Hazlitt remarking :

With respect to the suspension of the war in consequence

of the treaty of Amiens, it certainly had this good effect (on the supposition that it was absolutely necessary to go on with the contest) that it gave those who had been enemies of the old war, and had afterwards been disgusted with the conduct of the French, but did not like to relinquish their opinion while the original cause of dispute remained – it gave all persons of this class (of which there were great numbers) an opportunity to quit the ranks of discontent without exposing themselves to the charge of inconsistency. As it was a new war, they thought they had a fair right to have a new opinion about it; and they exercised their freedom of election as eagerly in approving the conduct of ministers in entering upon the present war, as they had done in condemning their continuance of the former one. For myself, I confess I have always looked upon the present war as a continuance of the last, carried on upon the same principles and for the same purposes.

For this opinion, as one whose training had been in metaphysics, he may have felt entitled to find some support in circumstances at a moment when the recent personal aggrandisement of Napoleon was being very openly regarded, not as having put peace further out of the question, but as having brought it sensibly nearer.[1] However this may be, with this passage before us we need no longer wonder, I think, if his stay in the Lakes in 1803 had proved chequered.

On the general question, of course, he was of Fox's opinion –

1. 'France under an Emperor seemed no longer to represent a new principle in European politics.' – *Political History of England*, XI. 46. The implications of this statement, of course, concede very nearly everything that Hazlitt was to spend his political life in fighting for. We may compare the *Life of Napoleon* of 1828: 'It has been usual (as men remember their prejudices better than the truth) to hold up the Coalition of the Allied Powers as having for its end and justification the repressing of the horrors of the French Revolution; whereas, on the contrary, those horrors arose out of the Coalition, which had for its object to root out not the evil, but the good of the Revolution in France. History will confirm this sentence.'

that France had been made into a great military nation by her
enemies. It is for a full, contemporary, and persuasive presenta-
tion of that point of view, in relation to the hopes of peace of
1806, that his political pamphlet is notable. 'It has been said,' he
remarked, 'that "there is wisdom in a multitude of counsellors";
but if they only raise a clamour by repeating all of them the
same thing, I do not see how this advantage can be obtained.'
We have not the space to make the quotation here, but the
reader who wishes to appreciate the continuity of Hazlitt's political opinions will turn to it in its place. He will find that, late
as his start had been, he had not been long in attaining to the
pen of the ready writer. For the Character of Pitt with which his
pamphlet concluded he made acknowledgement to the writer
Coleridge had been in the year 1800.

VIII

On 4 July Miss Lamb writes to her young lady: 'Charles and
Hazlitt are going to Sadler's Wells, and I am amusing myself
in their absence with reading a manuscript of Hazlitt's; but
have laid it down to write a few lines, to tell you how we are
going on.' She adds: 'Sunday morning. I am cooking a shoulder
of Lamb (Hazlitt dines with us); it will be ready at two o'Clock,
if you can pop in and eat a bit with us.' In this invitation Miss
Lamb was not to be taken seriously, for Miss Stoddart was at
Winterslow; but it was not long, we may be sure, before such
an offer was proffered and accepted in earnest.

The appearance of the *Free Thoughts* (through J. Budd, of
Pall Mall) must have synchronized almost exactly with Coleridge's return. At the beginning of the year, at the request of
its author, there had been included in a parcel of books for the
Lakes 'W. Hazlitt's book about Human Action, for Coleridge';
but it does not seem probable that the exile can have been cheered
by that work, for in the previous September he had left Malta,
having quarrelled with Stoddart. After wintering in Naples and
Rome under circumstances which have defeated even his most

skilful biographer, he fled from Italy in June before Napoleon's triumphant advance, and arrived in London unheralded in August. Without plans, without means, and almost without hope, he threw himself upon that universal refuge, the Lambs. 'It was,' says Mr Dykes Campbell, 'the saddest of homecomings.'

At his brother's house in Great Russell Street Hazlitt got on with his work. From here, on 30 August, there is a note to the publisher Johnson, which still, in spite of Lamb's letter of the first month of the year, has reference to the *Light of Nature.* 'I have sent you,' we read, 'the abridgement I have made of the two first volumes. ... I find that in going on in the way I have done, I can insert almost every thing that is worth remembering in the book. I give the amusing passages almost entire. In fact I have done little more than leave out repetitions, and other things that might as well never have been in the book. But whether I have done it properly or no, you will be able to determine better than I.' In addition, his early interest in politics now fully revived, he was at work on the *Eloquence of the British Senate* – his 'piece of justice due to the mighty dead'. In this summer, we may note, Crabb Robinson, now reporting for Walter of *The Times,* had made the acquaintance of the Lambs. His introduction came through the Clarksons, but he had first heard of them, he says, from Hazlitt, with whom his interrupted friendship had no doubt been resumed immediately on the return of the latter from the country.

October gives us the following from Miss Lamb to Miss Stoddart: 'I have received a long letter from your brother on the subject of your intended marriage. He says, that if Mr D. is a worthy man he shall have no objection to become the brother of a farmer, and he makes an odd request that I shall set out to Salisbury to look at and examine into the merits of the said Mr D. and speaks very confidently as if you would abide by my determination. ... You have gone too far in this affair for any interference to be at all desirable and if you had not, I really do not know what my wishes would be. When you bring Mr

Dowling at Christmas, I suppose it will be quite time enough for me to sit in judgement upon him, but my examination will not be a very severe one. If you fancy a very young man, and he likes an elderly gentlewoman; if he likes a learned and accomplished lady, and you like a not very learned youth, who may need a little polishing, which probably he will never acquire; it is all very well, and God bless you both together and may you be both very long in the same mind.'

Our next news of any kind is of the production of *Mr H.* at Drury Lane on 10 December. Hazlitt, the author, his sister, and Crabb Robinson were in the theatre together; and of the event the first-named wrote his recollection fifteen years after in *On Great and Little Things* :

I remember when Lamb's farce was damned (for damned it was, that's certain) I used to dream every night for a month after (and then I vowed I would plague myself no more about it) that it was revived at one of the Minor or provincial theatres with great success, that such and such retrenchments and alterations had been made in it, and that it was thought *it might do at the other House* [Covent Garden] ... How often did I conjure up in recollection the full diapason of applause at the end of the Prologue, and hear my ingenious friend in the first row of the pit roar with laughter at his own wit! Then I dwelt with forced complacency on some part in it which had been doing well; then he would consider (in concert) whether the long tedious opera of the *Travellers,* which preceded it, had not tired people beforehand, so that they had not spirits left for the quaint and sparkling 'wit skirmishes' of the dialogue, and we all agreed it might have gone down after a Tragedy, except Lamb himself, who swore he had no hopes of it from the beginning, and that he knew the name of the hero when it came to be discovered could not be got over. – *Mr H.,* thou wert damned! Bright shone the morning on the playbills that announced thy appearance, and the streets were filled with the buzz of persons asking one another if they

would go to see *Mr H.*, and answering that they would certainly; but before night the gaiety, not of the author, but of
his friends and the town was eclipsed, for thou wert damned!

An early intimation of this news also was sent to Miss Stoddart
in the country. If she came up for Christmas, we must suppose
that she came without Mr Dowling.

IX

The year 1807 opens with a letter. Since everything that we
can learn of this somewhat obscure year has its interest for us,
we may have it in full.

Hazlitt to His Father

Tuesday.

My dear Father,—I have just seen Tom Loftus, who told
me to my surprize that he left you last Friday. He called last
night, but I was out. I was rather surprized, because, though I
knew of his going into Wales, I did not think of his going
your way. He seemed much pleased with his reception, and
with his journey altogether. He has brought home some Welsh
mutton with him, which I am going to eat a part of tonight.
He stopped a whole day at Oxford, which he thinks a finer
place than Wem or even Shrewsbury. I have just finished the
cheeks which I had dressed last Friday for my dinner after I
had taken a walk round Hampstead and Highgate. I never
made a better dinner in my life. T. Loftus came to help me
off with them on Saturday, and we attacked them again at
night, after going to the Opera, where I went for the first
time and probably for the last.[1] The fowls I took to Lamb's
the night I received them, and the pickled pork. They were

---

1. 'The Opera ... proceeds upon a false estimate of taste and morals; it
supposes that the capacity for enjoyment may be multiplied with the objects
calculated to afford it. It is a species of intellectual prostitution; for we can
no more receive pleasure from all our faculties at once than we can be in
love with a number of mistresses at the same time.' – *The Opera* (1818).

very good. But I found only one tongue in the basket, whereas you seem to speak of two.

The book I took to John's yesterday. The preface to Search is finished and printed to my great comfort. It is very long, and for what I know very tiresome. I am going on with my criticisms [for the *Eloquence of the British Senate*] and have very nearly done Burke. I do not think I have done it so well as Chatham's. I showed the one I did of him to Anth. Robinson, who I understand since was quite delighted with it, and thinks it a very fine piece of composition. I have only Fox's to do of any consequence. Pitt's I shall take out of my pamphlet, which will be no trouble.

I am to settle with Budd tomorrow, but I doubt my profits will be small. These four viz. Burke, Chatham, Fox, Pitt, with Sir R. Walpole's will be the chief articles of the work, and if I am not mistaken they will be confounded good ones. I am only afraid they will be too good, that is, that they will contain more good things than are exactly proper for the occasion. Have you seen it[1] in any of the papers? It was in the *M. Chronicle*. It is a pretty good one. I might if I was lazy take it, and save myself the trouble of writing one myself. I supped at Godwin's on New Year's day and at Holcroft's on Sunday.

I am going to dinner at Hume's tomorrow, where I also was on Christmas day, and had a pleasant time enough. It was much such a day as it was two years ago, when I was painting your picture.[2] *Tempus preterlabitur.* I am afraid I

1. Mr W. C. Hazlitt's text, which is here followed, contains this lacuna. The reference is evidently to Godwin's *Character of Fox* contributed on the death of that statesman to the *Morning Chronicle* of 22 November 1806. See Mr Kegan Paul's *Life*. In the *Eloquence of the British Senate* Hazlitt's own Character has a note appended making acknowledgement to Godwin's, one passage of which, he says, 'is taken as nearly as I could recollect it'. It is not easy, however, to find the passage in question.

2. He had been at Wem, as we have seen, for the Christmas of 1805 also, but the picture of his father which he remembered with satisfaction had presumably been painted a year earlier.

shall never do such another. But all in good time: I have
done what I wanted in writing and I hope I may in painting.

My mother I suppose was much pleased to see T. Loftus.
He said that he intended returning the same day, having no
time to spare, but that you pressed him so much to stop. Did
not you think him a good deal like me? He intends calling
on John to say that he has seen you.

I can think of nothing more but my best love to my Mother
and Peggy, and that I am your affectionate son,

W. HAZLITT.

Hazlitt's cousin Tom Loftus was the son of his mother's brother,
the 'old hair-brained uncle' with a taste for *Tristram Shandy*
of whom we read in more than one of the essays. Shortly before
this letter was written he had moved into rooms of his own at
34 Southampton Buildings. Here, in the new year, he brought
his two big books to completion, the first *An Abridgement of
the Light of Nature Pursued, by Abraham Tucker, Esq., originally published in seven volumes, under the name of Edward
Search, Esq.,* with a preface 'by the author of the *Principles of
Human Action*'; the second, *The Eloquence of the British
Senate; or, Select Specimens from the Speeches of the Most Distinguished Parliamentary Speakers, from the Beginning of the
Reign of Charles I to the Present Time.* The preface to the one,
and the preface and critical notes to the other, we may regard
as his earliest completely characteristic pieces of writing.

He had done, he told his father, 'what he wanted in writing';
but here he reckoned without himself and the circumstances of
the moment. There was an opponent in the field who had not
yet with any effect been answered. All that Mackintosh, all that
Burke even, had done to overturn the optimistic hopes based on
the French Revolution, was as nothing compared with the success which had attended the Reverend T. R. Malthus. His attack
was all the more powerful for being indirect: here was evidence,
adduced with all the authority of science, that things were as
they were bound to be, and that hopes of human improvement

were chimerical. The *Essay on the Principle of Population*, first published in 1798, had lately been reissued in augmented and triumphant form, and to the mood of resignation in which the upper classes of the country were settling down to the indefinite continuance of the war it was proving a notable contributor. Hazlitt tackled it, as it required to be tackled, with spirit. He was no 'perfectibility' man; but for the author of this work in his character of 'conscience-keeper to the rich and great', he had a contempt which is infectious. We may best appreciate his views by means of a quotation:

Mr Malthus desires his readers to look at the enormous proportion in which the poor-rates have increased within the last ten years. But have they increased in any greater proportion than the other taxes, which rendered them necessary, and which I think were employed for much more mischievous purposes? I would ask, what have the poor got by their encroachments for the last ten years? Do they work less hard? Are they better fed? Do they marry oftener, and with better prospects? Are they grown pampered and insolent? Have they changed places with the rich? Have they been cunning enough, by means of the poor-laws, to draw off all their wealth and superfluities from the men of property? Have they got so much as a quarter of an hour's leisure, a farthing candle, or a cheese-paring more than they had? Has not the price of provisions risen enormously? Has not the price of labour almost stood still? Have not the government and the rich had their way in every thing? Have they not gratified their ambition, their pride, their obstinacy, their ruinous extravagance? Have they not squandered the resources of the country as they pleased? Have they not heaped up wealth on themselves, and their dependents? Have they not multiplied sinecures, places, and pensions? Have they not doubled the salaries of those that existed before? Has there been any want of new creations of peers, who would thus be impelled to beget heirs to their titles and estates, and saddle the younger branches of their rising families, by means of their new influence, on the country at large? Has there been any want of contracts, of loans, of monopolies of corn, of good understanding between the rich and the powerful to assist one another, and to fleece the poor? Have the poor prospered? Have the rich declined? What then have they to complain of? What ground is there for the apprehension, that wealth is secretly changing hands, and that the whole property of the country will shortly be absorbed in the poor's fund? Do not the poor create their own fund? Is not the necessity for such a fund first occasioned by the unequal weight with which the rich press upon the poor, and has not the increase of that fund in the last ten years been occasioned by the additional exorbitant demands, which have been made upon the poor and industrious, which without some assistance from the public they could not possibly have answered? Whatever is the increase in the nominal amount of the poor's fund, will not the rich always be able to throw the burthen of it on the poor themselves? But Mr Malthus is a man of general principles. He cares little about these circumstantial details, and petty objections. He takes higher ground. He deduces all his conclusions, by an infallible logic, from the laws of God and nature. When our Essayist shall prove to me, that by these paper bullets of the brain, by his ratios of the increase of food and the increase of mankind, he has prevented one additional tax, or taken off one oppressive duty, that he has made a single rich man retrench one article at his table, that he has made him keep a dog or a horse the less, or part with a single vice, arguing from a mathematical admeasurement of the size of the earth, and the number of inhabitants it can contain, he shall have my perfect leave to disclaim the right of the poor to subsistence, and to tie them down by severe penalties to their good behaviour on the same profound principles. But why does Mr Malthus practise his demonstrations on the poor only? Why are they to have a perfect system of rights and duties prescribed to them? I do not see why they alone should be put to live on these *metaphysical* board-wages, why they should be forced to submit to a course of *abstraction*; or why it should be meat and drink to them, more than to others, to do the will of God. Mr Malthus's gospel is preached only to the poor!

He addressed himself first to the question in three letters, between March and May, in the columns of Cobbett's *Political Register,* which lately, from being a Tory organ, had asserted its proprietor's independence by becoming a Radical one. The letters were promptly taken up by Longman, and, with much additional matter, they formed his third publication of this year, *A Reply to the Essay on Population, by the Rev. T. R. Malthus.*

In the midst of all this literary activity we find him, in a short note which has survived, seeing his father's sermons through the press and engaging to paint the portrait of the publisher Johnson. For the rest, we do not see him at all. The Lamb correspondence, falling silent towards the end of 1806, remains silent throughout 1807 until October. Crabb Robinson, following the Berlin Decrees of the preceding November, had been appointed by Walter to represent *The Times* at the ensuing Baltic operations; and in the interval between his appointment and his departure we find him writing to his brother Thomas at Bury: 'I have seen since none of my friends but W. Hazlitt and Amyot. I shall keep as much aloof as possible.' In February Robinson left for Altona. Other sources of information failing to open themselves to us, it is with all the force of dramatic surprise that we come in October to the first letter from Miss Lamb to her young woman which we have read for a twelvemonth:

'You know, I make a pretence not to interfere; but like all old maids I feel a mighty solicitude about the event of love stories. I learn from the Lover that he has not been so remiss in his duty as you supposed. His Effusion, and your complaints of his inconstancy, crossed each other on the road. He tells me his was a very strange letter, and that probably it has effronted you. That it was a strange letter I can readily believe; but that you were effronted by a strange letter is not so easy for me to conceive, that not being your way of taking things. But however it be, let some answer come either to him, or else to me, showing cause why you do not answer him. And pray, by all means, preserve the said letter, that I may one day have the pleasure of seeing how Mr Hazlitt treats of love. ...

'Yesterday evening we were at Rickman's; and who should we find there but Hazlitt; though, if you do not know it was his first invitation there, it will not surprise you as much as it did us. We were very much pleased, because we dearly love our friends to be respected by our friends. The most remarkable events of the evening were, that we had a very fine pine-apple; that Mr Phillips, Mr Lamb, and Mr Hazlitt played at Cribbage in the most polite and gentlemanly manner possible – and that I won two rubbers at Whist.

'Farewell – Determine as wisely as you can in regard to Hazlitt, and, if your determination is to have him, Heaven send you many happy years together. If I am not mistaken, I have concluded letters on the Corydon Courtship with this same wish. I hope it is not ominous of change; for if I were sure you would not be quite starved to death, nor beaten to a mummy, I should like to see Hazlitt and you come together, if (as Charles observes) it were only for the joke sake.'

Hazlitt had not been only enunciating principles in opposition to those of the Rev. Mr Malthus. Miss Lamb and the lady's 'secrecy' assisting, he had formed, it is evident, the sudden resolution to put them into practice.

CHAPTER V

INTERREGNUM

(1808–11)

*

He who does nothing, renders himself incapable of doing any thing; but while we are executing any work, we are preparing and qualifying ourselves to undertake another.

On Application to Study.

I

LAMB, who had a macabre taste, recorded his friend's decision to undertake matrimony by means of a supposititious extract from the *Morning Post*:

Last night Mr H., a portrait painter in Southampton Buildings, put an end to his existence in a shocking manner. It is supposed that he must have committed his purpose with a pallet-knife, as the edges of the cicatrice, or wound, were found besmeared with a yellow consistence, but the knife could not be found. The reasons of this rash act are not assigned; an unfortunate passion is mentioned; but nothing certain is known. The deceased was subject to hypochondria, low spirits, but he had lately seemed better, having paid more than usual attention to his dress and person. Besides being a painter, he had written some pretty things in verse and prose.

The pretty things in verse we do not know; nor, we may be certain, did Lamb either. He may be found repeating the pleasantry, in a letter of the following summer, to George Dyer: 'William Hazlitt, your friend and mine, is putting to press a collection of verses, chiefly amatory, some of them pretty enough. How these painters encroach on our province!'

To his friend's account of him the dead man demurred. 'Perhaps he belonged', he wrote, 'to the class of *nondescripts* rather than any other. The opinion of the world was divided; some persons being inclined to consider him as a gentleman and others as a low fellow. It is hard to say whether he ought to be considered as an author or a portrait-painter. It is certain that he never painted any pictures, but those of persons that he hired to sit for him, and though he wrote a number of books it does not appear that they were ever read by any body.' The reader who will turn to the Suicide Joke, between Lamb and Hume, with Hazlitt responding, in the pages of Mr W. C. Hazlitt's little book, *Lamb and Hazlitt,* will find it to contain a number of hints for a portrait of the latter in his thirtieth year. When Lamb, in further characterizing the deceased, refers to him as one who was 'naturally of a discoursible and communicative temper (though of a gloomy and close aspect, as born under Saturn), a great repeater of conversations which he generally carried away verbatim & would repeat with syllabic exactness in the next company where he was received (by which means I that have staid at home have often reaped the profit of his travels without stirring from my elbow chair)'; or when Hume, indignantly repudiating the dead man's strictures upon the 'difficult' nature of his own conversation, avers: 'We, who are judges of good argument, know that he was all illumination: *lucidus ordo* was his maximus Apollo; more especially – *latterly*' – we may conclude, I believe, that in the year that had closed Hazlitt had emerged somewhat notably within view of his friends.

II

Now that he is as good as married, we shall not need to linger unduly over the intervening stages. In the preceding summer Miss Stoddart's brother, the King's Advocate (henceforward, from his degree of D.C.L., to be known as 'the Doctor'), had come back from Malta, had married very suitably the daughter of a clergyman who was also a baronet, and had resumed his practice at the Bar. In a letter of December we learn that he 'is at present on very friendly visiting terms with Hazlitt', but he has not yet been told of the engagement, and Miss Lamb is fearful of the consequence of delay in the disclosure. In these circumstances, in January, when Hazlitt is still confined to his rooms with the ill-health which provided the basis of Lamb's rumour, we come to the following. Those who, unlike Miss Lamb, have a diffidence in overlooking other people's love-letters, may take the letter as read.

Hazlitt to Miss Stoddart

Tuesday night.

My Dear Love,—Above a week has passed, and I have received no letter — not one of those letters 'in which I live, or have no life at all'. What is become of you? Are you married, hearing that I was dead (for so it has been reported)? Or are you gone into a nunnery? Or are you fallen in love with some of the amorous heroes of Boccaccio? Which of them is it? Is it with Chynon, who was transformed from a clown into a lover, and learned to spell by the force of beauty? Or with Lorenzo, the lover of Isabella, whom her three brethren hated (as your brother does me), who was a merchant's clerk? Or with Federigo Alberigi, an honest gentleman, who ran through his fortune, and won his mistress by cooking a fair falcon for her dinner, though it was the only means he had left of getting a dinner for himself? This last is the man; and I am the more persuaded of it, because I think I won your good liking myself by giving you an entertainment — of sausages, when I had no money to buy them with. Nay now, never deny it! Did not I ask your consent that very night after, and did you not give it? Well, I should be confoundly jealous of those fine gallants, if I did not know that a living dog is better than a dead lion : though, now I think of it, Boccaccio does not in general make much of his lovers : it is his women who are so delicious. I almost wish I had lived in those times, and had been a little *more amiable.* Now, if a woman had written the book, it would not have had this effect upon me : the men would have been heroes and angels, and the women nothing at all. Isn't there some truth in that? Talking of departed loves, I met my old flame the other day in the street. I did dream of her *one* night since, and only one : every other night I have had the same dream I have had for these two months past. Now, if you are at all reasonable, this will satisfy you.

Thursday morning.—The book is come. When I saw it I thought that you had sent it back in a *huff,* tired out by my sauciness and *coldness,* and delays, and were going to keep an account of dimities and sayes, or to salt pork and chronicle small beer as the dutiful wife of some fresh-looking rural swain; so that you cannot think how surprised and pleased I was to find them all done. I liked your note as well or better than the extracts; it is just such a note as such a nice rogue as you ought to write after the *provocation* you had received. I would not give a pin for a girl 'whose cheeks never tingle' nor for myself if I could not make them tingle sometimes. Now, though I am always writing to you about 'lips and noses' and such sort of stuff, yet as I sit by my fireside (which I do generally eight or ten hours a day), I oftener think of you in a serious, sober light. For indeed, I never love you so well as when I think of sitting down with you to dinner on a boiled scrag-end of mutton, and hot potatoes. You please my fancy more then than when I think of you in – no, you would never forgive me if I were to finish the sentence. Now I think of it, what do you mean to be dressed in when we are married? But it does not much matter ! I wish you would let your hair grow; though perhaps nothing will be better than 'the same air and look with which at first my heart was took'. But now to business. I mean soon to call upon your brother *in form,* namely, as soon as I get quite well, which I hope to do in about another *fortnight* : and then I hope you will come up by the coach as fast as the horses can carry you, for I long

mightily to be in your ladyship's presence – to vindicate my
character. I think you had better sell the small house, I mean
that at 4.10, and I will borrow £100. So that we shall set off
merrily in spite of all the prudence of Edinburgh.

Goodbye, little dear!   W. H.

The interest of a passage in this letter is that it points to one
of the only two well-attested love-affairs of Hazlitt's life. In the
Reply to Malthus of the preceding summer, among passages
more cogent to the argument, he had written : 'I never fell in
love but once; and then it was with a girl who always wore her
handkerchief pinned tight round her neck, with a fair face,
gentle eyes, a soft smile, and cool auburn locks. I mention this,
because it may in some measure account for my temperate, tractable notions of the passion, compared with Mr Malthus's.' That
the 'temperate, tractable notions' were inserted for the benefit of
his friends, I think we may conclude from an entry in Mrs
Hazlitt's (née Stoddart) Journal of the *Liber Amoris* affair
(17 July 1822): 'I told him it was like his frenzy for Sally Shep-
hard; he said *that* was but a fleabite, nothing at all to this, for
she had never pretended to love him, but all along declared she
did not, but this was the only person who ever really seemed
and professed to be fond of him.' Here, no doubt, we have the
name of Hazlitt's 'old flame'. When we go on, however, with
Mr W. C. Hazlitt, to identify the young lady in question with
the daughter of Dr Shepherd of Gateacre, and the same with a
Miss Shepherd who is mentioned as the companion of Hazlitt's
earliest studies at Liverpool, we are met with a difficulty. Dr
Shepherd (b. 1768, minister of the Old Puritan Chapel, Gateacre
from 1792) was Hazlitt's senior by only ten years, and to provide
him with a marriageable daughter by the year 1807 would seem
as much as, if not more than, the probabilities could manage.
All we can safely conclude, I think, until some more of the
Lamb correspondence for this year comes to light, is that the
first Mrs Hazlitt secured her husband on the rebound.

The task of setting off, however, was not going to prove quite so simple. In February, while still far from well, and strictly against Miss Lamb's injunctions, Hazlitt went down to Winterslow, where he executed a drawing of the 'cottage or tenement' which (as we may find him confessing in the correspondence of January) he 'hoped one day to call his own'. This drawing, forwarded by the Lambs to Wem, whither they believed him to have resorted in order to be nursed, is the subject of some anxious correspondence between Lamb and the old minister which is well known. At the end of the month the truant is back, and Lamb informs Manning in China : 'A treaty of marriage is on foot between William Hazlitt and Miss Stoddart. Something about settlements only retards it. She has somewhere about £80 a year, to be £120 when her mother dies. He has no settlement except what he can claim from the Parish. *Pauper est Cinna, sed amat.* The thing is therefore in abeyance.' The thing was in abeyance, we may be certain, until Miss Stoddart's property was safely secured to herself and issue, by the intervention of her brother.

Under the will of her father, the late Lieutenant John Stoddart, R.N., Sarah Stoddart inherited property as follows : (1) A 'house, malt-house, and garden', in St Anne's Street, Salisbury; (2) a 'small house', also in St Anne's Street; (3) 'all my property in the 5% Annuities'. For the annual value of these items we may no doubt accept Lamb's figure of £80; and we may note that they were left in trust to her brother and another for the use and benefit of the said Sarah Stoddart 'until she shall have attained the age of twenty-five or marry with their consent and approbation'. On the decease of her mother, Sarah Stoddart would become further entitled to : (1) 'my present dwelling-house and pleasure garden'; (2) 'the unexpired term of the lease of my garden in Bugmore'; and (3) a half share, with her brother, of the residue of the estate. These items together would presumably produce Lamb's further £40. At the moment in question, Miss Stoddart's mother was still living; but she herself had attained her thirty-third year. We may therefore conclude that she was free to 'sell the small house', as Hazlitt suggested;

and generally was in enjoyment of complete liberty to dispose as she wished of her property and person.[1]

The next difficulty was over the wedding, which, as first conceived, was to take place from the Lambs', and to dispense with fraternal assistance. But this is soon put a stop to. 'The Doctor,' writes Miss Lamb, 'expressed a strong desire that you should not come to town to be at any other house than his own, for he said that it would have a very strange appearance. ... If you are to be married, he wishes that you should be married with all the proper decorums, *from his house*.' But this, for the most excellent reasons, will entail a delay of three months. Miss Lamb, while not anxious to quarrel with Miss Stoddart's brother, adds, 'Let there be a clear necessity shewn, and we will quarrel with anybody's brother'. It is not altogether with surprise, since this ultimatum appears to hang upon a point of London domicile, that we next learn, in the middle of March, of a project for a Winterslow wedding. Miss Lamb, as the bride's maid, is in two minds between a gown sprigged by her friend and a silk sent by Manning from China. A worked border, from the former hand, Miss Lamb insists upon resigning to Margaret Hazlitt. 'Her brother William is her great favourite, and she would be pleased to possess his bride's last work.' The question is asked : 'What has Charles done that nobody invites him to the wedding?' But once more a foot is put down, and although, with the coming of Miss Stoddart to town, our letters are at an end, we may be sure that it was the Doctor's. When the marriage took place, it

1. It will be noted that in the above (for which I am indebted to the researches of the late Mr J. Rogers Rees, communicated to *Notes and Queries*, X series, X 61), there is no mention of property in the village of Winterslow, and it is probable that Miss Stoddart's cottage there had been acquired by herself, or was included in the residue of his estate which the testator did not think worth specifying. At all events, the generally received, but never very credible, account of 'cottages at Winterslow, which produced the annual sum of £120' (Birrell, *Hazlitt*, p. 83) must be considered as displaced by the above. My own researches into Miss Stoddart's birth date have failed of their object, but in this matter the information of Mr W. C. Hazlitt, that she was three years her husband's senior, may no doubt be relied upon.

took place in London, with, again we may be sure, all the proper decorums.

One appearance, however, the pair have yet to make before the shades of matrimony close over them. In March and April of this year Wordsworth was in town, receiving homage in the somewhat regal manner which, as all observers note, was fast growing upon him. On 19 April he writes to Coleridge (midway in his second short residence in the Lakes): 'I come now to "The White Doe". In compliance with frequent entreaties, I took the MS. to the Lambs, to read it, or part of it, one evening. There unluckily I found Hazlitt, and his beloved; of course, though I had the poem in my hand, I declined, nay absolutely refused to read it. But as they were very earnest in entreating me, I at last consented to read one book, and when it was done, I said – ' But what Wordsworth said of the 'White Doe' we need not here concern ourselves with; and what any one else said is not recorded.

On Sunday, 1 May 1808, at St Andrew's Church, Holborn, William Hazlitt and Sarah Stoddart were married.

III

While Hazlitt departs for the country we may take here his picture of the society he was leaving, from *On the Conversation of Authors,* written twelve years afterwards:

'When a set of adepts, of *illuminati,* get about a question, it is worth while to hear them talk. They may snarl and quarrel over it, like dogs; but they pick it bare to the bone, they masticate it thoroughly.

'This was the case formerly at L[amb]'s – where we used to have many lively skirmishes at their Thursday [Wednesday] evening parties. ... There was L[amb] himself, the most delightful, the most provoking, the most witty and sensible of men. He always made the best pun, and the best remark in the course of the evening. His serious conversation, like his serious writing, is his best. No one ever stammered out such fine, piquant, deep, eloquent things in half a dozen half sentences as he does. His jests scald like tears : and he probes a question with a play upon words. What a keen, laughing, hair-brained vein of home-felt truth! What a choice venom! How often did we cut into the haunch of letters, while we discussed the haunch of mutton on the table! How we skimmed the cream of criticism! How we got into the heart of controversy! How we picked out the marrow of authors! ... Need I go over the names? They were but the old everlasting set – Milton and Shakespeare, Pope and Dryden, Steele and Addison, Swift and Gay, Fielding, Smollett, Sterne, Richardson, Hogarth's prints, Claude's landscapes, the Cartoons at Hampton-Court, and all those things that, having once been, must ever be. The Scotch Novels had not then been heard of : so we said nothing about them. In general, we were hard upon the moderns. The author of the Rambler was only tolerated in Boswell's Life of him; and it was as much as any one could do to edge in a word for Junius. L[amb] could not bear Gil Blas. This was a fault. I remember the greatest triumph I ever had was in persuading him, after some years' difficulty, that Fielding was better than Smollett. On one occasion he was for making out a list of persons famous in history that one would wish to see again[1] – at the head of whom were Pontius Pilate, Sir Thomas Browne, and Dr Faustus – but we black-balled most of his list! But with what a gusto would he describe his favourite authors, Donne, or Sir Philip Sidney, and call their most crabbed passages *delicious!* He tried them on his palate as epicures taste olives, and his observations had a smack in them, like a roughness on the tongue. With what discrimination he hinted a defect in what he admired most – as in saying that the display of the sumptuous banquet in Paradise Regained was not in true keeping, as the simplest

1. Which occasion Hazlitt made the subject of another essay, *On Persons One Would Wish to Have Seen* (1826), which dates itself equally clearly as belonging to the pre-Winterslow era of recollection. Its *personæ* are, with the addition of Joseph Hume and George Dyer, the same as those of the essay above quoted. It is, of course, a mistake to bring Leigh Hunt into it, who was not a Mitre-Courtier.

fare was all that was necessary to tempt the extremity of hunger
– and stating that Adam and Eve in Paradise Lost were too
much like married people. He has furnished many a text for
C[oleridge] to preach upon. There was no fuss or cant about
him : nor were his sweets or his sours ever diluted with one particle of affectation. I cannot say that the party at L[amb]'s were
all of one description. There were honorary members, lay-
brothers. Wit and good fellowship was the motto inscribed over
the door. When a stranger came in, it was not asked, "Has he
written any thing?" – we were above that pedantry; but we
waited to see what he could do. If he could take a hand at
piquet, he was welcome to sit down. If a person liked any thing,
if he took snuff heartily, it was sufficient. He would understand,
by analogy, the pungency of other things, besides Irish blackguard, or Scotch rappee. A character was good any where, in a
room or on paper. But we abhorred insipidity, affectation, and
fine gentlemen. There was one of our party who never failed to
mark "two for his Nob" at cribbage, and he was thought no
mean person. This was Ned P[hillips], and a better fellow in his
way breathes not. There was R[ickman], who asserted some
incredible matter of fact as a likely paradox, and settled all controversies by an *ipse dixit,* a *fiat* of his will, hammering out many
a hard theory on the anvil of his brain – the Baron Munchausen
of politics and practical philosophy :– there was Captain
B[urney], who had you at an advantage by never understanding you – there was Jem White, the author of Falstaff's Letters
... there was A[yrton], who sometimes dropped in, the Will
Honeycomb of our set – and Mrs R– –, who being of a quiet
turn, loved to hear a noisy debate. An utterly uninformed person might have supposed this a scene of vulgar confusion and
uproar. While the most critical question was pending, while
the most difficult problem in philosophy was solving, P[hillips]
cried out, "That's game," and M[artin] B[urney] muttered a
quotation over the last remains of a veal-pie at a side-table. Once,
and once only, the literary interest overcame the general. For
C[oleridge] was riding the high German horse, and demonstrat-

ing the Categories of the Transcendental philosophy to the author of the Road to Ruin; who insisted on his knowledge of German, and German metaphysics, having read the Critique of Pure Reason in the original. "My dear Mr Holcroft," said C[oleridge], in a tone of infinitely provoking conciliation, "you really put me in mind of a sweet pretty German girl, about fifteen, that I met with in the Hartz forest in Germany – and who one day, as I was reading the Limits of the Knowable and the Unknowable, the profoundest of all his works, with great attention, came behind my chair, and leaning over, said, What, *you* read Kant? Why, *I* that am German born, don't understand him!" This was too much to bear, and Holcroft, starting up, called out in no measured tone, "Mr C[oleridge], you are the most eloquent man I ever met with, and the most troublesome with your eloquence!" P[hillips] held the cribbage-peg that was to mark him game, suspended in his hand; and the whist table was silent for a moment. I saw Holcroft downstairs, and, on coming to the landing-place in Mitre-court, he stopped me to observe, that he thought Mr C[oleridge] a very clever man, with a great command of language, but that he feared he did not always affix very precise ideas to the words he used. After he was gone, we had our laugh out, and went on with the argument on the nature of Reason, the Imagination, and the Will. ... Those days are over!'

We have here the Lamb circle – Captain (afterwards Admiral) Burney and Martin his son, now in his twentieth year; William Ayrton, musician and musical critic; James White, Lamb's schoolfellow at Christ's Hospital, now engaged in the treasurer's office of that institution; John Rickman, clerk to the Speaker; Edward Phillips, clerk to John Rickman, and, on the latter's promotion in 1814, his successor. To these names those of George Dyer, scholar and poet, and Joseph Hume, civil servant and humorist, must be added. The days in question date themselves, so far as Coleridge is concerned, at the winter of 1806–7, or that of 1807–8. In the March following Hazlitt's departure to the country, Thomas Holcroft died.

IV

The seven months' silence which follows the marriage is broken by Mary Lamb on 10 December: 'I hear of you from your brother; but you do not write yourself, nor does Hazlitt. ... You cannot think how very much we miss you and H. of a Wednesday evening. All the glory of the night, I may say, is at an end. Phillips makes his jokes, and there is no one to applaud him; Rickman argues, and there is no one to oppose him. The worst miss of all to me is, that, when we are in the dismals, there is now no hope of relief from any quarter whatsoever. Hazlitt was most brilliant, most ornamental, as a Wednesday-man; but he was a more useful one on common days, when he dropt in after a quarrel or a fit of the glooms. ... Charles is come home, and wants his dinner, and so the dead men must be no more thought on.' A postscript is added by Lamb to say: 'There came this morning a printed prospectus from S. T. Coleridge, Grasmere, of a weekly paper to be called The Friend – a flaming prospectus – I have no time to give the heads of it – to commence first Saturday in January. There came also a notice of a Turkey from Mr Clarkson, which I am more sanguine in expecting the accomplishment of.' The first number of *The Friend* appeared in June 1809, and the last in March 1810. There are pointed inquiries in Miss Lamb's letter which we may answer by saying that a child of the marriage was born on 15 January.

Hazlitt, a metaphysician and a painter, who did not as yet know what else he was, had retired to the country, but not to be idle. His work for the year 1808 makes itself known to us from the letter which follows and the prospectus of his *History of English Philosophy* which accompanied it:

Hazlitt to Rt. Hon. William Windham, M.P.
Winterslow, near Salisbury.
Feby. 15, 1809.[1]
Sir, – I take the liberty to offer to your notice the enclosed

1. From the original in the British Museum.

Prospectus. I have no other excuse to make for this intrusion than that I believe the design of the work is such as may meet with your approbation — & the natural wish of every one that what has employed many years of his life & many anxious thoughts may not be entirely lost. My principal view in it would be to chastise the presumption of modern philosophy. The advocates of this system, however, by an exclusive & constant claim to the privilege of reason, have so completely satisfied themselves, & so very nearly persuaded others to believe that they are the only rational persons in the world, that any attempt to disprove their doctrines is looked upon as flying in the face of reason itself & an attack upon first principles. An attempt like the present must therefore I believe fail of success, without some particular support; and my object in soliciting the names of a few persons distinguished for liberal knowledge, & elevated powers of mind as subscribers to the work, was to shew that an opposition to the fashionable paradoxes was not the same thing as formally declaring one's-self on the side of ignorance & error. I know no name, Sir, that would contribute to this end more than your own; the permission to make use of which would be thankfully & proudly acknowledged by, Sir, your obedient, very humble servant,

W. HAZLITT.

Windham, whom Lord Rosebery has called 'the greatest English gentleman', had been Secretary for War throughout Pitt's administration, and the suggestion that he among others should be approached may have come from Crabb Robinson, whose friend Amyot was Windham's private secretary. For the latter's character and pursuits, as distinguished from his politics and oratory, Hazlitt seems to have entertained a regard throughout his life, as readers of *The Fight* may remember. He did not, however, I think we may say, support the *History of English Philosophy* : nor do we know of any one else who did.

We pass to June, in which month Miss Lamb broaches the subject of the visit of herself and Charles, with Phillips and

Martin Burney, to Winterslow. 'Martin says, if you can borrow a blanket or two, he can sleep on the floor, without either bed or mattress, which would save his expenses at the Hut; for, if Phillips breakfasts there, he must do so too, which would swallow up all his money. And he and I have calculated that, if he has no Inn expenses, he may as well spare that to give you for a part of his roast beef. We can spare you also just five pounds. You are not to say this to Hazlitt lest his delicacy should be alarmed; but I tell you what Martin and I have planned, that if you happen to be empty pursed at this time, you may think it as well to make him up a bed in the best kitchen. I think it very probable that Phillips will come; and if you do not like such a crowd of us, for they both talk of staying a whole month, tell me so, and we will put off our visit till next summer.' The visit was put off, though not till next summer. Within a few days of writing this, Mary Lamb was taken ill; and on 5 July the Hazlitts' child died.

However, for the month of October the party came. We have little information concerning the 'dear, quiet, lazy, delicious month' (as Mary Lamb called it), save in one or two after references. Lamb, to Coleridge, on 30 October, says: 'I have been with Mary on a visit to Hazlitt. The journey has been of infinite service to her. We have had nothing but sunshiny days and daily walks from eight to twenty miles a-day: have seen Wilton, Salisbury, Stonehenge &c. Her illness lasted but six weeks; it left her weak, but the country has made us whole.' Mary wrote: 'I assure you, I never passed such a pleasant time in the country in my life, both in the house & out of it, the card playing quarrels, and a few gaspings for breath after your swift foot-steps up the high hills excepted, and those draw-backs are not unpleasant in the recollection. ... We had a good cheerful meeting on Wednesday; much talk of Winterslow, its woods & its nice sun flowers. I did not so much like Phillips at Winterslow, as I like him now for having been with us at Winterslow.' Hazlitt himself tells us a little more in his *Farewell to Essay-Writing*: 'I used to walk out at this time with Mr & Miss

L[amb] of an evening, to look at the Claude Lorraine skies over our heads, melting from azure into purple and gold, and to gather mushrooms, that sprung up at our feet, to throw into our hashed mutton at supper. I was at that time an enthusiastic admirer of Claude, and could dwell for ever on one or two of the finest prints from him hung round my little room; the fleecy flocks, the bending trees, the winding streams, the groves, the nodding temples, the air-wove hills, and distant sunny vales; and tried to translate them into their lovely living hues. ... I will not compare our hashed mutton with Amelia's; but it put us in mind of it, and led to a discussion, sharply seasoned and well sustained, till midnight, the result of which appeared some years after in the *Edinburgh Review*.' Mary Lamb's letter, of 7 November, concludes: 'Farewell. Love to William, and Charles's love and good wishes for the speedy arrival of the Life of Holcroft, & the bearer thereof.' We here learn of Hazlitt's third literary activity at Winterslow. His second, *A New and Improved Grammar of the English Tongue,* for Godwin, had been already completed.

It was with Godwin that his literary business during this summer had been transacted, and two short notes, or portions of notes, survive. The first puts one or two unimportant queries regarding circumstances in the early life of Holcroft; and the second has reference to the *Grammar.* 'As to the attack upon Lindley Murray,' we read, 'I have hit at him several times, and whenever there is mention of a blunder, "his name is not far off". Perhaps it would look like jealousy to make a formal set at him. Besides, I am already noted by the reviewers for want of liberality, and an undisciplined moral sense.' The reference here would be to the *Reply to Malthus.* Godwin was proposing to add to the book a supplementary letter under his prudential name of Baldwin; on which Hazlitt said: 'Assuredly the works of William Godwin do not stand in need of those of E. Baldwin for vouchers and supporters. The latter (be they as good as they will) are but dust in the balance as compared with the former. Coleridge talks out of the Revelations of somebody's "new name from Heaven"; for my own part, if I were you, I should not wish for any but my old one.' He signs; 'I am, dear Sir, very faithfully and affectionately yours.' *A New and Improved Grammar of the English Tongue, for the use of Schools, in which the Genius of our Speech is especially attended to, And the Discoveries of Mr Horne Tooke & other Modern Writers on the Formation of Language are for the first time incorporated. By William Hazlitt. Author of an Essay on the Principles of Human Action, etc., etc., etc. To which is added a New Guide to the English Tongue, by Edward Baldwin, Esq.,* was published in November, as we may know from the following note on the 23rd of the month from Godwin to the publisher Constable: 'I have just forwarded to the proprietors of the *Edinburgh Review* a Grammar I have given to the public, written by one of my inward friends, Mr William Hazlitt. He is a man of singular acuteness and sound understanding, and I think he has brought some new materials to elucidate a most ancient subject. I never saw the Parts of Speech so well defined (I could almost say at all defined) before. I need not say that it would be of the greatest advantage to me if the writers of the *Edinburgh Review* felt disposed to speak of the book according to what I hold to be its merits.' The writers of the *Edinburgh Review* did not feel so disposed, and Hazlitt's *Grammar* was left to enjoy the private approval of Charles Lamb and the attention of the discriminating. Its philology only, which he took from Horne Tooke, is outmoded: its case against Lindley Murray may be found summarized in *The Spirit of the Age*: 'He confounds the genius of the English language, making it periphrastic and literal, instead of elliptical and idiomatic. According to Mr Murray, hardly any of our best writers ever wrote a word of English.'

Our next information is derived from a letter to Crabb Robinson, who now once more comes into the narrative. After his return from the Baltic, Robinson had been for *The Times* to Corunna; and since his second return he had acted for a short time as Foreign Editor to that journal. He had now, however,

parted from Walter on terms of friendship which he always
maintained; and, before turning to the law as a profession, was
acting in a sub-editorial capacity to the dramatist Richard Cumberland on a short-lived quarterly called the *London Review*,
set up by the publisher Samuel Tipper. Robinson had, in the
previous year, made the acquaintance in London of both
Southey and Wordsworth. Of the former he reports: 'I was
charmed with his person and manners, and heartily concurred
with him in his opinions of the war'; and of the latter (whose
Convention of Cintra was just published): 'My perfect agreement with him in politics, and my enthusiastic and unconcealed
admiration of his poetry, gave me speedy admission to his
confidence.' It will be evident that Robinson, like the poets, had
travelled some little distance from the opinions of his youth;
but that he had not yet travelled far enough to throw over his
old friends at the behest of his new ones, will be equally evident
from the following letter, dated by himself 4 December 1809:

Hazlitt to Crabb Robinson

Sunday afternoon.[1]

Dear Robinson, – I did not receive your friendly letter till
this morning. There is sometimes a delay of one or two days
in the post, & I shall therefore send you this in a parcel by the
coach, so that you will have it tomorrow. I am obliged to you
for thinking of me for a coadjutor in the Review; and I am
willing to try what I can do in the way you proposed to the
editor. I am only afraid I shall disgrace your recommendation,
& shew that you have more good nature than discretion in
your opinions of your friends. I shall have done Holcroft's
Life in a fortnight when I shall bring it up to town, & it will
then be time enough to talk of the book or books to be reviewed. With respect to Opie's Lectures, I suppose you know
that they are transcribed with little variation from Fuseli's
printed ones, & that the delivery of them was what nobody
but Opie would have undertaken, & that nobody but Mrs

1. From the original (unpublished) in Dr Williams' Library.

Opie would have thought of their publication. However, there is good scope for criticism in them, & there being a mixture of scandal in it would not perhaps be the worse; but of this, as of all other questions of what may or may not answer I am quite ignorant. Be it remarked that I have at the same time a good opinion of Opie. There is only one way in which the Life of Holcroft can interfere with the review, which is that there are in a Diary of H's, which is to be put in as an Appendix, one or two most excellent stories about Cumberland, which I should be loth to leave out, but which Cumberland, without being the most irritable man in the world, might be disposed to complain of. Indeed I am afraid I shall get into more than one scrape of this kind, in consequence of the philosophical & philanthropical studies of my author on his acquaintance in the above-named Diary. I am sorry Miss Lamb looked so low, but I hope it was only the effect of the Wednesday nights smoking, & sitting up. I am pushing hard to get Holcroft done (all but correcting & Heaven knows there will be enough of that wanted) by Tuesday, & I must therefore return to a most pathetic account of his being blown up by aqua fortis in 1800. I am tired to death of the work, having been at it unceasingly the last fortnight, & I hope you will therefore excuse brevity & stupidity. I am glad to hear you see A. Robinson often, when you do again, make my best respects to him. I received a very friendly, I may say affectionate, letter from him in the summer. I believe I have said all that was necessary about the Review. With Mrs H's compliments, I am yours truly,

W. HAZLITT.

My reason for not calling when in town was the fear of not finding you at home, & my being in [the] country makes me more *nervous*, as they call it, than I generally am.

The *London Review* ran for four numbers only, and contained no contributions from Hazlitt, for the excellent reason that after

the date of this letter no further issue appeared. He finished the
Life of Holcroft, inscribed its preface 'January, 1810',[1] and took
the work up to London.

In the letter which follows we find him just returned from
his visit:

Hazlitt to Crabb Robinson

Winterslow, near Salisbury
Feb. 26.[2]

Dear Robinson,

Yesterday as soon as you were gone, it occurred to me that
I had forgot to mention a circumstance which might perhaps
turn to account. Mrs Holcroft when I was there the other day
was shewing me & praising a work called the Martyrs by the
famous Chateau Briand, which I believe has not been trans-
lated. It was published 1809. It is in three vols & is as far as
I understand from her account & what I read a sort of poetical
romance (in prose) founded on the persecutions against the
Christian Religion, something in the style of the death of
Abel, or more properly in his own style, if you are acquainted
with it. I was thinking that a translation might sell, & that it
would possibly be in Tipper's way to engage in such a work.
The subject is orthodox, & the style as fine as can be. If you
could take the trouble to mention it to him, & he thought the
plan feasible, I should be glad to attempt it at any rate you

1. The *Life of Holcroft* was not published until 1816. We find the
reason in an undated letter from Godwin to Mrs Holcroft which Mr Kegan
Paul prints: 'For myself, I can fairly say that if I had known that every
time I dined or called upon Mr Holcroft, I was to be recorded in a quarto
book, well printed and with an ornamental frontispiece, in the ridiculous
way of coming in to go out again fifty times, I would not on that penalty
have called upon or dined with him at all. ... I will be no part or party
to such a publication.' Thus Godwin's respect for the 'singular acuteness
and sound understanding' of his 'inward friend' did not extend to the
performance of his editorial functions. Fortunately when the book did
appear, it did so (so far as we can judge) as it had left the hands of Hazlitt.
For Mr W. C. Hazlitt's statement that he did not finish it there is no
warranty which is discoverable.

2. From the original (unpublished) in Dr Williams' Library.

could procure for me, 2½ guineas, 2, or 1½ per sheet. One more push I must make, & then I hope to be afloat, at least for a good while to come. I had also before this last project started up, thought of turning the History of E. Philosophy into a volume of Essays on the subjects mentioned in the prospectus, making the history subservient to the philosophy, which I believe is what I should do best, but I suspect that this is a subject to which Tipper would not very seriously incline his ear. I have in short many plots & projects in my head, but I am afraid none of them good ones. Such as they are, you will I hope excuse my troubling you with them, & believe me to be yours affectionately

                                        W. HAZLITT.

In neither of these projects, we must suppose, did he receive encouragement, and the year 1810 was spent mostly in painting.

It is so, at least, that we find him engaged in April, in a letter to his wife who was making a stay with the Lambs:[1] 'Both parcels of prints came safe, & I need hardly say that I was glad to see them & thank you exceedingly for getting them for me. I am much obliged to you for your trouble in this as well as about the pictures. Your last letter but one I did not receive in time to have come up to see them before Friday (the day then fixed for the sale), & though I got your letter on Friday time enough to have been with you yesterday morning, I did not feel disposed to set out. The day was wet & uncomfortable, & the catalogue did not tempt me so much as I expected. There were a parcel of Metzus & Terburghs & boors smoking & ladies at harpsichords, which seemed to take up as much room as the St Cecilia, the Pan & St George, the Danae, & the Ariadne in Naxos. Did Lamb go to the sale, & what is the report of the pictures? But I have got my complete set of Cartoons, "here I

1. This letter must be read in full in *Lamb and Hazlitt*, where it is dated by Mr W. C. Hazlitt April 1809 (i.e. between the birth of the Hazlitts' child and its death). It belongs, no doubt, to April 1810, where we have placed it.

sit with my doxies surrounded," & so never mind. I just took out my little copy of Rembrandt to look at, & was so pleased with it, I had almost a mind to send it up, & try whether it might not fetch two or three guineas. But I am not at present much in the humour to incur any certain expense for an uncertain profit. With respect to my painting, I go on something like Satan, through moist & dry, sometimes glazing & sometimes scumbling, as it happens, now on the wrong side of the canvas & now on the right, but still persuading myself that I have at last found out the true secret of Titian's golden hue & the oleaginous touches of Claude Lorraine. I have got in a pretty good background, & a *conception* of the ladder which I learned from the upping stone on the down, only making the stone into gold, & a few other improvements. I have no doubt there was such another on the field of Luz, & that an upping stone is the genuine Jacob's ladder. But where are the angels to come from? ... It is supper time, my dear, & I have been painting all day, & all day yesterday, & all the day before, & am very very tired, & so I hope you will let me leave off here, & bid you goodnight. I enclose a £1 note to Lamb. If you want another, say so. But I hope your partnership concern with Mr Phillips will have answered the same purpose.' The postscript is: 'Before you come away, get Lamb to fix the precise time of their coming down here'.

The Lamb correspondence for the first half of this year is nearly a blank, but on 10 July, when Charles breaks the silence to Basil Montagu, it is from Mr Hazlitt's, Winterslow, near Sarum, that he does so. 'My head has received such a shock by an all-night journey on the top of the coach, that I shall have enough to do to nurse it into its natural pace before I go home. I must devote myself to imbecility. ... We purpose setting out for Oxford Tuesday fortnight, and coming thereby home.' This programme would seem to have been carried out in its entirety. It was on this occasion that the local tailor (as Hazlitt records in the *Character of the Country People*) 'was ordered to make a pair of brown or snuff-coloured breeches for my friend Charles

Lamb; – instead of which the pragmatical old gentleman (having an opinion of his own) brought him home a pair of "lively Lincoln-green", in which he rode in triumph in Johnny Tremain's cross-country caravan through Newbery, and entered Oxford, "fearing no colours," the abstract idea of the jest of the thing prevailing in his mind (as it always does) over the sense of personal dignity.' And in *On Going a Journey* we read: 'I once took a party to Oxford with no mean *éclat* – shewed them that seat of the Muses at a distance,

> "*With glistering spires and pinnacles adorn'd,*"

descanted on the learned air that breathes from the grassy quadrangles and stone walls of the halls and colleges – was at home in the Bodleian; and at Blenheim quite superseded the powdered Ciceroni that attended us, and that pointed in vain with his wand to common-place beauties in matchless pictures.' On 9 August Lamb writes to him: 'Our pleasant excursion has ended sadly for one of us. You will guess I mean my sister. ... I have lost all wish for sights. God bless you. I shall be glad to see you in London.'

V

Hazlitt had now spent two years in his 'little room' hung with the Claudes and Raphaels, with his occasional (and by no means successful) literary occupations, his painting, the plain at hand for walking, and the Lambs for summer visitors; and we should be the last to assert that he had not been happy.[1] But he was not afloat. He had married a certain (or possibly an uncertain)

---

1. 'One of the most delightful parts of my life was one fine summer, when I used to walk out of an evening to catch the last light of the sun, gemming the green slopes or russet lawns, and gilding tower or tree, while the blue sky gradually turning to purple and gold, or skirted with dusky grey, hung its broad marble pavement over all, as we see it in the great master of Italian landscape [Claude].' – *On the Pleasure of Painting*. We can have very little doubt that it is the summer of 1809, and no earlier one, which is commemorated in this passage.

number of pounds a year and a cottage; but he had not, in a time of war prices, married an independency. The *History of English Philosophy,* on which he had leaned, had failed him; and the 'one more push', of which he had spoken to Crabb Robinson, was as far from being given as ever. It was with this realization in his heart, no doubt, that he went to London some time after Mary Lamb's recovery at the end of September. He did not stay long this time, but he stayed long enough to become aware that the *Edinburgh Review* had at last taken notice of his *Reply to Malthus,* in its issue dated August, and to write a further letter to the *Political Register.* By 28 November he is back, and a Winterslow pig, doubtless a return for hospitality received, has arrived at Inner Temple Lane. Lamb writes : 'I sent you on Saturday a Cobbett, containing your reply to the *Edinburgh Review,* which I thought you would be glad to receive as an example of attention on the part of Mr Cobbett to insert it so speedily. Did you get it? We have received your pig, and return you thanks; it will be dressed in due form, with appropriate sauce, this day. ... Coleridge is in town, or at least at Hammersmith. He is writing or going to write in the *Courier* against Cobbett, and in favour of paper money.' Lamb signs himself 'Yours ever' and adds : 'I think your paper is complete'.

Among the more important resolutions for the new year was that of Crabb Robinson to keep a diary. For this decision it would not be entirely fanciful to hold Hazlitt responsible. It was, Crabb Robinson tells us, as a result of the interest with which he read Holcroft's diary in the previous summer that he decided to keep something of the same kind himself; and he doubtless read that diary as one of the consultative committee which sat upon it as it came from the hands of Hazlitt, and was still sitting upon it, so that it had become known to the Lambs as the 'Life Everlasting'. At all event, Crabb Robinson's diary immediately becomes serviceable to us, and it is by its aid that we know that early in the year Hazlitt was in town, was established again at his old rooms in Southampton Buildings, and was once more and for the last time professionally engaged in the painting of portraits.

We may make a beginning upon its entries:

'18 February: — Called for Thomas [the diarist's brother, of Bury] at W. Hazlitt's, to whom he was sitting for a portrait.'

'4 March: — Took tea with W. Hazlitt and had two hours pleasant chat with him. He spoke of Coleridge with the feelings of an injured man.' The rest of this entry, which was the occasion on which Hazlitt recalled Coleridge's fickleness in Sir George Beaumont's company in the Lakes, we have taken on an earlier page (p. 95). That he had other and more recent ground of complaint against Coleridge, I think we may realize if we turn to De Quincey, who, as a young man at Oxford, had met Coleridge in the year following his return from Malta, had presented him with £300, and had followed him to the Lakes, where from 1809 he rented Dove Cottage from Wordsworth. De Quincey had recently been in London, seeing through the press the *Convention of Cintra*; but he did not meet Hazlitt until 1821. Writing in 1838 of the latter's first book, he lets fall the remark: 'Thirty years ago I looked into it slightly, but my reverence for Hartley offended me with its tone, and hearing that Coleridge challenged for his own most of what was important in the thoughts, I lost all interest in the essay'. Again, in his other article (1845) written ostensibly in praise of Lamb, but principally in disparagement of Hazlitt: 'His *Essay on the Principles of Human Action,* and his polemic esssay against the Hartlean theory, supposing even that these were not derived entirely from Coleridge[1] (as Coleridge used to assert) — could at the best, be received only as evidences of ingenuity and a natural turn for philosophizing.' Five years later than the present date, Hazlitt was to refer publicly to Coleridge as 'the

1. 'Till I began to paint, or till I became acquainted with the author of the Ancient Mariner, I could neither write nor speak. He encouraged me to write a book, which I did according to the original bent of my own mind.' — *On the Causes of Popular Opinion* (1828). This I think we may say that we have seen to be the truth.

dog-in-the-manger of literature', and I think we may already understand by these references a little of what he meant. In the meantime it was, in some sense, a new Coleridge whom he had found, after three years; a Coleridge who, after some mysterious passages following on the last number of the *Friend,* had turned up in London with powder in his hair, looking, as Lamb wrote to Wordsworth, 'like Bacchus, Bacchus ever sleek and young'. To add to the irony of events, the former master and the former pupil were living almost next door to one another, for Coleridge, although nominally resident with the Morgans at Hammersmith, had taken a lodging at 32 Southampton Buildings in order, as he said, to be nearer his work. Of the results of that work, for the Tory *Courier* at extremely irregular intervals over the next two years, I do not think that the most uncompromising of Coleridge's admirers has ever quite dared to be proud.

We may resume from Crabb Robinson:

'6 March: — After dinner called on C. Lamb; heard from him that George Burnett had died wretchedly in a workhouse. Hazlitt and Coleridge were there and seemed sensibly affected by the circumstance. There certainly was every reason for strong sympathy, founded on similarity of pursuits and a like want of fortune, and dependence on literary talents for support.'

'8 March: — Called on W. Hazlitt. Learnt that Miss Lamb had had a renewal of her attack. H. thinks that Burnett's death occasioned the present relapse. He had applied a little while before to C. L. for money which C. L. had not sent him, for he had before received relief from him with a promise not to apply again for six months. This circumstance agrees with what Mrs C. Aikin related to me on Tuesday — he had offended them by an improper application to which they had shewn no attention.[1] H. thinks that poor Miss Lamb as well as her brother is

---

1. Mr Lucas here (*Life of Lamb,* p. 308), by a slip very easy to excuse, has circulated an inaccuracy. By printing this entry in two separate parts, and losing sight of the sequence, he has convinced himself, and persuaded his readers, that it was Hazlitt who had 'offended by an improper appli-

injured by Coleridge's presence in town, and their frequent visits and constant company, which keep their minds in perpetual fever.' This view is separately endorsed by Crabb Robinson, whom we find writing at this date in a letter to his brother Thomas: 'Poor Mary Lamb has been attacked again by her shocking malady. It has been, I fear, precipitated by Coleridge's company, which I think has a dreadful effect upon her nerves and shatters her frame.'

'10 March: — Had a call from W. Hazlitt. I shewed him Blake's Young — he saw no merit in them as designs. I read him some of the Poems — he was much struck with them and expressed himself with his usual strength and singularity.'

'23 March: — Called on W. Hazlitt, having secured Mr Howel to sit to him for his picture.'

'29 March: — I spent the evening with W. Hazlitt. Smith, his wife and son, Hume, Coleridge, and afterwards Lamb was there. Coleridge philosophized as usual. He and Hazlitt joined in an obscure statement about abstract ideas. Hazlitt said he had learnt from painting that it is difficult to form an idea of an individual object — that we first have only a general idea; that is a vague, broken, imperfect recollection of the individual object. This I observed was what the mob meant by a general idea, and Hazlitt said he had no other. We talked of politics.' Of the Smith of this entry we seem to know little, save that he was a Scotsman, an acquaintance of Godwin's, and, according

cation'. So far is this from being the case, that the statement regarding Burnett is paraphrased by the diarist from Hazlitt's own words, as appears clearly in the above transcription. Hazlitt may have borrowed from Lamb in the course of their friendship, and no doubt did, but he did not do so on this occasion; and Mr Lucas's general inference from this piece of evidence, as to the cause of any subsequent occasional coolnesses between them, therefore falls to the ground. As a matter of fact, Hazlitt's character in money matters would seem to have been rather completely the opposite of that which has been too easily supposed. We have already seen Lamb's allusion to his 'delicacy' (p. 135); and Patmore says: 'He had an almost childish horror of owing money, and was always ready to pay it away, even to the last guinea, the moment he received the proceeds of any considerable work'.

to Lamb, 'of a most literal understanding'. We do not meet him again.

'30 March: — Accompanied C. Lamb to the Lyceum. On returning to C. L.'s, found Coleridge and W. Hazlitt there, and had a half hour's chat. Coleridge spoke feelingly of Godwin and the unjust treatment he had met with. In apology for Southey's review of Godwin's Life of Chaucer, Coleridge ingeniously observed that persons who are themselves very pure are sometimes on that account *blunt* in their moral feelings. This I believe to be a very true remark indeed.' It is not the less true because the diarist himself provides a somewhat notable instance of it.

The next entry is a little obscure: —

'15 April: — In the evening I was for a short time with Godwin. ... G. related me an anecdote concerning H[azlitt]. The painting he had made of — —, a handsome young man, had been sent home with an abusive letter by the mother. Poor H[azlitt] left town in great agony. He has not sent my brother's picture and I fear does not mean to let it go out of his hands; perhaps he has already destroyed it. And I fear he has not the money to refund. I saw also to-day Mr Howel's portrait. It is a good caricature likeness but a coarse painting. I fear poor H. will never succeed. With very great talents and with uncommon powers of mind I fear he is doomed to pass a life of poverty and unavailing repinings against society and his evil destiny.' We should find it hard to be certain from this whether Godwin's 'anecdote' had reference to something which had just happened, or which had happened in the past; but the fact is that from this point Hazlitt vanishes from the diary until the autumn. We may just note that on 16 May Robinson's friend Mrs Pattison had 'received Mr Howel's picture and seemed quite satisfied with it'.

According to a hint conveyed by Robinson in another place, it was in this year that Hazlitt painted the portrait of Thomas Clarkson. While the sittings may, of course, have been at Bury, they are more likely to have been in London, where the Clarksons were frequent visitors. Clarkson, says Robinson, 'had heard that Hazlitt was more able to paint like Titian than any living painter. Some one had said that his portrait of Lamb had a Titianesque air about it.' If the interest of Clarkson amounted to patronage, it had come too late to save Hazlitt for painting. Certainly this hurried departure for Winterslow is more like that gesture of 'disgust and despair' which attended his abandonment of the art than anything we have encountered, or shall encounter.

He has been at Winterslow perhaps a couple of months when the curtain is lifted:

Hazlitt to Thomas Robinson
Winterslow, July 10.[1]

Dear Sir, — I was quite ashamed to receive your letter, & know not what to answer. I have the picture by me, & brought it down with a full intention to set about improving it immediately. I have however put it off from day to day & week to week first from an unfortunate habit that what I ought to do, I seldom do, & secondly from a fear of doing away what likeness there is without mending the picture. I will however do what I can to it before I come to town in October, & will then leave it with your brother. Till then I do not forget that I am your debtor.

I am glad to hear that Mr Clarkson's picture is thought like, & only wish that it were what it should be. Hoping you will excuse this lame answer, & with respects to Mrs Robinson, I remain, Dear Sir, your obliged humble servant,

W. HAZLITT.

On 26 September, at Winterslow, Hazlitt's son William was born, and the letters of the Lambs on the occasion, which have survived in a year otherwise bare of their correspondence, are well known. Charles wrote: 'Well, my blessings and heaven's be upon him, and make him like his father, with something a

1. From the original (unpublished) in Dr Williams' Library.

better temper and a smoother head of hair, and then all the men and women must love him.' We may assume, I think, that in flinging off from London in the spring Hazlitt had to some extent flung off from the Lambs.

Within a few days, however, he was in town again, according to plan. Coleridge was in this month arranging to lecture on Shakespeare and Milton, and at the same time concerning himself, characteristically, about Lamb's drinking too much. 'I am right glad,' he writes to Rickman in a letter of October which Mr Orlo Williams prints, 'that something effective is now done – tho' permit me to say to you in confidence, that as long as Hazlitt remains in town I dare not expect any amendment in Lamb's health, unless luckily H. should grow moody and take offence at being desired not to come till 8 o'clock. It is seldom, indeed, that I am with Lamb more than once in the week – and when at Hammersmith, most often not once a fortnight, and yet I see what harm has been done even by me – what then if Hazlitt – as probably he will – is with him five evenings in the seven? Were it possible to wean C. L. from the pipe, other things would follow with comparative ease, for till he gets a pipe, I have regularly observed, that he is content with porter – and that the unconquerable appetite for spirit comes in with the tobacco.' This is an exceptional effort, even for Coleridge. The things which hardly require to be said about it are, first, that whereas Hazlitt was in town for at most a few days after five months' absence, Coleridge had been at hand throughout the summer, with a continuation of the effects that have been noted, and with the recent consequence of new defensive measures; and, second, that Lamb's young Bacchus was himself at this time, while talking much of reformation, continuing to 'pour down goblet after goblet'. Coleridge, in fact, is here exemplifying somewhat perfectly the trait which he possessed in common with all those who have lost moral control : he is peculiarly alive in others, by a process of unconscious self-defence, to the precise weaknesses of which he himself is guilty. It was so, as long as seven years before, in a moment's jauntiness before departure for Malta, that he had reported to Southey a meeting with George Burnett, 'so nervous, so helpless, with such opium-stupidly-wild eyes'. The Coleridge who, by fixing his very grave attention on Charles Lamb's tobacco pipe, hoped to conceal from himself his own more serious 'unconquerable appetite', is a Coleridge whom it is necessary to hold very clearly before us. Lamb was able to do so, and to regard him not only with tolerance but with affection. We shall find in due time that Hazlitt reached a point at which he was not.

Crabb Robinson was out of town for the first half of this month, and the absence of Hazlitt from his diary when he returns is explained by the letter which follows:

Hazlitt to Crabb Robinson

Winterslow, near Salisbury.
October 29, 1811.[1]

Dear Robinson,—One of the things which I meant to do on coming to town was to call upon you: which I suppose was the reason, that is to say, cause I did not. In truth, I was held in durance vile all the time I was there by one of the greatest miseries of human life, I mean a tight pair of boots,[2] which made it impossible for me to move a step without being put in pain & out of humour, so that after a journey of a mile, I should not have had spirits left to open my case, which is

1. From the original (unpublished) in Dr Williams' Library.

2. It is open to the moralist, I am afraid, to affirm that the boots were not paid for. In a short note without date which Mr W. C. Hazlitt prints, Hazlitt is to be found writing to Thomas Hardy, political reformer and bootmaker: 'Dear Sir,—I was obliged to leave London without discharging my promise, the reason of which was that I was myself disappointed in not receiving £20 which was due to me, £10 for a picture, & £10 for revising a manuscript. I am at present actually without money in the house. If you can defer it till October, when I shall be in London to deliver some Lectures, by which I shall pick up some money, I shall esteem it a favour, and shall be glad to pay you the interest from the time I was in London last.' This is attributed by Mr W. C. Hazlitt to 1820, but it belongs quite evidently to this summer, the picture for which Hazlitt was disappointed of ten pounds being, no doubt, that of 'the handsome young man' mentioned in Crabb Robinson's entry of 15 April.

briefly this. That I am going (in spite of the muse that pre-
sides over eloquence, I do not know her name) to deliver lectures, that I have got 30 subscribers, & want ten or a dozen
more if I can possibly get them. If therefore you could assist
me by picking up one or two names, I can only say I shall be
much obliged to you, & that the lectures will be as good as
I can make them. The subjects of them will be nearly as
follows, I have written 6. Lecture 1. On Hobbes's writings
with a general view of philosophy since his time, shewing that
succeeding writers have done little more than expand, illustrate, & apply the metaphysical principles distinctly laid down
by him. Lect. 2. On Locke's Essay on the Human Understanding, or on the nature of *ideas,* shewing that all ideas
necessarily imply a power for which sensation or simple perception does not account, *viz.* an understanding or comprehending faculty.

Lect. 3. On Berkeley's Principles of human knowledge, &
on abstract ideas. In these two lectures I should attempt to
prove in opposition to the modern opinion that we can have
no complex or abstract ideas, that there are in reality no
others, i.e. none which do not imply a power, to a certain
extent, both of comprehension & abstraction.

Lect. 4. On self-love & benevolence.

Lect. 5. On Helvetius's doctrine on the same subject, & on
Hartley's attempt to resolve all our affections & faculties into
association of ideas.

6. On Bishop Butler's theory of the mind, or an account
of the different original springs which move that various
machine, such as sensibility, understanding, will, or the love
of pleasure, the love of truth, & the love of action.

7. On the controversy between Price & Priestley or on
materialism & necessity.

8. The same subject continued.

9. On Tooke's Diversions of Purley – theory of language &
nature. 10. An argument on natural religion.

The price to each subscriber is two guineas, & they will be

delivered about January. I remain, Dear Robinson, yours sincerely,

W. HAZLITT.

At the end of November he is in town again, leaving his family presumably in the country. We come at once to Crabb Robinson:

'30 November: Called on W. Hazlitt. Chatted with him on his intended lectures.

'4 December: At Captain Burney's. The Captn. unwell. Cards with Hazlitt, Phillips, etc.

'7 December: A call on W. Hazlitt to pay him Subscription Money for his Lectures. I found him alone and gloomy: he showed me a new edition of Hobbes on Human Nature, edited, I understand, by Mallet.'

A week later, in a letter to his brother Thomas, the diarist is somewhat more expansive: 'W. Hazlitt is come to town. He means to spend the winter here, and on my asking him what he meant to do with your picture, he mumbled out that he should try to do something to it, or else he must – –. The truth is that poor H. is so poor and so unhappy that I can't but feel more pity than displeasure. He announced you know lectures on the history of philosophy and wrote to me to procure him subscription. I informed him J. Buck and J. Collier would subscribe. He first sent me three tickets and then wrote to beg I would pay for them. J. B. and J. C. consented and I left the six guineas. When the lectures will be delivered I can not tell. He means to deliver them as he does to deliver your picture, and will probably do both sooner or later, but we must wait his time.'

In this the diarist spoke with justice, possibly without intending to do so. After all, Hazlitt had had, and still had, to wait his own time; and few men have waited longer.

CHAPTER VI

THE JOURNALIST (I)

(1812–14)

*

Something I did, *took*, and I was called upon to do a
number of things all at once.

Conversations of Northcote.

I

His first appearance as a public lecturer was duly made in spite
of the scepticism of Robinson. The year 1812, indeed, opened
well for that indefatigable waiter upon other men's good things.
Coleridge, at the Philosophical Society's rooms in Fleet Street,
on Mondays and Thursdays, had not finished his course, when,
on the second Tuesday in January, Hazlitt opened at the Russell
Institution, Great Coram Street, Brunswick Square. We may
immediately begin to be as busy as the diarist happily found
himself.

'13 January: – Accompanied Mrs C. Aikin to Coleridge's
lecture.

'14 January: – Tea with C. Lamb. ... From him I went to
Hazlitt's first lecture on the History of English Philosophy. He
read ill a very sensible book: and as he seems to have no conception of the difference between a lecture and a book his lectures cannot possibly be popular, hardly tolerable. He read a
sensible and excellent introduction on philosophy and on
Hobbes: but he delivered himself in a low monotonous voice,
with his eyes fixed intently on his book, not once daring to

look on his audience. He read too so rapidly that no one could possibly follow him; at the same time the matter he read was of a kind to require reflection. No subject is in itself less adapted to a lecture than Metaphysical philosophy; no manner less adapted to recommend abstruse matter than Hazlitt's. So that it is impossible H's lectures should not altogether fail of their subject unless he should alter his style and delivery, which I fear is hardly in his power. With all these exceptions to his lectures, as such, the matter was in general, as far as I could force my attention to comprehend, very excellent.

'15 January : – Tea with the Lambs. An evening at cards. ... Hazlitt there; much depressed. Dr Stoddart had left a letter of advice to him on his lecture which hurt him apparently. And the conversation that afterwards took place irritated him greatly. He seemed disposed to give up the lectures altogether, at least at the Russell Institution. He blamed himself for yielding to Dr Stoddart in delivering them there and considered the size of the room, the nature of the audience, &c., as the occasions of his not succeeding; he was told by Flack, the secretary, as he began to lecture, that he must limit himself to an hour. This made him read so rapidly. I observed on the difference between a book and a lecture, and perhaps more than I intended betrayed my opinion. I spoke of the compassion I felt beholding H. so oppressed in delivering the lecture and this he misunderstood. For Miss Lamb told me the following day that he had been hurt by this, and in consequence I wrote a letter to him explaining what I had said.'

'16 January : – At Coleridge's lecture. ...

'17 January : – At 10 went to Barron Field's. C. Lamb and Leigh Hunt ... there. Lamb and Hunt, I found, had had a contest about Coleridge. H[unt] had spoken of him as a bad writer, L[amb] as of the first man he ever knew. The dispute was revived by me, but nothing remarkable was said. C. L., who soon became tipsy, in his droll extravagant way abused everyone who

denied the transcendency, while H. dryly denied the excellency
of his writings and expressed his regret that he did not know
him personally. H. took L's speeches in good part, evidently
by his manner showed his respect for his talents, while C. L. to
make his freedom endurable praised Hunt's remarks on Fuseli
(a praise H. seemed to relish). I spoke about Hazlitt's lectures
in terms of great praise, but C. L. would not join me, and I
fear I did not succeed in my object. I left C. L. getting very
drunk, and I understand the party remained up till late.' What
the diarist's 'object' can have been in commending Hazlitt to
Lamb (who heard no lectures, neither Coleridge nor Hazlitt)
would be hard to say, and he does not enlighten us; so that we
may turn to note the two names in this account which are new
to us. Both, like Lamb, were Christ's Hospital boys, both were
eight or more years his junior, and all three had recently come
together over Leigh Hunt's quarterly magazine, the *Reflector*.
In addition, Hunt had been for nearly four years the editor of
his brother John's journal the *Examiner,* a weekly which was
fast rising into eminence. That he and Lamb were as yet but
little known to one another is made clear in Robinson's diary,
and is indeed evident from this passage.

We may resume:

'21 January: — Lounged in my room till Hazlitt's second lecture, which I heard. He delivered himself well; that is loud, and
with a tone of confidence which being forced had sometimes the
air of arrogance; this however did not offend (except perhaps a
few) and he was interrupted by applause several times. His lecture was on Locke. Mr Burrell had abridged it.' Of Burrell we
know little, save that he was a barrister and a friend of Dr Stoddart's, for whom we find him acting six years before in the
Malta dispute with Coleridge. The diarist continues: 'On the
whole H. improved vastly in his present lecture and I hope he
will now get on. He read half his first lecture at B. Montagu's
last night; he was to read the whole, but he abruptly broke off

and could not be persuaded to read the remainder. Lamb and other friends were there.'

'28 January: – Tea with C. Lamb. Returned to chambers till half past 8 when I went to Hazlitt's lecture, which was on Locke, and not less impressively delivered than the last.

'4 February: – At Hazlitt's fourth lecture; still on Locke. Mortified to find that my quickness in perceiving the import and comprehending metaphysical reasoning was greatly lessened by the neglect of these pursuits. Hazlitt's manner is now very respectable.

'11 February: – Evening at Hazlitt's: a lecture on Disinterestedness. The matter of his book *On the Motives of Human Action* was incorporated in this lecture, which however did not apparently please so much as others of less worth in reality. The attendance was thin.

'18 February: – Took tea with Flaxman, and accompanied Mrs Flaxman to Hazlitt's lecture. It was a continuation of the lecture on Self Love, very dull though it concluded eloquently.

'25 February: – Accompanied Miss Benger to Hazlitt's lecture. H. this evening gave his lecture on Hartley. It was to me very dull.' We are not told what it was to Miss Elizabeth Ogilvie Benger, author of the *Life of Anne Boleyn* and other works, and a member of the Aikin-Barbauld circle with which Robinson was familiar.

'3 March: – At Hazlitt's lecture. An interesting and animated lecture on Helvetius and on the doctrine of Selfishness.

'10 March: – W. H. wrote to say he is obliged to postpone his lectures and I fear his debts oppress him so that he cannot proceed. I wish I could afford him assistance, for I know no state of suffering more dreadful than that of indigent genius.

'16 March: – To Charles Lamb, with whom were Barron

Field, Leigh Hunt and Barnes. The latter with a somewhat *feist* appearance, has a good countenance, and is a man who, I dare say, will make his way in the world. He has talents and activity, and inducements to activity. He has obtained high honours at Cambridge, and is now a candidate for a fellowship. He reports for Walter.' Thomas Barnes, one year junior to Leigh Hunt, was another of the Christ's Hospital and *Examiner* group, who became within five years editor of *The Times*. Lamb, Robinson notes, 'wrote last week in the *Examiner* some capital lines, "The Triumph of the Whale," and this occasioned the conversation to take more of a political turn than is usual with Lamb. Leigh Hunt is an enthusiast, very well-intentioned, and I believe, pre- pared for the worst. He said, pleasantly enough, "No one can accuse me of not writing a libel. Everything is a libel, as the law is now declared, and our security lies only in their shame." He talked on the theatre and showed on such points a great superiority over the others.

'17 March: – Instead of Hazlitt's lecture went to see Mrs Clarkson at J. B[uck]'s, and had a pleasant Whist lounge.

'31 March: – Hazlitt's lecture on Free Will and Necessity. He maintained a qualified necessity or rather an explained necessity. I did not hear the whole of the lecture.'

After the break of three weeks noted by Crabb Robinson (of which his explanation may or may not have been the correct one) the lectures appear to have proceeded smoothly to their close. The diarist was somewhat evidently tiring, but he turned out once more:

'27 April: – At Hazlitt's last lecture. Very well delivered, and full of shrewd observation. At the close, he remarked on the utility of metaphysics. He quoted and half assented to Hume's sceptical remark, that perhaps they are not worth the study, but that there are persons who can find no better way of amusing themselves. He then related an Indian legend of a Brahmin, who was so devoted to abstract meditation, that in the pursuit of philosophy he quite forgot his moral duties, and neglected ablution. For this he was degraded from the rank of humanity and transformed into a monkey. But even when a monkey he retained his original propensities, for he kept apart from the other monkeys, and had no other delight than that of eating cocoanuts and studying metaphysics. "I too," said Hazlitt, "should be very well contented to pass my life like this monkey, did I but know how to provide myself with a substitute for cocoanuts." '

It was in taking the steps necessary to provide himself with a substitute for cocoanuts that he was to stumble, almost by accident, upon the true work of his life.

II

His start in journalism, in his thirty-fifth year, is not unduly obscure to us. Immediately, no doubt, having come to town only 'to spend the winter', he returned to Winterslow. With or without his family (of which there is no mention until the end of the year), he was back in town in June. Our information is once more derived from Crabb Robinson :

'30 June : — Called at W. Hazlitt's, who was operating on Thomas [Robinson].

'1 July : — Called on W. Hazlitt, who at last did make a finish of Thomas's picture, which is now more tolerable than before, though still it has somewhat of the fierceness of the Saracen.' This, we may be certain, was the last professional portrait which Hazlitt ever painted.

'23 July : — Went to Captain Burney's with Miss Lamb, not having for a long time before visited the party. ... Hazlitt spoke freely but I have no doubt justly of Mallet. "He is a fellow who has a great reputation," said he, "because he did nothing. What can we think of a man, who being quite independent in his fortune, makes an abridgement of Locke and edits a book of

Hobbes, and at the same time thinks he is doing nothing? I do not mean to say that it is necessary for a man to do anything. He may be a very excellent man without it." ' This is a very characteristic opinion of Hazlitt's, and it no doubt derived its point at this juncture from the circumstance that he himself was very well understood to be under the necessity of 'doing something'.

Our diarist absenting himself for the vacation, we have to wait for our next information until September. It requires to be prefaced by the statement that Hazlitt's brother-in-law, finding the Bar too restricted an arena for his powerful political opinions, had in March of this year joined the staff of *The Times* in an advisory capacity similar to that held for a short time by Robinson. We come to the latter's next entries:

'21 September: – Called at Dr Stoddart's with a view to speak to him about W. Hazlitt, but he was not at home.

'28 September: – A call on Dr Stoddart to consult about Hazlitt & getting him a situation under Walter.

'30 September: – Met Dr Stoddart with Miss Lamb, with whom I chatted about Hazlitt. H., at the same time that he went to Perry & received from him a conditional promise of being employed as a reporter sent Dr S. to Walter. And Walter has promised to do something for H., but by this injudicious conduct H. has exposed himself to the likelihood of offending either W. or P. However, the prospect of him finding the means of subsistence is by this greatly improved. Wrote to H. He had written to me to – –.' The diarist here relapses into his shorthand.

We may make what we choose of these entries, but what we are tempted to make of them is that Hazlitt, driven somewhat desperate, had suffered the interposition of Robinson between himself and his brother-in-law. In the meantime, however – enormously to his relief, as we may imagine – the Lambs had ascertained in a chance conversation with Mrs Collier that a position might be secured on the *Morning Chronicle.* Lamb's letter to her husband, the Foreign Editor of that journal under Perry, survives the general fate which has overtaken the Lamb correspondence of this period, and is as follows:

Lamb to John Dyer Collier

Sunday morning.

Dear Sir, – Mrs Collier has been kind enough to say that you would endeavour to procure a reporter's situation for W. Hazlitt. I went to consult him upon it last night, and he acceded very eagerly to the proposal, and requests me to say how very much obliged he feels to your kindness, and how glad he should be for its success. He is, indeed, at his wits' end for a livelihood; and, I should think, especially qualified for such an employment, from his singular facility in retaining all conversations at which he has been ever present. I think you may recommend him with confidence. I am sure I shall *myself* be obliged to you for your exertions, having a great regard for him.

Yours truly, C. LAMB.

If Hazlitt received two offers, he accepted the one which gave him the greater prospect of political sympathy, and which did not come, even indirectly, from the hand of his brother-in-law. He settled down straightway to his new duties.

The cheerfulness with which the author of *The Eloquence of the British Senate* took his seat in the Press Gallery as a reporter is to his credit. It was now, we may suppose, that he entered upon the tenancy of the house in Westminster which was to be his home for the next eight years. The house, No. 19 York Street (a site now covered by the more remarkable erection of Queen Anne's Mansions), was Milton's house, it was the property of the philosopher Bentham who lived close by, and it had until recently been in the free occupation of Bentham's disciple, James Mill. Here, before the end of the year, Mrs Hazlitt and the child were installed. On 24 December Robinson looked in at Lamb's. 'The party there: Hazlitt, I was gratified by finding in high spirits, he finds his engagement with Perry as Parliamentary Reporter very easy, and the four guineas per week keep his head above water. He seems quite happy.' And on 2 January 1813: 'In the evening at Hazlitt's. The Burney and Lamb party were there, and I found H. in a handsome room and his supper was comfortably set out. Enjoyments which have sprung out of an unmeaning chat with Mrs C[ollier] at Lamb's. On what frivolous accidents do the important events of our lives depend.'

III

The paper in which Hazlitt contentedly sunk himself from the autumn of 1812 to the autumn of 1813 was the leading Whig organ and the natural *vis-à-vis* of *The Times*. It was, under James Perry, a good paper, remarkable for its contributors – including at one time and another Sheridan, Mackintosh, Porson (who married Perry's sister), Lamb, Coleridge, Moore, Campbell and Byron – and for the virtual invention of the modern or relay system of Parliamentary reporting. Perry himself, in every respect except personally, Hazlitt knew well. He had recently written a book (which was not yet published) in which, as an early friend of Holcroft, and one who had stood his own political trial, Perry figured extensively. Ten years later than the present date, when Perry was dead and the editorship of the *Chronicle* had passed to his own colleague of the Press Gallery, John Black, Hazlitt wrote of his first editor again, in his account of *The Periodical Press*.

The late Mr Perry [we there read] who raised the *Morning Chronicle* into its present consequence, held the office of Editor for nearly forty years; and he held firm to his party and his principles all that time – a long term for political honesty and consistency to last! He was a man of strong natural sense, some acquired knowledge, a quick tact; prudent, plausible, and with great heartiness and warmth of feeling. ... Perry was more vain than proud. This made him fond

of the society of lords, and them of his. His shining countenance reflected the honour done him, and the alacrity of his
address prevented any sense of awkwardness or inequality of
pretensions. He was a little of a coxcomb, and we do not think
he was a bit the worse for it. A man who does not think well
of himself, generally thinks ill of others; nor do they fail to
return the compliment. Towards the last, he, to be sure, received visitors in his library at home, something in the style of
the Marquis Marialva in Gil Blas. He affected the scholar. On
occasion of the death of Porson, he observed that '*Epithalamia*
were thrown into the coffin'; of which there was an awkward
correction next day – 'For *Epithalamia* read *Epicedia!*' The
worst of it was, that a certain consciousness of merit, with a
little overweening pretension, sometimes interfered with the
conduct of the paper. Mr Perry was not like a contemporary
editor [Walter], who never writes a sentence himself, and
assigns, as a reason for it, that 'he has too many interests to
manage as it is, without the addition of his own literary
vanity'. The Editor of the *Morning Chronicle* wrote up his
own paper; and he had an ambition to have it thought, that
every good thing in it, unless it came from a lord, or an
acknowledged wit, was his own. If he paid for the article
itself, he thought he paid for the credit of it also. This sometimes brought him into awkward situations. He wished to be
head and chief of his own paper, and would not have anything behind the editor's desk greater than the desk itself. He
was frequently remiss himself, and was not sanguine that
others should make up the deficiency.

Such was Hazlitt's first editor, and it is easy to see that he bore
him only a very little malice.

What Hazlitt, from his place in the gallery, thought of the
House of Commons, may be studied in the essay *On the Difference between Writing and Speaking* (1820):

Practice makes perfect. He who has got a speech by heart on any particular occasion, cannot be much gravelled for lack of matter on any similar occasion in future. Not only are the topics the same; the very same phrases — whole batches of them — are served up as the Order of the Day; the same parliamentary bead-roll of grave impertinence is twanged off, in full cadence, by the Honourable Member or His Learned and Honourable Friend; and the well-known, voluminous, calculable periods roll over the drowsy ears of the auditors, almost before they are delivered from the vapid tongue that utters them! It may appear, at first sight, that there are a number of persons got together, picked out from the whole nation, who can speak at all times upon all subjects in the most exemplary manner; but the fact is, they only repeat the same things over and over on the same subjects ... Instead of an exuberance of sumptuous matter, you have the same meagre standing dishes for every day in the year. You must serve an apprenticeship to a want of originality, to a suspension of thought and feeling. You are in a go-cart of prejudices, in a regularly constructed machine of pretexts and precedents; you are not only to wear the livery of other men's thoughts, but there is a House of Commons jargon which must be used for everything. A man of simplicity and independence of mind cannot easily reconcile himself to all this formality and mummery; yet woe to him that shall attempt to discard it! You can no more move against the stream of custom, than you can make head against a crowd of people; the mob of lords and gentlemen will not let you speak or think but as they do. You are hemmed in, stifled, pinioned, pressed to death — and if you make one false step, are 'trampled under the hoofs of a swinish multitude!' Talk of mobs! Is there any body of people that has this character in a more consummate degree than the House of Commons? Is there any set of men that determines more by acclamation, and less by deliberation and individual conviction? That is more *en masse,* in its aggregate capacity, as brute force and physical number? That judges with more Midas ears, blind and sordid, without discrimination of right and wrong? The greatest test of courage I can conceive, is to speak truth in the House of Commons.

This was, of course, the unreformed House of Commons. Hazlitt was in the Gallery for about a year, and it is a year that is almost devoid of personal history.

On his return from the country he had resumed his attendances at the studio of the old painter Northcote, in Argyll Place. Hard by, in Great Marlborough Street, the young painter Benjamin Robert Haydon was established. 'Hazlitt came in at Northcote's one day (1812)', writes the latter, 'and as he walked away with me he praised Macbeth. I asked him to walk up'. It is hardly needful to state, since the subject is Haydon, that the Macbeth which was praised was his own painting of that name, completed in the previous year to the order of Sir George Howland Beaumont. Haydon, aged at this date twenty-seven, was regarded as the rising hope of the 'historical' school, but, with no lack of talent or of patronage, his career was already jeopardized by his overweening egotism and by his constitutional inability to live within his means. He had quarrelled three years before with the authorities over the hanging of a picture, and henceforward three-fourths of his activities were to be expended on the non-essentials of his art. When in his *Autobiography*, put together two years before his death by his own hand (1846), Haydon took upon himself to sum up Hazlitt's career which had ended by the force of nature fourteen years earlier, he did so as follows:

With no decision, no application, no intensity of self-will, he had a hankering to be a painter, guided by a feeble love of what he saw, but the moment he attempted to colour or paint, his timid hand refused to obey from want of practice. Having no moral courage, he shrank from the struggle, sat down in hopeless despair, and began to moralize on the impossibility of art being revived in England – not because the people had no talent, not because they had no subject-matter, not because

there was no patronage, but because he, W. H., did not take
the trouble which Titian took, and because he was too lazy to
try. Mortified at his own failure, he resolved as he had not
succeeded no one else should, and he spent the whole of his
after life in damping the ardours, chilling the hopes, and dim-
ming the prospects of patrons and painters, so that after I
once admitted him, I had nothing but forebodings of failure
to bear up under, croakings about the climate, and sneering at
the taste of the public.

This is a witness, I think we may say, whom we may fairly be
on our guard against. The fact remains that Hazlitt liked
Haydon, despite his absurdities; and, badly as he has served his
memory, we shall find Haydon confessing that he could not but
like Hazlitt.

At the opening of the year 1813 two events occurred of which
the latter was no more than an interested spectator. The first of
these was the production, on 23 January, of Coleridge's *Remorse* at Drury Lane; the second, the trial of the Hunts on the
charge of libelling the Prince Regent which ended, on 3 February, in their conviction. Hazlitt got on with his Parliamentary
reporting.

Coleridge, as regarded his own play, could not believe this.
We find him writing on 25 January to Rickman: 'I have not yet
read what the *remorseless* critics of the *"ano abstersurae chartae"*
[a pleasing periphrasis for the *Examiner,* one presumes] say of
the play, but I know that Hazlitt in the *Morning Chronicle* has
sneered at my presumption in entering the lists with Shakespeare's *Hamlet,* in Teresa's description of the two brothers:
when (so help me the Muses) that passage never occurred to my
conscious recollection, however it may, unknown to myself,
have been the working idea within me. But mercy on us! Is
there no such thing as two men's having similar thoughts on
similar occasions?' I have tried hard to make this passage the
ground for establishing that Hazlitt contributed original matter
to the *Morning Chronicle* as early as January in this year, and

have not succeeded. The columns of the paper afford no evidence for such a contention. In addition, the question would have to be answered why, in reprinting his dramatic criticisms *in extenso* in the *View of the English Stage,* he included nothing earlier than October. We shall see in a moment Crabb Robinson's remarks in April, and also Hazlitt's own statement that his literary services to Perry were comprised in 'a single half-year' — an estimate which coincides exactly with our own observation. The conclusion appears irresistible that Coleridge was mistaken. The review of *Remorse* in the *Chronicle* consists of two columns which may very well have come from the pen of Hazlitt's predecessor, a Mr Mudford, and it would puzzle any one but Coleridge to find a 'sneer' intended in the passage to which he points.

The year is a blank in the Lamb correspondence, and Crabb Robinson, much engaged in his legal studies, gives us only two entries:

'14 January: — Again at chambers all day and in the evening, after which I called at Lamb's where I found the Hazlitts, &c., and chatted pleasantly enough with them.'

'29 April: — Spent the evening, which I had not done for a long time before, at C. Lamb's — at whist as usual. Chat with Hazlitt, who finds himself made comfortable by a situation which furnishing him with the necessaries of life keeps his best faculties not employed but awake. And I do not think it is much to be feared that his faculties will therefore decline. He has a most powerful intellect and needs only encouragement to manifest this to the world by a work which could not be overlooked.'

The latest speech which we can be certain (from his essay *On the Present State of Parliamentary Eloquence*) that Hazlitt heard from his place in the Gallery was the maiden effort, on 20 December 1813, of Sir James Mackintosh, recently returned from a judgeship in India. But before this date he had already gradu-

ated from the Parliamentary Report to the general columns of
the newspaper.

IV

His emergence, when it happened, was, as we should expect,
neither half-hearted nor mistakable. In the month of September
some so-called 'Common-places' – *On the Love of Life, On*
Classical Education – begin to make their appearance; and
simultaneously there is a note on the acceptance by Southey of
the office of Poet Laureate. This is followed immediately by
two letters under the heading *The Stage*.[1] It was these last, we
may imagine, which led Hazlitt's editor to conclude, however
reluctantly, that he might be entertaining on his staff a dramatic
critic unawares. Within a month of his appearance he is duly
installed in that office; and from this moment he never looks
back, but marches from department to department of Mr Perry's
paper, making each one of them his own.

Of his start in dramatic criticism we may read in *On Patronage and Puffing* (1822):

When I formerly had to do with these sort of critical ver-
dicts, I was generally sent out of the way when any *debutant*

1. Here *was* something by Hazlitt, and signed with his initials. On the
date of the appearance of the first letter (25 September) we have Coleridge,
on the eve of his three years' disappearance to Bristol and Calne, writing to
Stuart of the *Courier* in animadversion upon the 'anti-patriotism' of the
Morning Chronicle, and adding: 'In the same paper there is what I should
have called a masterly essay on the causes of the downfall of the Comic
Drama, if I was not perplexed by the distinct recollection of having conversed the greater part of it at Lamb's'. Coleridge's very free charges of
plagiarism from his own conversation are by their nature somewhat difficult to investigate, but if he had grounds for this one, they must be sought
in the period prior to the *Reply to Malthus*. In that book Hazlitt's theory
of comedy was first suggested; it was developed in these two letters; made
into a 'Round Table', under the title of *On Modern Comedy*; and finally
incorporated into the *English Comic Writers*. If it was not his own, he
may be said to have made it his own. But I think it conceivable that the
reader may have grown somewhat tired of Coleridge's endeavours, having
ruined his own career, to prevent Hazlitt from having one.

had a friend at court, and was to be tenderly handled. For the rest, or those of robust constitutions, I had *carte blanche* given me. Sometimes I ran out of the course, to be sure. Poor Perry! what bitter complaints he used to make, that by *running-a-muck* at lords and Scotchmen I should not leave him a place to dine out at! The expression of his face at these moments, as if he should shortly be without a friend in the world, was truly pitiable. What squabbles we used to have about Kean and Miss Stephens, the only theatrical favourites I ever had! Mrs Billington had got some notion that Miss Stephens would never make a singer, and it was the torment of Perry's life (as he told me in confidence) that he could not get any two people to be of the same opinion on any one point. I shall not easily forget bringing him my account of her first appearance in the Beggar's Opera. I had been down on a visit to my friends near Chertsey, and on my return, had stopped at an inn at Kingston-upon-Thames, where I had got the Beggar's Opera and had read it overnight. The next day I walked cheerfully to town. It was a fine sunny morning, in the end of autumn, and as I repeated the beautiful song, "Life knows no return of spring", I meditated my next day's criticism, trying to do all the justice I could to so inviting a subject. I was not a little proud of it by anticipation. ... I deposited my account of the play at the *Morning Chronicle* office in the afternoon, and went to see Miss Stephens as Polly.

The *Beggar's Opera* was Hazlitt's second professional visit to the theatre: his first had been to see the same actress in Arne's opera *Artaxerxes*. His 'friends near Chertsey', we are able to say, were his father, mother, and sister, who, on the retirement of the Rev. William Hazlitt from the ministry, had removed in this year from Wem to Addlestone in Surrey.

His account of Miss Stephens may be read in the *View of the English Stage*. He resumes:

When I got back, after the play, Perry called out, with his

cordial, grating voice, 'Well, how did she do?' and, on my speaking in high terms, answered, that 'he had been to dine with his friend the Duke [of Sussex], that some conversation had passed on the subject, he was afraid it was not the thing, it was not the true *sostenuto* style; but as I had written the article' (holding my peroration on the Beggar's Opera carelessly in his hand) 'it might pass!' I could perceive that the rogue licked his lips at it, and had already in imagination 'bought golden opinions of all sorts of people' by this very criticism, and I had the satisfaction the next day to meet Miss Stephens coming out of the Editor's room, who had been to thank him for his very flattering account of her.

The essay passes to Kean, whose first appearance on the London stage was on 26 January 1814:

I was sent to see Kean the first night of his performance in Shylock, when there were about a hundred people in the pit, but from his masterly and spirited delivery of the first striking speech, 'On such a day you called me dog', &c., I perceived it was a hollow thing. So it was given out in the *Chronicle,* but Perry was continually at me as other people were at him, and was afraid *it would not last;* yet I am in the right hitherto. It has been said, ridiculously, that Mr Kean was written up in the *Chronicle.*[1] I beg leave to state my opinion that no actor can be written up or down by a paper. An author may be puffed into notice, or damned by criticism, because his book may not have been read. An artist may be over-rated or undeservedly decried, because the public is not much accustomed to see or judge of pictures. But an actor is judged by his peers, the play-going public, and must stand or fall by his own merits or defects. The critic may give the tone or have a casting voice where popular opinion is divided; but he can no more *force* that opinion either way, or wrest it from its base in

1. 'The belief of the time was that Hazlitt received £1,500 from the management of Drury Lane for these articles. They made Kean's reputation, and saved the theatre.' (L'Estrange, *Mitford*, II. 47.)

common sense and common feeling, than he can move Stonehenge.

Hazlitt was perhaps lucky that his *début* synchronized so nearly with that of an actor such as Kean. But if he was lucky, Kean was lucky too.

His *début* as a dramatic critic, however, synchronized also with the Battle of Leipsic, and he was in little danger of giving up to the theatre what was meant for mankind. For six years he had written no word on politics, but he had not thought the less. The situation at the moment at which he found himself with a pen in his hand may be readily summarized. The defeat of Napoleon had been followed by a disposition on the part of the British government to bring the war to an end, and from his place in the Gallery Hazlitt had heard the Prime Minister announce that terms of peace would be proposed 'consistent with the honour, rights, and interests of France — such a peace as we in her situation should be disposed to grant'. The words were the signal for one of those stampedes with which the student of English political history is familiar. *The Times,* now under the editorship of Dr Stoddart, called in its inspired letter-writer of the moment, 'Vetus' (Edward Sterling), to charge ministers with war-weariness and to set up a cry of 'No Peace with Buonaparte'. It was essential, according to this writer, that the war should be waged to the bitter end, and admit of no conclusion short of the unconditional surrender of France and the restoration of the Bourbons. To this contention Hazlitt addressed himself in his *Illustrations of Vetus*:

This patriot logician in a letter to *The Times* of Friday, labours to stifle the most distant hope of peace in its birth. He lays down certain general principles which must for ever render all attempts to restore it vain and abortive. With the watchword of *Eternal war with Buonaparte* blazoned on his forehead, in the piety of his pacific zeal, he challenges Buonaparte as the wanton, unprovoked implacable enemy of the peace of mankind. We will also venture to lay down a maxim, which is — That from the moment that one party declares and acts upon the avowed principle that peace can never be made with an enemy, it renders war on the part of that enemy a matter of necessary self-defence, and holds out a plea for every excess of ambition or revenge. If we are to limit our hostility to others only with their destruction, we impose the adoption of the same principle on them as their only means of safety. There is no alternative. But this is probably the issue to which Vetus wishes to bring the question. ... The events which have lately taken place on the Continent, and the moderate and manly tone in which those events have been received by Ministers, have excited the utmost degree of un-easiness and alarm in the minds of certain persons, who re-double the eagerness of their cries for war. The cold blooded fury and mercenary malice of these panders to mischief, can only be appeased by the prospect of lasting desolation.

The duel thus opened proceeded on its course, and would not be without instruction if we could afford due space to illustrate it here. In asserting his contention, that 'the only legitimate basis of a treaty, if not on the part of the continental Allies, at least for England herself, is that she should conquer all she can, and keep all she conquers', Vetus was no doubt stating what he sin-cerely believed; and in opposing this contention, and applying to it the name 'exclusive patriotism', Hazlitt was not less sincere. To Vetus's protestation, that he was 'at a loss to understand the patriotism which is not exclusive', he responded with a defini-tion :

We will tell Vetus what we mean by exclusive patriotism, such as (we say) his is. We mean by it then, not that patriotism which implies a preference of the rights and welfare of our country, but that which professes to annihilate and proscribe the rights of others — not that patriotism which supposes us to be the creatures of circumstance, habit, and affection, but

that which divests us of the character of reasonable beings –
which fantastically makes our interests or prejudices the sole
measure of right and wrong to other nations, and constitutes
us sole arbiters of the empire of the world – in short, which,
under the affectation of an overweening anxiety for the welfare of our own country, *excludes* even the shadow of a pretension to common sense, justice, and humanity. It is this
wretched solecism which Vetus would fain bolster up into
a system, with all the logic and rhetoric he is master of.

Vetus countered this by an excursus upon 'the men who in
some degree precipitated the French Revolution ... the mongrel
race of metaphysical enthusiasts, who undertook to change the
objects of human feeling, that they might disappoint more effectually the ends for which it was bestowed'. A 'sucker from the
root of this poisonous vegetable' he professed to find 'again in
blossom', but whether it was Lord Liverpool or Hazlitt who
was thus designated is not altogether apparent. The 'stupid
impertinence' was, however, Hazlitt's, which, said Vetus, 'has
no relation to the *Morning Chronicle,* with which I am disposed
to part in peace. One feels a tolerance towards that paper, for
the talents which once adorned it; and of the continuance of
which I should rejoice to see more proof in its late attacks on
Vetus'. To which Hazlitt responded : 'As to the talent shewn
in our attacks on him, we are ready to admit that it is little
enough; but we at the same time think that if it had been
greater, it would have been more than the occasion required'.
Events upon the Continent, however, did not wait upon either
of the disputants; and if the Allied statesmanship, by undertaking to respect the integrity of France and leaving the choice
of a constitution to the French people, disappointed Vetus, the
apparent prompt decision of the latter against Buonaparte was
at least an equal disappointment to Hazlitt. In the light of
events, it is more than a little likely that the good Perry conceived his contributor to have been running away with the
paper. Whatever the cause of difference, it now soon came to a

head. As has been suggested, Hazlitt's progress from field to
field of his interests, once he had started, had been rapid, and
for a brief period of months we find his dramatic criticisms, art
criticisms, political letters and leading articles, 'Common-
Places', and contributions from 'An English Metaphysician', all
going up together in Mr Perry's columns. That the latter's disturbance was not limited to political considerations is suggested,
in a letter of four years later (28 December 1818), by an independent observer on Mr Perry's own hearth:

> I have just been reading Hazlitt's *View of the English Stage*
> – a series of critiques originally printed in the different news-
> papers, particularly the *Chronicle*. ... I was at Tavistock House
> at the time, and well remember the doleful visage with which
> Mr Perry used to contemplate the long column of criticism,
> and how he used to execrate 'the d – d fellow's d – d stuff'
> for filling up so much of the paper in the very height of the
> advertisement season. I shall never forget his long face. It
> was the only time of the day that I ever saw it long or sour.
> He had not the slightest suspicion that he had a man of
> genius in his pay – not the most remote perception of the
> merit of the writing – nor the slightest companionship with
> the author. He hired him as you hire your footman; and
> turned him off (with as little or less ceremony than you would
> use in discharging the aforesaid worthy personage) for a very
> masterly but damaging critique on Sir Thomas Lawrence,
> whom Mr P., as one whom he visited and was being painted
> by, chose to have praised.

The observer was Miss Mitford, not yet the author of *Our
Village*, but a literary young woman who almost alone among
her contemporaries appears to have observed the outset of Hazlitt's journalistic career with something of the surprised admiration it deserved.

We must not, however, forget Crabb Robinson. If the diarist,
on account of political divergencies, was not always to follow

Hazlitt's career with admiration, he was rarely to fail for long to follow it. In December we duly find him recording the opinion : 'His Illustrations of Vetus which have lately appeared in the *Chronicle* are not equal to his articles on the Drama'. The next entry of interest to us is the following :

'29 April : — Called on C. Lamb. Dr Stoddart there : I stayed to tea. The Dr & I exchanged a few words about our common friend Walter. He seemed quite pleased & comfortable. He says that the anonymous stanzas of an ode lately published are by Southey, and that they originally belonged to the Carmen [Triumphale] but it was thought indecorous that the Laureate should avow such sentiments. The stanzas deprecate a peace with Buonaparte, and exhort the French to execute justice on the Miscreant. Lamb says that Hazlitt is confounded by the conduct of Buonaparte : he is ashamed to show his face.'

For our remaining information we must go forward to an entry very near the end of the year. The subject of Hazlitt's professional employment happening on that occasion (17 November) to be raised, the diarist gives us the following : 'He [Hazlitt] complains bitterly of Perry's treatment of him, and I believe his statement, for he is too proud and high minded to lie. He says that during the last six months [i.e., of his engagement, to May] he wrote seventy columns for the *Morning Chronicle,* that Perry himself confessed to him that he had done more for the paper than all the other writings, and in consequence of his approbation of what H. had done advanced him £100, of which £50 are due. I had understood from the Colliers that Perry had not actually dismissed H., but that he abstained from coming. H. states the fact thus. P. said to him expressly that he wished H. to *look out for another situation.* The affronting language H. could not easily forget, as he was not fit for a reporter. H. said he thought he could do miscellaneous things. Perry said he would think of it. However when H. afterwards went to the office for his salary he was told Mr P. wished to speak with him. He went to P.'s room. P. was not alone, and desired H. to wait. H. went to another room. P. then seeing H.

went out of the house. H. in consequence never called again. As there [has been] no express refusal either to pay or to accept his services in another way than as reporter, P. has an excuse for saying he did not dismiss H.

'H. also mentions instances of P.'s insolent behaviour to him which must render dependence on such a man a galling servitude. He called on H. one evening to answer on the spot an article or speech about the liberty of the Press. H. wrote one, he says not a good one. P. looked it over. "This is the most pimping thing I ever read. If you cannot do a thing of this kind off hand you won't do for me." Yet on former occasions he had been vastly pleased with H.'s articles and had turned them into leading articles. H. says P.'s conduct is to be ascribed to the fall of Buonaparte, "by which", says he, "my articles were made in the event very unfortunate. But it is hard to make me suffer for that." Whether H.'s offence was not writing in other papers I can't tell, but certainly P. who has no delicacy or regard for the feelings of others would not have scrupled to insist on H.'s leaving off, if such had been his real objection to him.' 'How different a man is Walter!' Crabb Robinson begins to add – an opinion which Hazlitt showed himself willing to second when he came later for a short time to work for him.

The above is all confirmed as nearly as need be by a passage in an essay of six years later, *On the Qualifications Necessary to Success in Life*: 'A writer whom I know very well ... having written upwards of sixty columns of original matter on politics, criticism, belles-lettres, and *virtu* in a respectable Morning Paper, in a single half-year, was, at the end of the period, on applying for a renewal of his engagement, told by the Editor "he might give in a specimen of what he could do". One would think sixty columns of the *Morning Chronicle* were a sufficient specimen of what a man could do". But while this person was thinking of his next answer to Vetus, or his account of Mr Kean's performance of Hamlet, he had neglected to "point the toe", to hold up his head higher than usual (having acquired a habit of poring over books when young), and to get a new velvet collar to an old-fashioned great-coat. These are "the graceful ornaments to the columns of a newspaper – the Corinthian capitals of a polished style!" This unprofitable servant of the Press found no difference in himself before or after he became known to the readers of the *Morning Chronicle,* and it accordingly made no difference in his appearance or pretensions.'

The spectacle of Hazlitt just a little sorry for himself in recollection is a more profitable one than that of Crabb Robinson penning trite maxims in the heat of the occasion. 'It is quite painful,' he adds, 'to witness the painful exertions for a livelihood which H. is condemned to make, and how strongly it shows that a modicum of mechanical marketable talent outweighs an ample endowment of original thought and the highest powers of intellect, when a man does not add to that endowment the other of making it turn to account. How many men are there connected with Newspapers who live comfortably with not a tithe of H.'s powers as a writer.' How many indeed, most excellent diarist!

V

Hazlitt's case, however, was not really so desperate. Thanks to his first editor, he was no longer in ignorance of what he could do. He had now fleshed and exercised his pen in all fields in which he was henceforward to wield it; and if what he could do was not good enough for Perry, it was good enough for others. On walking out of the *Chronicle* office, he had but to walk into the columns of two other journals.

His first meeting with Leigh Hunt, we may say with some certainty, had been at Lamb's in the spring of 1812. It was not immediately followed by intimacy, for reasons which, on Hazlitt's side, we can very easily guess. Leigh Hunt at twenty-eight could, and did, pass easily anywhere as an extremely successful young man; Hazlitt, at thirty-four, was no longer quite young, and was certainly not successful. His first apprenticeship to regular journalism, which Leigh Hunt had passed somewhat brilliantly eight years before, had still to be undergone; and in the preliminaries which preceded it it does not surprise us that Leigh Hunt took no part. This in spite of the fact that before the end of the year 1812 the two were meeting with frequency at the studio of Haydon.

Before Hazlitt could become intimate with Leigh Hunt, it was necessary that, so far as the world of journalism was concerned, he should stand upon his own feet. This, as we have seen, he had very speedily managed to do. In the meantime Leigh Hunt, as we have also seen, in the course of pursuing his somewhat airy way as a political journalist, had trodden once too often on the ministerial coat which as assiduously trailed for him. Twice before the ministry had indicted the *Examiner*, and twice had failed to secure a conviction. On the first occasion, in February 1810, the *Morning Chronicle* had been brought to trial first, for reproducing the offending statement; and, on the refusal of the jury to convict, the action against the *Examiner* had fallen to the ground. A year later the paper was again proceeded against, this time on account of an article against military flogging reprinted from a provincial journal, the *Stamford News*, of which one John Scott was editor; but Hunt's friend Brougham appeared in the defence and the verdict was Not Guilty. The ministry awaited their chance, caught Leigh Hunt napping in a reference to the Prince Regent's morals and figure, and, at a suitable moment, secured their conviction. Leigh Hunt went to pass a period of two years in the Surrey Gaol, his brother John a period similar in Coldbath Fields; while each was condemned to pay a fine of £500.

The *Examiner*, as a result of all this, was an important paper,[1] and Leigh Hunt in prison a famous man. He was, as we at this distance are able to see, at the age of twenty-nine at the height of his career. All his life he had been something of the infant prodigy, and it is the fate of the infant prodigy to decline in

1. A letter of Bentham's in 1812 shows us the position it had gained. He says, speaking of the weeklies: 'The *Examiner* is the one that at present, especially among the high political men, is most in vogue. It sells already between 7,000 and 8,000.' (Bain, *Mill*, p. 123.)

interest as he approaches middle age. This, however, was as yet some way ahead. A poet at sixteen, a clerk in the War Office at twenty, a journalist who had revived the light discursive essay and struck out a new line in theatrical criticism at twenty-one, and editor of the *Examiner* three years later, Leigh Hunt's career up to the present had been about as different from that of his new contributor as it would be possible for one career to be from another. While Byron brought him food and his own poems, while the philosopher Bentham played at shuttle-cock with his children in the prison-yard, while young Shelley at Oxford sent him offers of financial assistance, Leigh Hunt, seated in his gaoler's room, on the ceiling of which he had caused a blue sky with white clouds to be painted, while the walls were decorated with trellised roses, continued to edit the *Examiner* and to write his poem 'Rimini'. It was here, he says in his *Autobiography,* that Hazlitt 'first did me the honour of a visit', and 'would stand interchanging amenities at the threshold, which I had great difficulty in making him pass. I know not which kept his hat off with the greater pertinacity of deference, I to the diffident cutter-up of Tory dukes and Kings, or he to the amazing prisoner and invalid who issued out of a bower of roses'. The scene was thus set, by a course of action which we feel on both sides to be characteristic, for a re-meeting of equals which we may date with some confidence at the spring of 1814.

It was not to Leigh Hunt, however, that Hazlitt carried the first articles which he took away from the *Morning Chronicle.* In all the respects in which he had made a reputation in the preceding winter, the *Examiner* was to some extent provided. Leigh Hunt, from prison, continued to do politics, the theatre he handed over to Barnes, the fine arts were attended to by the third Hunt, Robert. There was another paper which was more ready for him. In January 1813 the *Stamford News* came to town as *Drakard's London Paper,* bringing its editor with it; and a year later it underwent another change into the *Champion.* It is to the pages of John Scott's *Champion* that we find

Hazlitt most immediately transferring himself, as his tenure of Mr Perry's columns becomes uncertain. The first article which we find him taking away is that *On the Late War*, which is really the conclusion of the Vetus series, in the first week of April. For a further two months he continues in the *Chronicle*, but only on the theatre and the fine arts. His last contribution is at the end of May, by which date the *contretemps* spoken of by Miss Mitford may be presumed to have occurred.[1]

In the meantime he had made a start on the *Examiner*, with his 'Common-Places' transferred from the *Morning Chronicle*. In July an article on *Mr Kean's Iago*, making its appearance between two appearances of the regular dramatic critic, and containing some observations on the character of Desdemona, 'not a little startled some of our readers', as Leigh Hunt wrote from prison. 'It may be observed,' he added, 'that all plain-speaking inquiries into the nature of ourselves and our passions are apt to be startling – at least in the first instance'. The article led to controversy between Barnes and Hazlitt, of which the latter got the better. Immediately afterwards, he became the dramatic critic of the *Champion*. He had already taken over from the editor (Scott) the department of the Fine Arts, his opening article on the President of the Royal Academy's *Picture of Christ Rejected* (26 June) causing something of a sensation. This he followed with a series of articles reinforcing the views on modern painters and modern painting which he had already expressed, under the title of *The Fine Arts, Whether they are Promoted by Academies and Public Institutions*.

Henceforward, to the end of the year and beyond it, we have to picture him cultivating his double field, and few weeks passed in which he did not make his contribution to both journals. We must pause only at the most salient; and one of these immediately presents itself. Hazlitt's *Character of Mr Wordsworth's new Poem, the Excursion*, brings Lamb out of

1. The critique in question ('The Royal Academy', *Morning Chronicle*, 3 May 1814) will be found recovered and reprinted in *New Writings: Second Series*.

the comparative seclusion into which, since the former's accession to journalism, their relation has fallen. As Mr Lucas has
shown, these were busy professional years with Lamb, leaving
him little leisure for literary activity, so that the arrangement
into which he had entered to write for Scott at the same time as
Hazlitt, resulted in only one contribution and then had to be
cancelled. We come to his letter to Wordsworth, of 19 September. 'The nature of my work,' we read, 'puzzling and hurrying,
has so shaken my spirits, that my sleep is nothing but a succession of dreams of business I cannot do, of assistants that give me
no assistance, of terrible responsibilities. I reclaimed your book,
which Hazlitt has uncivilly kept, only two days ago, and have
made shift to read it again with shatter'd brain. It does not lose
– rather some parts have come out with a prominence I did not
perceive before, but such was my aching head yesterday (Sunday) that the book was like a Mountn. Landscape to one that
should walk on the edge of a precipice. I perceived beauty
dizzily. Now what I would say is, that I see no prospect of a
quiet half day or hour even till this week and the next are past. I
then hope to get four weeks' absence, and if *then* is time enough
to begin I will most gladly do what you require.' What Wordsworth required was that Lamb should review the 'Excursion',
by Southey's influence, in the *Quarterly*.

Lamb goes on: 'The unlucky reason of the detention of Excursion was, Hazlitt and we having a misunderstanding. He
blowed us up about six months ago,[1] since which the union
hath snapt, but M. Burney borrow'd it for him and after re-
iterated messages I only got it on Friday. His [Hazlitt's]
remarks [in the *Examiner*] had some vigor in them, particu-

1. Six months from September is April, and it was in that month that
we found Crabb Robinson recording: 'Lamb says that Hazlitt is confounded by the conduct of Buonaparte: he is ashamed to show his face'.
Hazlitt, that is to say, having taken badly the events of the spring, had
'blown up' Lamb for his political indifference. A couple of months afterwards, he had gone out of his way to praise him in his *Examiner* article
(19 June) on Hogarth. This, their first difference in ten years of which we
know, is a type of all subsequent ones.

larly something about an old ruin being *too modern for your Primeval Nature,* and about a lichen, but I forget the Passage, but the whole wore a slovenly air of dispatch and disrespect. That objection which M. Burney had imbibed from him about Voltaire, I explained to M. B. (or tried) exactly on your principle of its being a characteristic speech.' This is a cool manner of writing, partly accounted for by the context, partly by the circumstance that Hazlitt, for the purpose of his review which came out in three parts, had detained a book which Lamb himself intended reviewing. Wordsworth, we must suppose, noted the coolness, and wished to convert it into a breach; for by return he supplied Lamb with that account of the misdoings of Hazlitt's youth which we have considered in an earlier chapter. If this was his wish, he reckoned without his man; and Lamb, on writing again, by a more careful adoption of tone (*ante,* page 106) showed conclusively enough that the attempt had not been successful.

A 'slovenly air of dispatch and disrespect' is not altogether the impression the modern reader takes away from Hazlitt's first published estimate of Wordsworth — from his first written word, indeed (if we except one or two strictures on the Odes of the Laureate), on the poetry of his contemporaries. Lamb, as we may satisfy ourselves very easily, had read no more than its opening paragraph. But Hazlitt had said of the 'Excursion': 'In power of intellect, in lofty conception, in the depth of feeling, at once simple and sublime, which pervades every part of it and which gives to every object an almost preternatural and preterhuman interest, this work has seldom been surpassed.' He had said of the author: 'There is in his general sentiments and reflections on human life a depth, an originality, a truth, a beauty and grandeur both of conception and expression, which place him decidedly at the head of the poets of the present day, or rather which place him in a totally distinct class of excellence.' He had concluded, after doing the work of Wordsworth the most practical form of service which it could receive in 1814, that of extensive quotation: 'About as many fine things have passed through Mr Wordsworth's mind, as, with five or six exceptions, through any human mind whatever'. But he had not cared for the poet's description of Voltaire's *Candide*, the book enjoyed by the Solitary in his rural retirement, as the 'dull product of a scoffer's pen';[1] and he had had his own reasons of loyalty as well as of judgement for saying so.

The chief of these reasons we may learn, I believe, from a note to the 'Excursion' which Wordsworth dictated thirty years later than the date we have now reached. The character of the Solitary, he said, was 'drawn from several persons':

The chief of these was, one may *now* say, a Mr Fawcett, a preacher at a dissenting meeting house at the Old Jewry ... an able and eloquent man. He published a poem on war, which had a good deal of merit, and made me think more about him than I should otherwise have done. But his Christianity was probably never very deeply rooted; and, like many others in those times of like showy talents, he had not strength of character to withstand the effects of the French Revolution, and of the wild and lax opinions which had done so much towards producing it, and far more in carrying it forward in its extremes. Poor Fawcett, I have been told, became pretty much such a person as I have described; and early disappeared

1.   'The book, which in my hand
        Had opened of itself ...
                          ... I found to be a work
        In the French tongue, a Novel of Voltaire,
        His famous Optimist. "Unhappy Man!"
        Exclaimed my Friend ...
                          ... How poor,
        Beyond all poverty how destitute,
        Must that Man have been left, who, hither driven,
        Flying or seeking, could yet bring with him
        No dearer relique, and no better stay,
        Than this dull product of a scoffer's pen,
        Impure conceits discharging from a heart,
        Hardened by impious pride!'

The words, it is true, are those of the Wanderer in the poem; but the Author says nothing to dissent from them.

from the stage, having fallen into habits of intemperance which I have heard (though I will not answer for the fact) hastened his death.

Little, as we have seen, is known of Fawcett, and between Hazlitt's 'death hastened by the disappointment of his hopes' and Wordsworth's 'hastened, I have heard (though I will not answer for the fact) by intemperance', a choice must be made of the end best suited, in the individual judgement, to the opinions. What is clear to us is that 'poor Fawcett' was a sympathiser with the French Revolution, who had died at a moment which had placed his reputation singularly at the mercy of his political opponents. The only difference of which we are aware, so far as his memory was concerned, between 1814 and 1844, was that in the former year Hazlitt was not dead. So far was he from being dead, that in a public sense he had only just come to life; and, while he was not going to give the lie to the perception of Wordsworth's qualities as a poet which he had held from his twenty-first year, he equally was not willing to conceal his consciousness of the gulf which had opened between them.

It is with a knowledge of these facts[1] that we may approach the passage in this article which has been deemed best worthy of remembrance. He has quoted the poet's aspiration for the future of society (*Excursion*, IV. 260 seq.), and continues:

In the application of these memorable lines, we should perhaps, differ a little from Mr Wordsworth; nor can we indulge with him in the fond conclusion afterwards hinted at, that one day *our triumph,* the triumph of humanity and liberty, may be complete. For this purpose, we think several things neces-

1. Of which, we may note, Lamb afterwards (page 227) showed his customarily generous, if tardy, appreciation. We need not, any more than Crabb Robinson, believe that Hazlitt 'cried' over the composition of his review of the *Excursion*: but that he found himself powerfully divided between allegiance to the work of a poet whom he had loved and studied and to a cause which he believed to be even more important than that of poetry, I do not think that we need doubt.

sary which are impossible. It is a consummation which cannot happen till the nature of things is changed, till the many become as united as the *one*, till romantic generosity shall be as common as gross selfishness, till reason shall have acquired the obstinate blindness of prejudice, till the love of power and of change shall no longer goad man on to restless action, till passion and will, hope and fear, love and hatred, and the objects proper to excite them, that is, alternate good and evil, shall no longer sway the bosoms and business of men. All things move, not in progress, but in a ceaseless round; our strength lies in our weakness; our virtues are built on our vices; our faculties are as limited as our being; nor can we lift man above his nature more than above the earth he treads. But though we cannot weave over again the airy, unsubstantial dream, which reason and experience have dispelled,

> '*What though the radiance which was once so bright*
> *Be now for ever taken from our sight,*
> *Though nothing can bring back the hour*
> *Of glory in the grass, of splendour in the flower,*'

yet we will never cease, nor be prevented from returning on the wings of imagination to that bright dream of our youth; that glad dawn of the day-star of liberty; that spring-time of the world, in which the hopes and expectations of the human race seemed opening in the same gay career with our own; when France called her children to partake her equal blessings beneath her laughing skies; when the stranger was met in all her villages with dance and festive songs, in celebration of a new and golden era; and when, to the retired and contemplative student, the prospect of human happiness and glory were seen ascending like the steps of Jacob's ladder, in bright and never-ending succession. The dawn of that day was suddenly over-cast; that season of hope is past; it is fled with the other dreams of our youth, which we cannot recall, but has left behind it traces, which are not to be effaced by

Birthday and Thanksgiving Odes, or the chanting of *Te Deums* in all the churches of Christendom. To those hopes eternal regrets are due; to those who maliciously and wilfully blasted them, in the fear that they might be accomplished, we feel no less what we owe – hatred and scorn as lasting!

This duty to himself and to the memory of his friend performed, Hazlitt thought that he had spoken well of the *Excursion*.

VI

We may conclude the year with a number of arrears from Crabb Robinson:

'7 June: – Dined with Collier, and walked in the evening with Mrs Collier and the Lambs to Alsager's. We spent the evening at cards and very pleasantly. Mitchell and Hazlitt were there. Mrs C. joined us from the Hunts. Lamb was very pleasant.' Mitchell was Thomas Mitchell, the friend of Leigh Hunt and translator of Aristophanes. This is the first mention of Thomas Alsager, a colleague of Barnes on *The Times,* who now comes into the narrative through the circumstance that his residence closely neighboured Leigh Hunt's temporary one, in Horsemonger Lane. It was the Hunt family in gaol, of course, that Mrs Collier had stepped across to visit.

'4 July: – Took early tea with Flaxman, to whom I read an admirable criticism by Hazlitt on West's picture of the Rejection of Christ.[1] A bitter and severe but most excellent performance. Flaxman was constrained to admit the high talent of the criticism, though he was unaffectedly pained by its severity; but he was himself offended by West's attempt to represent this sacred subject.'

During August and September, like the good barometer he

1. This passage was given by Dr Sadler in his 1869 edition of Robinson's *Diary, Reminiscences and Correspondence*. In spite of this plain pointer, the article escaped the attention of Hazlitt's successive editors and bibliographers. It will be found reprinted in *New Writings: Second Series*.

was, Robinson was in Paris, rejoicing in the superior advantages
accruing to tourists from 'that great event, the restoration of
the French monarchy, after twenty-five years of Revolution'.
On his return, he does not cease to serve us as barometer.

'15 October : – Rose early, and having breakfasted in my
chambers spent the day on the roof of the Bury coach. I do not
know when the day has passed so rapidly while travelling. ... I
read almost the whole day with interest the *Examiners* for the
last three months. They contain an excellent review of Wordsworth's poem by Hazlitt. ... He has also written in the
Examiner a review of the character of Iago, very ably executed.
Barnes answered his criticism with good sense but marked in-
feriority of talent.

'26 October [at Bury] : – Walked to the Library, and read the
last number of the *Edinburgh Review*. A review of Northcote's
Life of Reynolds containing many thoughts exactly resembling
Hazlitt's sentiments in his observations on West's great picture
but very inferior indeed both in energy and beauty.

'29 October : – I dined with Mrs Barbauld. Mr and Mrs C.
Aikin ... were of the party. We had a pleasant afternoon. I read
some extracts from Wordsworth's poem out of [Hazlitt's review in] the *Examiner*, but it did not seem to please greatly,
nor was Hazlitt's criticism on West's picture approved of; perhaps I had praised both too highly before I read them.

'11 November : – Took notes and also read in Court some of
Hazlitt's articles in *Champion* and *Examiner*. One a bitter but
well written sneering article against the allied powers reproaches
them with sinking back into their ancient tyrannical habits.
Also some happy strictures on Rochefoucauld's Maxims, introducing excellent remarks on *envy*. How lamentable that so fine
a writer should want a fit field for his exertions!'

Our concluding entry is one of which we have taken a portion already on an earlier page. We now have its beginning :

'17 November : – After nine, I went to C. Lamb's, whose
parties are now once a month only. I played a couple of rubbers
pleasantly and afterwards chatted with Hazlitt till one o'clock.

He is become an *Edinburgh Reviewer* through the recommendation of Lady Mackintosh, who had sent to the *Champion*
office to know the author of the articles on Institutions.[1] H. sent
those and other writings to Jeffrey and has been in a very flattering manner enrolled in the corps. This has put H. in good
spirits: he now again hopes that his talents will be appreciated
and become a subsistence to him.'

The fit field had arrived, in the opinion of the diarist.

1. The manner of this start is confirmed by an unpublished letter from
Lady Mackintosh to John Scott, in the possession of Major S. Butterworth:
'Lady Mackintosh has the pleasure to send Mr Scott [in Paris] the letter
she spoke of for St Germain's. ... Lady M. has written a strong recommendation of Mr Hazlet [*sic*] as a clever writer to Mr Jeffrey, and will
communicate his answer as soon as she receives his [Scott's] direction at
Paris.'

CHAPTER VII

THE JOURNALIST (II)

(1815–16)

*

Is truth then so variable? Is it one thing at twenty, and another at forty? ... Not so, in the name of manhood and of commonsense!

The Spirit of the Age.

I

THE opening of 1815 found Hazlitt in full employment on the *Champion* (the theatre and the fine arts), the *Examiner* (miscellaneous essays), and the *Edinburgh Review*. The last named, twelve years after its foundation, was at the height of its power, a power which, exerted on the Liberal side so far as politics were concerned, had called into being five years before, through the longsightedness of a bookseller and the unofficial support of the Government, the rival effort of the *Quarterly*. In 1815 the *Edinburgh* was still pre-eminent in its own field, and accession to the ranks of its writers was something like a professional and social hall-mark. This Hazlitt had obtained within two years of his coming to London, and little more than a year of his start in periodical writing.

At the beginning of the year, while the Congress of the Powers was assembled at Vienna, Leigh Hunt, in anticipation of approaching release from his two years' imprisonment, was making new plans for the *Examiner*. In pursuance of these he took over the theatre from Barnes, and seated himself with Hazlitt at the Round Table – a feature which was designed to give his own easy sketches of men and manners in alternation with the more searching form of the essay practised by his new contributor. 'But our plan,' as readers of the latter will remember, 'had been no sooner arranged and entered upon, than Buonaparte landed at Frejus, *et voilà la Table Ronde dissoûte*. Our little congress was broken up as well as the great one; Politics called off the attention of the Editor from the Belles Lettres; and the task of continuing the work fell chiefly upon the person who was least able to give life and spirit to the original design.'[1] The release of Leigh Hunt was on 3 February; the return of Napoleon from Elba on 1 March; and an event which served directly to draw Hazlitt into closer association with the *Examiner* contributed indirectly to the same end by severing his connection with the *Champion*.

Once more, with the return of Napoleon, English liberalism found itself confronted with a divided path. We may go forward in order to hear of it. Writing at the end of 1815 his political survey of *The Concluding Year*, John Scott said:

It was maintained by some, between whom and ourselves there had hitherto been little else than coincidence of senti-

1. The earliest stages of a famous partnership are not without their illumination upon character. On 1 and 8 January Leigh Hunt, with much pleasant 'business', spreads the cloth for the Round Table. On the 15th Hazlitt rewrites *On the Love of Life*. The fourth, fifth, and sixth instalments are by Hunt, and concern themselves with 'Egotists' and some invented correspondence on the same subject. The seventh is by Hazlitt, *On Classical Education*, which ends (in the newspaper) with a passage on the education of women. In the eighth Hunt defends the feminine character: 'A Knight, and attack the ladies! One of *us*, and not be perfectly amiable and high-minded! ... We looked at his eyes, but they were whole — we looked at his hair, but it was in good and plentiful condition — we looked at him as far as the Table would let us, but there he was, sitting in as complacent a style, and looking as fine and conclusive, as if he had been rescuing forty damsels from insult!' The picture of a 'complacent' Hazlitt, looking 'fine and conclusive', is perhaps worth rescuing at this juncture; and in other respects the regard of L. H. for 'the profound though sometimes rash thinker' W. H. is apparent. In the issue for 12 March, which contains the news of Elba, there is no Round Table; and it is from this point forward, when the feature is sustained by Hazlitt, that the business of knights and chivalry makes a not unexpected disappearance.

ment, that Buonaparte's return was, upon the whole, the
triumph of popular right over usurped power, that, in point
of fact, he was supported by France generally, and that, therefore, he would be invulnerably defended against his enemies.
It was further said, that, in the very outset, he brought a large
portion of political reform into the Government of France;
that it was likely he would either keep, or be kept to, all his
engagements, in favour of liberty; that the attack preparing
against him would be made on the independence of the
French nation, that it would be ruinous to the aggressors, the
chief of whom was England, and glorious for the intended
victim, the once depressed, but again surmounting, Napoleon. We did not see or feel things in this way, and we
took the liberty of saying so. ... Some have called this *trim-
ming*.

Among the 'some', we may be quite sure, was Hazlitt. His
concluding article in the *Champion* was on 5 March, *On Mr
Wilkie's Pictures*: and at the same moment, in further relief
of Leigh Hunt, whose health had suffered by imprisonment, he
took over the *Examiner's* theatre. That the transfer was not immediately an unfriendly one the contemporary files of both
newspapers present us with evidence. Henceforward for more
than two years, so far as weekly journalism was concerned,
Hazlitt's eggs were to be all in one basket.

We may now turn to Crabb Robinson, who as usual affords
us some enlightenment :

'5 February (Sunday): – Went to Alsager's to dinner. The
party consisted of Sergt and Mrs Rough, Ayrton, M. Burney,
W. Hazlitt. It was a pleasant afternoon. Hazlitt, while he continued sober, was excellent company. He talked a little about
German literature, and abused Goethe for writing expressly on
the principle of producing no effect. Egmont, said he, is as
cold and unimpressive as possible. I objected that this fault is not
common. He asserted that the Germans knew no medium between gross effect and none at all.' For a development of this

assertion, the reader will turn to the *Edinburgh Review* article, *Schlegel on the Drama,* of the following February. 'Afterwards he became warm on politics and declaimed against the friends of liberty for their apostasy. He attacked me, but was at the same time civil. He expressed his pleasure at the present conduct of the Sovereigns of Europe as confirming his anticipation.' The anticipation in question had been expressed in the *Champion* article, *Whether the Friends of Freedom can Entertain any sanguine Hopes of the Favourable Results of the ensuing Congress,* which we found Crabb Robinson reading in Court. Hazlitt had remarked: 'We believe this, that princes are princes, and that men are men; and that to expect any very great sacrifices of interest or passion from either in consequence of certain well-timed and well-sounding professions drawn from them by necessity, when that necessity no longer exists, is to belie all our experience of human nature.' The Peace Conference of February 1815, as a matter of history, was principally concerned in quarrelling over the appropriation of Poland and Saxony. We may note that this entry contains Robinson's earliest reference to Hazlitt's habit, held in common with his friend Charles Lamb, of sometimes drinking too much. His year in the Press Gallery has been credited with the not altogether unusual effect of strengthening this habit; but finding within a few months of this date that it was doing his health no good, he gave it up altogether, as, for once, every witness is in agreement.

'15 April: — I called at the Colliers, and found that Miss Lamb was gone to Alsager's, from whom I had an invitation. I went as a duty. There was a largish party, and I stayed till near two, playing whist ill, for which I was scolded by Capt. Burney, and *vingt un* unfortunately. And debated with Hazlitt, in which I was not successful, as far as the talent of the disputation was involved: though H. was wrong as well as offensive in almost all he said. When pressed, he does not deny what is bad in the character of Buonaparte, and yet he triumphs and rejoices in the late events. H. and myself once felt alike on politics, and now our hopes and fears are directly opposed.' The late events were by now of course the return from Elba and the triumphal re-entry of Napoleon into Paris.

'24 April: – Read this morning Hazlitt's article on the great Novelists in the *Edinburgh Review*. A very interesting article. His discrimination between Fielding and Le Sage is particularly excellent. His characters of Cervantes, Richardson, and Smollett are also very capital. But his strictures on Sterne are less pointed, and his obtrusive abuse of the politics of the King as occasioning the decline of novel writing during the present reign is very far fetched indeed. He is also severe and almost contemptuous towards Miss Burney, whose Wanderer was the pretence for the article.'

This was the article, itself 'sharply seasoned and well sustained', which was the fruit of conversation with Lamb at Winterslow. We may perhaps see what it was that Hazlitt had ventured to say of Miss Burney:

There is little other power in Miss Burney's novels, than that of immediate observation; her characters, whether of refinement or vulgarity, are equally superficial and confined. The whole is a question of form, whether that form is adhered to or violated. It is this circumstance which takes away dignity and interest from her story and sentiments, and makes the one so teasing and tedious, and the other so insipid. The difficulties in which she involves her heroines are indeed 'Female Difficulties' – they are difficulties created out of nothing. The author appears to have no other idea of refinement than that it is the reverse of vulgarity; but the reverse of vulgarity is fastidiousness and affectation. There is a true, and a false delicacy. Because a vulgar country Miss would answer 'yes' to a proposal of marriage in the first page, Mad. d'Arblay makes it a proof of an excess of refinement, and an indispensable point of etiquette in her young ladies, to postpone the answer to the end of five volumes, without the smallest reason for their doing so, and with every reason to

the contrary. The reader is led every moment to expect a de-
nouement, and is as constantly disappointed on some trifling
pretext. The whole artifice of her fable consists in coming to
no conclusion. Her ladies stand so upon the order of their
going, that they do not go at all. They will not abate an ace
of their punctilio in any circumstances, or on any emergency.
They would consider it as quite indecorous to run down stairs
though the house were in flames, or to move off the pavement though a scaffolding was falling. She has formed to
herself an abstract idea of perfection in common behaviour,
which is quite as romantic and impracticable as any other idea
of the sort; and the consequence has naturally been, that she
makes her heroines commit the greatest improprieties and
absurdities in order to avoid the smallest. In contradiction to a
maxim in philosophy, they constantly act from the weakest
motive, or rather from pure affectation.

These remarks are illustrated from the *Wanderer*, and Hazlitt
adds :

We are sorry to be compelled to speak so disadvantageously
of the work of an excellent and favourite writer; and the
more so, as we perceive no decay of talent, but a perversion of
it. There is the same admirable spirit in the dialogues. ... But
these do not fill a hundred pages in the work; and there is
nothing else good in it. In the story, which here occupies
the attention of the reader, Madame d'Arblay never excelled.

The impropriety of which he was guilty, of course, was of
writing his true opinion of a lady, in her capacity of public
entertainer, who was the sister of a choleric gentleman with
whom he had been playing whist at intervals for ten years, and
with whom he would be playing it in the month of the appearance of the article. If criticism has to take account of these social
considerations, Hazlitt was at no time afraid of the consequences

of disregarding them. The Captain's letter, by some chance, is preserved.

Captain Burney to Hazlitt

May 17, 1815.

Sir,—It would be strange, if not wrong, after years of intimate acquaintance, that cause of offence should happen between us, and be so taken, and be passed over in silence, and that acquaintance still continue. Your attack on my Sister's early publications dissatisfied me, and the more in coming from a quarter I had been in the habit of believing friendly. If I had seen it before publication, I should have remonstrated against some of your remarks, because I think them unjust. Your publication of such a paper showed a total absence of regard towards me, and I must consider it as the termination of our acquaintance.

JAS. BURNEY.

As to the diarist's finding of 'strictures' on Sterne, there are not any: 'My Uncle Toby', says Hazlitt, 'is one of the finest compliments ever paid to human nature'. The affront to the King is a not very much more serious business than the affront to Captain Burney. Hazlitt had attributed the almost simultaneous appearance of four great English novelists to the era of peace and hobby-riding that followed on the accession of the House of Hanover; and he added: 'But since that period, things have taken a different turn. His present Majesty during almost the whole of his reign, has been constantly mounted on a great War-horse; and has fairly driven all competitors out of the field'. One such competitor, Miss Austen, he unaccountably overlooked; nor, much to his own loss we may be certain, did he ever repair the omission. The first of the Waverley novels was only just published.

Having steered successfully one first-rate article into the *Edinburgh*, Hazlitt got on immediately with another, which came to him as a consequence of the inability of the poet

Thomas Moore to perform it.[1] This was the article on Sismondi's *Literature of the South,* not, in Hazlitt's hands, so perfect a subject, but one which enabled him to be at his best on Boccaccio, and incidentally on Chaucer and Spenser. The translations from the Italian in the course of this article, which came out in the June number, we should suppose to have been from the pen of Leigh Hunt.

A short note to a member of the Hunt circle, which is without date but which belongs evidently to the month in which this article was written, has the interest which attaches to the only line of Hazlitt's personal handwriting which we possess in this year.

Hazlitt to Charles Ollier

19 York Street,
Saturday morning.

Dear Sir, – I feel myself exceedingly obliged by your kind attention with respect to your musical treat. I am afraid from unavoidable circumstances I shall not be able to avail myself of it. I have to get something done by the end of next week, which obliges me to practise a great deal more self-denial than I like. If I do not pay my respects to Corelli, it is because I am held fast by half-a-dozen of his countrymen. If I can, however, I will escape from them.—I am, dear Sir, your obliged very humble servant,

W. HAZLITT.

In May and June, Wordsworth was in town. In March, the

---

1. Jeffrey to Moore, 18 September 1814 (Russell, *Memoirs,* II. 41). An earlier letter from Jeffrey to Rogers, in which the co-operation of Moore is solicited (II. 13), gives us some interesting particulars regarding remuneration: 'And now I have only to add, that our regular allowance to contributors of the first order is about twenty guineas for every printed sheet of sixteen pages; but that for such articles as I have now hinted at, we should never think of offering less than thirty, and probably a good deal more. I have some discretion in this matter, which I am not disposed to exercise very parsimoniously'. Jeffrey's pay was, for his day, consistently generous – or for ours either, for that matter, for the same class of work.

first Collected Edition of his works had appeared, with a dedication to Sir George Beaumont and a pair of frontispieces from
the brush of that baronet; and Wordsworth had taken the opportunity, in an essay supplementary to the preface, of retorting
upon his 'adversaries'. On 16 April we find Robinson looking
over the volumes, and remarking: 'The supplement to his Preface I wish he had left unwritten. His reproaches of the bad
taste of the times will be ascribed to merely personal feelings
and to disappointment'.

On 9 May the diarist was invited to the Lambs, to meet the
poet. 'Wordsworth spoke of the changes in his new poems. He
has substituted *ebullient* for *fiery* speaking of the Nightingale,
and *jocund* for *laughing* applied to the Daffodils. We agreed
in preferring the original reading. But on my gently alluding
to the lines, "Three feet long and two feet wide", confessing
that I dared not read them out in company, he said, "They
ought to be liked". Hazlitt said in his ferocious way at Alsager's
that if Lamb in his criticism of the *Excursion* [in the
Quarterly] had found but one-fault with W. he would never
have forgiven him. And some truth there is in the extravagant
statement.' But this is the latest occasion on which the diarist is
to be found admitting it. On 1 June he had Wordsworth to
breakfast and a select party to meet him; and from this moment
dated his thick and thin partisanship of the poet.

Wordsworth, whose view of the dangers attaching to the
liberty of the Press was only less extreme than that of Southey,
had so far forgotten the Editor of the *Examiner* in Leigh Hunt
the poet, as to send the latter, on the assurance of Brougham
that he was an admirer, the Collected Poems. This he followed,
on Sunday, 11 June, by a visit to Hunt, who was still in indifferent health, at his rooms in the Edgware Road. In his *Autobiography* of 1850 (that book in which, as his son says, 'the
silence is broken almost in inverse proportion to the intimacy of
his relations'), Hunt has left an account of the occasion:

He came to thank me for the zeal I had shewn in advocating the cause of his genius. I had the pleasure of shewing him his book on my shelves by the side of Milton; a sight which must have been the more agreeable, inasmuch as the visit was unexpected. He favoured me, in return, with giving his opinion of some of his contemporaries, who would assuredly have not paid him a visit on the same ground on which he was pleased to honour myself ...

Mr Wordsworth, whom Mr Hazlitt designated as one that would have had the wide circle of his humanities made still wider, and a good deal more pleasant, by dividing a little more of his time between his lakes in Westmoreland and the hotels of the metropolis, had a dignified manner, with a deep and roughish but not unpleasing voice, and an exalted mode of speaking. He had the habit of keeping the left hand in the bosom of his waistcoat; and in this attitude, except when he turned round to take one of the subjects of his criticism from the shelves (for his contemporaries were there also) he sat dealing forth his eloquent but hardly catholic judgements. In 'his father's house' there were not 'many mansions'. He was as sceptical on the merits of all kinds of poetry but one, as Richardson was on those of the novels of Fielding.

The 'zeal' mentioned by Hunt, so far as we can see, had at this date been principally exemplified in the *Examiner* by Hazlitt's notice of the *Excursion* of the autumn before. Hunt's 'Feast of the Poets', indeed, as first printed in the *Reflector,* had submitted Wordsworth to ridicule, and although on revising it for republication while in prison he had altered some of its poetical judgements, he had committed himself afresh to its political ones. 'Mr Southey', he had said, 'and even Mr Wordsworth, have both accepted offices under government, of such a nature as absolutely ties up their independence. Mr Coleridge, in pamphlets and newspapers, has done his best to deserve likewise; and yet they shall all tell you that they have not diminished their free spirit a jot. In like manner they are as violent and intolerant against their old opinions, as ever they were against their new ones, and without seeing how far the argument carries, shall insist that no man can possess a decent head or respectable heart who does not agree with them. ... The persons of whom we have been speaking have been always in extremes, and perhaps the good they are destined to perform in their generation, is to afford a striking lesson of the inconsistencies naturally produced by so being. Nothing remains the same but their vanity'. It is of some importance to note that these opinions, often treated as though they were a unique expression of Hazlitt's 'perverseness' or 'malignity', were Leigh Hunt's independently.

'The conversation', adds Hunt, 'turned upon Milton': but he did not remember, or does not say, that it turned also upon a footnote to Hazlitt's dramatic article in that day's *Examiner*. Hazlitt had written no word on Wordsworth since his review of the 'Excursion'. The effect of that review (the effect, indeed, as we are forced to conclude, of his emergence at all as a writer) had been unfortunate. It had taken the form of a request on Wordsworth's part that for the term of his London visit Hazlitt should be excluded from Lamb's, a request with which Lamb, under protest, had felt forced to comply. We need not wonder, I think, that if Hazlitt had formerly admitted a delicacy in writing about Wordsworth, it was by this course of action removed. In concluding a notice of a performance of *Comus* with some remarks on the consistency of Milton's political character, he added the footnote:

In the last edition of the works of a modern poet, there is a sonnet to the King, complimenting him on his 'royal fortitude'. The story of the Female Vagrant, which very beautifully and affectingly describes the miseries brought on the lower classes by war, in bearing which the said 'royal fortitude' is so nobly exercised, is very properly struck out of the collection.

Both these statements were true: in his 'November 1813', written to congratulate King George III on living to see the

Battle of Leipsic, Wordsworth had achieved a somewhat syco-
phantic sonnet; and his early poem, 'An Evening Walk', which
Hazlitt had known for seventeen years, was omitted from this
first edition of his Collected Works. The saying so by Hazlitt,
however, amounted to that 'malignant attack' for which Hunt,
'in a manly way', repudiated editorial responsibility on this
Sunday morning; and which led Wordsworth, on the Thursday
following, to acquaint Crabb Robinson with the true and sufficient reason of 'his coolness towards H.' (*ante* p. 100). If the
reader will at this point turn back to the chapter in which this
matter was considered, he will be in a position to appreciate the
degree in which the reputation of Hazlitt lay within Wordsworth's power in this somewhat critical summer.

We come to Crabb Robinson's next entry: '17 June (Saturday):—I went late to Lamb's. His party were there, and a
numerous & odd set they were – for the most part interesting
and amusing people. Geo. Dyer, Captain & Martin Burney, Ayrton, Phillips, Hazlitt & wife, Alsager, Barron Field, Coulson,
John [Payne] Collier, Talfourd, White, Lloyd, & Basil Montagu. Montagu I had never before been in company with. His
feeling face & gentle tones are very interesting, but it is said
that those tones are all adopted ad captandum. Perhaps in B. M.
affection is become habit & so lost its nature. Wordsworth says
he is a *Philanthropised courtier.*' The poet's reference, of course,
was to Basil Montagu's birth, as the natural son of the Earl of
Sandwich. Although a new acquaintance of the diarist's, he was
an old member of the Godwin and Holcroft circle, and Hazlitt
had known him, no doubt, since the opening years of the century. At this date in his forty-fifth year, Montagu was a barrister
with an extensive practice in Chancery and bankruptcy, and
henceforward we shall see a good deal of him. The diarist adds:
'Hazlitt & Capt. Burney met for the first time since their quarrel
about H.'s review of the Wanderer. They did not speak.' The
date was the eve of Waterloo.

With the names that are old there are others that are new
in the above account. Among them is that of Talfourd, a young

man aged twenty who had newly arrived from the country to read law and pursue literature, and was doing both on the next staircase to Lamb's in Inner Temple Lane. Twenty-two years later, when he became Lamb's first biographer, he put on record an impression of Hazlitt which is celebrated:

'When I first met Hazlitt in the year 1815, he was staggering under the blow of Waterloo. The reappearance of his imperial idol on the coast of France, and his triumphal march to Paris, like a fairy vision, had excited his admiration and sympathy to the utmost pitch; and though in many respects sturdily English in feeling, he could scarcely forgive the valour of the conquerors; and bitterly resented the captivity of the Emperor in St Helena, which followed it, as if he had sustained a personal wrong. On this subject only, he was "eaten up with passion"; on all others, he was the fairest, the most candid of reasoners. His countenance was then handsome, but marked by a painful expression; his black hair, which had curled stiffly over his temples,[1] had scarcely received its first tints of grey; his gait was awkward; his dress was neglected; and, in the company of strangers, his bashfulness was almost painful – but, when in the society of Lamb and one or two others, he talked on his favourite themes of old English books or old Italian pictures, no one's conversation could be more delightful. The poets, from intercourse with whom he had drawn so much of his taste, and who had contributed to shed the noble infection of beauty through his reasoning faculties, had scarcely the opportunity of appreciating their progress. [Talfourd here tactfully refers to the refusal of Wordsworth, in particular, to meet Hazlitt, of which we have read.] It was, in after years, by the fireside of

1. Taltourd, of course, was by temperament and training a rhetorical rather than an observant writer, and we may gather, for what the point is worth, that Hazlitt's hair did not 'curl stiffly'. This account, in a form only slightly varied, was first written for the *Literary Remains* of 1836, and was submitted by Hazlitt's son to the Montagus. In an unpublished letter, which is further quoted on page 368, Basil Montagu reports his wife's opinion: 'Mr Hazlitt's hair, she says, was soft, wavy, and very beautiful – totally unlike Mr Talfourd's description of it.'

the Lambs, that his tongue was gradually loosened, and his pas-
sionate thoughts found appropriate words. There, his struggles
to express the fine conceptions with which his mind was filled,
were encouraged by entire sympathy; there he began to stammer
out his just and original conceptions of Chaucer and Spenser,
and other English poets and prose writers, more talked of,
though not better known to their countrymen; there he was
thoroughly understood, and dexterously cheered, by Miss Lamb,
whose nice discernment of his first efforts in conversation were
dwelt upon by him with affectionate gratitude, even when most
out of humour with the world.' Hazlitt's first efforts in conversation, of course, had belonged to a period when Talfourd was
not yet in knickerbockers.

We have yet, however, to meet the news of Waterloo, and
this we may allow to be painted for us by that ill-disciplined but
lively talent, Haydon's: '23 June: — I had spent the evening
with John Scott, who lived in the Edgware Road. I had stayed
rather late, and was coming home to Great Marlborough Street,
when in crossing Portman Square a messenger from the Foreign
Office came right up to me and said, "Which is Lord Harrowby's? The Duke has beat Napoleon; taken one hundred and fifty
pieces of cannon, and is marching to Paris." "Is it true?" said
I, quite bewildered. "True!" said he; "which is Lord Harrowby's?" Forgetting in my joy this was not Grosvenor Square, I
said, "There," pointing to the same point in Portman Square,
as Lord Harrowby's house occupies in Grosvenor Square, which
happens to be Mrs Boehm's, where there was actually a rout.
In rushed the messenger, through servants and all, and I ran
back again to Scott's. They were gone to bed, but I knocked
them up and said, "The Duke has beat Napoleon, taken one
hundred and fifty pieces of cannon, and is marching to Paris."
Scott began to ask questions. I said, "None of your questions;
it's a fact," and both of us said "Huzza!"

'I went home and to bed; got up and to work. Sammons, my
model and corporal of the 2nd Life Guards, came, and we tried
to do our duty; but Sammons was in such a fidget about his

regiment charging, and I myself was in such a heat, I was obliged to let him go. Away he went, and I never saw him till late next day, and then he came drunk with talking. I read the *Gazette* the last thing before going to bed. I dreamt of it and was fighting all night; I got up in a steam of feeling, and read the *Gazette* again, ordered a *Courier* for a month, called at the confectioner's and read all the papers till I was faint. ... "Have not the efforts of the nation," I asked myself, "been gigantic? To such glories, she only wants to add the glories of my noble art to make her the grandest nation in the world, and these she shall have if God spare my life."

'25 June : – Read the *Gazette* again, till I now know it actually by heart. Dined with Hunt. I give myself great credit for not worrying him to death at this news; he was quiet for some time, but knowing it must come by-and-by, and putting on an air of indifference, he said, "Terrible battle this, Haydon". "A glorious one, Hunt." "Oh, yes, certainly," and to it we went.

'Yet Hunt took a just and liberal view of the question. As for Hazlitt, it is not to be believed how the destruction of Napoleon affected him; he seemed prostrated in mind and body, he walked about unwashed, unshaved, hardly sober by day, and always intoxicated by night, literally, without exaggeration, for weeks; until at length, wakening up as it were from his stupor, he at once left off all stimulating liquors, and never touched them after.'

'Haydon', we may find Hazlitt remarking to Northcote, quite generally and many years later, 'should have been the boatswain of a man-of-war; he has no other ideas of glory than those which belong to a naval victory, or to vulgar noise and insolence; not at all as something in which the whole world may participate alike.' It is to Haydon and Talfourd, nevertheless, that posterity has turned for its picture of him in Waterloo year. Crabb Robinson does not materially assist us. 'Glorious! This is indeed most glorious!' he exclaims; and, adding 'Godwin, Capel Lofft, and Thelwall are the only three persons I know, except Hazlitt, who grieve at the late events,' he takes his departure to view, in the course of an extended Continental tour, the sufficiently recent battlefield.

II

From this point forward to the end of the year it so happens that we see little of Hazlitt except in his work. It is there, of course, if we are wise, that we shall look for him.[1] He was writing an article on the theatre every week, and in addition continuing at the Round Table to pour out those stores which he had accumulated in twenty years of reading, of thinking, and of painting. If his spirits were low, as we know that they were, he kept the fact from his readers, and got on with his job like a practical journalist.

It is not until September that his political views quite casually obtrude themselves. In that month, writing on Chateaubriand, he happens to drop an allusion which by students of Napoleon will be readily taken. Napoleon had 'assassinated' the Duc d'Enghien (in 1804) he said, 'because he was not willing that he should assassinate him.' For this, he was promptly fallen upon by a certain 'Fair Play', who accused him of 'defending murder by aid of calumny'. A lively correspondence ensued, which protracted itself throughout the months of October, November and December, and Hazlitt's part in which was conducted over the signature of 'Peter Pickthank'. He happened, he said, 'to be acquainted with the Gentleman who invented the nickname of "the Corsican" for Bonaparte, and who used to boast that this nickname, notwithstanding its absurdity, had done more to promote the war, and make a bugbear of the person to whom it was applied, than any other circumstance.' The gentleman in question was Coleridge, and the occasion that 'Letter to Fox' which we made an opportunity to notice on an earlier page. But the

1. For his 'prostration' by Waterloo we may allow, apparently, just two issues of the *Examiner* (9 and 16 July). From this point forward his appearances both at the theatre and at the Round Table (*On Milton's Versification, On the Tendency of Sects, On John Buncle*, etc.) are regular and without intermission.

discussion took general grounds, and was promptly raised by Hazlitt to the plane of metaphysics:

> Lastly, Sir, I object to the signature of *Fair Play*, which your correspondent has assumed. There is no such character nor no such thing. ... Whoever supposes himself to be free from all bias and prejudice in questions of this kind is deficient in self-knowledge; as he who supposes that mere abstract reason, without passion or prejudice, can ever be a match for strong passion and inveterate prejudice with all the aids of venal sophistry to boot, must be ignorant of human affairs and human nature. ... The love of freedom is no match for the love of power, because the one is urged on by passion, while the other is in general the cold dictate of the understanding. With this natural disadvantage on the side of liberty, I know what I have to expect from those persons who pique themselves on an extreme scrupulousness in the cause of the people. I find none of this scrupulousness in the friends of despotism; *they* are in earnest, the others are not. Such persons, while they remain in the minority, are scrupulous in the extreme, because their love of a general principle is not strong enough to make them incur popular odium or risk their private interest. It would be well if they stopped here. But these gentlemen are apt to change, and when they get once into the beaten track, they shake off their scruples with their party. They are as impudent on the profitable side of the question as they were cautious on the losing.

With this hint of what certain people might have to expect when he began in earnest to write about them, Hazlitt withdrew from his only political activity in Waterloo year. 'Fair Play's' share in the controversy need hardly concern us. 'He takes leave of me,' says Hazlitt, in his concluding letter of 10 December, 'by wishing me better principles and a better temper. I despair of either. For my temper is so bad as to be ruffled almost as much by the roasting of a Protestant as by the spoiling of my dinner; nor have I better hopes of mending my principles, for they have never changed hitherto.' The allusion is to the Massacre of Nîmes which followed hard upon the Restoration of the Bourbons.[1]

To conclude the year, Crabb Robinson gives us an isolated entry:

'9 December: — At 7, went to Alsager's, another long delayed visit – several months. There I met the Lambs, Hazlitt, Burrell, Ayrton, Coulson, Sly & Godwin. I enjoyed the evening. Hazlitt was sober, argumentative, acute & interesting – I had no conversation with him, but I enjoyed his conversation with others. Lamb was good humoured & droll, with great originality as usual. Coulson was a new man almost to me. He is said to be a prodigy of knowledge, a young élève of Jer. Bentham – a reporter for the *Chronicle*. Sly was unwell – he has had a fall from his horse which I fear has hurt his mind, for the moment at least. He sat a long time looking at our play instead of listening to Hazlitt's conversation.' We do not know much of Sly, but there is the suggestion here that if one was in one's right mind Hazlitt's conversation was something that one listened to.

In November his third child had been born.

III

We begin the year 1816 with some correspondence. Constable had taken over the *Encyclopædia Britannica,* and, being in negotiation for a collection in volume form of the Round Table papers, he invited Hazlitt to contribute the article on the Fine Arts. On 10 January there is a letter to Macvey Napier, the Editor of the Supplement to the work: 'I mentioned to Mr Constable that I would do such an article as you require by the middle of February, if I could possibly. I am now pretty sure of being able to do it by that time. I shall endeavour to supply what is wanting on the subject of the Fine Arts in the original article in the Encyclopædia Britannica.' On 10 February there is a

1. This correspondence has not been reprinted.

further letter: 'I propose to make the article turn on the styles of the different great works of art, on the causes that have produced them, and on the prospect of their revival at the present period. If you see any fault in this idea, you would oblige me by suggesting any alteration.' We may suppose that no fault was found, for on 20 March we read: 'I enclose the remainder of the article, and am anxious to know your opinion of it. It contains the best part of what I know about art. As to political innuendos, and one or two other things relating to proposed articles, you can omit or retain them at your pleasure.' The only political innuendo we find in the published article is a reference to pictures of 'red coats at Waterloo'.

We come next to the following:

Hazlitt to Macvey Napier

34 Southampton Buildings,
Holborn.   April 2.[1]

Dear Sir,—I was exceedingly gratified by the receipt of your very flattering letter of last week. I dare say that your objections to several of the observations are well founded. I confess I am apt to be paradoxical in stating an extreme opinion when I think the prevailing one not quite correct. I believe however this way of writing answers with most readers better than the logical. I tried for some years to express the truth & nothing but the truth, till I found it would not do. The opinions themselves I believe to be true, but like all abstract principles, they require deductions, which it is often best to leave the public to find out. If you could let me have a proof, I would return it by the next day's mail: otherwise I should be obliged by your letting me have a copy at your convenience. The immediate purport of my writing was the following, which your

1. This, and the preceding letters (first published by the present writer in the *Athenæum*, 8 August (1919), from the originals in the British Museum. Hazlitt's article on the 'Fine Arts' has hitherto been dated 1824, the year in which the Supplement to the fourth and fifth editions of the *Encyclopædia Britannica* was completed.

candour will excuse. I understood you to state in a former
letter as the bookseller's arrangement that the money for any
article would be paid when the article was printed. I suppose
you will have nearly got through this so as to know the general
size of it by this time. I have, Sir, a bill to take up to-morrow
week 10 April, & if you could possibly transmit me fifteen
pounds by that time, it would be a great assistance to me. The
stagnation of money matters in this town is such that it is impossible to procure either by loan or anticipation, a single sixpence. I find this circumstance press particularly hard upon
me at a time when I am clearing off the arrears into which my
affairs had fallen owing to the aforesaid *logical way of writing*.
With every apology for this intrusion, I am, Dear Sir, with
respect, your obliged humble servant.

W. HAZLITT.

P.S. — I received the proofs of the Round Table from Mr
Constable, & shall return them to-morrow, or next day. I was
thinking just now that the words *Colouring, Drawing, Ideal
& Picturesque* would make proper articles under the head of
the Fine Arts, the metaphysics of which is in a very confused
state at this day.

Why this letter, unlike those which preceded it, should have been
written from Hazlitt's old rooms at Southampton Buildings, instead of from his house at Westminster, is a matter on which we
can only speculate. His article on the Fine Arts, making its appearance in the first volume of the Supplement in this summer,
afterwards became an integral part of the *Encyclopædia,* remaining so until, with the inevitable development of that work, its
manner of treatment although not its principles became outmoded.

Noticing in passing one of the ablest of all Hazlitt's *Edinburgh Review* papers, that on *Schlegel on the Drama* in the issue
for February, we may make a return to the *Examiner.* Leigh
Hunt, removed in this spring to Hampstead, had begun the

political year as he meant to continue it. In February he re-printed Southey's 'Battle of Blenheim', dedicating it 'to the Author of the Account of the Battle of Waterloo in the last *Quarterly Review*'; and he followed it in the same month with an article from his own pen entitled 'Heaven Made a Party to Earthly Disputes – Mr Wordsworth's Sonnets on Waterloo'. One of the results of this editorial policy was a widening of the breach between the *Examiner* and the *Champion,* so that we find John Scott writing in April: 'As public writers we once felt that we were enlisted with the *Examiner* on the side of sound politics and the best English sentiments. ... It has since become, in our view, a grossly anti-English publication'. During the four months which preceded this verdict (partly to be accounted for by an acquaintance between Scott and Wordsworth formed dur-ing the latter's visit to town in the preceding summer), Hazlitt had continued to be as good as his word, leaving politics to Leigh Hunt while he proved the mainstay of the paper in other directions.

The condition of the country in this year is no secret from us. The consequences of twenty-two years of war were just begin-ning to make themselves unmistakably felt, when, in April, Wordsworth threw down the political gauntlet. In the preface to his 'Thanksgiving Ode, 18 January 1816, with other Short Pieces, chiefly Referring to Public Events,' he wrote:

If the author has given way to exultation, unchecked by these distresses, it might be sufficient to protect him from a charge of insensibility, should he state his own belief that these sufferings will be transitory. ... There will doubtless be no few ready to indulge in regrets and repinings, and to feed a morbid satisfaction, by aggravating these burthens in imag-ination, in order that the calamity so confidently prophesied, as it has not taken the shape which their sagacity has allotted to it, may appear as grievous as possible under another.

Disposing thus in advance not merely of the opposition of his political opponents, but of the facts themselves[1] the poet went on 'to encourage a martial spirit in the bosoms of his countrymen', and to advocate 'an assiduous cultivation of military virtues'. His philosophic attribution to the Deity of war as a method –

> *But Thy most dreaded instrument*
> *In working out a pure intent,*
> *Is Man – arrayed for mutual slaughter –*
> *– Yea, Carnage is Thy Daughter!* [2]

might have been deemed more permissible if it had not been accompanied in the same volume with specific recommendations for the increase of the standing army. It is of this work (which Lamb, with his customary magnificent disregard of men's mere opinions, had been seeing through the press) that we find Crabb Robinson recording: 'Of the integrity of Wordsworth I have no doubt as of his genius I have an unbounded admiration,

1. 'The nation was in fact [i.e., despite appearances which misled the rejoicing poets] entering upon a period of unprecedented depression and discontent, which lasted through the last four years of George III's reign. ... So long as the war lasted, low as the rate of wages might be, there was generally employment enough in the fields or the factories for nearly all the hands willing to labour. When the inflated war prices came to an end, and wheat fell below 80s. or even 70s. a quarter, until it reached 52s. 6d. early in 1816, labourers were turned off and wages cut down still further; bread was not proportionately cheapened, and agrarian outrages sprang up. The continent, impoverished by the war, no longer required British goods for military purposes, and, as its own domestic industries revived, ceased to absorb British products flung in profusion on its markets. Hence came a reduction of 16 per cent in the export trade, and of nearly 20 per cent in the import trade, which resulted in bankruptcies and the dismissal of workpeople. If we add to these causes of distress, the influence of over-speculation, the accession of disbanded soldiers to the ranks of the unemployed, and the substitution of the factory system with machinery for domestic manufactures with hand labour, we can partly understand why Great Britain, never harried by invading armies, should have suffered more than France itself from popular misery and disaffection for several years after the restoration of peace.' – *Political History of England*, XI. 171–2.

2. 'Ode, 1815', revised by Wordsworth in a less fierce mood thirty years later.

but I doubt the wisdom and discretion of his latest political writings.'

It was this moment which Coleridge chose for his re-emergence from Calne, his sixteen-year-old masterpieces in one hand and a number of social panaceas in the other. We first hear of him in a letter from Lamb to Wordsworth of 26 April: 'Coleridge spent a fortnight at, or in the neighbourhood of, the Murray, with what he calls a vision, Kubla Khan – which said vision he repeats so enchantingly that it irradiates and brings heaven and Elysian bowers into my parlour, while he sings or says it, but there is an observation, "Never tell thy dreams", and I am almost afraid that Kubla Khan is an owl that won't bear daylight, I fear lest it should be discovered by the lantern of typography and clear reducting to letters, no better than nonsense or no sense. ... He is at present under the medical care of a Mr Gilman (Killman?) a Highgate Apothecary, where he plays at leaving off Laud ... m. I think his essentials not touched : he is very bad, but then he wonderfully picks up another day, and his face when he repeats his verses hath its ancient glory, an Archangel a little damaged.' Before proceeding to Highgate, Coleridge spent a fortnight at, or in the neighbourhood of, the Lambs'. We do not know what may have passed between him and Hazlitt there, but in the three years in which he had done nothing Hazlitt had got upon his own feet. That the latter was very little likely, in this year of all others, to put up with a resumption of Coleridge's peculiarities, I think we may understand.

'Christabel' fell for review as the first of a new department of 'Literary Notices', pretty plainly designed as a political appanage to the *Examiner* in this summer, and shared by Hazlitt and Leigh Hunt. This one is without signature, but we may say that it is by Hazlitt. 'The fault of Mr Coleridge,' we read, 'is that he comes to no conclusion. He is a man of that universality of genius, that his mind hangs suspended between poetry and prose, truth and falsehood, and an infinity of other things, and from an excess of capacity he does little or nothing. Here are two unfinished poems and a fragment.' Here *were* two unfinished poems and a fragment. In 'Christabel' Hazlitt was willing to find, as he had doubtless always found,[1] 'a great deal of beauty, both of thought, imagery, and versification'; while of 'Kubla Khan' he was very much of Lamb's opinion – 'It is not a poem but a musical composition. We could repeat the opening lines to ourselves not the less often for not knowing the meaning of them.' The objection which has been taken to this review finds its justification less in what was said than in what was not said. The fact is, of course, that Hazlitt made the mistake, which it is very easy for us not to make, of reviewing the man Coleridge was in 1816 instead of the poet he had been in 1800.

One other work of a contemporary poet he reviewed at the same moment – Leigh Hunt's 'Rimini' in the *Edinburgh* for June. We may say that he reviewed it, because we shall after-wards find him claiming credit for the good nature shown in the act; but in the review itself, by the time it had left Jeffrey's hands, there was so much of Jeffrey that he afterwards thought he had written it. It was an ill business, if you valued personal judgements higher than guineas, writing on contemporary poetry in the *Edinburgh Review*.

Throughout the month of June, Hazlitt was throwing him-self into the campaign on behalf of the acquisition of the Elgin Marbles for the nation, in the face of official apathy. In the midst of this distressful summer, on 19 June, his younger child died. 'The day the child died,' notes his grandson, 'he cut off a lock of his hair, enclosing it in a piece of paper, and writing upon it to show what it was. I have that paper, and that writing now [1867] before me; my grandfather's words are: "My dear little John's hair, cut off the day he died".'

1. It is by means of this review that we are able to supply the 253rd line which Coleridge removed from the poem. A MS. copy of 'Christabel' in his wife's hand (dating, no doubt, from the visit of her brother to the Lakes in 1800, when, by carrying the poem to Scott, he made 'Christabel' the spiritual mother of the 'Last Minstrel') was used by Hazlitt as a note-book during his Parliamentary reporting, and presented by him to his colleague of the Press Gallery, John Payne Collier.

IV

It was now, at the moment when Cobbett brought down the *Political Register* from a shilling to twopence, that Hazlitt turned his attention to politics. While Leigh Hunt continued to skirmish in editorials, he took as his subject *Speeches in Parliament on the Distresses of the Country*:

We have said that the expenses of the war might as well have been sunk in the sea; and so they might, for they have been sunk in unproductive labour, that is, in maintaining large establishments, and employing great numbers of men in doing nothing or mischief; for example, in making ships to destroy other ships, guns and gunpowder to blow out men's brains, pikes and swords to run them through the body, drums and fifes to drown the noise of cannon and the whizzing of bullets; in making caps and coats to deck the bodies of those who live by killing others; in buying up pork and beef, butter and cheese, to enable them to do this with more effect: in barracks, in transport-ships, in horses, bridles, and saddles, in suttlers and followers of the camp, in chaplains of the regiment, in common trulls, and the mistresses of generals and commanders-in-chief; in contractors, in army and navy agents, their partners, clerks, relations, dependants, wives, families, servants in and out of livery, their town and country houses, coaches, curricles, parks, gardens, grottos, hot-houses, green-houses, pictures, statues, libraries; in treasury scribes, in secretaries and under-secretaries of state, of the foreign, colonial, and war departments, with their swarms of underlings, all of whom are maintained out of the labour and sweat of the country, and for all of whom, and for all that they do (put together) the country is not one pin the better, or at least, one penny more in pocket, than if they were at the bottom of the Channel. The present may have been the most just and necessary war, in a political, moral, and religious point of view, that was ever engaged in; but it has also been the most expensive; and what is worse the expense remains just the same, though it may have been the most unjust and unnecessary in the world. We have paid for it, and we must pay for it equally in either case, and wholly out of our own pockets. The price of restoring the Pope, the Inquisition, the Bourbons, and the doctrine of Divine Right, is half of our nine hundred millions of debt. That is the amount of the Government bill of costs, presented to John Bull for payment, not of the principal but the interest; that is what he has got by the war; the load of taxes at his back, with which he comes out of his five and twenty years' struggle, like Christian's load of sins, which whether it will not fall off his back like Christian's, into the Slough of Despond, will be seen before long. The difference between the expense of a war or a peace establishment is just the difference between a state of productive and unproductive labour. Now this whole question, which from its complexity puzzles many people, and has given rise to a great deal of partly wilful and partly shallow sophistry (see an article on this subject in Mr Coleridge's *Friend*), may be explained in two words. Suppose I give a man five shillings a day for going out in a boat and catching fish for me. This is paying for productive labour : that is, I give him so much for what he does, or a claim upon so much of the public stock : but in taking so much from the stock by laying out his five shillings, he adds so much to it by his labour, or the disposal of his time in catching fish. But if I, having the money to do what I please with, give him five shillings a day for shooting at crows, he is paid equally for his trouble, and accordingly takes so much from the public stock, while he adds nothing to it, but so much carrion. So if the government pay him so much a day for shooting at Frenchmen and Republicans, this is a tax, a loss, a burthen to the country, without any thing got by it; for we cannot, after all, eat Frenchmen and Republicans when we have killed them. War in itself is a thriving, sensible traffic only to cannibals! Again — if I give a man five shillings for making a pair of shoes, this is paying for productive labour, viz. for labour that is useful, and that must be performed by some one; but if I give the same man five shillings for standing on his head or behind my chair while I am picking my teeth, or for running up a hill and down again for a wager – this is unproductive labour, nothing comes of it, and though the man who is thus idly employed lives by it, others starve, upon whose pittance and whose labour he lives through me. Such is the nature and effect of war; all the energies of which tend to waste, and to throw an additional and heavy burthen upon the country, in proportion to the extent and length of time that it is carried on. It creates so many useless members of the community; every man paid by the war out of the taxes paid by the people, is, in fact, a dead body fastened to a living one, that by its weight drags it to the earth. A five and twenty years' war, and nine hundred million debt, are really a couple of millstones round the neck of a country, that must naturally press her down a little in the scale of prosperity. That seems to be no riddle. We defy any sophist to answer this statement of the necessary tendency of war in its general principle to ruin and impoverish a country. We are not to wonder, when it does so; but when other causes operate to counteract or retard this tendency. What is extraordinary in our own case is, that the pernicious effects of war have been delayed so long, not that they have come upon us at last.

It is not a nice thing, when you have propounded a theory that 'Carnage' is 'God's daughter', to have your political deductions jeopardized by a counter theory that 'war is a thriving, sensible traffic only to cannibals'. It is no wonder that Southey confided to Robinson, who spent a part of his vacation holiday this year in the Lakes, that 'he considered the Government seriously endangered by the writings of Cobbett, and still more by the *Examiner*'; and the sincerity of this opinion we need not suppose to have been affected by the handling his own Ode on the marriage of Princess Charlotte had just received at the hands of the latter. 'His lay is ten times as long,' said Hazlitt, 'and he thinks it is therefore ten times better than an ode of Mr Pye's.'

Hazlitt, once started, was not likely to stop. 'The rich and the poor,' he wrote, 'may at present be compared to the two classes of frequenters of pastry-cooks' shops, those on the outside and those on the in. We would seriously advise the latter, who see the gaunt faces staring at them through the glass-door, to recollect that though custard is nicer than bread, bread is the greatest necessary of the two.' It was in this situation that Coleridge was somewhat extensively advertised by new publishers as being about to bring out 'A Lay-Sermon on the Distresses of the Country, addressed to the Middle and Higher Orders'. Without waiting to review the publication, Hazlitt wrote a 'Literary Notice' reviewing the advertisement – and the character of the author:

We seen no sort of difference between his published and his unpublished compositions. It is just as impossible to get at the meaning of the one as the other. No man ever yet gave Mr Coleridge 'a penny for his thoughts'. His are all maiden ideas; immaculate conceptions. He is the 'Secret Tattle' of the press. Each several work exists only in the imagination of the author, and is quite inaccessible to the understandings of his readers – 'Yet virgin of Proserpina from Jove'. We can give just as good a guess at the design of this Lay-Sermon, which is not published, as of *the Friend,* the Preliminary Articles in *the Courier, the Watchman,* the *Conciones ad Populum,* or any of the other courtly or popular publications of the same author. Let the experiment be tried, and if, on committing the manuscript to the press, the author is caught in the fact of a single intelligible passage, we will be answerable for Mr Coleridge's loss of character. But we know the force of his genius too well. What is his *Friend* itself but an enormous title-page; the longest and most tiresome prospectus that ever was written; an endless preface to an imaginary work; a table of contents that fills the whole volume; a huge bill of fare of all possible subjects, with not an idea to be had for love or money? One number consists of a grave-faced promise to perform something impossible in the next; and the next is taken up with a long-faced apology for not having done it. Through the whole of his work Mr Coleridge appears in the character of the Unborn Doctor; the very Barmecide of Knowledge; the Prince of preparatory authors!

'*He never is – but always to be* wise'

He is the Dog in the Manger of literature, an intellectual Mar-Plot, one who will neither let any body else come to a conclusion, nor come to one himself.

To sum the matter up he concluded: 'Mr Shandy would have settled the question at once: – "You have little or no nose, sir".' The reader will now turn to the portrait in *The Spirit of the Age,* to see how much of all this Hazlitt was willing to let stand as his considered judgement, after his anger had cooled.

What should be said, is said, as usual, by Lamb, in a letter to Wordsworth of 23 September: 'Have you read the review of Coleridge's character, person, physiognomy, &c., in the *Examiner* – his features to his *nose* – O horrible licence beyond the old Comedy. He is himself gone to the sea side with his favourite Apothecary, having left for publication as I hear a prodigious mass of composition for a Sermon to the middling ranks of people to persuade them they are not so distressed as is commonly supposed. Methinks he should recite it to a congregation of Bilston Colliers – the fate of Cinna the Poet would instantaneously be his. God bless him, but certain that rogue-Examiner has beset him in most unmannerly strains. Yet there is a kind of respect shines thro' the disrespect that to those who know the rare compound (that is the subject of it) almost balances the reproof, but then those who know him but partially or at a distance are so extremely apt to drop the qualifying part thro' their fingers.' Lamb adds: 'There was a cut at me a

few months back by the same hand, but my agnomen or agni-
nomen not being calculated to strike the popular ear, it dropt
anonymous, but it was a pretty compendium of observation,
which the author has collected in my disparagement, from some
hundreds of social evenings which we had spent together —
however in spite of all, there is something tough in my attachment to H., which these violent strainings cannot quite dis-
locate or sever asunder. I get no conversation in London that is
absolutely worth attending to but his.' This being so, we do not
quite see why Lamb (not for the first time) should play up to
Wordsworth's very different feelings. The 'cut' at him was
shared by Hazlitt's editor, and had made its appearance in a
note at the end of the *Lay of the Laureate,* 'This article falls
somewhat short of its original destination, by our having been
forced to omit two topics, the praise of Buonaparte, and the
abuse of poetry. The former we leave to history: the latter we
have been induced to omit from our regard to two poets of our
acquaintance. We must say they have spoiled sport. One of
them has tropical blood in his veins, which gives a gay, cordial,
vinous spirit to his whole character. The other is a mad wag —
who ought to have lived at the Court of Horwendillus, with
Yorick and Hamlet — equally desperate in his mirth and his
gravity, who would laugh at a funeral and weep at a wedding,
who talks nonsense to prevent the headache, who would wag
his finger at a skeleton, whose jests scald like tears, who makes
a joke of a great man, and a hero of a cat's paw.' We should
not have thought that Lamb would have been made angry by
this; and we cannot help feeling that he might have remembered against it a note of cordial praise which Hazlitt had gone
out of his way to introduce into his *Encyclopædia Britannica*
article at much the same moment, and which had not 'dropt
anonymous'.

Robinson, having imbibed somewhat deeply of the Lake point
of view, returned to town in October. On his way he paused
long enough among old friends at Norwich to give us an entry:
'14 October: — I read to the party Hazlitt's article against

Coleridge and an equally admirable notice of Owen of Lanark's View of Society – an article full of acuteness, wit, malignity [the diarist's favourite epithet], and scorn. William Taylor had never before heard any of Hazlitt's compositions. He declared these to be masterpieces of banter.' William Taylor, of the *Monthly Review,* the early friend of Southey, and the subject of a passage in Borrow's *Lavengro,* never to our knowledge met Hazlitt, but his opinion is of interest. In reviewing (not favourably) the work of the first English Socialist, whose industrial Utopia was receiving a great deal of patronage at this moment from people who were putting in hand the post-Waterloo home policy, Hazlitt had remarked : 'A man that comes all the way from the banks of the Clyde acquires a projectile force that renders him irresistible'.

Early in October he took a brief respite out of town – the only one we receive any evidence of between his leaving Winterslow in 1812 and his return there in 1818. We trace him on this occasion to Gloucester and Bath,[1] and have little hesitation in associating his visit with the removal of his parents in this year from Addlestone to the latter town, before their final settlement in Devonshire in the following year. It was at Bath that Miss Emmet, sister of the Irish patriot, was taken into the family, with which she continued to live until her death in 1824. With

1. To Gloucester, by means of an *Examiner* article, 'A Modern Tory Delineated', dated from there on 1 October; to Bath, by means of an allusion in a *Times* critique (unreprinted) of the following September : 'We may add, that we saw this gentleman [Mr Stanley] (to great advantage) in some characters at Bath, about a year ago'. I cannot help regarding it as an example of the not very intelligent depreciation with which Hazlitt's memory has been followed that Mr Birrell should base on the absence of surviving correspondence (apparently) a charge that he 'found it easier to write splendid disquisitions about the essential grandeur of his father's character for money, than to drop the old man an occasional line of greeting for love'. ('Hazlitt', *English Men of Letters,* p. 143.) For three years, as we have seen, his parents had been living within easy reach of London, and the moment they remove to Bath we obtain clear evidence of his visiting them there. The splendid disquisition to which Mr Birrell refers as having been written during the lifetime of Hazlitt's father will be found in *On Court Influence* (1818).

changing times the old Unitarian minister had not changed, and evidence is not lacking that the deferred emergence of his second son had been such as to bring him both pride and pleasure.

Robinson, back in town, gives us several entries in succession :

'2 November : – Called on the Lambs. Martin Burney was there, and we played a rubber and afterwards Talfourd stepped in. We had a long chat together. ... We talked of Hazlitt's late ferocious attack on Coleridge, which Lamb thought fair enough between the parties, but he was half angry with M. Burney for asserting that the praise was greater than the abuse. Nobody, said Lamb, will care about or understand the "taking up the deep pauses of conversation between Seraphs and Cardinals", but the satire will be unmercifully felt. Such an article is like saluting a man, "Sir, you are the greatest man I ever saw," and then pulling him by the nose.' A couple of months later, when Hazlitt repeated this procedure, we shall find Lamb adopting precisely Martin Burney's line of defence.

'12 November : – Lounged at the Surrey Institution. Read a very stupid review of Christabel in the [September] *Edinburgh Review*.' A discussion of the authorship of this review has been relegated to an Appendix.

'24 November (Sunday) : – Breakfasted with Basil Montagu. ... Read at M.'s Coleridge's beautiful Fire, Famine, & Slaughter, written in his jacobinical days, & now reprinted to his annoyance by Hunt in the *Examiner*. Also an article on Commonplace Critics by Hazlitt. His definition of good company excellent – "Those who live on their own estates & other people's ideas".

'15 December (Sunday) : – After one I went to Montagu's. He gave me a no. of the *Examiner* published this morning containing two capital articles by Hazlitt. A gross attack on Dr Stoddart and remarks on Coriolanus in which with great spirit and effect he shews that poets as such are inclined to favour kings. These articles interested me much.

'21 December: — Found Coleridge at home, and enjoyed his conversation for an hour and a half. ... He mentioned Hazlitt's attack with greater moderation than I expected. He complains with reason, I think, of Lamb, who, he says, ought not to admit a man into his house who abuses the confidence of private intercourse so scandalously. He denies H. however originality, & ascribes to Lamb the best ideas in H.'s articles.[1] He was not displeased to hear of his being knocked down by John Lamb lately.' The accident which Hazlitt met with at the hands of Lamb's brother (Talfourd's 'burly Ajax Telamon') — who, despite all the investigations of Mr Lucas, is so shadowy a figure to us — we hear about otherwise from the Journal of Thomas Moore, under date 9 September 1820: 'Kenney told me that John Lamb (the brother of Charles) once knocked down Hazlitt who was impertinent to him, and on those who were present interfering and begging of H. to shake hands and forgive him, H. said, "Well, I don't mind if I do. I am a metaphysician and nothing but an *idea* hurts me".' The Kenney of this passage is James Kenney the dramatist, second husband of Mrs Holcroft, who left London in 1818 to live in Paris, where Moore's entry was made. From Talfourd we learn that the difference of opinion concerned the colouring of Holbein and Vandyke, and had nothing to do with politics.

In defining *Common-place Critics* in the article admired by Robinson, Hazlitt had said: 'The secret of their unanimity and strict accord, is, that not any one of them ever admits any opinion that can cost the least effort of mind in arriving at, or of courage in declaring it'. The second cost at least he was incurring in this month by his series, *Illustrations of The Times Newspaper*. In the course of these articles, in which the activities of the Holy Alliance in this winter were very faithfully dealt

1. The charge of plagiarism, it will be seen, had now been transferred to a quarter where it apparently remained throughout Coleridge's life. In his *Table Talk*, under date 6 August 1832, he may be found reported as saying: 'Compare Charles Lamb's exquisite criticisms on Shakespeare with Hazlitt's *round and round imitations of them*'.

with, Hazlitt may be found developing a theory which he had forgone earlier in the year, and which the diarist noted in the article on *Coriolanus*. 'The spirit of poetry,' he said, 'is in itself favourable to humanity and liberty; but, we suspect, not in times like these – not in the present reign. ... The object of poetry is to please : this art naturally gives pleasure, and excites admiration. Poets, therefore, cannot do well without sympathy and flattery. It is, accordingly, very much against the grain that they remain long on the unpopular side of the question. They do not like to be shut out when laurels are to be given away at court – or places under government to be disposed of, in romantic situations in the country. They are happy to be reconciled on the first opportunity to prince and people, and to exchange their principles for a pension.' A theory which the diarist admired *in abstracto,* he could not abide when it was treated in the second of Hazlitt's articles *in concretis*.

He had spoken his mind of Coleridge : he now turned to Wordsworth. 'The secret of the Jacobin poetry and the anti-Jacobin politics of this writer,' he said, 'is the same.'

He tolerates nothing but what he himself creates; he sympathizes only with what can enter into no competition with him, with 'the bare earth and mountains bare, and grass in the green field'. He sees nothing but himself and the universe. He hates all greatness, and all pretensions to it but his own. His egotism is in this respect a madness; for he scorns even the admiration of himself, thinking it a presumption in any one to suppose that he has taste or sense enough to understand him. He hates all science and all art; he hates chemistry, he hates conchology; he hates Sir Isaac Newton; he hates logic, he hates metaphysics, which he says are unintelligible, and yet he would be thought to understand them; he hates prose, he hates all poetry but his own; he hates Shakespeare, or what he calls 'those interlocutions between Lucius and Caius', because he would have all the talk to himself, and considers the movements of passion in Lear, Othello, or Macbeth as im-

pertinent, compared with the moods of his own mind; he
thinks everything good is contained in the Lyrical Ballads,
or, if it is not contained there, it is good for nothing; he hates
music, dancing, and painting; he hates Rubens, he hates
Rembrandt, he hates Raphael, he hates Titian, he hates Vandyke; he hates the antique; he hates the Apollo Belvidere; he
hates the Venus de Medicis. He hates all that others love and
admire but himself. He is glad that Buonaparte is sent to St
Helena, and that the Louvre is dispersed for the same reason
– to get rid of the idea of any thing greater, or thought
greater, than himself. The Bourbons, and their processions
of the Holy Ghost, give no disturbance to his vanity; and he
therefore gives them none.

In this comprehensive indictment (which he afterwards very
handsomely withdrew)[1] he was drawing, no doubt, in equal
measure upon his memories of the poet's public and his private
utterances. We come immediately to the sequel:

'22 December (Sunday): – After tea went to Basil Montagu's.
Hazlitt was there. I could not abstain from adverting to a
scandalous article in this morning's *Examiner* in which he
attacks Wordsworth. H. without confessing himself the author
spoke as if he were but did not vindicate himself boldly. He
said, "You know I am not in the habit of defending what I do
– I do not say all that I have done is right." In the same tone
and after I had said I was indignant at certain articles I had
read, and at the breach of private confidence in the detail of
conversation, H. said: "It may be indelicate, but I am forced

1. 'It has been said of Mr Wordsworth that "he hates conchology, that
he hates the Venus of Medicis". But these, we hope, are mere epigrams
and *jeux d'esprit,* as far from truth as they are free from malice; a sort
of running satire or critical clenches.' – *The Spirit of the Age* (1823). The
particular 'violation of friendship' which Crabb Robinson could not forgive was, somewhat evidently, not any of those occurring in the above
passage, but that relating to Wordsworth's political opinions in the year
1800 (*ante,* page 101, footnote), which had appeared in Hazlitt's article of
the preceding week.

to write an article every week, and I have not time to make one
with so much delicacy as I otherwise should". To this I replied
by alluding to the anecdote of the French Minister, who
answered the libeller who said he must live, "I do not see the
necessity". H. then made a distinction. He said he would never
take advantage of a slip in a man's conversation and repeat
what was not such a person's real opinion; but where what he
had said was his notorious opinion, not said to one person but
generally, he thought such things might without injustice be
repeated. I said, "One aggravation is wanting in such a case.
And your distinction amounts to this: I won't lie, I will only
violate the confidences of friendship." H. then adverted to the
tergiversation of these persons. He thought it, he said, useful to
expose people who otherwise would gain credit by canting and
hypocrisy. I admitted the attack on Southey's Carmen Nuptiale
[the *Lay of the Laureate*] to be unexceptionable. But H. admitted that he believes Southey to be still a perfectly honest
man. Wordsworth was not named. Coleridge he seemed very
bitter against.

'Basil Montagu seemed inclined to take part with Hazlitt.
He said, "It is difficult to draw the line in such cases. If I were
in the House of Commons and I heard a man applaud a measure of government publicly which he had privately reprobated
to me the day before, should I be censurable in rising up and
declaring this?"

'I carefully abstained from shaking hands with Hazlitt. We
were of course stiff towards each other. And I having praised
a picture by Domenichino engraved by Muller of St John, he
said "A very bad thing, Ma'am".'

This was the end.

'After this evening,' adds the diarist in his Reminiscences, 'I
never to my recollection exchanged a word with Hazlitt.' In
this, as we shall see, he was far from accurate. 'I often met him
at Lamb's but we never spoke. He lived twelve [fourteen]
years afterwards, and not many years before his death he said
to Mary Lamb, "Robinson cuts me, but in spite of that I shall

always have a kind feeling towards him for he was the first person that ever found out there was anything in me".' Again: 'I have heard Mary Lamb say, after I had cut him, "You are rich in friends — we cannot afford to cast off our friends because they are not all we wish"; and I have heard Lamb say, "Hazlitt does bad actions without being a bad man".'

CHAPTER VIII

THE JOURNALIST (III)

(1817)

*

My opinions have been sometimes called singular: they are
merely sincere. I say what I think: I think what ᴵ feel. I
cannot help receiving certain impressions from things; and
I have sufficient courage to declare (somewhat abruptly)
what they are. This is the only singularity I am conscious of.

A View of the English Stage.

I

I F we thought that Hazlitt, by his 'bad actions' of 1816, had
placed himself by common consent outside the pale, we should
make a mistake. His attack on the politics of *The Times* had
two consequences, or at least sequels; the first, the removal of
his brother-in-law Dr Stoddart from the editorship; the second,
his own appointment to the position of dramatic critic to that
journal.

We may continue, however, to take events in their order. In
the last days of the year Coleridge's Lay Sermon had really
appeared, under the title, as it proved, of 'The Statesman's
Manual; or the Bible the Best Guide to Political Skill and Fore-
sight. A Lay Sermon, addressed to the Higher Classes of
Society'. Hazlitt had said, 'We have by anticipation given some
account of this Sermon', and had proceeded to show that the
work itself was a reasonable deduction from his own account
of its author's present political character. At the same time, he
reviewed it for the *Edinburgh*. If the modern reader will have
some regard to the condition of the country in this winter, and

consider Coleridge's manual as seriously addressed to it, he will not have much difficulty, I think, in admitting these two articles as fair political comment.

In the first days of the new year *The Round Table* was published, by Constable in Edinburgh and Longmans in London. Of the fifty-two essays forming its two volumes, forty were by Hazlitt and twelve by Leigh Hunt, as the preface by the former plainly stated. On the title-page, Hazlitt's name stood alone. This was his first published book since the *Grammar* of 1810, if we make an exception of the *Life of Holcroft,* which, under circumstances that are not very clear to us, had made its appearance through Longmans in the preceding summer.

We may pass to Crabb Robinson, whose pages are still full of last year's reverberations:

'29 January: — Late, I called on Charles Lamb. Mrs Morgan & Miss Brent [of Hammersmith] were there. The conversation was on Hazlitt's attack on Coleridge & Wordsworth. Lamb spoke strongly in apology for H. and *at* me. He represented the praise of Coleridge as an ample set-off, and he thought both C. & W. had deserved this at his hands. At the same time he declared he had quarrelled with Hazlitt about it. He had sent the article against C. to W. who had written about it with feeling. And he appeared to have been much offended with C. for not noticing as it deserved what L. had related to him about H., viz. that when he sat down to write a critique on the Excursion he actually cried because he was disappointed and could not praise it as it deserved. To which C. gave no answer but by going on with the sentiment that the Excursion was a falling off. I saw no reason for this displeasure by L. I do not believe the fact that Hazlitt cried, and I hardly think L. serious in his vindication of H. At least, it is but a momentary feeling.'

That Lamb was right when he said that in Hazlitt's view of Coleridge 'a kind of respect shines through the disrespect' we may very easily believe when, in the week after his own article on the Lay Sermon, he writes to the *Examiner* the letter which is the germ of *My First Acquaintance with Poets.* If the reader can see no respect in the opening passage of that essay (*ante,* page 58), beginning 'It was in January 1798 [just nineteen years ago, as the letter adds] that I rose one morning before daylight, to walk ten miles in the mud, and went to hear this celebrated person preach' – he will find it nowhere. This opening passage is the letter which Hazlitt wrote at this moment. It was signed 'Semper Ego Auditor', and went on to ask why Mr Coleridge, 'having preached such a sermon as I have described, has published such a sermon as you have described?'

What right, Sir, has he or any man to make a fool of me or any man? I am naturally, Sir, a man of plain, dull, dry understanding, without flights or fancies, and can just contrive to plod on, if left to myself; what right then has Mr C., who is just going to ascend in a balloon, to offer me a seat in the parachute, only to throw me from the height of his career upon the ground, and dash me to pieces? Or, again, what right has he to invite me to a feast of poets and philosophers, fruits and flowers intermixed – immortal fruits and amaranthine flowers – and then to tell me it is all vapour, and, like Timon, to throw his empty dishes in my face? No, Sir, I must and will say it is hard. I hope between ourselves, there is no breach of confidence in all this, nor do I well understand how men's opinions on moral, political, or religious subjects can be kept a secret, except by putting them in the *Correspondent.*

With a hit at Crabb Robinson, and another at his brother-in-law (whose paper the *Correspondent* was) thus neatly contained in a single sentence, Hazlitt rode off from that full avowal of his sentiments towards Coleridge which he only brought himself to make six years later.

Two further entries of the diarist's follow:

'24 February: – After dinner I went to the Surrey Institution, and there I read in the [December] *Edinburgh Review* Hazlitt's review of Coleridge's Lay Sermon – an article made up of his personal attack on Coleridge in the *Examiner*. And also [in the *Quarterly*] Southey's article on the liberty of the press – a high-tory article which did not even amuse me.' Southey, in the article in question, 'On Parliamentary Reform', was very seriously in favour of 'the crime of seditious libel' – in other words, of the writings of Cobbett and Hazlitt – being made punishable by transportation.[1]

'3 March : – I called on Miss Lamb, and had a long chat with her. I found her very bitter towards Walter. She had heard Mrs Stoddart's story. ... I am satisfied that on the whole Walter has treated Stoddart as he deserves.' Here is Hazlitt's brother-in-law's tragedy, who through an excess of zeal in what he had taken to be the right cause had lost the editorship of *The Times*.

'At the close of the last year,' says Crabb Robinson in his Reminiscences, 'Mr Walter, having after long and not groundless cause of dissatisfaction dismissed Dr Stoddart from the literary superintendence of *The Times,* the Doctor claimed a compensation and the amount was referred to the arbitration of Burrell of the Northern circuit and myself. It is needless to advert to the grounds of the claim now – I remark merely that I had for a length of time been the depositary of Walter's complaints. I always laboured to mitigate his resentment, reminding him that it was he, Walter, not Stoddart, who had changed his sentiment. The Doctor's hatred of Buonaparte was fixed and unalterable, and his furious expression of it caused his having the popular title of *Dr Slop* – as his vituperation, it was thought, could have no fitter parallel. Walter's hostility yielded to the force of circumstances, and the nation was as tired as himself of

---

1. 'Why is it that this convicted incendiary [Cobbett], and others of the same stamp, are permitted week after week to sow the seeds of rebellion, insulting the Government, and defying the laws of the country? ... Men of this description, like other criminals, derive no lessons from experience. But it behoves the Government to do so, and curb sedition in time.' – Southey, *On Parliamentary Reform*. The reader who is inclined to deprecate the violence of some of Hazlitt's political writing during these years will do well, of course, to study equally the violence of the political writing which provoked it.

the anti-Napoleonism of the *Times* leaders. But after a time, when the Doctor continued to write in the same fierce tone, though his articles were continuously rejected and even their place supplied by others of an opposite character, I thought Mr Walter was warranted in giving him his discharge. Burrell and I had several meetings, and my humanity might have encroached on my sense of strict commercial justice in my concessions to the poorer man, when I was relieved from this trial by an act of flagrant wrong. Stoddart made secret arrangements for setting up a rival paper to *The Times*, and then wrote a short note addressed to Burrell and me, thanking us for the trouble we had taken and declining to accept of any compensation, as the *New Times* would be set up on the following Saturday – and in fact on Saturday the 15th of February appeared the *Day and New Times*. The Doctor in an introductory article written in the worst taste announced himself as the person who had written for some time the leading articles in *The Times*, and having left the conduct of that paper purposed to conduct the *Day and New Times* alone without any restraint or hindrance whatever. I copy this from my journal of the 16th: "Treacherous towards Mr Walter, and quackishly puffing about himself, his article was grossly indecent. I shared Mr W's feelings of resentment." The *New Times* did not flourish, as *The Times* ever did since, and still does [1851] if possible more than ever.'

This being the situation of *The Times*, Crabb Robinson was authorized by Walter 'to enquire of Southey whether he would undertake the editorship on liberal terms'. Southey's letter of refusal of 13 March, stating that he would not give up a country life and the pursuit of literature for any emolument, and justifying the inroads already made upon his time by 'temporary politics' solely on the ground of the importance of the interests at stake, concludes: 'We are in danger of an insurrection of the Yahoos: – it is the fault of governments that such a cast should exist in the midst of civilized society, but till the breed can be mended it must be curbed, & that too with a strong hand'.[1]

1. From the original (unpublished) in Dr Williams' Library.

Southey, always vehement, had an exceptional reason for his
vehemence at this moment. His early 'Wat Tyler' had just been
got hold of and published by the Radical bookseller Hone, and
on 9 March Hazlitt reviewed it, placing it in somewhat deadly
conjuncture with the Laureate's *Quarterly* article.

The author of Wat Tyler was an Ultra-jacobin; the author
of Parliamentary Reform is an Ultra-royalist; the one was a
frantic demagogue; the other is a servile court-tool; the one
maintained second-hand paradoxes; the other repeats second-
hand commonplaces; the one vented those opinions which
gratified the vanity of youth; the other adopts those prejudices
which are most conducive to the convenience of age; the one
saw nothing but the abuses of power; the other sees nothing
but the horror of resistance to those abuses: the one did not
stop short of general anarchy; the other goes the whole length
of despotism; the one vilified kings, priests, and nobles; the
other vilifies the people: the one was for universal suffrage
and perfect equality; the other is for seat-selling and the increasing influence of the Crown: the one admired the preaching of John Ball; the other recommends the Suspension of the
Habeas Corpus, and the putting down of the *Examiner* by the
sword, the dagger, or the thumb-screw; for the pen, Mr
Southey tells us, is not sufficient. We wonder that in all this
contempt which our prose-poet has felt at different times for
different persons and things, he has never felt any dissatisfaction with himself, or distrust of his own infallibility. Our
differing from others sometimes staggers our confidence in
our own conclusions: if we had been chargeable with as many
contradictions as Mr Southey, we suppose we should have had
the same senseless self-sufficiency. A changeling is your only
oracle. Those who have undergone a total change of sentiment on important questions, ought certainly to learn modesty
in themselves, and moderation towards others; on the contrary, they are generally the most violent in their own
opinions, and the most intolerant towards others.

Southey applied for an injunction against his own work, but failed to secure it, on the somewhat surprising ruling that the poem was so mischievous in tendency that its publicity could not be interfered with at the suit of the author.

This brought Coleridge into the field. A letter written by him, on 22 March, to Street, the co-proprietor with Stuart of the *Courier,* is sufficiently relevant to come in here :

What injudicious advisers must not Southey have had! It vexes me to the quick. ... With the exception of one outrageously absurd & frenetic passage, the Thing contains nothing, that I can find, that would not have been praised and thought all very right *forty years ago* at all the Public Schools in England, had it been written by a lad in the first form, as a *Poem.* For who in the Devil's name ever thought of reading Poetry for any political or practical purposes till these Devil's Times that *we* live in? The *publication* of the work is the wicked thing. Briefly, my dear Sir! every one is in the right to make the best he can, honourably, of a bad business. But the Truth is the Truth. The Root of the Evil is *a Public* – and take my word for it, this will wax more and more prolific for the State to suffer any truth to be published, because it will be certain to convey dangerous falsehood to 99 out of a hundred. Then we shall come round to the *esoteric* (interior, hidden) doctrines of the Ancients, and learn to understand what Christ meant when he commanded us not to cast Pearls before Swine. – Take four fifths of the Wat Tyler for instance – 'Tis a wretched mess of Pigsmeat, I grant, but yet take it, and reduce it to single assertions – how many of them, think you, would bear denying, *as truths*? But if Truth yelps and bites at the Heels of a Horse that cannot stop, why, Truth may think herself well off if she only gets her teeth knocked down her throat. It is for this reason, that I entertain towards the Jeffries, Cobbetts, Hunts, and all these creatures – and to the [*illegible*] who have fostered the vipers – a feeling more like Hatred than I ever bore to other Flesh and Blood, so clearly do I see and always have seen, that it must end in the suspension of Freedom of all kind. Hateful under all names these wretches are most hateful to me as liberticides.[1]

A strange theory, differing somewhat totally from what the Coleridge of 1794 had written in the *Conciones ad Populum* : 'For Truth should be spoken at all times, but more especially at those times, when to speak Truth is dangerous'. Coleridge's published letters for the defence, in the *Courier,* took two main lines : that the author was only nineteen when he wrote the poem, and that it was really written, under the influence of Spenser, in honour of the chastity of Wat Tyler's daughter. To which Hazlitt replied, in the further article he wrote on the subject, first : 'A person who forgets all the sentiments and principles to which he was most attached at nineteen, can have no sentiments ever after worth being attached to'; and, second : 'Mr C. might as well tell us the Laureate wrote Wat Tyler as an Epithalamium on his own marriage. There is but one line on the subject from beginning to end.'

The matter might have been allowed to rest here, if Mr William Smith, the member for Norwich, had not got up in the House with the *Quarterly Review* in one hand and 'Wat Tyler' in the other. Perhaps he had been reading the *Examiner*; more likely the inspiration was his own. At all events, the occasion, which was a debate on the censorship of the press, provided Southey with an excuse for his 'Letter' to this gentleman; and Southey's Letter rendered inevitable further articles by Hazlitt. As he said, 'We are always disposed to quarrel with ourselves for quarrelling with him, and yet we cannot help it, whenever we come in contact with his writings'. That this was indeed the effect of Southey upon Hazlitt, we can believe most implicitly. If Southey had not vindicated himself, with great and almost overpowering dignity, he would not have pointed the finger of scorn at those who 'had turned their faces towards the East in the morning, to worship the rising sun, and in the evening were

1. From the original (unpublished) in the British Museum.

looking eastward still, obstinately affirming that still the sun was there. I, on the contrary, altered my position as the world went round.' If Southey had not written this, Hazlitt would not have written: 'The sun indeed, passes from the East to the West, but it rises in the East again: yet Mr Southey is still looking in the West – for his pension'. We should, in a word, have been the poorer of some admirable polemics; and of one reference, to 'withered bay-leaves and contemptible grey hairs', which, in view of what Hazlitt was himself to suffer from, we could sooner have spared.[1]

On 7 April Wordsworth writes to Haydon: 'The miscreant Hazlitt continues, I have heard, his abuse of Southey, Coleridge, and myself, in the *Examiner*. I hope that you do not associate with the fellow; he is not a proper person to be admitted into respectable society.' The reply of Haydon, who had met Wordsworth during the latter's visit to town in the preceding summer, and had been much flattered by a sonnet which the poet had addressed to him in the columns of the *Champion*, is an exceedingly curious document. We cannot introduce it better than by saying that Haydon and Hazlitt had been engaged together in the Elgin Marbles campaign of 1816, and more recently (November) in the attack on the Catalogue Raisonné of the British Institution, in which, in the supposed interest of living painters, an attempt had been made to limit the public opportunities of

1. 'Mr Southey's self-love, when challenged to the lists, does not launch out into the wide field of wit or argument: it retires into its own littleness, collects all its slender resources in one poor effort of pert, pettifogging spite, makes up by studied malice for conscious impotence, and attempts to mortify others by the angry sense of his own insignificance. ... His "Letter" is a concentrated essence of a want of self-knowledge. It is the picture of the author's mind in little. In this respect, it is a "psychological curiosity"; a study of human infirmity. As some persons bequeath their bodies to the surgeons to be dissected after their death, Mr Southey publicly exposes his mind to be anatomized while he is living. He lays open his character to the scalping-knife, guides the philosophic hand in its painful researches, and on the bald crown of our *petit tondu*, in vain concealed under withered bay-leaves and a few contemptible grey hairs, you see the organ of vanity triumphant – sleek, smooth, round, perfect, polished, horned, and shining, as it were in a transparency.'

viewing old masters. In both of these matters Haydon, in his
Autobiography, pays a handsome tribute to Hazlitt; but in the
letter which he wrote at this moment he said: 'My turn will
come with Hazlitt, for he has the malignant morbidity of early
failure in the same pursuit. I have had several side stabs about
"great" pictures, &c., and the absurdity of Art ever existing in
England, but he shall see, if he cuts me openly, it shall not be
with impunity. In the Edinburgh Encyclopædia, speaking of
English Art, he mentioned every living painter now eminent,
but me! By leaving me out, the blockhead, he made people remark it, and so he has, in fact, done me good. One night, when
I saw him half-tipsy, and so more genial than usual, I said to
him, "Why do you sneer so at the prospects of English Art?
You know this is the country where it will next succeed." "I dare
say it will," he replied, "but what is the use of predicting success?" He served me a dreadful trick with Wilkie. He asked of
me a letter of introduction to see Wilkie's pictures. I gave it, and
the very next Sunday out came an infamous attack on Wilkie's
genius! You may depend, my dear Sir, that men of eminence
are considered food for such propensities and nothing better.
However, enough of him. I hope soon to have the pleasure of
seeing Mr Southey.' At the date at which this letter was written,
and throughout this year, Haydon and Hazlitt were meeting
constantly, on the latter's part in good faith. The article on
Wilkie to which the former refers is that in the *Champion* of
5 March 1815, which, it need not perhaps be said, was not an
'infamous attack', but a reasoned comparison between the merits
of Wilkie and Hogarth, by no means ungenerous to the former.

It is with some relief, I think, that we turn from these letters
about Hazlitt to read one from him.

Hazlitt to Macvey Napier

March 13, 1817.[1]

Dear Sir, – I conceive that nobody has been to blame in this
business but myself. In fact, I have been very ill all the winter,

1. From the original in the British Museum.

& have had more to do than I could have got through properly, if I had been well. I will send you Burger[1] in the course
of next week, & shall be happy at any time to do what I can
for the Supplement. But I would have you to understand at
first that I am a very unscientific person, & am therefore always liable to blunder on such matters. All that I know anything about (except things of amusement) is metaphysics, & I
know more of my own metaphysics than anybody else's. I
should think that the article Buonaparte might be made something of a little different from the Biography. I am, Dear Sir,
very respectfully your obliged humble servant,

W. HAZLITT.

This is our first intimation that he had been ill, but not our
first intimation that he had been busy. In addition to all his
journalistic work, and to the work of which we here learn, he
had written during this winter his Characters of Shakespear's
Plays. In April or May the book came out, printed by Charles
Reynell, the brother-in-law of John Hunt, published by the new
firm of Charles and James Ollier, and dedicated 'as a mark of
old friendship and lasting esteem, to Charles Lamb, Esq.'. It
sold well and immediately.

II

Our following to its conclusion of Hazlitt's campaign against
the political influence of the poets has taken us forward. We
may now go back to the Examiner of 1 December 1816, in which

1. The last of six articles contributed by Hazlitt to the second volume
of the Encyclopædia Britannica Supplement – James Barry, J. B. Base-
dow, John Beckmann, Xavier Bettinelli, G. B. Bilfinger, and Gottfried
August Bürger. With the exception of the first, the subjects allow Hazlitt's
characteristic interests little scope, and can certainly not have been of his
own choosing. The articles which he had offered to write (ante, page 208)
had not been entrusted to him, one or two of them being written instead
by Jeffrey. When Napier next approaches him (post, page 269) we shall
find, not greatly to our surprise, that he has had enough of Encyclopædia
writing.

Leigh Hunt had written on 'Young Poets'. 'The object of the present article,' he had said, 'is merely to notice three young writers who appear to us to promise a considerable addition of strength to the new school.' The young writers in question were Shelley, Keats, and John Hamilton Reynolds, each of whom, as the result of this article, entered the Leigh Hunt circle in this winter.

Shelley it is pretty certain that Hazlitt must have met, at Godwin's, between 1812 and 1814. The first – and, indeed, the only – evidence we possess of their meeting is contained in a couple of entries in Mary Shelley's journal, during their stay at Hunt's cottage in the Vale of Health in this spring. On Sunday, 9 February, we read: 'Walk with Shelley and Hunt to Brougham's in the morning. ... Several of Hunt's acquaintances come in the evening. Music. After supper a discussion until three in the morning with Hazlitt concerning Monarchy and Republicanism.' Another arrival of this moment in the Leigh Hunt circle, Charles Cowden Clarke, informs us that the case of republicanism was shared by Shelley and Hazlitt, while Hunt and Walter Coulson defended the monarchy. On the following Sunday, the 16th, Mary Shelley says: 'Mr and Mrs Hazlitt, B. Montagu, and Godwin dine: in the evening others come in. Music'. That this was the occasion on which Hazlitt first met the work of Keats we may say with some certainty on comparing a passage in Hunt's *Lord Byron and His Contemporaries* (1828): 'Having the pleasure of entertaining at dinner Mr Godwin, Mr Hazlitt, and Mr Basil Montagu, I showed them the verses of Keats.' Keats, in his twenty-first year and with his first *Poems* as yet unpublished, was much at Hunt's and much at Haydon's during this winter. His earliest reference to Hazlitt is in a letter of March to his friend Reynolds: 'It's the finest thing by God – as Hazlitt would say'. His second is in May, when he has left town for the summer: 'I must mention Hazlitt's Southey. O that he had left out the grey hairs.'

The *Examiner's* campaign against the poets was not for long to go unpunished. It had, of course, been a concerted campaign,

and while Hazlitt had written the articles we have seen Leigh
Hunt had written others. In its issue dated April, the *Quarterly*
discovered the *Round Table*. Since the article is one that was to
set a fashion, we may devote a little attention to it here. It began:

> Whatever may have been the preponderating feelings with
> which we closed these volumes, we will not refuse our acknow-
> ledgements to Mr Hazlitt for a few mirthful sensations which
> he has enabled us to mingle with the rest, by the hint that his
> essays were meant to be 'in the manner of the *Spectator* and
> *Tatler*'. The passage in which this is conveyed happened to be
> nearly the last to which we turned; and we were about to rise
> from the *Round Table* heavily oppressed with a recollection of
> vulgar descriptions, silly paradoxes, flat truisms, misty sophis-
> try, broken English, ill humour, and rancorous abuse, when
> we were first informed of the modest pretensions of our host.
> Our thoughts then reverted with an eager impulse –

to, of course, Addison, with the reflections of the reviewer upon
whom we need not concern ourselves. The article continued:

> Amongst the objects which Mr Hazlitt has thought it worth
> while for the good of mankind to take under his special super-
> intendence, the 'Manners' of the age have the first place.
> [Here Hunt's 'On a Day by the Fire' is quoted.] We are
> happy to have it in our power to state that the objects of his
> most sedulous care are of the softer sex. It is not indeed the sex
> in general, but it is a highly interesting and amiable part of
> it – that, namely, which passes under the denomination of
> 'washerwomen'.

A page of extracts from Hunt's essay of that title followed; after
which the reviewer ridiculed Hazlitt's definition of *gusto,* and
asserted, on evidence taken mostly from the twelve papers by
Hunt, that 'Mr Hazlitt is a very eminent creator of words and
phrases':

Our readers are, perhaps, by this time as much acquainted with the style of this author as they have any desire to be; and their curiosity may have been a little excited to know what the man is. It may be told in two words: he is a sour jacobin: a fact which he is so good as to disclose in the following pathetic lamentation over the French Revolution. [The concluding passage from *Mr Wordsworth's Excursion* (*ante*, page 184) is quoted.] As we might expect from this confession of feeling, the waters of bitterness flow around this unhappy person unceasingly. There is nothing in the world which he seems to like, unless we except 'washerwomen', for whom he does appear to have some regard. [Hazlitt's characters of Pitt and Burke, which he had reprinted from the *Eloquence of the British Senate,* are quoted.] We are far from intending to write a single word in answer to this loathsome trash; but we confess that these passages chiefly excited us to take the trouble of noticing the work. The author might have described washerwomen for ever; complimented himself unceasingly on his own 'chivalrous eloquence' [Hunt]; prosed interminably about Chaucer; written, if possible, in a more affected, silly, confused, ungrammatical style, and believed, as he now believes, that he was surpassing Addison – we should not have meddled with him; but if the creature, in his endeavours to crawl into the light, must take his way over the tombs of illustrious men, disfiguring the records of their greatness with the slime and filth which marks his track, it is right to point him out that he may be flung back to the situation in which nature designed he should grovel.

Having pointed 'Hazlitt' out, the *Quarterly* concluded in the following manner:

We learn from the Preface, that a few of these essays were written by Mr Hunt, the editor of the *Examiner* newspaper. We really have not the time to discriminate between the productions of the two gentlemen, or to mete out to each his own due portion of praise : we beg that they will take the trouble to decide it themselves according to their respective claims. We can only mention here that Mr Hunt sustains the part of the droll or merry fellow in the performance. ... *It is he who devotes ten or twelve pages to the dissertation on 'washer-women'*, and who repeats, no doubt from faithful memory, the dialogues which pass between Betty and Molly, the maid-servants, when they are first called in the morning, and describes, from actual observation (or, it may be, experience) the 'conclusive digs in the side' with which Molly is accustomed to dispel the lingering slumber of her bedfellow.

We have been at some pains to see the worst that Hazlitt had found to say about those of his contemporaries from whom he was divided by powerful political feeling, and may admit that there is something here which is new to us in the ethics of literary and political commentary.[1]

It would be too simple to suppose that these remarks, although dated April, were made public in that month. They were almost certainly both written and published subsequently to what Hazlitt had found to say about the *Quarterly* in his articles on Southey in the first two weeks of May; and had not very long been out, one imagines, when in September Keats wrote from Oxford to Reynolds: 'How is Hazlitt? We were reading his *Table* last night. I know he thinks himself not estimated by ten people in the world – I wish he knew he is. I am getting on famous with my third Book – have written 800 lines thereof, and hope to finish it next week.' This was *Endymion*.

So far from Hazlitt not being estimated, he was just now receiving his first solid testimony to the contrary. The opening fusillade from the *Quarterly* did not suffice even to shake him.

---

1. In his *Life of Lamb* Mr E. V. Lucas makes one remark with which I do not agree : 'The word loyalty was not in Hazlitt's dictionary; it was in italics in Lamb's'. I do not know a better example of loyalty in its essentials than Hazlitt's reply to this review, in the *Letter to Gifford*. His concealment of his consciousness that he had suffered by association with Leigh Hunt's very different, if equally estimable qualities, is perfect.

At the end of June his long and regular association with the *Examiner* came to an end, and he became dramatic critic to *The Times*. That the appointment was made directly by Walter, as a consequence of the social success of the *Characters of Shakespear's Plays,* we should suppose; but something may have been owing also to Thomas Barnes, who had now, in succession to Stoddart, been installed in the editorship. Somewhat surprisingly, Crabb Robinson, who perhaps did not approve of the appointment, says nothing about it. The *Examiner's* theatre, to which Hazlitt had attended week in and week out for two and a half years, was resumed by Leigh Hunt.

III

Of the second half of this year, spent by Hazlitt in the service of *The Times,* we learn all that we know, I think, from the preface to the *View of the English Stage* of the following spring: 'The volume here offered to the public, is a collection of Theatrical Criticisms which have appeared with little interruption, during the last four years, in different newspapers – *The Morning Chronicle,* the *Champion,* the *Examiner,* and, lastly, *The Times.* How I came to be regularly transferred from one of these papers to the others, sometimes formally and sometimes without ceremony, till I was forced to quit the last-mentioned by want of health and leisure, would make rather an amusing story, but that I do not choose to tell "the secrets of the prison-house". I would, however, advise any one who has an ambition to write, and to write his *best,* in the periodical press, to get if possible, "a situation" in *The Times* newspaper, the Editor of which is a man of business, and not of letters. He may write there as long and as good articles as he can, without being turned out for it.' We may be quite certain that Hazlitt was not on this occasion turned out, but that he left *The Times* at the end of six months for the reasons specified, and with respect and goodwill on both sides.

While Hazlitt is engaged in the service of *The Times,* we cannot do better than take the testimony of another arrival in both the Leigh Hunt and the Lamb circles in this summer – Bryan Waller Procter ('Barry Cornwall'). Procter, at this date in his thirtieth year, is that rare and welcome entrant upon the scene, an objective observer who carries conviction. He first wrote of Hazlitt at his death (the only one of his friends who troubled to do so), in some 'Recollections' contributed to the *New Monthly Magazine* for November 1830. 'Mr Hazlitt,' he says, 'was first pointed out to me about fourteen or fifteen years ago: I was afterwards introduced to him, at the house of (I think) Mr Charles Lamb; and during some years of my life I knew him well. He had previously been described to me as something fierce and unsocial; but I knew that, if he were so, there was also much in him of a finer quality, and I did not care to pin my faith upon others, in cases where I had an opportunity of judging for myself. It was at an exhibition (or some other public place) that I first saw him, and I remember going towards him with a mixture of curiosity and respect. I was young then and forward enough to admire an "author", whatever his pretensions might be. Time has now cured me of my indiscriminate respect for the makers of books; but it has not diminished my respect for the talents of William Hazlitt.

'At the time I refer to (it must, I think, have been in the year 1816) he was publishing, in the *Examiner*, some of his papers called the *Round Table*. His name was not so extensively circulated then as it since has been; but he was, nevertheless, well known to be a first-rate critic in matters connected with art and the theatres; and by his associates (some of them not too ready to admit the claims of literary candidates), he was characterized as an acute and profound thinker. His countenance did not belie this opinion. His figure was indeed indifferent, and his movements shy and awkward; but there was something in his earnest irritable face, his restless eyes, his black hair, combed backwards and curling (not too resolutely) about a well-shaped head, that was very striking. They would have made an excellent picture. Had the painter whom he most loved (Titian) been then living,

he would have been well pleased to have had such a countenance whereon to exercise his art, nor would he have disdained
to hand down to posterity the features of his eloquent admirer.'

Others of Procter's earliest written recollections we may find
room for at a later date. In his *Autobiographical Fragment* he
makes it clear that his introduction to Hazlitt was not through
Lamb but at supper at Leigh Hunt's, at the house in the New
Road, Paddington, into which the latter moved in July of this
year. He goes on: 'I expected to see a severe, defiant-looking
being. I met a grave man, diffident, almost awkward in manner,
whose appearance did not impress me with much respect. He
had a quick, restless eye, however, which opened eagerly when
any good or bright observation was made; and I found at the
conclusion of the evening, that when any question arose, the
most sensible reply always came from him. Although the process was not too obvious, he always seemed to have reasoned
with himself before he uttered a sentence. ... His grey eyes, not
remarkable in colour, expanded into great expression when occasion demanded it. Being very shy, however, they often evaded
your steadfast look. They never (as has been asserted by some
one) had a sinister expression; but they sometimes flamed with
indignant glances, when their owner was moved to anger; like
the eyes of other angry men. At home, his style of dress (or un-
dress) was perhaps slovenly, because there was no one to please;
but he always presented a very clean and neat appearance when
he went abroad. His mode of walking was loose, weak, and un-
steady; although his arms displayed strength, which he used to
put forth when he played at racquets with Martin Burney and
others. He played in the old Fives Court (now pulled down) in
St Martin's Street; and occasionally exhibited impatience when
the game went against him. It was here that he witnessed the
play at fives of the celebrated John Cavanagh, of whom he has
written so delightfully.'

Again, in his *Charles Lamb* of 1866 Procter wrote: 'I meet,
at present, with few persons who recollect much of Hazlitt.
Some profess to have heard nothing of him except his prejudices;

but his prejudices were few, and his violence (if violence he had), was of very rare occurrence. He was extremely patient, indeed, although earnest when discussing points in politics, respecting which he held very strong and decided opinions. But he circulated his thoughts on many other subjects, whereon he ought not to have excited offence or opposition. ... Besides being an original thinker, Hazlitt excelled in conversation. He was, moreover, a very temperate liver: yet his enemies proclaimed to the world that he was wanting in sobriety. During the thirteen years that I knew him intimately, and (at certain seasons) saw him almost every day, I know that he drank nothing stronger than water; except tea, indeed, in which he indulged in the morning. Had he been as temperate in his political views as in his cups, he would have escaped the slander that pursued him through life.'

Finally, on Lamb, Hazlitt, and Leigh Hunt, we may listen to Procter: 'Hazlitt (who was ordinarily very shy) was the best talker of the three. Lamb said the most pithy and brilliant things. Hunt displayed the most ingenuity. All three sympathised often with the same persons and the same books; and this, no doubt, cemented an intimacy that existed between them for so many years. Moreover, each of them understood the others, and placed just value on their objections when any difference of opinion (not infrequent) arose between them. Without being debaters, they were accomplished talkers. ... Politics (especially party politics) were seldom admitted. Lamb disliked them as a theme for evening talk; he perhaps did not understand them scientifically. And when Hazlitt's impetuosity drove him, as it sometimes did, into fierce expressions on public affairs, these were usually received in silence, and the matter thus raised up for assent or controversy allowed to drop.' But writing on Lamb's advantages Procter says: 'Hazlitt gave him daring'.

Procter's mention of politics reminds us that Hazlitt was not able, or willing, to put the whole of himself into *The Times*. If we look for the rest of him during these months we find it no longer in the *Examiner* but once more in the *Champion*. The latter journal, on its sale by John Scott early in this summer,

passed for a short term into the hands of a certain R. D.
Richards, of whom we know nothing except that he gave the
occasional articles of Hazlitt a flattering prominence. Here, between August and the end of the year, *On the Effects of War
and Taxes, On the Regal Character, What is the People?* and
other political essays made their appearance. The dramatic critic
of the journal at this period was John Hamilton Reynolds, and
it is to Reynolds, no doubt, that we should attribute the enthusiastic review of the *Characters of Shakespear's Plays* with which
the reappearance of Hazlitt in the *Champion* was heralded:
'This is the only work ever written on Shakespeare that can be
deemed worthy of Shakespeare'.

For exterior information upon the rest of this year we are
dependent upon Crabb Robinson:

'2 October: — At night I read, as I did last night, the last
[August] number of the *Edinburgh Review*. I was interested by
the review of Coleridge's Life written by Hazlitt, for which it is
said he has received 50 guineas. Jeffrey has added a note with
the initials of his name replying to the personalities in Coleridge's book. Jeffrey of course being a discreet & artful man has
the advantage over Coleridge in a personal dispute who has so
many infirmities of mind which lay him open to the attack of
an adversary, but Jeffrey confesses enough to fix on himself the
imputation of gross flattery & insincerity towards C. He says that
he saw C. liked compliments & therefore gave them — he advised
the publication of Christabel, on the report of others, and then
suffered Hazlitt to heap every species of obloquy upon it in his
review (see Appendix iv). He certainly shews the hospitality of
Southey not to have been of a kind to demand any very vehement gratitude. There is a very puffing review of Hazlitt's own
book, but at the same time it is an able article. These are the
interesting articles of the number.' The review of the *Characters
of Shakespear's Plays,* from Jeffrey's own pen, would hardly
have struck us as 'very puffing'. Its tone may be sufficiently suggested by an extract: 'He continually appears acute, desultory,

and capricious – with great occasional felicity of conception and expression – frequent rashness and carelessness – constant warmth of admiration for his author – and some fits of extravagance and folly, into which he seems to be hurried, either by the hasty kindling of his zeal as he proceeds, or by a self-willed determination not to be baffled or balked in any thing he has taken it into his head he should say'.

We have, as a matter of fact, one further sidelight on Jeffrey in his capacity as editor, in a letter of this month to Godwin. Godwin, after many years, had written a novel, *Mandeville*, and would seem to have been taking measures of prudence with regard to its reception. Jeffrey writes to him, on 30 October: 'I know nothing whatever of any arrangement for committing your work, which I am very impatient to see, either into the hands of Mr Hazlitt or of Sir James Macintosh; and as it is generally my office to offer or propose these tasks to my several contributors, I rather imagine it will be left for me to undertake the determination in this case also. Now, before deciding such a matter, I really must first see the book myself. I really do not quite agree with you in the opinions you seem to hold as to the critical qualifications of the two gentlemen you have alluded to. If the one is somewhat too cautious and discursive, and afraid of offending, the other is far too rash and exaggerated, and too exclusively studious of effect to be a safe, exemplary reviewer. Will you permit me to add that if there be any particular intimacy between Mr Hazlitt and you, or if you have communicated together on the project of his being your reviewer, I must certainly consider that as a serious objection to his being entrusted with the task. I have no doubt of his fairness and impartiality, so far as intention is concerned, but he seems to be a person whose judgement is somewhat at the mercy of partialities and prejudices – and, besides, the thing is of ill example, and affects the purity of our tribunal.' There is a postscript: 'I have burned your letter, and shall not speak of it to anybody'.

On Sunday, 2 November, Robinson 'dined late in Bedford Square (at B. Montagu's). ... Hazlitt too came in. He studi-

ously avoided me and would not speak. I am not at all sorry
that he should be offended & affronted with me. It is what I
wished. He talked much at his ease to Mrs Montagu & is greatly
improved in his manners. He is almost gentlemanly compared
with what he was.'

To conclude the year, the diarist gives us two entries which
cast their shadows before them:

'4 December: — I had a letter from Coleridge asking my advice about the expediency of prosecuting for a libel on him in
the *Edinburgh Magazine*.' This was *Blackwood's Edinburgh
Magazine*, to whose beginnings we shall come in the next chapter.

'31 December: — At Surrey Institution looked over *Blackwood's Magazine*. The publisher had written cringing letters to
Wordsworth & then published letters of sheer vulgar abuse
without any criticism or knowledge of any kind whatever.'

In this year Haydon put Hazlitt's head, 'looking at Christ as
an investigator', into his picture of the Entry into Jerusalem,
upon which he had been engaged since 1814.

CHAPTER IX

THE LECTURER

(1818–19)

*

Neither the outcry *for* or *against* moves me a jot: I do not
say that the one is not more agreeable than the other.
Farewell to Essay-Writing.

I

ON 2 January we find Crabb Robinson 'reading for an hour in
Hazlitt's Shakspeare', an evidence, if we required it, that the
vogue of that work continued. On the second Tuesday in the year
his lectures on the English Poets opened at the Surrey Institution.

Our first information is from Keats, in a letter of 23 January
to his brothers at Teignmouth: 'I went last Tuesday, an hour
too late, to Hazlitt's Lecture on Poetry, got there just as they
were coming out, when all these pounced upon me – Hazlitt,
John Hunt and son, Wells, Bewick, all the Landseers, Bob
Harris, aye and more. ... Sunday I dined with Hazlitt and
Haydon.' This was at Haydon's new studio at Lisson Grove,
whither he had recently removed from Great Marlborough
Street. John Hunt we know; his son Henry was now in the
Examiner office, and later carried on his father's publishing
business with Charles Cowden Clarke as partner. All the Landseers would no doubt include John Landseer, painter and en-
graver, who had himself delivered a course of lectures at the
Surrey Institution in 1815 on the Philosophy of Art, and his sons
Thomas and Edwin, both pupils of Haydon. William Bewick,
who six years later made a well-known drawing of Hazlitt, had
also recently become one of Haydon's pupils. In his *Life* by

Thomas Landseer (1871) we may read, dated February, a letter from the young painter to his family which gives us a very fresh picture of literary society in this circle at this moment: 'I have been at two or three very intellectual dinners. ... Amongst the company were Horatio Smith (author of Rejected Addresses), Keats the poet, Hazlitt the critic, Haydon, Hunt the publisher, &c., &c. ... Hazlitt is giving lectures on poetry; they are said to be the finest lectures that ever were delivered. He gave me a ticket of admission: I have attended. He is the Shakespeare prose writer of our glorious country; he outdoes all in truth, style, and originality – you must read his Shakespeare's Characters.' To complete the circle of young men who surrounded Hazlitt at this date, we must add the name of Charles Jeremiah Wells, now in his twentieth year and in a solicitor's office, who, without at any time emerging into prominence, is understood to have given Hazlitt a dozen years of personal devotion. Of Bob Harris I am not aware that we know anything.

Crabb Robinson attended Hazlitt's third lecture: '27 January: – Went to the Surrey Institution, where I heard Hazlitt lecture on Shakespeare & Milton. He delighted me much by the talent he displayed, but I was equally disgusted with the malignant spirit that broke through in the covert attack on Wordsworth. Without naming him, he was very abusive, reproaching modern poets for their vanity and incapacity of admiring and loving anything but themselves. He was applauded at this part of his lecture, but I know not whether he was generally understood.' Robinson then rushed off, and was in time to hear Coleridge's opening lecture on Shakespeare at Fleur-de-Luce Court. 'I was gratified unexpectedly by finding a large & respectable audience, generally of very superior persons – in physiognomy rather than dress. But the lecture was heavy.'

On Sunday, 15 February, the diarist called at Basil Montagu's: 'I found Hazlitt there. We did exchange a few words together.' On the following Tuesday he heard the sixth lecture: 'He spoke of the writers about Queen Anne, and was bitter, sprightly, and full of political & personal allusion. He also was almost obscene in treating of Prior, and quoted his [Gay's] unseemly verses against Blackmore to a congregation of saints. He drew an ingenious but not very intelligible parallel between Swift, Rabelais, & Voltaire, and even eulogized the modern infidel, so indiscreet and reckless is the man.' The 'modern infidel' was, of course, Voltaire. This was the lecture of which Keats reports: 'I hear Hazlitt's lectures regularly, his last was on Gray, Collins, Young, &c., and he gave a very fine piece of discriminating Criticism on Swift, Voltaire, and Rabelais. I was very disappointed at his treatment of Chatterton. I generally meet with many I know there.'

The diarist, of course, was looking for cause of offence, and he found it more satisfactorily in the next lecture. This is the lecture (it is one of the small evidences we have that Keats's esteem for Hazlitt was returned) which opened with a reconsideration of the case of Chatterton, since 'I am sorry that what I said in the conclusion of the last Lecture respecting Chatterton should have given dissatisfaction to some persons with whom I would willingly agree on all such matters'. It went on to Burns, and, almost inevitably, to Wordsworth's 'Letter to a Friend' of that poet. 'He was so contemptuous, speaking of his letter about Burns,' says Robinson, 'that I lost my temper and hissed, but I was on the outside of the room. I was led to burst out into declamations against H. which I afterwards regretted, though I uttered nothing but the truth. Hazlitt abused Wordsworth in a vulgar style, imputing to him the mere desire of representing himself as a superior man.[1] I hurried away to attend Mrs Smith

1. He said: 'Indeed (if I may be allowed to speak my whole mind, under correction) Mr Wordsworth could not be in any way expected to tolerate or give a favourable interpretation to Burns's constitutional foibles – even his best virtues are not good enough for him. He is repelled and driven back into himself, not less by the worth than by the faults of others.' The elder poet had just been driven back into himself by Keats. Keats, full of admiration, had first met Wordsworth at Haydon's in December, and on several occasions afterwards. In his letter of 21 February to his brothers he says: 'I am sorry that Wordsworth has left a bad impression wherever he visited in town by his egotism, vanity, and bigotry. Yet he is a great poet, if not a philosopher.' This, all said and done, was Hazlitt's opinion.

to Coleridge's lecture.' These were busy days for the diarist. If he could have brought himself to attend the next, and last, lecture, he would have heard Hazlitt read the whole of 'Hart-Leap Well', and remark: 'As Mr Wordsworth's poems have been little known to the public, or chiefly through garbled extracts from them, I will here give an entire poem (one that has always been a favourite with me), that the reader may know what it is that the admirers of this author find to be delighted with in his poetry. Those who do not feel the beauty and the force of it, may save themselves the trouble of inquiring farther.'

Lamb, who did not attend lectures, we find reporting to Wordsworth on 18 February his reasons: 'W. H. goes on lecturing against W. W. and making copious use of quotations from said W. W. to give zest to said lectures. S. T. C. is lecturing with success. I have not heard either him or H. ... Lectures are not much to my taste, whatever the Lecturer may be. If *read*, they are dismal flat, and you can't think why you are brought together to hear a man read his works which you could read so much better at leisure yourself; if delivered extempore, I am always in pain lest the gift of utterance should suddenly fail the orator in the middle, as it did me at the dinner given in honour of me at the London Tavern.'

We have not yet heard Talfourd, who in drawing on his memories of three courses of lectures delivered by Hazlitt, succeeds in principally illuminating this first one: 'Mr Hazlitt delivered three courses of lectures at the Surrey Institution ... before audiences with whom he had but "an imperfect sympathy". They consisted chiefly of Dissenters, who agreed with him in his hatred of Lord Castlereagh, but who "loved no plays"; of Quakers, who approved him as the opponent of Slavery and Capital Punishment, but who "heard no music"; of citizens devoted to the main chance, who had a hankering after the "improvement of the mind", but to whom his favourite doctrine of its natural disinterestedness was a riddle; of a few enemies, who came to sneer; and a few friends, who were eager to learn and to admire. The comparative insensibility of the bulk of his audi-

ence to his finest passages, sometimes provoked him to awaken
their attention by points which broke the train of his discourse,
after which he could make himself amends by some abrupt
paradox which might set their prejudices on edge, and make
them fancy they were shocked. He startled many of them at the
onset, by observing that, since Jacob's dream, "the heavens have
gone further off, and become astronomical" — a fine extravagance, which the ladies and gentlemen who had grown astronomical themselves under the preceding lecturer, felt called on to
resent as an attack on their severer studies. When he had read a
well-known extract from Cowper, comparing a poor cottager
with Voltaire, and had pronounced the line, "A truth the brilliant Frenchman never knew", they broke into a joyous shout
of self-gratulation, that they were so much wiser than a wicked
Frenchman. When he passed by Mrs Hannah More with observing that "she had written a great deal which he had never read",
a voice gave expression to the general commiseration and surprise, by calling out "More pity for you!" They were confounded
at his reading with more emphasis, perhaps, than discretion,
Gay's epigrammatic lines on Sir Richard Blackmore, in which
scriptural persons are freely hitched into rhyme; but he went
doggedly on to the end, and, by his perseverance, baffled those
who, if he had acknowledged himself wrong by stopping, would
have hissed him without mercy. He once had an edifying advantage over them. He was enumerating the humanities which
endeared Dr Johnson to his mind, and at the close of an agreeable catalogue, mentioned, as last and noble, "his carrying the
poor victim of disease and dissipation on his back through Fleet
Street" — at which a titter arose from some who were struck by
the picture as ludicrous and a murmur from others, who
deemed the allusion unfit for ears polite. He paused for an instant, and then added in his sturdiest and most impressive
manner, "an act which realized the parable of the Good Samari-
tan", at which his moral and delicate hearers shrank rebuked
into deep silence. He was not eloquent in the true sense of the
term; for his thoughts were too weighty to be moved along by

the shallow stream of feeling which an evening's excitement can arouse. He wrote all his lectures, and read them as they were written; but his deep voice and earnest manner suited his matter well.'

Procter adds to this account: 'He read his lectures in an abrupt yet somewhat monotonous voice, but they were very effective. If he failed in communicating, by his manner, the lighter graces of his authors, he established their graver beauties, and impressed on his auditors a due sense of their power. Keats, the poet, who used to go there to hear him, remarked to a friend of mine that he reminded him of Kean.' And Bewick, remarking that Hazlitt 'became a favourite at the Surrey Institution, and stood up in his place at the lecture-table with all confidence, in the consciousness of having friends and admirers about him', recalls how, on occasions when disapprobation was expressed, he would 'calmly look towards the place whence the hissing came, turning back the leaf of his copy, and deliberately repeating the sentiments with greater energy and a voice more determined than before'.

That Hazlitt's vogue at this moment was by no means limited to the circles Talfourd would have us suppose, we may learn if we take at this point the continuation of a letter of which we read the beginning on an earlier page. The writer is Miss Mitford, and the date of her letter the December following. After describing the manner of his leaving the *Morning Chronicle* (*ante,* page 174), she goes on: 'Hazlitt's revenge was exceedingly characteristic. Last winter, when his *Characters of Shakespear* and his lectures had brought him into fashion, Mr Perry remembered him as an old acquaintance,[1] and asked him to dinner, and a large party to meet him, to hear him talk, and to show him off as the lion of the day. The lion came – smiled and bowed – handed Miss Bentley to the dining-room – asked Miss

---

1. Hazlitt had, as a matter of fact, signalized the retirement of his old editor by contributing to the *Morning Chronicle* under John Black a series of articles *On the Spy System* in the preceding summer. In these articles, reprinted in *Political Essays,* the exploits of the Government agent Oliver – recently submitted to investigation by Mr and Mrs J. L. Hammond – will be found very faithfully dealt with.

Perry to take wine – said once "Yes" and twice "No" – and never uttered another word the whole evening. The most provoking part of this scene was, that he was gracious and polite past all expression – a perfect pattern of mute elegance – a silent Lord Chesterfield; and his unlucky host had the misfortune to be very thoroughly enraged, without anything to complain of.' While Miss Mitford was not in the ordinary way a young lady upon whose evidence we should place implicit reliance, or in whose opportunity of judging what was or was not 'characteristic' of Hazlitt we should believe very strongly, she was here describing, we may take it, a scene at which she had been present. We trace her, at least, to have been on a further visit to the Perrys during this January and February.

Hazlitt, as we may suppose, had conceded nothing to his success. From the outset of this year, his short connection with the *Champion* having come to an end with the re-sale of that journal, he had engaged himself in a new enterprise with John Hunt. Anyone who will take the trouble to turn over the pages of that pleasing little weekly, *The Yellow Dwarf*, in the bound volume containing Hazlitt's own connections which is preserved in the British Museum, can have small doubt that it was designed to float to success on his new-found reputation. His own principal articles – *On Court Influence*, *The Clerical Character*, *The Regal Character* – are signed with his name, and the next subject on his list is announced very prominently. In addition, there are regular extracts from the course of lectures proceeding simultaneously. *The Yellow Dwarf* ran for twenty-one numbers, and from a good many signs I conclude John Hamilton Reynolds to have had a principal hand in it.

We know of no positive difference with Leigh Hunt that had caused Hazlitt to withdraw from the *Examiner* on his appointment to *The Times* in the preceding summer, but that he may have preferred to go his own way after the *Round Table* review would not surprise us. He did so too late to escape being tarred with the Leigh Hunt brush. In this winter the latter's *Foliage* had been published, and the curious reader will find among the

epistles in verse which that work contains one whose addressee
is Hazlitt:

> *Dear Hazlitt, whose tact intellectual is such*
> *That it seems to feel truth, as one's fingers do touch, –*
> *Who in politics, arts, metaphysics, poetics,*
> *To critics in these times, are health to cosmetics,*
> *And nevertheless, – or I rather should say,*
> *For that very reason, – can relish boy's play,*
> *And turning on all sides, through pleasures and cares,*
> *Find nothing more precious than laughs and fresh airs.*

The poem goes on to achieve the intimacy of 'Dear Will', and to
allude to the pleasure which the poet-editor obtained from 'a
few droppers-in like my Cousin and you.' It was this kind
of thing, of course, which gave lamentable ground for that
belief in a Cockney school already promulgated from Edinburgh.

On 18 April Crabb Robinson gives us an entry: 'I returned to
Lamb's again. There was a large party, – the greater part of
those who are usually there, but also Leigh Hunt and his wife.
... He, though a man I very much dislike, did not displease me
this evening. He has improved in manliness and healthfulness
since I last saw him, some years ago. There was a glee about him
which evinced high spirits, if not perfect health, and I envied
his vivacity. He imitated Hazlitt capitally, Wordsworth not so
well. Talfourd was there, and injudiciously loquacious.'

That Keats for his part was finding something unprofitable
in Leigh Hunt at this date we know. He had gone to Teignmouth, from where he writes on 23 March to Haydon: 'It is a
great Pity that People should by associating themselves with the
finest things, spoil them. Hunt has damned Hampstead and
masks and sonnets and Italian tales. Wordsworth has damned
the lakes. ... Ollier has damned music. Hazlitt has damned the
bigotted and blue-stockinged; how durst the Man? he is your
only good damner, and if ever I am damn'd – damn me if I

shouldn't like him to damn me.' There is, and is intended to
be, a *non sequitur* in this indictment: bigotry and blue stockings were not, for Keats, among the 'finest things', nor had
Hazlitt been associating with them. To this letter Haydon replies with the news that 'Hazlitt is going to lecture at Crown
and Anchor tavern in the Strand. – I am sorry for it, tho' he
will get money, it is letting his talents down a little.' This proposal eventuated in April, with a repetition of the English
Poets series; and it was here that Coleridge lectured in the following winter.

In April Keats wishes to be remembered, through Haydon, to
'Hazlitt and Bewick'. Later in the month he writes to Reynolds
of his intention to learn Greek, and perhaps Italian, 'and in
other ways prepare myself to ask Hazlitt in about a year's time,
the best metaphysical road I can take'. In May, in acknowledg-
ing from Reynolds the news of the town, he notes as evidence
that there is something real in the world, 'Moore's present to
Hazlitt – I like that Moore, and am glad I saw him at the
Theatre just before I left town'. We do not know what Moore's
present to Hazlitt can have been, unless it was a copy of *The
Fudge Family in Paris,* which Moore sent at this time, and
which, as a tribute of respect from a fashionable poet to the
leading spirit of *The Yellow Dwarf,* was not unacceptable. Hazlitt reviewed the book, with equal acceptability, in the pages of
that paper; but if Moore supposed, as he seems to have done,
that the gift would cause Hazlitt to revise his opinion that 'Mr
Moore ought not to have written Lalla Rookh, even for three
thousand guineas', he found himself, on the publication of the
Lectures, disappointed.

The letter of Keats in May from which we have already
quoted goes on to introduce us to a name with which we shall
become familiar. Developing a metaphor in explanation of the
vagaries of his more intimate correspondence, Keats says: 'I
must play my draughts as I please, and for my advantage and
your erudition, crown a white with a black, or a black with a
white, and move into black or white, far and near as I please.

— I must go from Hazlitt to Patmore. ... "from Gray to Gay, from Little to Shakespeare".'

Peter George Patmore, who is thus introduced in an anti-thesis, and who had become by this date, we must suppose, sufficient of a familiar in the Keats-Reynolds circle for the allusion to be taken, had first met Hazlitt, as we know from his own account, in the course of the arrangements for the lectures at the Surrey Institution, of which he was at this time the secretary. He was in his thirty-fourth year, and combined with this office, or did so very shortly afterwards, the function of London theatrical correspondent to the newly established *Blackwood's Edinburgh Magazine*. It was in this capacity that, at the opening of the year, he had proposed to Hazlitt to prepare a report of the lectures from the manuscript; and since the interview which ensued upon this proposal serves the purpose of giving us one of our very few views of the Hazlitt domestic interior, we may take it here with the warning that, like most that Patmore writes, it must not be too implicitly relied upon :

I went to him in York Street, in consequence of the note referred to above; and, though I have never since (until this moment) attempted to recall the scene, it lives before me now as if it were of yesterday. On knocking at the door, it was, after a long interval, opened by a sufficiently 'neat-handed' domestic. The outer door led immediately from the street (down a step) into an empty apartment, indicating an unin-habited house, and I supposed I had mistaken the number; but, on asking for the object of my search, I was shown to a door which opened (a step from the ground) on to a ladder-like staircase, bare like the rest, which led to a dark bare landing-place, and thence to a large square wainscotted apart-ment. The great curtainless windows of this room looked upon some dingy trees; the whole of the wall, over and about the chimney-piece, was entirely covered, up to the ceiling, by names written in pencil, of all sizes and characters, and in all directions – commemorative of visits of curiosity to 'the house of Pindarus'. There was, near to the empty fire-place, a table with breakfast things upon it (though it was two o'clock in the afternoon); three chairs and a sofa were standing *about* the room, and one unbound book lay on the mantelpiece. At the table sat Hazlitt, and on the sofa a lady, whom I found to be his wife.

My reception was not very inviting; and it struck me at once (what had not occurred to me before) that in asking facilities for criticizing William Hazlitt in *Blackwood's Magazine* I had taken a step open to the suspicion of either mischief or mystification, or both. However, I soon satisfied him that my object and design were anything but unfriendly. To be what he called 'puffed' in so unlooked-for a quarter was evidently deemed a god-send; it put him in excellent humour accordingly; and the 'Lake Poets' being mentioned, and finding me something of a novice in such matters (and moreover an excellent listener), he talked for a couple of hours, without intermission, on those 'personal themes', which he evidently 'loved best', and with which, in this instance, he mixed up that spice of malice which was never, or rarely, absent from his discourse about his quondam friends, Wordsworth, Coleridge, and Southey. ...

This first lengthened interview of mine with Hazlitt ended by his promising to let me have the MS. of his lectures, to do what I pleased with, and we parted on a better footing than we had met; though evidently with as little prospect as before of our ever becoming intimate associates : — for the way in which he handled his quondam friends, as above described, did anything but decrease the dread I had been taught to entertain of his personal character.

Hazlitt wrote to Patmore : 'Dear Sir, — I am very well satisfied with the article, and obliged to you for it. I am afraid the censure is truer than the praise. It will be of great service, if they insert it entire, which, however, I hope. Your obliged, W. HAZLITT.' That the article did come out, in the February *Black-*

wood, followed by further reports of a respectful nature in March and April, and that the inadvertence was amply atoned for, we shall find when we come in a moment to review the activities of that magazine.

In the meantime Hazlitt, whose thoughts were turning more and more to lectureship, seems to have based on the false appearance of favour which Patmore had secured him in Edinburgh a notion that he might lecture with acceptability in that city. A letter from Jeffrey, which possesses the interest of being the first direct communication we have between editor and contributor, must have gone some little way to prepare him for the more complete disillusionment to follow.

Jeffrey to Hazlitt

Edinburgh, 3d May, 1818.

My dear Sir, — I am sorry you ascribe so much importance to the omission of your little paper on Dr Reid's book. I did certainly intend to have inserted it, but the monstrous length of some other articles, and your unavoidable absence from home when the No. was finally filled up, prevented me. I think I shall give it a place in the next, though there is not much interest in the subject:[1]

I feel that I am extremely to blame for not answering a former letter of yours on a subject more personal to yourself, and assuredly I do not feel it the less for your delicacy in saying nothing about it in your last; but I can safely say that it was not owing to indifference or unwillingness to give you all the information I had, but to a feeling of great uncertainty as to the justness of any information I had, and the hazard of great error in any advice I might found on it. This made me

1. The review by Hazlitt of Thomas Reid's *Inquiry into the Human Mind* was still unpublished in September, and it did, in fact, never appear in the *Edinburgh Review*. There is a reference to the subject in *On the Causes of Popular Opinion* (1828): 'When I wished to unburthen my mind in the Edinburgh by an article on English (not Scotch) metaphysics, J[effrey], who echoes this *florid* charge, said he preferred what I wrote for effect, and was afraid of its being thought heavy — by the side of Macculloch!'

hesitate, and resolve to reflect and inquire before I made any answer, and then came in the usual vice of procrastination and the usual excuse of other more urgent avocations, till at last it was half forgotten, and half driven willingly from my conscience when it recurred.

Perhaps you care nothing about the subject any longer, or have received information to decide you from quarters of higher authority, but I still think myself bound to answer your questions as they were put, and therefore I say that in general I think Edinburgh the worst place in the world for such experiments as you seemed to meditate, both from the extreme dissipation of the fashionable part of its population, and from a sort of conceit and fastidiousness in all the middling classes, which, originating at least as much in a coldness of nature as in any extraordinary degree of intelligence, makes them very ready to find fault and decry.

Most lectures have accordingly failed entirely in this place, and the only exhibitions of the sort which have taken have been such as pretended to reveal some wonderful secret, like Feinagle, or to give a great deal of information in a short and popular way, like some teachers of Astronomy and Chemistry, though their success has been always very moderate.

Estimating the merit of your Lectures as highly as I am sincerely inclined to do, I could by no means insure you against a total failure; but I think it much more likely that you might find about forty or fifty auditors – not of the first rank or condition – and be abused as a Jacobin and a raving blockhead by a great many more, if you seemed in any danger of – [MS. torn here.] We are quite provincial enough for that, I assure you, notwithstanding the allowance of liberality and sense that is to be found among us. If this prospect tempts you, pray come. I shall willingly do all I can for you, but I fear it will not be very much.

In the meantime I am concerned to find your health is not so good as it should be, and that you could take more care of it if your finances were in better order. We cannot let a man of genius suffer in this way, and I hope you are in no serious danger. I take the liberty of enclosing £100, a great part of which I shall owe you in a few weeks, and the rest you shall pay me back in reviews whenever you can do so without putting yourself to any uneasiness. If you really want another £100 tell me so plainly, and it shall be heartily at your service. – Believe me always, with the greatest regard, your obliged and faithful servant,

J. JEFFREY.

This, we may fairly say, is an admirable letter. We may only wish that Jeffrey had been as able to recognize the merits of his contributors as he was willing to remunerate them.

On 28 May Keats, who had just returned to town, writes to Bailey: 'Yesterday I dined with Hazlitt, Barnes, and Wilkie, at Haydon's. The topic was the Duke of Wellington – very amusingly pro-and-con'd.' That the *Lectures on the English Poets* were out at this date Crabb Robinson, who had gone on circuit before the concluding lecture of the course was delivered, gives us evidence. 'I read to-day,' he says on 29 May, 'Hazlitt's last lecture on the Poets, in which he flippantly & cavalierly but with eloquence occasionally breaks the staff over the heads of the living poets.' The book was brought out by Taylor and Hessey, who had just published *Endymion*; and it contained the advertisement, 'This day is published, *Characters of Shakespear's Plays*, by William Hazlitt. Second Edition.' Simultaneously appeared, through another publisher, his collected dramatic criticisms, *A View of the English Stage,* from the preface to which we have already quoted.

It is at this point that Crabb Robinson does for us a further service – he gives a date for the actual appearance of the *Quarterly* for January of this year.[1] On 10 June he says: 'Lounged for an hour at the Surrey Institution, reading

1. Punctuality was not among the merits of this redoubtable organ of opinion. Dr Smiles tells the story of how Gifford got so far behind on one occasion that a quarter had to be omitted altogether.

Quarterly Review, in which Hazlitt's Lectures on Shakespear are most unjustifiably abused.'

The spectacle of the *Quarterly* making a second mouthful of Hazlitt is one which need not long detain us. 'Sometimes,' the public were informed, 'he breaks forth into a poetical strain, but more frequently he descends to that simpler style of eloquence which is in use among washerwomen, the class of females with whom, as we learn from the *Round Table,* he and his friend Mr Hunt more particularly delight to associate.'

We should not have condescended to notice the senseless and wicked sophistry of this writer, or to point out to the contempt of the reader his 'didactic forms' and 'logical diagrams' [the reviewer had taken objection to Hazlitt's style] had we not considered him as one of the representatives of a class of men by whom literature is more than at any former period disgraced, who are labouring to effect their mischievous purposes *non vi sed saepe cadendo;* and therefore conceived that it might not be unprofitable to show how very small a portion of talent and literature was necessary for carrying on the trade of sedition. The few specimens which we have selected of his ethics and his criticism are more than sufficient to prove that Mr Hazlitt's knowledge of Shakespeare and the English language are on a par with the purity of his morals and the depth of his understanding.

This was the blow which, coming with a force behind it which our differently organized modern literary society finds hard to credit,[1] laid low, in Hazlitt's view, the expectations just raising themselves on his new-found reputation.

1. 'Taylor and Hessey told me that they had sold nearly two editions of the *Characters of Shakespear's Plays* in about three months, but that after the *Quarterly Review* of them came out, they never sold another copy. – *On Living to One's Self* (1821). The substantial accuracy of this statement has been questioned, but in view of other evidence which we possess of the power of the *Quarterly* during the post-Waterloo reaction we do not know why it should have been. When Southey, reviewing the *Essays of*

II

It is high time, however, that we gave some attention to the magazine which had definitely set itself to better the *Quarterly's* example. *Blackwood's* had made its start early in the year 1817, and was about to be abandoned with its sixth number when its proprietor made the acquaintance of two young men about the town of Edinburgh, John Wilson and John Gibson Lockhart. Much has been made of the youth of Mr Blackwood's young men : they were, at the time they joined him, in their thirty-third and twenty-fourth years respectively. Mr Blackwood's former Editors went over to Constable, starting in August a new series of an old magazine under the title of the *Edinburgh Magazine*; while Wilson and Lockhart settled down to the production of Mr Blackwood's celebrated seventh number, that for October.

With the merely local excitement caused by Mr Blackwood's young men we need not concern ourselves : the 'Chaldee Manuscript' is of interest to us only incidentally as declaring the feud now entered upon between the new editors and the old. But the number contained also Wilson's article on Coleridge (about which we found him consulting Crabb Robinson) and Lockhart's 'On the Cockney School of Poetry No. I'. The former is merely personal to the writer : it is the latter article which indicates a method :

> Mr Hunt is not disqualified by his ignorance and vulgarity alone, for being the founder of a respectable sect in poetry. He labours under the burden of a sin more deadly than either of these. The two great elements of all dignified poetry, re-

Elia, remarked that it was a book 'which wants only a sounder religious feeling to be as delightful as it is original', we find Crabb Robinson writing to Dorothy Wordsworth (31 October 1823): 'Stewart Rose says that the sale of his *Letters from Italy* was stopped at once on account of a hint in the Quarterly that there were some *improprieties* in the book, and I have no doubt that Southey has utterly ruined the sale of Elia, and perhaps the popularity of Lamb for ever as a writer, by his article'.

ligious feeling and patriotic feeling, have no place in his mind.
... The poetry of Mr Hunt is such as might be expected from
the personal character and habits of its author. ... His poetry
is that of a man who has kept company with kept-mistresses.
He talks indelicately like a tea-sipping milliner girl. Some
excuse for him there might have been, had he been hurried
away by imagination or passion. But with him indecency is a
disease, and he speaks unclean things from perfect inanition.
The very concubine of so impure a wretch as Leigh Hunt
would be to be pitied, but alas! for the wife of such a husband! For him there is no charm in simple seduction; and he
gloats over it only when accompanied with adultery and
incest.

This is but carrying one step further the method of the
Quarterly, which we have already seen applied by that review
to Hunt, just before the coming into office of Mr Blackwood's
young men.

The ostensible cause of the moral indignation was of course
'Rimini'; and it was on this account that Hazlitt came into the
tail of the article:

The very culpable manner in which his chief poem was reviewed in the *Edinburgh Review* (we believe it is no secret, at
his own impatient and feverish request, by his partner in the
Round Table) was matter of concern to more readers than
ourselves. ... Mr Jeffrey does ill when he delegates his important functions into such hands as those of Mr Hazlitt. It
was chiefly in consequence of that gentleman's allowing Leigh
Hunt to pass unpunished through a scene of slaughter which
his execution might so highly have graced, that we came to
the resolution of laying before our readers a series of essays on
the Cockney School – of which here terminates the first.

Hunt contemplated proceedings, but, probably on account of his
financial embarrassment, he abandoned these, and inserted in-

stead a formal and dignified notice in the *Examiner*. At the same time we find him writing to Jeffrey : 'I trouble you with this, to say, that since my last I have been made acquainted with the atrocious nonsense written about me in *Blackwood's Magazine*, and that nothing can be falser than what is said respecting my having asked and pestered Mr Hazlitt to write an article upon my poem in the *Edinburgh Review*. I never breathed a syllable to him on the subject, as anybody who knows me would say for me at once, for I am reckoned, if anything, somewhat over fastidious and fantastic on such matters.'

Hazlitt's name, introduced thus early into Mr Blackwood's pages, did not make its reappearance there – and this notwithstanding that the burlesque vendetta against Hunt was carried on from number to number without intermission – until Patmore procured the insertion of his favourable reports of the first lectures in February. In the meantime Hazlitt had been praised in Constable's *Edinburgh Magazine* for November (in an article which took occasion to vindicate Hunt from the aspersions cast upon him in a 'contemporary work'), and in December he complied with the overtures of the editors and contributed the first of a series of papers to that magazine. Whether this was the circumstance which caused the change of *Blackwood's* tone towards him, or whether Wilson was nursing all the time the information derived from the period of his own residence in the Lakes, and waiting only to divulge it for encouragement such as was provided by the *Quarterly* in June, we shall probably never know. A combination of the two hypotheses would appear probable; in conjunction with which may be taken the possibility that Blackwood had thoughts of handling the Scottish end of the published *Lectures* as he afterwards handled (without known prejudice to his morals) *Table Talk*. If some such reason for restraint were removed with the March number, this would account for the suddenness of the appearance in that month of 'pimpled Hazlitt' in Mr Blackwood's more jocular pages, while the body of the magazine was still devoting space to the respectful consideration of his lectures. As for the belated insertion in June of a contributed article (from whose hand we know not) seriously appraising the merits of Hazlitt and Jeffrey, 'at present the two most eminent speculators on literary topics', it is hard to know to what freak of editorial inconsequence or revived commercial prudence to attribute it. For in the following month (the *Quarterly* on Hazlitt having appeared in the interval) the magazine makes no secret of the single-mindedness of its intentions. Leigh Hunt, we are told, is finished with. 'The pages of the *Edinburgh Review*, we are confident, are henceforth shut against him. One wicked Cockney will not again be permitted to praise another in that journal, which, up to the moment when incest and adultery were defended in its pages had, however openly at war with religion, kept at least upon decent terms with the cause of morality. It was indeed a fatal day for Mr Jeffrey, when he degraded both himself and his original co-adjutors, by taking into pay such an unprincipled blunderer as Hazlitt. He is not a coadjutor, he is an accomplice. The day is perhaps not far distant, when the Charlatan shall be stripped to the naked skin, and made to swallow his own vile prescriptions.'

Thus unequivocally heralded, so far as Hazlitt was concerned, *Blackwood's* for August made its appearance. It is a number that has been often turned to for the sake of Keats. While Lockhart dealt with the 'starved apothecary', Wilson relieved himself in regard to Hazlitt. We turn over a few pages from the fourth article of 'The Cockney School', and come to 'Hazlitt Cross-Questioned':

Mr Editor. — In the course of your practice as a critical sportsman, you have already had the merit of discovering, winging, and bagging some new kinds of game. Upon one of these, your additions to the sphere of amusement, I beg leave heartily to congratulate you. I mean that wild, black-bill Hazlitt.

You do not, I perceive, know what a paltry creature this is, otherwise you would either have said more or less about him than you have done. ... He is a mere quack, Mr Editor, and a mere bookmaker; one of the sort that lounge in third-rate bookshops, and write third-rate books.

There follow, presented with a tremendous appearance of formidability, eight queries:

I. Mr William Hazlitt, ex-painter, theatrical critic, review, essay and lecture manufacturer, London, Did you, or did you not, in the course of your late Lectures on Poetry, &c., infamously vituperate and sneer at the character of Mr Wordsworth[1] – I mean his personal character; his genius even you dare not deny. II. Is it, or is it not, true that you owe all your ideas about poetry or criticism to gross misconceptions of the meaning of his conversation; and that you once owed your personal safety, perhaps existence, to the humane and firm interference of that virtuous man, who rescued you from the hands of an indignant peasantry whose ideas of purity you, a cockney visitor, had dared to outrage?

Of the remaining queries, a selection will suffice:

In an essay of yours on the Ignorance of the Learned, do not you congratulate yourself, and the rest of your Cockney crew, on never having received any education?

Do not you, who cannot repeat the Greek alphabet, nay, who know not of how many letters it is formed, pretend to give an opinion of the literary character of Professor Porson?

Do you know what is English, or what is not English, any more than you know that Latin is not Greek?

Did you not insinuate, in an essay on Shakespeare in the *Examiner,* that Desdemona was a lewd woman, and after that dare to publish a book on Shakespeare?

Do you know the Latin for a goose?

---

1. One of the humours of this strange magazine is that Wilson himself *did,* both before and after this date, 'infamously vituperate' the character of Wordsworth. See Crabb Robinson's entries of 31 December 1817, and 31 October 1821; and, better still, the pages of the magazine in question.

The article concluded, 'As soon as Mr Hazlitt answers these eight simple questions, other eight of a more complex nature, and worded more gravely, await his attention', and it came from 'An Old Friend With a New Face, Greenwich'.

The interest of what, if it were not for Keats, might be termed Mr Blackwood's Hazlitt number, was completed by two other articles. The first was on 'Shakespeare's Sonnets', and was by way of being a notice of the *Characters of Shakespear's Plays.* 'To him,' [Hazlitt] we read, 'truth and falsehood are indifferent. He cannot write one syllable on any subject, unless he has an opinion before him, and then he very magnanimously and intellectually contradicts that opinion. He stands with his back turned on the whole writing world, and need not therefore be surprised to get an occasional kick or two.' The other was a review of the recently published 'Works' of Charles Lamb, who was, to these writers (for some reason best known to themselves) 'a man of virtue, and, we doubt not, a man of religion'. 'Once, and once only, he alludes to Hunt, in some very beautiful verses, addressed to the child of that person when in prison with his unhappy father; but to "pimpled Hazlitt", notwithstanding his "coxcomb lectures" on Poetry and Shakespeare, he does not condescend to say one syllable.' This might have been the occasion, had Lamb thought it worthy, of an earlier 'Letter to Southey'.

As for Hazlitt, he may or may not have been surprised by his 'kick or two'; but what is certain is that his 'Old Friend' was never heard of again with his promised further questions.

III

In June, *The Yellow Dwarf* having finished its career, his books being out, and having a number of commissions to execute, he had gone down to Winterslow. This was, so far as we know, his first return since he had left there in 1812. He had come to a sort of period, his work was to undergo a change, and to take a new start. There is something entirely suitable that he should be at Winterslow, the scene of *On Living to One's-Self,* at the

moment when there burst on his head all the accumulated retri-
butory storm we have been witnessing. He had taken notice of
the *Quarterly's* attack by writing for the *Examiner* of 15 June a
character-sketch, *The Editor of the Quarterly Review*. It is of
this first draft of the *Letter to Gifford* that we find Leigh Hunt
writing to Shelley in Italy: 'Hazlitt has written a masterly
character of Gifford, much more coolly done than these things
of his in general'.

He had returned, not to the cottage – that, we are given to
understand, along with his wife's other properties, had been
converted into an annuity by her brother at the time of the removal to London – but to the coaching inn, the Hut (now the
Pheasant), a mile out of the village on the London road. It is
here that we find him in a letter of August:

Hazlitt to Macvey Napier
Winterslow Hut, near Salisbury.
August 26, 1818.

My Dear Sir, – I am sorry to be obliged, from want of health
and a number of other engagements, which I am little able to
perform, to decline the flattering offer you make me. I have
got to write, between this and the end of October, an octavo
volume or a set of lectures on the Comic Drama of this country for the Surrey Institution, which I am anxious not to slur
over, and it will be as much as I can do to get it ready in time.
I am also afraid that I should not be able to do the article in
question, or yourself, justice, for I am not only without books,
but without knowledge of what books are necessary to be consulted on the subject. To get up an article in a Review on any
subject of general literature is quite as much as I can do without exposing myself. The object of an Encyclopædia is, I take
it, to condense and combine all the facts relating to a subject,
and all the theories of any consequence already known or advanced. Now, where the business of such a work ends, is just
where I begin, that is, I might perhaps throw in an idle speculation or two of my own, not contained in former accounts of

the subject, and which would have very little pretensions to rank as scientific. I know something about Congreve, but nothing at all of Aristophanes, and yet I conceive that the writer of an article on the *Drama* ought to be as well acquainted with the one as the other. If you should see Mr Constable, will you tell him that I am writing *nonsense* for him as fast as I can?

I remain, Dear Sir,

Your very respectful and obliged humble servant,

W. HAZLITT.

The subject of the Drama, which Hazlitt here declined, was offered to Sir Walter Scott, who wrote the article under that head in the third volume of the Supplement.

The 'nonsense' which Hazlitt wrote at this date for Constable comprised the earliest of his fully mature and characteristic essays, *On the Ignorance of the Learned,* which, making its appearance in the *Edinburgh Magazine* for July, accounted in part for the outburst of *Blackwood's.* It further comprised his papers *On Fashion, On Nicknames,* and *On Taste,* which came out in ensuing numbers. In the second of these he said : 'Any one who is without character himself may make himself master of the reputation of another by the application of a nickname, as, if you do not mind soiling your fingers, you may always throw dirt on another. No matter how undeserved the imputation, it will stick; for, though it is sport to the bye-standers to see you bespattered, they will not stop to see you wipe out the stains.' We may know from this that *Blackwood's* for August had now reached him. He did not address himself more directly to the subject, for he had already sent to the Editors of the *Edinburgh Magazine* a categorical reply to each of the eight queries of his cross-questioner.[1] Having done this, he put the *Comic Writers*

1. This reply (for reasons, probably, of expedience) was not published, and some extracts from it were given for the first time by Mr Charles Whibley in *Blackwood's Magazine* for September 1918. The MS. has since been published (*A Reply to Z,* First Edition Club, 1923). Mr Whibley's introduction must be regarded with caution.

on one side, came up to town, and instituted proceedings for libel.

On 20 September there is a letter from Jeffrey: 'I have just received your letter, and shall willingly hold myself retained as your counsel'. On the 21st, Keats, just back from his Scotch tour, writes to Dilke in the country: 'I suppose you will have heard that Hazlitt has on foot a prosecution against Blackwood. I dined with him a few days since at Hessey's – there was not a word said about it, though I understand he is excessively vexed.' *The Times* of the same date contains, in a prominent position, the following: 'Mr Hazlitt has directed a prosecution against the publishers of *Blackwood's Edinburgh Magazine,* for an alleged libel upon him in the last number. It is a book filled with private slander.'

Murray had taken over a share in the Magazine.[1] On the blowing over of the Hunt affair, at which time he held the position merely of friend and mentor, he had written to Blackwood: 'I cannot congratulate you on your victory. ... I will venture my existence that you are injuring your character in the opinion of every one whose good opinion is worth having. I cannot perceive your object in literally running amuck at every one; and I would not undergo your feelings for any worldly advantage.' After the appearance of the August number he writes: 'I have delayed writing for no other reason than that I was desirous of gathering from all quarters the opinion respecting our magazine, and you will believe how great my own regret is at finding the clamour against its personality almost universal. ... My hands are withered by it. I cannot offer the work without encountering the dread of reproachful refusal; and as to obtaining contributions from men of character, I might as soon ask them to let me stab them in their backs.' He requests that some change shall be made, or his name removed from the title-page. And this, it must be remembered, was from the publisher of the *Quarterly*.

1. A general reference may be given for the remainder of the section to the annals of the three publishing houses concerned (see Appendix I).

Mr Blackwood begins in high spirits. Enclosing, on 22 September, a communication received, he says: 'I suppose this fellow merely means to make a little bluster, and try if he can pick up a little money. There is nothing whatever actionable in the paper. ... The article on Hazlitt, which will commence next number, will be a most powerful one, and this business will not deprive it of any of its edge.' Three days later there is a trifle more concern in his tone: 'What are people saying about that fellow Hazlitt attempting to prosecute? There was a rascally paragraph in *The Times* of Friday last mentioning the prosecution, and saying the magazine was a work filled with private slander. My friends laugh at the idea of his prosecution.' In the meantime Mr Murray's strictures have begun to arrive, and he hastens to add: 'I perfectly agree with you in all you say about personality in expression. I have always been doing as much in this way as I can, and to-day I communicated to my friends what you say on the subject.' A few days later: 'Mr W[ilson] has called just now, and I have the happiness of enclosing you a most admirable letter which they have written this morning, and which, in fact, leaves me nothing almost to say'.

The admirable letter from Wilson and Lockhart (printed at length in Mrs Oliphant's book) cannot be here altogether passed over. They express much regret to Mr Murray, they are willing to take his opinion on the matter as decisive, they admit 'that something out of the common order has been done, and that something of an outcry does exist', and are only inclined to question whether that outcry has not been exaggerated. 'On this part of the subject,' goes on the former, 'allow me to remark that, with the exception of this last article on Hazlitt, the articles on the Cockney School are little if at all more severe than those in the *Quarterly Review,* and that they give more offence to the objects of their severity only on account of their superior keenness – above all, that happy name which you and all the reviews are now borrowing, the Cockney School. Hazlitt and Hunt conceived that they could crush an infant work, and knew that they were powerless against the *Quarterly*. Therefore against us did they pour their hottest phials.[1] Give yourself no uneasiness about this, however, as if the action is brought at all, it will be brought here. But do not condescend for a moment to think of giving Hazlitt either answer or satisfaction of any kind. Let him fret on; in the end he will do nothing.' Mr Murray replied: 'I will do anything if you will only be good, and keep the peace. ... Best compliments to Mr Wilson and Mr Lockhart.'

On 6 October Mr Blackwood writes: 'I have this instant received Hazlitt's summons for his action in the Court of Session, in which he claims £2,000 for damages! ... The matter sits very lightly upon me and our friends.' But a few days later he agrees that 'It will save a great deal of trouble and botheration if Hazlitt gives up his action, and I think there is every probability of his doing so. He never would have thought of it had he not been urged on by Constable, who must be at the whole expense if it proceeds. Our friends are to speak to Mr Scott, to tell C. strongly that he must give up this system of urging on actions, else it will be worse for him.' There is no evidence for supposing that Constable had anything to do with the action, nor has the next disturbance to Mr Blackwood's peace been placed successfully at his rival's door.[2] This was the pamphlet 'Hypocrisy Unveiled, and Calumny Detected: in a Review of *Blackwood's Magazine*', which made its appearance in the middle of October, and took what the modern world may agree to consider a sufficiently dispassionate view of this magazine's early activities. 'All the venom,' this writer says, 'which these malicious creatures could generate or collect has been spitefully thrown upon Mr

1. Hunt, as any one may satisfy himself who will take the trouble, had made no allusion to *Blackwood's* until he was attacked, and had then contented himself with a formal repudiation of its charges. Hazlitt's earliest public recognition of the magazine's existence was the passage in *On Nicknames* which we have quoted.

2. The pamphlet has been variously but not, so far as I am aware, decisively attributed. A copy in the British Museum, formerly in the possession of Lord Cockburn, bears the following MS. note: 'I have been told, on something like good authority, that this most efficacious castigation was the work of two excellent persons, who are now Professors in two Universities'.

Jeffrey, Mr Playfair, Mr Brougham, Mr Hazlitt, Mr Napier, Mr [Lord] Murray and others who have been guilty of writing for the *Edinburgh Review*, the *Encyclopædia Britannica*, or the *Edinburgh Magazine*.'

The libeller of Mr HAZLITT avows himself to be an *old friend* with a *new face*, – a face which certainly, whatever features it may have at one time displayed, exhibits only those of a demon. We pretend not to know what Mr Hazlitt is as a man, but we know that this vilifier of Mr Hazlitt cannot be a good one. The facts which he invidiously recals and publishes, whether true or not, are facts which he must have come to the knowledge of under circumstances that either imposed secrecy or implied trust and confidence. The attack on Mr Hazlitt comes with a worse grace from these persons, inasmuch as they praised him warmly in the outset, holding him up as the first poetical critic of the day, and afterwards devoting an article to a parallel between him and Mr Jeffrey; but the secret of all is, that Mr Hazlitt furnished several very able articles to the *Scots* or *Edinburgh Magazine;* – articles which display more original thinking than all that have yet appeared in Blackwood's work. ... Hazlitt is an abomination in their sight because he is rising into consequence.

A pair of challenges to mortal combat were promptly delivered, through his publisher, to the author of this pamphlet – which was just what he wanted for an appendix to his further editions: so that in future, with the names of John Wilson and John Gibson Lockhart duly set out there, the Veiled Editorship of *Blackwood's Magazine* was not quite the mystery it had formerly been.

Mr Murray was much incensed: 'I really can recollect no parallel to the palpable absurdity of your two friends. If they had planned the most complete triumph to their adversaries, nothing could have been so successfully effective. They have actually given up their names, as the authors of the offences

charged upon them, by implication only, in the pamphlet. ...
The means thus put into the hands of Hunt, Hazlitt, &c., are
enormous, and they will now turn the tables upon them.' The
correspondence, chiefly concerned with the merits of the magazine as chastened by Murray, proceeds throughout November.
At the end of that month, there is a sharp return to the business
which concerns us. Murray writes to Blackwood: 'Your letter
has occupied my whole morning. Nothing can be worse than
your inattention to so important a matter. Even at this late
period you omit to send me any one document on which counsel
can form an opinion. What is the accusation? What can you
prove? How you could let it fall in this manner at your door, I
cannot conceive. ... I have had a long consultation with Mr
Turner, and I have sent after, and searched myself after, the
works which the fellow has written. Mr Turner will write tonight. To neglect such a thing as this when three-fourths of the
talent of the Bar are in hostility to you, and when any jury will
be prejudiced against you, is very reprehensible. The magazine
is very far superior to the former one, and is liked by every one
who has seen it.'

In December we learn that Mr Sharon Turner is 'in regular
negotiation with Mr Patmore (Hazlitt's friend)', and in active
correspondence with Blackwood. On the 16th we learn from the
latter the result of these negotiations: 'I have had two letters
from Mr Patmore, informing me that Mr Hazlitt was to drop
the prosecution. His agent has since applied to mine offering to
do this, if the expenses and a small sum for some charity were
paid. My agent told him he would certainly advise any client of
his to get out of court, but that he would never advise me to pay
anything to be made a talk of, as a sum for charity would be.
He would advise me, he said, to pay the expenses and a trifle to
Hazlitt himself privately. Hazlitt's agent agreed to this.' We
do not know what settlement Hazlitt's Edinburgh solicitor
agreed to, since the correspondence here fails us. It was not until
the first week of February, however, that the *Scotsman* announced: 'Mr Hazlitt's action against the Publishers of *Black*-

wood's Magazine has been withdrawn, they having agreed to pay him a certain sum as damages, and all expenses.' This intimation was copied into both *The Times* and the *Examiner*.

The effect of Hazlitt's action is to be clearly read in some months of agitated correspondence, and in the pages of the Magazine itself. 'The late Hot Weather', and 'Is the *Edinburgh Review* a Religious and Patriotic Work?' are Mr Blackwood's most dangerous matter for several months to come. That the 'most powerful article' on Hazlitt, due to appear in the October number, never in fact did appear, has been already stated. No prominent mention of his name, indeed, was made again in *Blackwood's Magazine* until March 1822, by which date Wilson was Professor of Moral Philosophy in the University of Edinburgh and Hazlitt was in that city for the purpose of his divorce.

IV

In his reply (which was not published) to the questions of his cross-questioner, in which he had been accused of lounging in third-rate bookshops, Hazlitt had said : 'I sometimes, indeed, lounge away my time in the Fives Court and play rackets instead of answering your questions'. It is here that we find him, an exact month after the institution of the proceedings which we have followed to their end – a month in which he may or may not have returned to Winterslow. On 22 October Keats, snatching one of his brief respites in this autumn from the nursing of his brother Tom, 'walked with Hazlitt as far as Covent Garden : he was going to play Rackets'.

Wherever Hazlitt had spent the month, he had completed his lectures on the Comic Writers. Their delivery began on the first Tuesday in November, at the Surrey Institution. With Keats prevented from attending, and with Crabb Robinson fallen largely into indifference, we hear less of them than of the previous course. It would be too much, however, to expect of the diarist complete abstention :

'10 November: — I hurried to the Surrey Institution to hear Hazlitt's second lecture on the Comic Writers of England. Shakespeare was part of the subject, but the lecture was not one of the best. It was but a dull performance. He raised a tumult by abusing Gifford, which a few hissed at and many applauded. But the best thing he did was reading a glorious passage from Ben Jonson's Alchemist in which the Alchemist riots in imagination on the wealth he is about to enjoy.' The passage in answer to the *Quarterly's* review of the *English Poets,* which appeared at this moment, does not figure in the printed lecture, and Hazlitt no doubt transferred it to the *Letter to Gifford.* The reviewer had said: 'Mr Hazlitt seems to have bound himself like Hannibal to wage everlasting war, not indeed against Rome, but against accurate reasoning, just observation, and precise, or even intelligible, language.'

'17 November: — I heard a lecture from Hazlitt at the Surrey Institution. It was not good. He is sinking fast as a lecturer.'

'8 December: — At 7 I went to Hazlitt's lecture. He spoke of Congreve, Wycherley, Vanbrugh, and Farquhar, making distinctions which may be true, but of which the evidence was not apparent, and betraying illaudable feelings which he uttered in offensive epigrams. He seems to delight in gently touching the sore points of the saints — being always on the brink of obscenity and palpably recommending works of the most licentious character. This lecture was after all but dull, and his audience grows thin.'

'15 December: — Called on Gurney and accompanied the Miss G.'s to Hazlitt's lecture. It was on the Essayists, Addison and Steele, and was for the greater part a repetition of the Round Table.'

If Keats had been able to attend, and if Crabb Robinson had been able to stay away, we should have had wiser and warmer words on the *Comic Writers.* Early in December Keats's brother Tom died, and soon after, having occasion to be in the neighbourhood of York Street, he 'called on Hazlitt'. He took away with him the Lectures, either in manuscript or in proof; for in

his last journal-letter of the year for America we find him tran-
scribing a long passage in illustration of their author's 'fiery
laconicism'. The transcription comes between those of his own
'Fancy' and 'Bards of Passion and of Mirth', and not for the
first or the last time Hazlitt's prose and Keats's verse go well in
a letter together.

V

On the first Tuesday of 1819 the Lectures on the Comic Writers
came to an end, and Hazlitt had an opportunity to look round
him. His reputation as a critic, he read in the *Morning Chronicle*
on the conclusion of the course, 'stood already high with the
public; but we are mistaken if these Lectures will not add to it.
He displayed the same boldness and originality of thinking; the
same critical acuteness, eloquence, and felicity of expression for
which his Lectures on our Poets were so eminently distinguished.
From the character which Mr Hazlitt has by universal assent
acquired, of being one of the ablest and most eloquent critics of
our nation (we may say of any nation), much was of course to
be expected from the employment of his talents on a branch of
literature in which the genius of our countrymen shines perhaps
with more distinguished lustre than in any other.' Hazlitt was
not more averse than other men to having pleasant things said
of him, at any time; but his comment on the universality of the
assent was to sit down and write *A Letter to William Gifford,
Esq., From William Hazlitt, Esq.* The work, brought out by
Miller of Burlington Arcade (no doubt at its author's expense)
was reviewed by Hunt in the *Examiner* of the 7th. But its most
delighted adherent was Keats: writing on the 12th of the month
to America, he quotes and cannot stop quoting. 'The force and
innate power with which it yeasts and works itself up – the
feeling for the costume of society, is in a style of genius. He hath
a demon, as he himself says of Lord Byron.' Concluding this
letter with a fanciful profession of literary faith, Keats, we find,
'doth not admire Sheil's play, Leigh Hunt, Tom Moore, Bob
Southey, and Mr Rogers: and does admire Wm. Hazlitt'. There

can be no doubt that the *Letter to Gifford* set the seal on that admiration.

When Hazlitt has a sword in one hand we generally find him with a racket in the other, and it was in the midst of the composition of the *Letter to Gifford* that he wrote for the *Examiner* (one of only two contributions in the year) on the *Death of Cavanagh*:

It may be said that there are things of more importance than striking a ball against a wall – there are things indeed which make more noise and do as little good, such as making war and peace, making speeches and answering them, making verses and blotting them; making money and throwing it away. But the game of fives is what no one despises who has ever played at it. It is the finest exercise for the body, and the best relaxation for the mind. The Roman poet said that 'Care mounted behind the horseman and stuck to his skirts'. But this remark would not have applied to the fives-player. He who takes to playing at fives is twice young. He feels neither the past nor future 'in the instant'. Debts, taxes, 'domestic treason, foreign levy, nothing can touch him further'. He has no other wish, no other thought, from the moment the game begins, but that of striking the ball, of placing it, of *making* it! This Cavanagh was sure to do. His eye was certain, his hand fatal, his presence of mind complete. He could do what he pleased, and he always knew exactly what to do. He saw the whole game, and played it; took instant advantage of his adversary's weakness, and recovered balls, as if by a miracle and from sudden thought, that every one gave for lost. He had equal power and skill, quickness, and judgement. He could either out-wit his antagonist by finesse, or beat him by main strength. Sometimes, when he seemed preparing to send the ball with the full swing of his arm, he would by a slight turn of his wrist drop it within an inch of the line. In general, the ball came from his hand, as if from a racket, in a straight horizontal line; so that it was in vain to attempt to overtake

or stop it. As it was said of a great orator that he never was
at a loss for a word, and for the properest word, so Cavanagh
always could tell the degree of force necessary to be given to
a ball, and the precise direction in which it should be sent. He
did his work with the greatest ease; never took more pains
than was necessary; and while others were fagging themselves
to death, was as cool and collected as if he had just entered the
court. His style of play was as remarkable as his execution. He
had no affectation, no trifling. He did not throw away the
game to show off an attitude, or try an experiment. ... Cobbett and Junius together would have made a Cavanagh. He
was the best *up-hill* player in the world; even when his adversary was fourteen, he would play on the same or better,
and as he never flung away the game through carelessness and
conceit, he never gave it up through laziness or want of heart.

Hazlitt's second non-apologetic activity for the year was the
collection of his *Political Essays,* undertaken at the instance of
the Radical bookseller William Hone. On 3 February there is a
letter from the latter: 'I dined at John Hunt's on Sunday, with
Mr Hazlitt for whose work on the prospectus I have just concluded a bargain, and given Mr Creery [*sic*] this morning copy
to begin with. Hazlitt is a De Foeite.' The acquaintance here
indicated is evidently a new one, and the prospectus to be supplied by Hazlitt (which may have been written, but which we
do not possess) was for Hone's History of Parody, which was
never completed. Hone was at this time at the height of his
prolific partnership with George Cruikshank in the production
of political squibs, and two years before had emerged with
triumph from his celebrated trials at the hands of the Government. The acquaintance now begun, with both Hone and Cruikshank, continued without interruption until Hazlitt's death.
Political Essays, published by Hone, printed by another stout
Radical McCreery, and dedicated to John Hunt, 'the tried,
steady, zealous, and conscientious advocate of the liberty of his
country', did not make its appearance till August, but the book

was announced, and the preface doubtless written, in the early months of the year.

With the preface to this book Hazlitt closed a chapter, but he closed it, in a manner characteristic of himself, not by huddling it out of sight, but by completing it and placing it on record. Henceforward he was to do no more journalism avowedly political; his connection with the daily and weekly organs of the Press was severed, and was never in the same spirit of henchmanship to be resumed. In 1819, the culminating year of the post-Waterloo home policy, as has since been recognized, Hazlitt's political pen was silent; but he was justified in thinking it had done enough. His record, from the controversy with Vetus, through his illustrations of the parts played by the poets, to his essays in the *Yellow Dwarf,* he was not ashamed of, and was willing to have investigated. 'I am no politician,' he wrote, in his preface, 'and still less of a party-man; but I have a hatred of tyranny, and a contempt for its tools, and this feeling I have expressed as often and as strongly as I could. ... I deny that liberty and slavery are convertible terms, that right and wrong, truth and falsehood, plenty and famine, the comforts or wretchedness of a people, are matters of perfect indifference. That is all I know of the matter; but on these points I am likely to remain incorrigible.'

VI

These, then, were the activities of the early part of the year, and Hazlitt, for the first and last time in his working life, was doing nothing for the newspapers and magazines. It would be pleasant to think that for this length of time Mr Blackwood's self-imposed penalty was doing its part in keeping him. There were in addition the proceeds of the *Lectures on the English Comic Writers,* published in April, the third of Hazlitt's works to be undertaken by Taylor and Hessey. Leigh Hunt, making it the subject of the *Examiner's* Literary Notice on 18 April, wrote: 'The reader will find in this book the usual characteristics of Mr Hazlitt's criticism – the same knowledge of human nature, the same contempt of prudery and self-love in displaying it, the same readiness to be pleased with what is reconciling and kind, the same metaphysical nicety, the same apparent love of paradox in his zeal to see fair play, and the same abrupt and powerful style, which like an oak-tree throws out its branches in short and pithy divisions, often terminating however in a profusion of poetical verdure.'

At the end of June or the beginning of July Hazlitt went down to Winterslow. We know this from the essay *On the Character of the Country People* which he sent to the *Examiner* of 18 July. 'If a stranger comes to live among country people,' we read, 'they have a bad opinion of him at first; and all he can do to overcome their dislike, only confirms them in it. ... Falstaff asks as a question not to be answered – "May I not take mine ease at mine inn?" But this was in Eastcheap. I cannot do so in the country; for while I am writing this, I hear a fellow disputing in the kitchen, whether a person ought to live (as he expresses it) by pen and ink; and the landlord the other day (in order, I suppose, the better to prepare himself for such controversies) asked me if I had any object in reading through all those books which I had brought with me, meaning a few odd volumes of old plays and novels.' If we were left to ourselves, we should have no hesitation in saying that the answer to the landlord's question, as regards the old plays at least, was to be found in the concluding series of lectures which Hazlitt had contracted to deliver in November – those on the Age of Elizabeth. But here we have to take into account the testimony of Procter, who in this summer published his *Dramatic Scenes*, a work which showed, in addition to a pleasing natural talent, a diligent study of the best Elizabethan models, and amounted, indeed, to a tribute to the contemporary influence of Lamb's *Specimens*. It was these two, the master and the pupil, to whom Hazlitt turned for guidance in approaching a period which, as we may find him confessing, was comparatively new ground to him. 'Hazlitt,' says Procter, 'spoke to Charles Lamb, and to myself, who were supposed by many to be well acquainted with those ancient writers. I lent him about a dozen volumes, comprehending the finest of the old plays; and he then went down to Winterslow Hut, in Wiltshire, and after a stay of six weeks came back to London, fully impregnated with the subject, with his thoughts fully made up upon it, and with all his lectures written. And he then appeared to comprehend the character and merits of the old writers more thoroughly than any other person, although he had so lately entered upon the subject.' We may find nothing to amend in this account save the term of six weeks.[1] It seems probable that Hazlitt was at Winterslow, more or less engaged upon this last course of his lectures, from early in July until late in September.

John Hunt, as we learn from a letter of Leigh's to Mary Shelley in March, had retired in the spring of this year with the younger members of his family to Somersetshire, leaving the conduct of the business side of the *Examiner* to his eldest son Henry. On 15 September he writes to Hazlitt: 'I take it for granted that you are at Winterslow Hut as Henry says you have left town, so I direct thither. You would gratify me much by coming over here. We have a bed at your service, a beautiful country to exercise in, and we would do our best to make you comfortable, not forgetting a total banishment of *veal* and *pork* from our table. Our beef and mutton are as good as that in London. You can have my little parlour to write in, which is a snug place for the purpose, being hung round with prints after Raphael, Titian, Correggio, and Claude, and looking over a piece of grass into a fine orchard, through a latticed window. What more is needful for a tasteful Jacobin? that is, if he be not immoderate in his desires. Come and try how you like it.'

1. It is possible, however, that Procter's period is accurate, and that the volumes of 'old plays' which Hazlitt had with him in July were for the purpose of his introductions to Oxberry's *New English Drama* (1818-21). A few of these introductions were drawn upon by his son in amplifying the text of the third (1841) edition of the *Comic Writers*. The remainder have been reprinted by the present writer (*New Writings: Second Series*).

On a matter of a £50 bill requiring to be taken up, Hazlitt wrote to Leigh Hunt, who replied on the 22nd: 'Your letter dated Saturday I did not receive till yesterday; and to-day I saw Mr Procter. He tells me that he had written me a letter enclosing the bill, and intrusted it to a friend, who kept it in his pocket for three or four days; upon which he enclosed it in another to you, directed to Southampton Buildings. Shall I call there for it? or what else shall I do? all that I can do I will: and your belief of this gives me great refreshment on these rascally occasions, though no more than I desire. I am glad to hear that you have broken the neck of the Elizabethan poets, and wished you could have knocked Lord Burleigh on the head by the way, in good earnest. As to Winterslow, it is hopeless to me just now, who have a wife just ready to be brought to bed, and literary births of my own without end. But I thank you most heartily for asking me.' Hunt's literary births, of which there were afterwards to be so many, were at this time the *Pocket Book* and the *Indicator*: the former, in Keats' view, 'full of the most sickening stuff you can imagine'. The fact is, of course, that although there were good things in his *Indicator* (which he would have been better employed in putting into the *Examiner*), Leigh Hunt was declining.

It is evident, from the foregoing, that the invitation to Taunton was not accepted in this autumn, and shortly afterwards, with his lectures completed, we may assume that Hazlitt returned to London. On 25 September Keats, who had been out of town for a similar period, and whose own financial position was giving him anxiety from a variety of causes which we need not go into, writes from Winchester to his friend Brown at Hampstead: 'I shall apply to Hazlitt, who knows the market as well as any one, for something to bring me in a few pounds as soon as possible'. This we may suppose he did during the fortnight in October which he spent with this end in view in lodgings at College Street, Westminster. But there was an influence stronger even than his regard for Hazlitt drawing Keats back to Hampstead. From there we find him, at the end of the month, writing to Severn that he is 'so very lax, unemploy'd, unmeridian'd, and objectless', that 'I even grudge indulging myself by going to Hazlitt's lecture'. We cannot positively assert that Keats did make the journey to attend any of this course, and, indeed, the state of his health may probably have precluded it. If he attended the first, he heard the justly celebrated 'general view' of the Age of Elizabeth.

We hear less of this course of lectures, delivered on Fridays throughout November and December, than of either of those which had preceded it. For one reason, Crabb Robinson did not attend it. The loan of books by Lamb and Procter was repaid at a high rate of interest. If Crabb Robinson did not attend, he is the means by which we know that the *Quarterly* (perhaps by accident) got in another blow which was well timed. The 'new' number, dated July, and published nearly six months afterwards by a custom which does not cease to surprise us, was read by the diarist on 11 December. 'A dull number,' he records, 'Hazlitt is scurvily treated, but it is mere retaliation, and what he merits.' What the *Letter to Gifford* merited, in the opinion of the diarist, was, as to one small part of it, the following. The work ostensibly under review was *Political Essays*:

At the close of another publication, in which he is more than commonly ridiculous, we are favoured with the writer's own opinion of himself, and he therein gravely informs the world that the object of his literary labours is the fame 'of a Pascal, a Leibnitz, or a Berkeley!' and plainly intimates that he expects to be classed with them after his death. There is something beyond all farce of caricature in this angry buffoon's self-satisfied assumption of a seat amongst these three great men, whom Religion, Genius, Philosophy, and Science raised almost above the nature of mortals – and this too, immediately after a more striking display than we remember to have seen elsewhere of Mr Hazlitt's peculiarities. We doubt whether a Dutch sign-painter would make his own apotheosis equally ludicrous even if he were to depict himself recumbent at the table of the Gods, with trunk hose, grasping a tobacco-pipe with one hand, and striving to purple his lips in nectar with the other.

Having got this slanderer of the human race in an attitude in which it is possible to smile at him, we willingly leave him there.

On 16 December Crabb Robinson 'went after nine to Lamb's. The party there: Hazlitt too. He and I exchanged a few words. I was the first to speak and he only answered me.' And on the 28th, our other sensitive recording instrument, Miss Mitford, writing to her admirer in the country, says: 'By the way, I never hear you talk of Hazlitt. Did you never read any of his works? Never read the *Round Table*? the *Characters of Shakespear's Plays*? the *Lectures on English Poetry*? or the *Lectures on the English Comic Writers*? The Quarterly Reviewers give him a bad character, but that merely regards politics, and politics ought not to weigh in works of general literature.'

VII

At the end of this year, to the best of our belief, Hazlitt terminated the tenancy of the house in Westminster which he had occupied for eight years.[1] Our latest view of him at this address is given by Procter: 'I went to visit him very often during his late *breakfasts* (when he drank tea of an astounding strength), not unfrequently also at the Fives Court, and at other persons' houses; and once I dined with him. This (an unparalleled occurrence) was in York Street [in 1819], when some friend had sent him a couple of Dorking fowls, of which he suddenly

---

1. We ought, perhaps, in view of the 'execution' of which we hear (*post,* page 321), to say that it was terminated for him. Hazlitt had concluded a somewhat lean year, and we shall learn in a moment that he was in want of 'a certain sum of money'. The failure of Leigh Hunt (who had received many favours from Bentham) to secure him an extension of tenure was possibly one among several causes which widened a breach between them from this date.

invited me to partake. I went, expecting the usual sort of
dinner; but it was limited solely to the fowls and bread. He
drank nothing but water, and there was nothing but water to
drink. He offered to send for some porter for me, but being out
of health at the time, I declined, and escaped soon after dinner
to a coffee-house, where I strengthened myself with a few.
glasses of wine.

'Do I mention this spare entertainment as a charge against
Hazlitt? Oh no, I do not; on the contrary, I was sure that the
matter had never entered into his mind. He drank water only,
and lived plainly, and not unreasonably assumed that what
sufficed for himself was sufficient for others. He had nothing
was parsimonious or mean in his character, and I believe
that he never thought of eating or drinking, except when
hunger or thirst reminded him of these wants. With the exception of a very rare dinner or supper with a friend or intimate,
his time was generally spent alone. After a late breakfast he took
his quire of foolscap paper and commenced writing (in a large
hand almost as large as text) his day's work. I never saw any
rough draft or copy. He wrote readily – not very swiftly, perhaps, but easily, as if he had made up his mind – the manuscript that I believe went to the printer. In his latter years he
dined generally at the Southampton Coffee-house, and was
much interested by the sayings of people whom he met there;
and would often repeat and comment on them when they served
to develope character.'

On two subjects, Hazlitt's methods of work, and his habits
of eating and drinking, we may feel that Patmore is a com-
petent authority. He says: 'When Hazlitt was regularly engaged on any work or article, he wrote at the rate of from ten
to fifteen octavo pages at a sitting; and never, or very rarely,
renewed the sitting on the same day, except when he was at
Winterslow – where, having no means of occupation or amusement in the evening part of the day, he used, I believe habitually, to write after his tea. And doubtless, one of his motives for
going there when he had any considerable work to get through,

was the knowledge that by that means alone he could persuade himself to work "double tides" ... He wrote rapidly, in a large hand, as clear as print, made very few corrections, and almost invariably wrote on an entire quire of foolscap; contriving to put into a page of his manuscript exactly the amount (upon an average) of an octavo page of print; so that he always knew exactly what progress he had made, at any given time, towards the desired goal to which he was travelling – namely, the end of his task. Unless what he was employed on was a review, he never had a book or a paper of any kind about him while he wrote.'

Again : 'For the last four or five years of life, Hazlitt never touched any other liquid but tea. During the previous four five years, he used to drink large quantities of cold water have frequently seen him take three or four quarts while sitting after supper – which was his favourite meal. Wine, and all fermented liquors, he had forsworn before I knew him; and he religiously kept to his resolution. *This,* he used to say, was the reason why Blackwood's people called him '"pimpled Hazlitt" – thus holding him up to the world as a dram-drinker ! "Had I really been a gin-drinker and a sot," I have heard him say, "they would have sworn I was a milk-sop".

'His breakfast and tea were frequently the only meals that Hazlitt took till late at night, when he usually ate a hearty supper of hot meat – either rumpsteak, poultry, or game – a partridge or a pheasant. This he invariably took at a tavern – his other meals (except his dinner sometimes) being as invariably taken at home.

'There were three or four houses only that he frequented; for he never entered the door of any one where his ways were not well known, or where there was any chance of his *bill* being asked for till he chose to offer payment of it. And when treated in a way that pleased him in the latter particular, he did not care what he paid. I have known him pay with cheerfulness accumulated sums of twenty or thirty pounds for suppers only or chiefly.

'The houses Hazlitt frequented were the Southampton Coffee-house, in Southampton Buildings, Chancery Lane; Munday's, in Maiden Lane, Covent Garden; and (for a short period) the Spring Garden Coffee-house. The first of these he has immortalized in one of the most amusing of his essays, *On Coffee-house Politicians*. Here, for several years, he used to hold a sort of evening levee, where, after a certain hour of night (and till a very *un*certain hour in the morning) he was always to be found, and always more or less ready to take part in that sort of desultory "talk" (the only thing really deserving the name of "conversation") in which he excelled every man I have ever met with.'

Procter, in his *Recollections* of 1830, to which reference has been made, brought together several memoranda in the hope of giving some idea of Hazlitt's conversation. We may take two or three of these here :

'He used to play at rackets for five or six hours at a time; sometimes quarrelling with his adversary, but not bearing malice. He liked a stout antagonist. "That fellow," said he, speaking of one who showed himself disheartened, "will never do anything in the world; he never plays well, unless he is successful. If the chances go against him, he always misses the ball : he cries *Craven* !" – "That," said some one, "is French courage." – "I don't call it courage at all," said H., "and certainly not French courage. The French have fought well; they have endured, too, more than enough – without your present imputation. Did you ever fight a Frenchman?" – "No." – "Then, don't make up your mind yet to your theory : reduce it to practice, and see if it be bullet-proof." '

'Miscalculating his expenses, he once found himself at Stamford reduced almost to his last shilling. He set off to walk to Cambridge, but having a new pair of boots on they gave him acute pain. In this predicament, he tried at twenty different places to exchange them for a pair of shoes or slippers of any sort, but no one would accommodate him. He made this a charge against the English. "Though they would have got treble the value by exchanging," said he, "they would not do it, because it would have been useful to me." – "Perhaps", said some one jestingly, "they did not know that you came honestly by them." – "Ah! true," said H., "that did not strike me before. That shakes my theory in this respect, if it be true; but then, it corroborates another part of it; so the fact is valuable either way. There is always a want of liberality, either in their thoughts or actions." (This was merely humour.)

'When I first knew Charles Lamb, I ventured one evening to say something that I intended should pass for wit. "Ha! very well; very well, indeed!" said he, "Ben Jonson has said worse things" (I brightened up, but he went stammering on to the end of the sentence) "– and – and – and – *better*!" A pinch of snuff concluded the compliment, which put a stop to my wit for the evening. I related the thing to Hazlitt afterwards, who laughed. "Ay," said he, "you are never sure of him till he gets to the end. His jokes would be the sharpest things in the world, but they are blunted by his good-nature. He wants malice – which is a pity."

'I remember calling upon him to admire a striking passage which occurred some years ago in *Blackwood's Magazine* in favour of Napoleon. It was written by Mr Lockhart or Professor Wilson, I believe, and I read it aloud to Hazlitt. "G–d!" he exclaimed, "that's good – that's fine; I forgive 'em all they've said of *me*."

'Several persons were regretting that [Leigh Hunt] (who we all agreed, was a singularly kind-hearted, vivacious, and intelligent man) should be eternally bruiting one opinion, that was disagreeable to everybody. "'Tis like a rash," said Hazlitt, "and comes out every summer. Why doesn't he write a book (if he has anything to say) and get rid of his complaints at once?" (The conversation afterwards continued to run upon the same individual, and nothing could be more handsome or just than Hazlitt's eulogy upon him.)

'It has been supposed', concludes Procter, 'that Hazlitt was dogmatical and fond of controversy, and that he resented any opposition to his opinions. This is an error. He liked *discussion* – fair, free talk, upon subjects that interested him; but few men ever yielded more readily to argument, for few ever sought truth more sincerely. He had no overweening sense of his own superiority; indeed, as far as I could perceive, he was utterly without vanity. He was very candid, and would hear his own opinions canvassed with the utmost patience. In his conversation he was plain, amusing, convincing. There was nothing of the ambitious or florid style which is sometimes perceptible in his writings. He was rarely eloquent. Once or twice, when stung by some pertinacious controversialist, I have known him exhibit eloquent and impetuous declamation; but in general he used the most familiar phrases, and made truth, rather than triumph, the object of discussion. He enjoyed anecdotes illustrative of character, spoke pithily upon occasion, and, when in good spirits and good humour, was the most delightful gossip in the world!'

CHAPTER X

THE ESSAYIST

(1820–1)

*

I intend these Essays as studies of human nature; and as, in the prosecution of this design, I do not spare others, I see no reason why I should spare myself.

On Means and Ends.

I

IN January, promptly upon the completion of their delivery, the *Lectures on the Dramatic Literature of the Age of Elizabeth* were brought out by Warren, a publisher of whom we know little. Hazlitt had done, to adapt a phrase used by himself in a very much earlier connection, what he wanted in lecturing. What he wanted to do next is perfectly clear to us, and it is equally clear that all that was lacking was the invitation. He had been available as the author of *Table Talk* at any time since *The Ignorance of the Learned*. The *Edinburgh Magazine,* for which he had shown himself willing to lay himself out, had failed him, and during the year which had elapsed no new receptacle had opened itself for his work. It was now about to do so.

When John Scott left the *Champion,* in 1817, he went abroad and remained abroad for two years, collecting materials for his book on the *Manners and Scenery of the French Provinces, Switzerland, and Italy*. At the end of 1819 he returned, published his book, and immediately engaged himself in a new literary venture. Whether the project of a new and improved *London Magazine* was in its origin Scott's, or that of the publisher Robert Baldwin, I am not aware that we know; but in the absence of evidence I think we may assume it to have been Scott's. *Blackwood's,* in form more happily than in manner, had inaugurated a new phase in periodical literature, and the proposal to rival it from the metropolis with a magazine at once popular and responsible was an attractive one. The success which attended Scott's undoubted abilities, until they were cut short in their prime, is famous. In slightly differing degrees, he turned Lamb into Elia and made Hazlitt the author of *Table Talk*.

When we remember the circumstances of political difference which had attended their separation five years earlier, there is interest in the first evidence of Scott's and Hazlitt's new approach. This survives in a letter from the former to his publisher, of the first days of January. 'I am sorry to say', we read, that I cannot honestly tell you that Mr Hazlitt's manuscript is likely to suit us in the mag. It falls into all those errors which I know are his besetting ones, but which I hope to keep him clear of when he is directed to particular topics, such as the drama, etc., His talent is undoubted, and his wish to serve us, I believe, at present very sincere. Since I last saw you, the friend at whose house I met Hazlitt on Sunday has called upon me to make a sort of semi-authorized communication from the gentleman. The fact is, as you surmised, that Mr H. is in want of a certain sum of money, and he says that, this sum in his power, he would be very free in every respect, and would devote the whole power of his mind to the preparation of the dramatic [articles], or anything else we might suggest. If so, he would be a very valuable contributor. What the sum is I do not know, but I apprehend the terms he asked for the volume (of which I am ignorant) reach the mark. If I could have told you that the Essays, of which a specimen has been forwarded, would surely suit us, the difficulty probably would be small; but although very anxious to find it so, I would not act fairly by you were I to give this as my opinion. At the same time, I will engage for the gentleman, from what I know of his character, that he would be most ready to listen to suggestions, and to strain every nerve for us in return for a service. He is naturally grateful, and although an original, is an honest one. I have not spoken to him for several years until last Sunday, but I see that in a very short time I shall be able to influence him to proper subjects and to a proper manner of handling them – I mean *proper* in regard to the Magazine, as, generally speaking, I should have little claim to be his judge or guide. Would it therefore suit you to say to him that, with regard to the Essays, of which one has been sent, you beg leave to think a little farther over the matter, and claim the privilege of suggesting what may occur to you; but that on the general score of dramatic articles, and such other contributions as might hereafter be arranged between himself and you on mutual agreement, you have no objection to treat as for the volume *immediately*?' We may learn from this that negotiations by which Hazlitt should become the dramatic critic of the new magazine were already in train – (his opening article indeed, containing 'an account of all the actors we have ever seen or heard of', was in the first number) – but that, as the writer of *Table Talk*, he was to be placed on probation.

A little further light on Scott's view of Hazlitt, and of his idea of the editorial function in general, we may derive from his review of the *Age of Elizabeth* in the Magazine's second number: 'Whatever faults Mr Hazlitt may have as a writer, want of meaning is not one of them. He has always something particular, and in his view, important, to say, when he attempts to say anything. Whether he may be deemed wrong or right in his opinions, they will always be found "cogent to the matter" – connected with the essential qualities of his subject, the fruit of thought, impelled by earnestness, and animated by feeling. We should say, judging by his style, that the wear and tear of his mind must be very considerable, and more than most people could support, for he never seems to avail himself of anything conventional, or conveniently ready for use : the whole force of his intellect seems always fairly put into play to elicit his sentiments, whatever the topic may be; so that we have nothing at second-hand from his pen, and he derives little or no advantage from any of the current saws, maxims, or principles, as they are called, of an enlightened and highly polished state of society. It is astonishing how much – and, as some think, how needlessly – he increases his labour by adhering to this process. A smart contributor to our Magazine, for instance, might take up a popular, interesting subject – fit for our Miscellany, and calculated to improve and instruct our readers – and he might put it in a very pleasing and prominent point of view; and yet perhaps, through the whole ten or twelve pages, the able writer might never seriously have asked himself what he was really about, or called up positive conviction from its slumbers, or considered any one point of doubt with that earnest exertion of the faculty of examination, which he would apply to a question, demanded of him out of doors, whether, to get to a certain street, it was necessary to take the second or the third turning to the left?

'We say that a smart contributor *could* easily do this for us (we do not say that such things are done), – but we do not think that Mr Hazlitt could, were he to try. Nevertheless, we have heard it said, that he writes in the *Edinburgh Review*, which puzzles us a little! It does not, however, at all puzzle us, that he should be abused in the *Quarterly*. It is difficult, indeed, to conceive, that the same period of the world's age has produced both Mr Hazlitt and the Review last named! To call them each the antipodes of the other, would not convey a just idea of their excessive dissimilarity and opposition. ... Each of the parties has peculiar merits as well as faults, and we wish we could pick and choose properties from the two, for our own use. What we should most like to cull from the *Quarterly* is, we believe, its *sale*; what we should decline robbing Mr Hazlitt of are his *politics*. We do not think that we need have any scruple to mention these latter, though our present business is with a literary work, for the author himself does not scruple to introduce them everywhere, and on all occasions: – they come, like a mastiff, by his side, into all companies he frequents, – whether of old poets, or modern players; and "love me, love my *dog*" is his maxim. To this he sturdily adheres, in spite of any symptoms of confusion or alarm amongst silk stockings and muslin petticoats. As we happen to have neither ourselves, we are very well inclined, so far as our own tastes go, to put up with the creature, that we may enjoy the pleasure which the talents of its master are calculated to afford.'

Having derived, by means of this somewhat long extract, a portrait of the portraitist as well as of his subject, we may proceed to see how the partnership worked out in practice.

II

Hazlitt did not take his temporary return to dramatic criticism too seriously. A little later in the year he announced a principle: 'The Drama is a subject of which we could give a very entertaining account once a month, if there were no plays acted all the year. But, as some artists have said of Nature, "the Theatres put us out". ... We like to be a hundred miles off from the Acted Drama in London.' This principle he put into practice before he enunciated it. His second and third articles might both have been written, so far as we can see, on an experience of playgoing extending but a very few days into February; and certainly long before the end of that month he was well on his way to pay the visit to John Hunt in Somersetshire for which he had received an invitation in the previous autumn. He went on, I think we may say, to visit his parents, now settled at Crediton; and on the road back, as we know from the account of his professional activities rendered in the last month of the year, he wrote his April article. 'In April [i.e. in the April magazine] (being at Ilminster, a pretty town in the Vale of Taunton, and thence passing on to the Lamb at Hindon, a dreary spot), we proved at these two places, sitting in an armchair by a seacoal fire, very satisfactorily, and without fear of contradiction, – neither Mr Maturin, Mr Sheil, nor Mr Milman being present –

that no modern author could write a tragedy.' He was back in town, in time to provide this article with a postscript, in the last days of March.

On the 25th of that month, 'after six years of struggle, ill health, and pecuniary distress', Haydon's picture of Christ's entry into Jerusalem came to the exhibition room, and Keats and Hazlitt, to the best of our knowledge, met for the last time. The picture was that in which both figured in the background, while, nearer the spectator, 'Voltaire sneered, and Wordsworth bowed in reverence and awe'. Haydon's account of the private view, although well known, is too characteristic an example of his style to be passed over :

'The tickets were all sold out. Saturday came at last. I stayed over at Hatchett's Coffee Room, went into the hall before the hour I had fixed, and seeing servants all at their posts, chairs all in a row, thought it odd nobody had come before twelve. I felt at any rate somebody ought to have been over-anxious. Then I got wretched and said "Perhaps nobody will come. Yes, nobody will come, that's clear." I went over to the coffee-room again, watching the clock inside the bar. At half past twelve I stole over again. Sammons looked knowing. "Anybody come?" said I. "Yes, sir; Sir William Scott is just gone in." "That will do, he always goes to every exhibition on earth, and brings everybody." Away I went and had a good lunch, drank a couple of glasses of sherry, and sallied forth about half past three, ready for anything. As I turned my anxious eyes towards the Hall, a crowd of carriages was blocking up Piccadilly. "Ha, ha, that will do", said I, and bounding over, I found the whole passage full of servants, and all the bustle and chat, and noise and hallooing of coachmen, of a regular rout at noonday ! Up I went, proudly; Sammons was seven feet high; there was no speaking to him. The room was full. Keats and Hazlitt were up in a corner, really rejoicing. At this moment in came the Persian ambassador and his suite : his fine manly person and black beard, with his splendid dress, made a prodigious show, and he said, in good English, and in a loud voice, "I like the elbow of soldier".' How Mrs Siddons turned the feeling of the room, how the artist took £1,760 7s. 6d. at the doors, and afterwards toured the picture in Scotland, may be read in the erratic artist's own pages. Hazlitt introduced one of his uniformly friendly references to Haydon's work into the article on Farington's Life of Reynolds which he wrote in the following month for the *Edinburgh Review*.

How do we know that this article, which came out in August, was written not later than April, and at Winterslow? The answer is contained in the article itself: 'In that short, but delightful season of the year, and in that part of the country where we now write, there are wild woods, and banks covered with primroses and hyacinths for miles together, so that you cannot put your foot between'. The latest date for Hazlitt's stay in town is given by Crabb Robinson: '20 April: – I took tea and spent the evening at Lamb's. Hazlitt and Leigh Hunt were there, people with whom I am not cordial, but I nevertheless enjoyed the evening.' Armed with the results of a month's playgoing, sufficient to last him into June, Hazlitt went down to Winterslow.

What took him there on this occasion we can say quite certainly. His period of probation was up, and he was at liberty to contribute Table Talks to the *London Magazine*. At the same time he had prevailed on Lamb (as Talfourd tells us, who would be in a position to know) to enter on a friendly rivalry. The first essay of Elia – 'Recollections of the South Sea House' – appeared in the Magazine for August; the first Table Talk – *On the Qualifications Necessary to Success in Life* – just two months earlier. It was immediately followed by *On the Difference between Writing and Speaking* and *On the Conversation of Authors*.

III

In a footnote attached to the first of his Table Talks in the magazine we find Hazlitt remarking: 'I would be permitted to say, that I am so sick of this trade of authorship, that I have a much greater ambition to be the best racket-player, than the best prose-

writer of the age.[1] The critics look askance at one's best-meant
efforts, but the face of a racket-player is the face of a friend.
There is no juggling here. If the stroke is a good one, the hit
tells. They do not keep two scores to mark the game, with Whig
and Tory notches. The thing is settled at once, and the applause
of the *dedans* follows the marker's voice, and seconds the
prowess of the hand, and the quickness of the eye. The accom-
plishments of the body are obvious and clear to all : those of the
mind âre recondite and doubtful, and therefore grudgingly acknowledged or held up as the sport of prejudice, spite, and folly.'
This confession, which he partly suppressed on reprinting the
essay, is our best indication of the mood in which he set out on
the chief work of his life.

We may see him at work in this summer, at his first-floor
window of the inn which may still be visited, in *On the Conversation of Authors* :

> Books are a world in themselves, it is true; but they are not
> the only world. The world itself is a volume larger than all
> the libraries in it. Learning is a sacred deposit from the ex-
> perience of ages; but it has not put all future experience on
> the shelf, or debarred the common herd of mankind from the
> use of their hands, tongues, eyes, ears, or understandings.
> Taste is a luxury for the privileged few; but it would be hard
> upon those who have not the same standard of refinement in
> their own minds that we suppose ourselves to have, if this
> should prevent them from having recourse, as usual, to their
> old frolics, coarse jokes, and horse-play, and getting through

1. This is confirmed for us by Procter : 'It must not be supposed that
Hazlitt spent all this period of his life [*circa* 1820] in writing or talking.
On the contrary, he was a furious racket player. The whole of many, and
the half of more days, were consumed in this amusement. The Fives
Court (now pulled down) was the arena where he was then ambitious to
figure; and rackets occupied almost his whole existence. The racket was
the only instrument with which he desired to conquer. If he ever thought
of that more formidable weapon, the goose-quill, it was unwillingly, and
in order only to provide for his wants, or that he might recount his suc-
cesses or reverses in his one favourite game.'

the wear and tear of the world with such homely sayings and shrewd helps as they may. Happy is it, that the mass of mankind eat and drink, and sleep and perform their several tasks, and do as they like without us – caring nothing for our scribblings, our carpings and our quibbles; and moving on the same, in spite of our fine-spun distinctions, fantastic theories, and lines of demarcation, which are like the chalk-figures drawn on ball-room floors to be danced out before morning! In the field opposite the window where I write this, there is a country-girl picking stones : in the one next it, there are several poor women weeding the blue and red flowers from the corn : farther on, are two boys, tending a flock of sheep. What do they know or care about what I am writing about them, or ever will – or what would they be the better for it, if they did?

To set against this passage, we may take one from *On the Difference between Writing and Speaking* :

To conclude this account with what perhaps I ought to have set out with, a definition of the character of an author. There are persons who in society, in public intercourse, feel no excitement,

> *'Dull as the lake that slumbers in the storm'*,

but who, when left alone, can lash themselves into a foam. They are never less alone than when alone. Mount them on a dinner-table, and they have nothing to say; shut them up in a room by themselves, and they are inspired. They are 'made fierce with dark keeping'. In revenge for being tongue-tied, a torrent of words flows from their pens, and the storm which was so long collecting comes down apace. It never rains but it pours. Is not this strange, unaccountable? Not at all so. They have a real interest, a real knowledge of the subject, and they cannot summon up all that interest, or bring all that knowledge to bear, while they have anything else to attend to. Till they can do justice to the feeling they have, they can do nothing. For this they look into their own minds, not in the faces of a gaping multitude. What they would say (if they could) does not lie at the orifices of the mouth ready for delivery, but is wrapped in the folds of the heart and registered in the chambers of the brain. In the sacred cause of truth that stirs them, they would put their whole strength, their whole being, into requisition; and as it implies a greater effort to drag their words and ideas from their lurking-places, so there is no end when they are once set in motion. The whole of a man's thoughts and feelings cannot lie on the surface, made up for use; but the whole must be a greater quantity, a mightier power, if they could be got at, layer under layer, and brought into play by the levers of imagination and reflection. Such a person then sees farther and feels deeper than most others. He plucks up an argument by the roots, he tears out the very heart of his subject. He has more pride in conquering the difficulties of a question, than vanity in courting the favour of an audience. He wishes to satisfy himself before he pretends to enlighten the public. He takes an interest in things in the abstract more than by common consent. Nature is his mistress, truth his idol. The contemplation of a pure idea is the ruling passion of his breast. The intervention of other people's notions, the being the immediate object of their censure or their praise, puts him out. What will tell, what will produce an effect, he cares little about; and therefore he produces the greatest. The *personal* is to him an impertinence; so he conceals himself and writes. Solitude 'becomes his glittering bride, and airy thoughts his children'. Such a one is a true author; and not a member of any Debating Club or Dilettanti Society whatever!

It was to put his whole strength into requisition that Hazlitt was to resort to Winterslow at frequent intervals during the next two years.

To think of the *London Magazine* as successfully maintained, or even very consciously set, at the standard of Lamb and Hazlitt, would be to flatter John Scott unduly, and to expect the impossible. It was not by accident that we found this good editor alluding to a 'smart contributor to our Magazine', for the fact is that of these he had several. Foremost among them was Thomas Griffiths Wainewright, *alias* Janus Weathercock, who made his appearance (without any probationary period) in the first number. That Lamb liked Wainewright, and thought his writings an adornment, we know;[1] but Hazlitt did not. A man who is going to be a murderer at thirty-six is not necessarily a bad writer at twenty-six; but Wainewright was a bad writer. We need not steal Talfourd's thunder and be angry with him after the verdict, because at this stage in his versatile career, aided by his hacks, his rings, and his finery, he 'seized on the critical department of the Fine Arts, both in and out of the Magazine, undisturbed by the presence or pretensions of the finest critic on Art who ever wrote – William Hazlitt'. What he seized on, in June of this year, was Hazlitt's theatrical article for March; and in July Hazlitt replied to him. In order to make clear work of the subject, he at the same time brought him into an essay, *On Vulgarity and Affectation*:

1. Leigh Hunt also, who wrote in the *Examiner* 22 (July 1821): 'There is a fellow after our own heart (if we may pay said heart such a compliment) who writes on the Fine Arts in the *London Mag*. Of three writers who render that publication precious in our eyes, he is one. Their names, Bunyanly-speaking, are "Fine Arts", Table Talk, and A Lie, alias Elia. ... The first loves Nature and Art, in doors and out of doors, trees, rooms and pictures, poetry and music, and fine eyes; finds enjoyment for himself and others at all seasons; in short, turns about, as they occur, with the ready sparkle of his animal spirits, to

" – all the fair variety of things."

We were afraid at one time he was going to be really vulgar, out of fear of being so, and libel our old friends the washerwomen, as well as the minor theatres; – but a rough hint from a critic who means kindlier than he sometimes appears to do, brought him to his "gentle senses".' The rough hint was Hazlitt's, as reproduced on p. 303. He had devoted his February article, as a consequence of the death of the King and the closing of the patent theatres, to a voyage of discovery among the minor houses: – a proceeding which had incurred the exquisite Weathercock's (perhaps humorous) displeasure.

'I like it,' says Miss Branghton in Evelina (meaning the Opera), 'because it is not vulgar.' That is, she likes it, not because there is any thing to like in it, but because other people are prevented from liking or knowing any thing about it. Janus Weathercock, Esq., laugheth to scorn and despitefully entreateth and hugely condemneth my dramatic criticisms in the *London,* for a like exquisite reason. I must therefore make an example of him *in terrorem* to all such hypercritics. He finds fault with me and calls my taste vulgar, because I go to Sadler's Wells ('a place he has heard of' – O Lord, Sir!) – because I notice the Miss Dennets, 'great favourites with the Whitechapel orders' – praise Miss Valancy, 'a bouncing Columbine at Ashley's and them there places, as his barber informs him' (has he no way of establishing himself in his own good opinion but by triumphing over his barber's bad English?) – and finally, because I recognize the existence of the Cobourg and Surrey theatres, at the name of which he cries 'Faugh' with great significance, as if he had some personal disgust at them, and yet he would be supposed never to have entered them. It is not his cue as a well-bred critic. *C'est beau ça.* Now this appears to me a very crude, unmeaning, indiscriminate, wholesale and vulgar way of thinking. It is prejudging things in the lump, by names and places and classes, instead of judging them by what they are in themselves, by their real qualities and shades of distinction. There is no selection, truth, or delicacy in such a mode of proceeding. It is affecting ignorance, and making it a title to wisdom. It is a vapid assumption of superiority. It is exceeding impertinence. It is rank coxcombry. It is nothing in the world else. To condemn because the multitude admire is as essentially vulgar as to admire because they admire. There is no exercise of taste or judgement in either case: both are equally repugnant to good sense, and of the two I should prefer the good-natured side.

So much for a man **Hazlitt** did not like: we may now turn

to one he did. He was at Winterslow when, on 4 May, Procter, now reading plays for Macready, wrote to Leigh Hunt as follows:[1] 'My dear Hunt, – A new Tragedy on a subject of Roman History is accepted and forthcoming at Covent Garden. As the Author is an old acquaintance of Hazlitt's (to whom I am going to write in a day or two about the matter) you will I know be glad to mention the thing, to say nothing of its being a piece of news for the paper. If you chose to rely at all on my report, I can safely say that it is the best Tragedy, as far as reading goes, that has yet been accepted by Covent Garden within my knowledge – it is very spirited and dramatic, and I hope that my friend Macready will shew it off to advantage. The name (which must *not* be mentioned) is *Virginius*.' Procter was doubtless as good as his word, and Hazlitt, having demonstrated earlier in the year the impossibility of any modern author writing a tragedy, came up to town in June to witness this surprising refutation by his old protégé. As he wrote in his July article, of which Virginius and Janus share the honours: 'We heard from good authority that there was a new tragedy worth seeing, and also that it was written by an old friend of ours. *That* there was no resisting.' This was, so far as we know, his first meeting with Sheridan Knowles since the latter's departure from London in 1808, since which date he had been for some time on the stage and latterly settled as a schoolmaster in Glasgow. If Hazlitt wrote of the author of 'Virginius' with caution, he never spoke of the man with anything but an affection which was reciprocated.

The news of his father's death in July, at the age of eighty-two, found Hazlitt still in town. In a letter addressed on the 28th to Winterslow Hut, his sister Margaret says: 'If we had known where to direct to you we should not have sent Mary [Hazlitt's niece, the daughter of John] to tell you of our father's death, but would have written to you directly; but neither your mother nor I were well enough to write at the time. ... He died on Sunday the 16th, about seven in the morning. To him his death was a release from a state of suffering: he made no com-

1. Leigh Hunt MSS., in the British Museum.

plaint, nor did he give one groan, but went on talking of glory, honour, and immortality, and talking with me to the last. His senses returned the last few hours, and when he could not speak, he took my hand and put it into mother's.' Hazlitt's mother, his sister says, wishes to know if he intends to write anything in the *Repository,* giving some account of his father – 'If you don't, somebody else will, and you can do it best'. He left the formal account to another hand, but almost immediately afterwards immortalized the old minister in *On the Pleasures of Painting.*

IV

From this point forward Hazlitt's personal movements in this year are less clear to us. We have the summary of his dramatic activities already alluded to, and this, no less than the articles themselves, would seem to make it plain that he was in town throughout August but not again until the end of October. In the middle of the former month we have the best of reasons for believing that he moved his town lodging to number 9, Southampton Buildings.[1] In the September magazine *On the Conversation of Authors* appeared, and is the subject of an undated note from Lamb: 'Dr H. – Lest you should come to-morrow, I write to say that Mary is ill again. The last thing she read was "Thursday nights", which seemed to give her unmixed delight, and she was sorry for what she said to you that night. The article is a treasure to us for ever.' We do not know what Mary Lamb said to Hazlitt, but we may think it not altogether unlikely that it was connected with his domestic affairs. Sarah Stoddart, we do not forget, was the friend of the Lambs before she was the wife of Hazlitt, and the marriage which had been welcomed for 'the joke sake' had recently lost any appearance of being successful which it had ever possessed. Very shortly after the receipt of this letter I think we may conclude that Hazlitt went once more to Winterslow.

1. 'When I sometimes think of the time I first saw the sweet apparition, August 16, 1820 … ' – *Liber Amoris.*

In the absence of further news of him, we may turn our attention to the fortunes of the magazine. Crabb Robinson, who was absent from town from July to October on an extended Continental tour in the company of Wordsworth, returns to give us an entry: '31 October: – Read in bed an able and crushing article on *Blackwood's Magazine* in the *London Magazine*. The writer (Scott) accuses directly Wilson with being the author of both the abusive and eulogistic articles on Wordsworth, a baseness that I believe W. thinks capable of though he is shy of expressing any opinion about Wilson.' The article which Crabb Robinson read in bed was that contained in the magazine for November. Scott had, at the outset, left his northern rivals severely alone, a sole reference, in his second number, being: 'We have to thank our brethren Editors of *Blackwood's* for a civil notice. ... If we have (as they say) imitated their *manner,* have they not, in return, taken some hints from us as to *manners?* May the interchange continue to be profitable to us both!' This pious expression of a hope was not for long to be justified. In his fifth number, writing on 'Newspapers', Scott had made, perhaps inadvisedly, some incidental reference to the part played by *Blackwood's* since its inception. The collaborators in that work, the one having in this year become son-in-law to Sir Walter, and the other, by the latter's influence, Professor of Moral Philosophy in the University of Edinburgh, were at the moment comporting themselves, as John Scott had remarked, with a more reasonable approximation to dignity. But in October the third anniversary of their first coming together under Mr Blackwood's banner was too much for them, and either one or both (but I think we may say Wilson) burst out into a panegyric on their own virtues, present and retrospective, of which the following are a few sentences:

> *We are absolutely coining money.* ... The publisher takes one half, and we the other, i.e. £4000 per annum. ... We have done more than all the periodical works that ever existed since the beginning of time (moderately speaking) to spread

the empire of genius and imagination upon earth. There is
no single man of genius whom we have not delighted to
honour. ... Of Baldwin's new bang-up concern we, at present,
just civilly ask the Jehu, John Scott, to keep his own side of
the road – not to be so fond of running races – and not to
abuse passengers who prefer going by another conveyance.

The circulation of *Blackwood's* was stated to be 'somewhere
below 17,000', and its readers were asked, to compare 'this
figure' with 'the known sales of other periodicals ... the
Quarterly, about 14,000; the *Edinburgh,* upwards of 7000, the
Gentleman's Magazine, about 4000, *Baldwin,* 1100, the *Scots*
[i.e., the *Edinburgh*] *Magazine,* as we have been assured by
authority that we think may be depended upon, 100 to 150.'
While Constable was told that he 'would act wisely to give up
altogether, and so leave the Periodical Literature of Scotland
entirely in the hands of us younger and abler men', Murray
learned (no doubt as much to his surprise as to our own) that
in the difference of two years before 'we took our pen, and
erased his name from our title-page'.

It was this strange compost of candour and impudence, and
in particular this claim to have made slander pay, which called
forth John Scott's 'able and crushing article'. He headed it with
a quotation. 'They do but jest – POISON IN JEST – no
offence i' the world!' and said:

In an early number of the *London Magazine,* we alluded
to the work in question, in a tone certainly less serious than
our present language; yet in that article we made it sufficiently
manifest, as we have reason to know, to the consciousness of
Blackwood's men that what it pleased themselves to term
(thus giving the word to certain credulous people, who, on
such subjects, can only speak as they are prompted) their
'foibles', their 'youthful indiscretions', hey-day irregularities
– only required to be seized hold of by an arm of moderate
power, to be shaken out of this flimsy disguise, and stand

exposed before the world as designing treacheries and sordid scandals.

'The honour of the literature of the present day', he concluded, 'we consider as now at stake', and having said so much, he had naturally to say more. Unfortunately, in saying it, he did not first make sure of his facts. His mistake lay in making the not unnatural assumption that Wilson's appointment had involved his withdrawal from the magazine; and the effect of his second article in December, entitled 'The Mohock Magazine', was to bring personally against Lockhart charges which would have been for the greater part justifiable if brought against the conductors of the magazine in general.

Here we may leave the matter for a space, as Lockhart left it. In December Hazlitt emerges again. He had returned to town, we may gather, in time to attend to the magazine's theatre for November, and in his concluding article for the year he wrote that summary of his dramatic activities to which reference has been made, prior to retiring from a post which had no doubt become irksome to him. On Sunday, 10 December, Crabb Robinson found him, with Procter, at Basil Montagu's, and had 'a very pleasant lounge there till past 12 o'clock'. On the 27th the diarist is more informative: 'Took tea, &c., at Lamb's. One of his monthly parties, less agreeable than usual. His vulgar brother there, whose manners are intolerable, and Phillips, and late, Ayrton. Also Talfourd stepped in, smartly dressed for a party. T. does not gain by personal decoration. I begin to think him personally vain. I have read his article on Wordsworth in the *New Monthly Mag.* It is all praise and luscious. ... John Scott on the other hand has in *Baldwin's London Mag.* eulogized with discrimination as well as with eloquence. It is an article that may convert a scorner; T. can only delight a disciple and partizan. T. has so much to write for the periodical works that he can hardly allow himself time to think. He is in danger of becoming a commonplace declaimer. He is to succeed Hazlitt as dramatic critic in the *London.* It will be, I fear, a falling off, for Hazlitt, though a mannerist in style, is a thinker at least. His Table-Talk in the *London* is full of acute observation.'

As a first fruit of the success of the *London Magazine* the publisher Colburn had acquired the *New Monthly* and, with the poet Campbell as editor, was starting it in a new series from January. The pushing young Talfourd was adding new worlds to his conquests.[1] He had written for the November *Edinburgh Review* a notice of the *Age of Elizabeth* which we should consider extremely patronizing, and even so, as we shall learn in a moment, Hazlitt was glad to have it there.

V

The first days of 1821 give us a letter:

Hazlitt to John Scott

Dear Sir, — I return the proof which I prefer to the philippic against Bentham. Do you keep the Past and Future? You see Lamb argues the same view of the subject. That 'young master' will anticipate all my discoveries, if I don't mind. The last No. was a very good one. The Living Authors was spirited and fine. Don't hold out your hand to the Blackwoods yet, after having knocked those blackguards down. My address after you receive this will be Winterslow Hut, near Salisbury. Send me the article on Past and Future, if you can spare it. Ask Baldwins if they would like the articles on Modern Philosophy, eight in number, at five guineas apiece.

W. H.

The proof which Hazlitt was returning was doubtless of *On Reading Old Books,* which came out in February; the essay he was withdrawing, containing the philippic against Bentham, *On People of Sense.* This letter enables us to see that he was

1. Miss Mitford, in a letter of 12 December, adds to our information: 'Colburn is making magnificent offers. He has proffered twenty guineas a sheet (five more than Hazlitt gets for the Table Talk in the *London*) to Horace Smith (one of the Rejected Addressers, you know) for any contribution, prose or verse, and he will give Talfourd his weight in gold rather than part with him.'

working a good deal ahead of the requirements of the *London Magazine,* and he was in fact now resorting to Winterslow to bring up the number of unused Table Talks to the requirements of the volume offered to Baldwin in the previous spring and now commissioned by Warren. Lamb's essay, in the January magazine which Hazlitt had just read, was 'New Year's Eve'. Scott's last Living Author was Byron. He had given no sign of holding out his hand to *Blackwood's* yet, but on the contrary, in a note in this issue, had proceeded from naming Lockhart by implication to naming him directly.

The sequel has been narrated so fully on behalf of Lockhart by Mr Andrew Lang that we need only summarize it here. On 10 January Scott found himself waited upon by Lockhart's friend Christie, a young barrister in London, with a demand for a dictated apology or satisfaction. The line taken by Scott is at first clear to us: his object was to bring the concealed editorship of *Blackwood's* into the light, and his reply, that Lockhart must 'distinctly declare the nature of his connection' with that magazine before he 'could consider his motives to be worthy of respect', was calculated to serve this end. If Scott had not changed this position, all might have been well; for it is hard to see how Lockhart, who 'would not condescend to offer any preliminary information whatever', could have avoided being forced into one of two alternatives – either of allowing the charges which had been laid at his door to remain there, or of having recourse to the law. But already on the 18th, Lockhart having come to town on what he understood to be Scott's suggestion, the latter so far advanced his position as to refer Christie conditionally to a second (Horace Smith); the condition being that Lockhart would assert as a preliminary that he had 'never derived money from any connection with the management of *Blackwood,* and that he never stood in any situation giving him directly or indirectly pecuniary interest in its sale'. This Lockhart would not (of course, could not) do; and having trailed his coat in every other respect in front of Scott over a week-end, he prepared to go back to Scotland. At this point however an old friend of ours intervened, and did not assist matters. Dr Stoddart, before Lockhart left town, secured from him for the *New Times* a copy of his final statement to Scott, and suggested the addition to it, 'for the public', of a form of words ingeniously contrived to come as near to the denial demanded by Scott as the facts of Lockhart's association with *Blackwood's* permitted. Unfortunately this statement as amended was allowed to appear without the explanation regarding the addition which was contemplated. Of the oversight Scott at once (31 January) took advantage, in a statement on his side which was intended to be final. Christie, reading this, took it to imply that if the copy of the statement received by Scott had contained the denial printed in the *New Times,* it would have taken him into the field; and he promptly wrote off to Horace Smith that if Scott would make the same journey to meet Lockhart as Lockhart had made to meet him, 'Mr Lockhart would give him a meeting instantly'. This letter, there seems reason to believe, Horace Smith suppressed. On 10 February Christie, having received no reply, felt himself justified in issuing a final statement on his own account, and this time he sent it to Patmore, a contributor to the magazine, who had been acting for Scott in some capacity that is not very clear to us since 20 January. Five days later Christie was waited on by Patmore with a demand that a sentence in this statement, imputing cowardice to Scott, should be publicly apologized for; on refusal, a challenge was presented. On the following evening an excellent editor lay mortally wounded in a field near Chalk Farm. In the duel itself Christie's part, and that of his second Traill, was unexceptionable: Patmore's marked by the worst faults of the amateur in an art which is going out of fashion.

Hazlitt, to the best of our knowledge, was well out of all this, writing Table Talks at Winterslow. Dating it '18th–19th January' he wrote *On Living to One's-Self*:

I never was in a better place or humour than I am at present for writing on this subject. I have a partridge getting

ready for my supper, my fire is blazing on the hearth, the air
is mild for the season of the year, I have had but a slight fit
of indigestion today (the only thing that makes me abhor myself), I have three hours good before me, and therefore I will
attempt it. It is as well to do it at once, as to have it to do for
a week to come. ...

What I mean by living to one's-self is living in the world,
as in it, not of it: it is as if no one knew there was such a
person, and you wished no one to know it: it is to be a silent
spectator of the mighty scene of things, not an object of attention or curiosity in it; to take a thoughtful, anxious interest in
what is passing in the world, but not to feel the slightest inclination to make or meddle with it. It is such a life as a pure
spirit might be supposed to lead, and such an interest as it
might take in the affairs of men, calm, contemplative, passive,
distant, touched with pity for their sorrows, smiling at their
follies without bitterness, sharing their affections, but not
troubled by their passions, not seeking their notice, nor once
dreamt of by them. He who lives wisely to himself and to his
own heart, looks at the busy world through the loop-holes of
retreat, and does not want to mingle in the fray.

He wrote other essays, sufficient to bring up to its full comple-
ment the first volume of *Table Talk*; and when his work was
done he came back to London.

Our earliest intimation of his return is given us by Crabb
Robinson. We may take here his only entries which concern us
over the period.

'2 February: — Read the last *Edinburgh Review*. This work
goes on sinking — I do not think that Talfourd will help to raise
it unless he corrects his tawdry commonplace diction. He has
written an article, Hazlitt, beginning well and with less trash
in it than usual, but ending in his worst way.' This was the review of the *Age of Elizabeth,* in the course of which Talfourd
(or conceivably Jeffrey) remarked: 'If Mr Hazlitt has not generally met with impartial justice from his contemporaries, we

must say that he has himself partly to blame. Some of the attacks of which he has been the object, have no doubt been purely brutal and malignant; but others have, in a great measure, arisen from feeling of which he has unwisely set the example. His seeming carelessness of that public opinion which he would influence – his love of startling paradoxes – and his intrusion of political virulence, at seasons when the mind is prepared only for the delicate investigations of taste, have naturally provoked a good deal of asperity, and prevented the due appreciation of his powers.'

'21 February: – I made a delightful purchase at Sotheby's, Raphael's Planets engraved by Dorigny. ... I took these to Lamb after dinner, but Lamb did not seem heartily to enjoy them. On the contrary, taking them to the Ader's they were delighted with them. On the other hand, bringing back to Lamb's the Bible of Raphael, L. and also Hazlitt who was there agreed in declaring them to be among the finest works of Raphael. ... Hazlitt & I now speak again, but he does not omit the *Sir* when he talks to me. I think he behaves with propriety & dignity towards me, considering the severity of my attack on him, which though warranted by my friendship with Wordsworth was not justified according to the customs of society.' A strange moment for the award of the *amende honorable* by our diarist, if Hazlitt could be supposed to have had more than the most remote connection with the duel which was now five days over.[1]

1. In the *Life* of Campbell which Cyrus Redding, the poet's subeditor, contributed to the *New Monthly Magazine* in 1848, he wrote (lxxix. 427): 'He [Campbell] never tolerated the remarks of this writer, although it cannot be denied that Hazlitt has commended his poetry in the highest terms; he has given the poet all but boundless praise. But his remarks were neutralized in Campbell's judgement by the discovery that one of the lines in the Pleasures of Hope was a borrowed line. ... This feeling exhibited itself in numberless instances. He declared to me that Hazlitt had been a means of irritating John Scott to such a degree that it was one cause of his going out in the duel where he fell: that Hazlitt was a dangerous man.' The point of this suggestion we take to be that Hazlitt had returned from the country between 10 and 15 February, and he may have done so; but if he did we may doubt, from what we have seen of their

On 27 February Scott died, and on 1 March there was the inquest. On the 3rd Crabb Robinson enters: 'C. L. seems to have felt acutely poor Scott's death. Talfourd was thinking of applying for the editorship, but C. L. agrees with me in thinking it incompatible with his profession'. The inquest was followed by the trial to which Christie and his second Traill surrendered themselves. The verdict of literary society is no doubt adequately rendered for us, on 22 March, by Miss Mitford: 'What a terrible affair this duel is! What a pity that poor John Scott did not fight at once with Horace Smith for his second; or, which would have been better still, say firmly that he would not fight at all in a literary quarrel. He is now the victim of his own contemptible second; a man who is a pawnbroker on Ludgate Hill[1] and a dandy in St. James's Street; and who egged on his unhappy friend to gratify his own trumpery desire of notoriety. I hope he will be severely dealt with.' In this desire Miss Mitford seems to have been disappointed. Indeed, it is not perfectly clear to us how the sensational Patmore got out of it.

VI

It was not Talfourd, but Hazlitt, who was turned to by the *London Magazine's* publisher on the death of Scott.

Robert Baldwin to Hazlitt

P.N. Row, March 5, 1821.

My dear Sir, – I must not any longer neglect to avail myself

relations, whether his influence upon Scott would have been as depicted. Simultaneously, however, in 1848, Horace Smith's 'Recollections of a Greybeard' were appearing in the magazine, and at the conclusion of his own account of the duel he said (lxxxi. 418): 'Before I quit this painful subject, let me allude to the following paragraph in Mr Cyrus Redding's Memoir of T. Campbell: "Campbell declared to me, &c." Campbell was too prone to believe whatever he might hear in disparagement of Hazlitt, and in this instance I have reason to think he had been misinformed.' We know of no reason why this statement should not be taken as conclusively as it was evidently intended to be.

1. In this Miss Mitford was not quite kind to Patmore: it was his father who was the pawnbroker.

of your kind offer to assist in filling up the chasm made by
the death of our lamented friend in the Magazine; and I know
not any subject which would be thought more interesting than
a continuation of the Living Authors, nor any pen so fitted
for the subject as yours. Pray select any one you may think
most fit, and render us your powerful assistance towards
making our next number equal to its predecessors.

In a day or two I shall probably request an interview with
you on the subject of an editor. – I am always, my dear Sir,
most faithfully yours,

ROBERT BALDWIN.

The editorial notes, the 'Lion's Head', for the month of April,
present distinct signs of being from his pen, while in the May
number there are no less than four of his contributions, including a Living Author, Crabbe.

While Hazlitt was engaged in his unaccustomed editorial
duties, *Table Talk; or, Original Essays,* was published. Of the
thirteen papers which composed it eleven were making a first
appearance, and there were thus some surprises for his acquaintance. Feeling temporarily out of patience with Leigh Hunt, for
reasons which are not altogether inexplicable to us, he had
brought him, under a sufficiently penetrable disguise, in at the
end of *On People with One Idea* :

There are persons who, without being chargeable with the
vice here spoken of, yet 'stand accountant for as great a sin' :
though not dull and monotonous, they are vivacious manner-
ists in their conversation, and excessive egotists. ... Whether
they talk of the town or the country, poetry or politics, it
comes to much the same thing. If they talk to you of the town,
its diversions, 'its palaces, its ladies, and its streets', they are
the delight, the grace, and ornament of it. If they are describing the charms of the country, they give no account of any
individual spot or object or source of pleasure but the circumstance of their being there. 'With them conversing, we forget

all place, all seasons, and their change.' They perhaps pluck a
leaf or a flower, patronize it, and hand it you to admire, but
select no one feature of beauty or grandeur to dispute the
palm of perfection with their own person. Their rural descriptions are mere landscape backgrounds with their own
portraits in an engaging attitude in front. They are not observing or enjoying the scene, but doing the honours as masters
of the ceremonies to nature, and arbiters of elegance to all
humanity. If they tell a love-tale of enamoured princesses, it is
plain they fancy themselves the hero of the piece. If they dis-
cuss poetry, their encomiums still turn on something genial
and unsophisticated, meaning their own style : if they enter
into politics, it is understood that a hint from them to the
potentates of Europe is sufficient. In short, as a lover (talk of
what you will) brings in his mistress at every turn, so these
persons contrive to divert your attention to the same darling
object – they are, in fact, in love with themselves; and, like
lovers, should be left to keep their own company.

In the portrait of a type Leigh Hunt recognized himself.[1] He

1. He had, of course, already had an opportunity of studying his own
portrait in *On the Conversation of Authors*: 'L. H. goes there [to Lamb's]
sometimes. He has a fine vinous spirit about him, and tropical blood in his
veins : but he is better at his own table. He has a great flow of pleasantry
and delightful animal spirits : but his hits do not tell like L[amb]'s; you
cannot repeat them the next day. He requires not only to be appreciated,
but to have a select circle of admirers and devotees, to feel himself quite
at home. He sits at the head of a party with great gaiety and grace; has
an elegant manner and turn of features; is never at a loss – *aliquando
sufflaminandus erat* – has continual sportive sallies of wit or fancy; tells
a story capitally; mimics an actor, or an acquaintance to admiration;
laughs with great glee and good humour at his own or other people's
jokes; understands the point of an equivoque, or an observation immediately; has a taste and knowledge of books, of music, of medals;
manages an argument adroitly; is genteel and gallant, and has a set of
bye-phrases and quaint allusions always at hand to produce a laugh : – if
he has a fault, it is that he does not listen so well as he speaks, is impatient of interruption, and is fond of being looked up to, without considering by whom. I believe, however, he has pretty well seen the folly
of this.'

conceived himself to have other ground of complaint.

On Paradox and Common-Place is a reasoned distinction between two types of character, each of which, in Hazlitt's opinion, served the cause of truth equally ineffectually. 'With one party, whatever is, is right: with their antagonists, whatever is, is wrong. These swallow every antiquated absurdity: those catch at every new, unfledged project – and are alike enchanted with the velocipedes or the French Revolution.' In choosing Shelley to illustrate the second character, he was perhaps guilty of rashness :

The author of the Prometheus Unbound (to take an individual instance of the last character) has a fire in his eye, a fever in his blood, a maggot in his brain, a hectic flutter in his speech, which mark out the philosophic fanatic. He is sanguine-complexioned, and shrill-voiced. As is often observable in the case of religious enthusiasts, there is a slenderness of constitutional *stamina,* which renders the flesh no match for the spirit. His bending, flexible form appears to take no strong hold of things, does not grapple with the world about him, but slides from it like a river –

> *'And in its liquid texture mortal wound*
> *Receives no more than can the fluid air.'*

The shock of accidents, the weight of authority make no impression on his opinions, which retire like a feather, or rise from the encounter unhurt, through their own buoyancy. He is clogged by no dull system of realities, no earth-bound feelings, no rooted prejudices, by nothing that belongs to the mighty trunk and hard husk of nature and habit, but is drawn up by irresistible levity to the regions of mere speculation and fancy, to the sphere of air and fire, where his delighted spirit floats in 'seas of pearl and clouds of amber'. There is no *caput mortuum* of worn-out, thread-bare experience to serve as ballast to his mind; it is all volatile intellectual salt of tartar, that refuses to combine its evanescent, inflammable essence with any thing solid or any thing lasting. Bubbles are to him the only realities: — touch them, and they vanish. Curiosity is the only proper category of his mind, and though a man in knowledge, he is a child in feeling.

The personal portrait points forward to the *Spirit of the Age,* but the personal portrait is the least part of the essay.

The publication of *Table Talk* with these and other essays in it had an immediate sequel:

Leigh Hunt to Hazlitt

Hampstead, April 20.

I think, Mr Hazlitt, you might have found a better time, and place too, for assaulting me and my friends in this bitter manner. A criticism on Table-Talk was to appear in next Sunday's *Examiner,* but I have thought it best, upon the whole, not to let it appear, for I must have added a quarrel-some note to it; and the sight of acquaintances and brother-reformers cutting and carbonadoing one another in public is, I conceive, no advancement to the cause of Liberal opinion, however you may think they injure it in other respects. In God's name, why could you not tell Mr Shelley in a pleasant manner of what you dislike in him? If it is not mere spleen, you make a gross mistake in thinking that he is not open to advice, or so wilfully in love with himself and his opinions. His spirit is worthy of his great talents. Besides, do you think that nobody has thought or suffered, or come to conclusions through thought or suffering, but yourself? You are fond of talking against vanity: but do you think that people will see no vanity in that very fondness — in your being so intolerant with everybody's ideas of improvement but your own, and in resenting so fiercely the possession of a trifling quality or so which you do not happen to number among your own? I have been flattered by your praises: I have been (I do not care what you make of the acknowledgement) instructed, and I thought bettered, by your objections; but it is one thing to be dealt candidly with or rallied, and another to have the whole

alleged nature of one's self and a dear friend torn out and
thrown in one's face, as if we had not a common humanity
with yourself. Is it possible that a misconception of anything
private can transport you into these – what shall I call them?
– extravagances of stomach? or that a few paltry fellows in
Murray's or Blackwood's interest can worry you into such outrageous efforts to prove you have no vanities in common with
those whom you are acquainted with? At all events, I am sure
that this sulky, dog-in-the-manger philosophy, which will
have neither one thing nor t'other, neither alteration nor want
of it, marriage nor no marriage, egotism nor no egotism, hope
nor despair, can do no sort of good to anybody. But I have
faith enough in your disinterestedness and suffering to tell
you so privately instead of publicly; and you might have paid
as decent a compliment to a man half killed with his thoughts
for others if you had done as much for me, instead of making
my faults stand for my whole character, and inventing those
idle things about [*illegible*] and hints to emperors. If you
wished to quarrel with me you should have done so at once,
instead of inviting me to your house, coming to mine, and in
the meanwhile getting ready the proof-sheets of such a book
as this – preparing and receiving specimens of the dagger
which was to strike at a sick head and heart, and others whom
it loved. There are more things in heaven and earth than are
dreamt of even in your philosophy; and if you had a little
more imagination, the very 'cruelty' of your stomach would
carry you beyond itself, and inform you so. If you did not
wish to quarrel with or to cut me, how do you think that
friends can eternally live upon their good behaviour in this
way, and be cordial and comfortable, or whatever else you
choose they should be – for it is difficult to find out – on pain
of being drawn and quartered in your paragraphs? I wish you
well.

LEIGH HUNT.

P.S. – Since writing this letter, which I brought to town

with me to send you, I have heard that you have expressed
regret at the attack upon myself. If so, I can only say that I
am additionally sorry at being obliged to send it; but I should
have written to you, had you attacked my friends only in that
manner. I am told also, that you are angry with me for not
always being punctual with you in engagements of visiting. I
think I have always apologized and explained when I have
not been so; but if not, surely a trifle of this kind, arising out
of anything but a sense of my being necessary to others, ought
not to make you tear one to pieces in this way for the sport
of our mutual enemies; and I must say, that since I got any
notion of your being annoyed by such things, I have come to
see you sometimes when I have been ready to drop in the
street with illness and anguish.

To this we possess the prompt reply:

Hazlitt to Leigh Hunt

Saturday night [April 21].
My dear Hunt, – I have no quarrel with you, nor can I
have. You are one of those people that I like, do what they
will; there are others that I do not like, do what they may. I
have always spoken well of you to friend or foe – viz. I have
said you were one of the pleasantest and cleverest persons I
ever knew; but that you teased any one you had to deal with
out of their lives. I am fond of a theory, as you know; but I
will give up even that to a friend, if he shews that he has any
regard to my personal feelings. You provoke me to think hard
things of you, and then you wonder that I hitch them into an
essay, as if that made any difference. I pique myself on doing
what I can for others; but I cannot say that I have found any
suitable returns for this, and hence perhaps my outrageous-
ness of stomach! For instance, I praised you in the *Edinburgh
Review,* and when in a case of life and death I tried to lecture,
you refused to go near the place, and gave this as a reason, saying it would seem a collusion, if you said any thing in my

favour after what I had said of you. 2. I got Reynolds to write in the *Edinburgh Review*, at a time when I had a great reluctance to ask any favour of Jeffrey, and from that time I never set eyes on him for a year and a half after. 3. I wrote a book in defence of Godwin some years ago, one half of which he has since stolen without acknowlegment, without even mentioning my name, and yet he comes to me to review the very work, and I write to Jeffrey to ask his consent, thinking myself, which you do not, the most magnanimous person in the world in defence of a cause. 4. I have taken all opportunities of praising Lamb, and I never got a good word from him in return, big or little, till the other day. He seemed struck all of a heap, if I ever hinted at the possibility of his giving me a lift at any time. 5. It was but the other day that two friends did all they could to intercept an article about me from appearing in the said *E. R.*, saying 'it would be too late', 'that the Editor had been sounded at a distance and was averse', with twenty other excuses, and at last I was obliged to send it myself, graciously, and by main force, as it were, when it appeared just in time to save me from drowning. Coulson had been backwards and forwards between my house and Bentham's for between three or four years, and when the latter philosophically put an execution in my house, the plea was he had never heard of my name; and when I theorized on this the other day as bad policy, and *felo de se* on the part of the Radicals, your nephew and that set said: 'Oh, it was an understood thing – the execution, you know!' My God, it is enough to drive one mad. I have not a soul to stand by me, and yet I am to give up my only resource and revenge, a theory – I won't do it, that's flat. Montagu is, I fancy, cut at my putting him among people with one idea, and yet, when the Blackwoods (together with your) shirking out of that business put me nearly under ground, he took every opportunity to discourage me, and one evening, when I talked of going there, I was given to understand that there was 'a party expected'. Yet after this I am not to look at him a little *in abstracto*. This is what has soured me, and made me sick of friendship and acquaintanceship. When did I speak ill of your brother John? He never played me any tricks. I was in a cursed ill humour with you for two or three things when I wrote the article you find fault with (I grant not without reason). If I complained to you, you would only have laughed; you would have played me the very same tricks the very next time; you would not have cared one farthing about annoying me; and yet you complain that I draw a logical conclusion from all this, and publish it to the world without your name. As to Shelley, I do not hold myself responsible to him. You say I want *imagination.* If you mean invention or fancy, I say so too; but if you mean a disposition to sympathize with the claims or merits of others, I deny it. I have been too much disposed to waive my own pretensions in deference to those of others. I am tired with playing at rackets all day, and you will be tired with this epistle. It has little to do with you; for I see no use in raising up a parcel of small, old grievances. But I think the general ground of defence is good.

W. H.

I have given [Jefferson] Hogg's papers to Baldwin, and wish you would write a character of me for the next number. I want to know why everybody has such a dislike to me.

The book which Hazlitt had written in defence of Godwin was the *Reply to Malthus,* and Godwin had now, after thirteen years, addressed himself to the same subject, in a work entitled *Of Population.* That Hazlitt had indeed taken all opportunities of praising Lamb we have seen; and the good word in return, in a public sense, is quite extraordinarily elusive. As for Basil Montagu, he was among the *People With One Idea* only in the same sense as Hunt; that is, by appropriation of the cap that fitted. Montagu was a voluntary and theoretic teetotaller, Hazlitt an enforced and practic one; and the former read: 'It is not pleasant, though it is what one submits to willingly from some people, to be asked every time you meet, whether you have quite

left off drinking wine, and to be complimented or condoled
with on your looks according as you answer in the negative or
affirmative.'

Leigh Hunt, at all events, by this letter was instantaneously
mollified:

Leigh Hunt to Hazlitt

· Monday [April 23].

Dear Hazlitt, – If you do not want to quarrel with me, I
certainly do not want to quarrel with you. I have always said,
to my own mind and to those few to whom I am in the habit
of speaking on such things, that Hazlitt might play me more
tricks than any man; and I conceive you have played me some.
If I have teased you, as you say, I have never revenged myself
by trampling upon you in public; and I do not understand
you when you say that there is no difference between having
an ill opinion of one in private and trying to make everybody
else partake it. But I am not aware how I can have teased you
to the extent you seem to intimate. How can anybody say that
I talked about the collusion you speak of? It is impossible. I
both spoke of your lectures in the *Examiner,* and came to hear
them; not indeed so often as I could wish, but Mrs Hunt knows
how I used to fret myself every evening at not being able to
go. [We may here take several lines about Hunt's health for
granted.] I am willing to be told where my attentions to a
friend are deficient; nor could you mistake me more when
you say I should have 'laughed' at you for complaining. On
the contrary, let but the word friendship be mentioned, and
nobody is disposed to be graver than myself – to a pitch of
emotion. But here I will let you into one of the secrets you
ask for. I have often said, I have a sort of irrepressible love for
Hazlitt, on account of his sympathy for mankind, his unmer-
cenary disinterestedness, and his suffering; and I should have
a still greater and more personal affection for him if he would
let one; but I declare to God I never seem to know whether
he is pleased or displeased, cordial or uncordial – indeed, his

manners are never cordial[1] — and he has a way with him, when first introduced to you, and ever afterwards, as if he said, 'I have no faith in anything, especially your advances; don't you flatter yourself you have any road to my credulity: we have nothing in common between us'. Then you escape into a corner, and your conversation is apt to be as sarcastic and incredulous about all the world as your manner. Now, egregious fop as you have made me out in your book, with my jealousy of anything bigger than a leaf, and other marvels — who is to be fop enough to suppose that any efforts of his can make you more comfortable? Or how can you so repel one, and then expect, not that we should make no efforts (for those we owe you on other accounts), but that it could possibly enter into our heads you took our omissions so much to heart? The tears came into the eyes of this heartless coxcomb when he read the passage in your letter where you speak of not having a soul to stand by you. I was very ill, I confess, at the time, and you may lay it to that account. I was also very ill on Thursday night, when I took up your book to rest my wits in, after battling all day with the most dreadful nervousness. This, and your attack on Mr Shelley, which I must repeat was most outrageous, unnecessary, and even, for its proffered purposes, impolitic, must account for my letter. But I will endeavour to break the force of that blow in another manner, if I can. As to the other points in your letter, if you wish me to say anything about them — everybody knows what I think of Godwin's behaviour, and of your magnanimity to boot, in such matters. But in sparing and assisting Godwin,

1. Hazlitt's comment upon this charge was made a year later: 'I know a person to whom it has been objected as a disqualification for friendship, that he never shakes you cordially by the hand. I own this is a damper to sanguine and florid temperaments, who abound in these practical demonstrations and "compliments extern". The same person, who testifies the least pleasure at meeting you, is the last to quit his seat in your company, grapples with a subject in conversation right earnestly, and is, I take it, backward to give up a cause or a friend.' — On the Knowledge of Character.

you need not have helped him to drive irons into Shelley's soul. Reynolds is a machine I don't see the meaning of. As to Lamb, I must conclude that he abstained from speaking of you, either because you cut so at Coleridge, or from thinking that his good word would really be of no service to you. Of the 'execution' you may remember what I have said; but I was assured again on Saturday that Bentham knew nothing of *it*. How can you say I 'shirked' out of Blackwood's business, when I took all the pains I could to make that raff and coward, Z, come forward? But I will leave these and other matters to talk over when I see you, when I will open myself more to you than I have done, seeing that it may not be indifferent to you for me to do so. At any rate, as I mean this in kindness, oblige me in one matter, and one only, and take some early opportunity of doing justice to the talents and *generous qualities* of Shelley, whatever you may think of his mistakes in using them. The attack on me is a trifle compared with it, nor should I allude to it again but to say, and to say most honestly, that you might make five more if you would only relieve the more respectable part of my chagrin and impatience in that matter. You must imagine what I feel at bottom with regard to yourself, when I tell you that there is but one other person from whom I could have at all borne this attack on Shelley; but in one respect that only makes it the less bearable.   Yours sincerely,

L. H.

Of his share in this correspondence, as one who was pleased with it, Leigh Hunt kept a copy. Shortly afterwards, we find him transmitting to his friend and benefactor in Italy an account of it, and adding: 'I was sorry for it on every account, because I really believe Hazlitt to be a disinterested and suffering man, who feels public calamities as other men do private ones; and this is perpetually redeeming him in my eyes. I told him so, as well as some other things; but you shall see our correspondence by and by.'

VII

This revealing interlude closed, we make a return to business. On 9 May there is a further letter from Baldwin: 'My dear Sir, – The arrangement with Messrs Taylor and Hessey is completed, and Mr Taylor will make an early opportunity of calling on you, unless you should think proper to look in upon them in a day or two. I sincerely hope that such an arrangement will be made as shall be quite satisfactory to yourself; I am sure it is to their interest that it should be so.' Three weeks later, on the 29th, there is a letter from Hessey: 'Mr Taylor was all this morning on the point of setting out to call upon you, as he wanted much to have some conversation with you, but a constant succession of callers-in prevented him. Will you do us the favour to take your breakfast with us in the morning, between nine and ten, when we shall have a chance of being uninterrupted for an hour or two?' We may reasonably suppose that Hazlitt breakfasted; and, as reasonably, that he declined the proposal then made to him. Thus came to an end his only experience of editorship, an experience we should suppose to have been little to his taste, and which nothing but the circumstances of Scott's end would have caused him to embark upon.

We may pass over the remaining months of the year more rapidly. Crabb Robinson gives us a couple of entries:

'16 May: – Spent the evening over the Whist table at Lamb's. Played with Hazlitt, and we now speak a little.'

'20 July: – Took tea and spent the evening at Lamb's. Hazlitt there – little or no conversation between us. – His fondness for his child, though it is a troublesome & forward child, is a good feature in his character. We played Whist and I stayed late.' The child was now nearly ten years old, and a pupil in Latin Grammar to Mary Lamb, as his fellow-pupil Mary Novello, afterwards Mary Cowden Clarke, informs us.

In July we obtain an extremely pleasant and not unuseful reminder that Hazlitt's life was not all spent among his literary acquaintances who have left reminiscences. The writer of the letter which follows is one who is not otherwise known to us, but who was doubtless none the less a good fellow on that account:

Thomas Pittman to Hazlitt

Canterbury, July 16, 1821.

In the old palace of King Ethelbert, in the ancient monastery of St Augustine are – two Racket-Players! who have found the true city of God, the court in respect whereof St James's with the approaching ceremony is nought. A massy stone wall of thirteen hundred years' duration, even as a board placed by the hand of modern art, fair and smooth as Belphœbe's forehead, forms its point. No holes or crannies throw out the well-directed ball. No jutting rocks or pendent precipices spoil the hit and the temper. All is smooth. Eleven yards from each other are two abutments, round which monks formerly prayed or seemed to pray, and courtiers lied, and seemed to speak the truth. These bound the court, and form delicious side-walls; but alas! they terminate abruptly before they have proceeded five yards. Endless, however, is the variety these quickly ending walls occasion. Of chalky foundation, firm, even, and hard is the ground; eighty-six feet in length, ever widening as it recedes from the wall. Close behind the court, but not too close, and down a slight descent, is a large square bowling-green, encompassed by old cloister walls covered with vines and trees, and edged with flowers of all sorts, the rose being one. Immense arches, ivy-covered towers, time mutilated, at magnificent distances – the house itself, like one of those chapels which we see adjoining cathedrals – all show the real forte of a monk to have been architecture, not divinity. The keep, the straggling abutments, all, all declare –

The wars they still remember of King Nine,
Of old Assaracus, and Inachus divine – [1]

but nothing gloomy, all cheerful, lively, pleasing, gay:

1. A favourite quotation of Hazlitt, from the 'Faerie Queene,' is here quoted back at him.

In spot more delicious, though but feigned,
Long or Jack Davies never played, or Spines
Or Hazlitt vollied.[1]

The inhabitants are not altogether unworthy of the place. For country people they are excellent. Racket is a great humanizer of the species, and ought to be encouraged. ...

Do come. You never saw so pretty a place. It beats Netley Abbey, and is older. The court is really admirable, and has the property of drying in two hours after the longest succession of hard rains. Good chalk has no fellow. The only false hops are in the beer, which is damnable; every thing else is fair. Do come, and inquire for 'John Austin, at The Old Palace'; he is our landlord, where we have bed and board, and he keeps the court. That ever I should live in a Fives Court! Come, and you will see fine play from yours very truly,

THOMAS PITTMAN.

One of the old racket-players here says: 'Jack Davies was the finest player I ever saw, and, by God, there is nobody can come near him'.

We may think that Hazlitt went to Canterbury. For the month of August, however, he was at Winterslow.[2] If he made the cross-country journey partly on foot, he may, as a result of it, have written *On Going a Journey*.

VIII

On his return from his customary vacation tour Crabb Robinson introduces us to a new figure: '31 October: – I called on De

1. It was at this stroke, we gather, that Hazlitt excelled. John Payne Collier is our informant: 'We of course often met at the *Morning Chronicle* Office and at the Fives Court, where I was fond of seeing him play. He was famous for what are called *volleys.*' – (Carew Hazlitt MSS., Letter of 2 June 1867.)

2. Our authority for this stay is an hotel bill for the month, formerly in the possession of Mr W. C. Hazlitt.

Quincey: a visit of duty. De Q. is a tiresome man, though certainly of great talent. He is necessitous, and will be in great distress soon, for his talents are not marketable. He is in ill health, is querulous, very strongly impressed with his own excellence, and prone to despise others.' The Opium Eater had made his first appearance in the *London Magazine* for September, and he and Hazlitt now met for the first time at one of the new proprietors' monthly dinners. During the ensuing four years of De Quincey's London residence there was, on the former's own showing, extremely little acquaintance between them.

'When Taylor and Hessey purchased the *London Magazine*,' notes Procter, 'they opened a house in Waterloo Place for the better circulation of the publication. It was there that the contributors met once a month, over an excellent dinner, given by the firm; and consulted and talked on literary matters together. ... Hazlitt attended once or twice; but he was a rather silent guest, rising into emphatic talk only when some political discussion (very rare) stimulated him. Mr De Quincey appeared at only one of these dinners. The expression of his face was intelligent, but cramped and somewhat peevish. He was self-involved, and did not add to the cheerfulness of the meeting. I have consulted this gentleman's three essays, of which Charles Lamb is professedly the subject; but I cannot derive from them anything illustrative of my friend Lamb's character. I have been mainly struck therein by De Quincey's attacks on Hazlitt, to whom the essays had no relation. I am aware that the two authors had a quarrel in 1823; Hazlitt having claimed certain theories or reasonings which the other had propounded as his own.'

From the best known of the essays to which Procter refers we may make a quotation:

His inveterate misanthropy was constitutional. Exasperated it certainly had been by accidents of life, by disappointments, by mortifications, by insults, and still more by having wilfully placed himself in collision from the first with all the interests that were in the sunshine of the world, and with all the persons that were then powerful in England; but my impression was, if I had a right to *have* any impression with regard to one whom I knew so slightly, that no change of position or of fortunes could have brought Hazlitt into reconciliation with the fashion of this world, or of this England, or of 'this now'. *Whatever is* – so much I conceive to have been a fundamental lemma for Hazlitt – *is wrong*. So much he thought it safe to postulate. *How* it was wrong might require an impracticable investigation; you might fail for a century to discover; but *that* it was wrong he nailed down as a point of faith that could stand out against all counter-presumptions from argument or counter-evidences from experience. A friend of his it was – a friend wishing to love him, and admiring him almost to extravagance – who told me, in illustration of the dark sinister gloom which sate for ever upon his countenance and gestures, that involuntarily, when Hazlitt put his hand within his waistcoat (as a mere unconscious trick of habit), he himself felt a sudden recoil of fear, as from one who was searching for a hidden dagger.

De Quincey, for reasons which are not particularly mysterious to us, obtained so long a start of Hazlitt in the world's favour and in the dignity of a Collected Edition, that one is loath to put a question mark to a piece of portraiture so celebrated.[1] We cannot lose sight of the fact, however, that the 'friend' here cited is Lamb, and Lamb is to be found pulling De Quincey's leg on

1. It has, however, already been put there: 'Shade of William Hazlitt, what hours were thine and mine in those early days! ... There was the library, and in it the *London Magazine,* and in the magazine Hazlitt's "Essays on Art". It is said in books we have read since then, that Hazlitt was a gloomy and rather dangerous-looking man, who seemed as if he were feeling for a dagger. We won't believe it. We will allow him to have been dark and solemn and quiet and Dantesque; but what was mistaken for sinister and malignant was only a knitting the sober brow of Il Penseroso frowning away "the brood of folly without father bred".' – The painter James Smetham's *Letters* (1891). As for De Quincey's 'fundamental lemma', the reader who will turn to the essay *On Paradox and Commonplace,* from which we quoted a little on page 317, will see that he had *not* much right to his impression.

so many occasions that we feel that he may have been pulling it
on this one. 'Mr De Quincey and Hazlitt', notes Procter in another place, 'thought poorly of each other. Hazlitt pronounced
verbally that the other would be good only "whilst the opium
was trickling from his mouth", but he never published anything
derogatory to the other's genius.'

Among the qualities in Hazlitt of which De Quincey has set
on record an adverse opinion is his style, including his habit of
'trite quotation'. He gives us Coleridge's phrase for it — 'paraly-
tic mouth-diarrhœa'. We may perhaps read Hazlitt *On Familiar
Style,* in an essay which he wrote at this moment:

It is not easy to write a familiar style. Many people mistake
a familiar for a vulgar style, and suppose that to write without affectation is to write at random. On the contrary, there is
nothing that requires more precision, and if I may say so,
purity of expression, than the style I am speaking of. It utterly
rejects not only all unmeaning pomp, but all low, cant phrases,
and loose unconnected, *slipshod* allusions. It is not to take the
first word that offers, but the best word in common use; it is
not to throw words together in any combinations we please,
but to follow and avail ourselves of the true idiom of the
language. To write a genuine familiar or truly English style,
is to write as any one would speak in common conversation,
who had a thorough command and choice of words, or who
could discourse with ease, force, and perspicuity, setting aside
all pedantic and oratorical flourishes. ... I conceive that words
are like money, not the worse for being common, but that it is
the stamp of custom alone which gives them circulation or
value. I am fastidious in this respect, and would almost as
soon coin the currency of the realm as counterfeit the King's
English. I never invented or gave a new and unauthorized
meaning to any word but one single one (the term *impersonal*
applied to feelings) and that was in an abstruse metaphysical
discussion to express a very difficult distinction. I have been (I
know) loudly accused of revelling in vulgarisms and broken

English. I cannot speak to that point: but so far I plead guilty
to the determined use of acknowledged idioms and common
elliptical expressions. I am not sure that the critics in question
know the one from the other, that is, can distinguish any
medium between formal pedantry and the most barbarous
solecism. As an author, I endeavour to employ plain words
and popular modes of construction, as were I a chapman and
dealer, I should common weights and measures.

To point the allusion of this passage, the Quarterly, reviewing
Table-Talk in its issue for October, affixed to its author the
epithet 'slang-whanger', and added: 'Mr Hazlitt having already
undergone the wholesome discipline of our castigation, without
any apparent benefit, a repetition of it would be useless, as far as
regards himself: for the sake of the younger class of readers,
however, it may not be entirely fruitless to take some brief notice
of these crude, though laboured lucubrations'.

On 20 November Crabb Robinson has an entry which we may
regard with some sympathy: 'I dined in the Hall, & then came
home to read Hazlitt's Table Talk, a delightful volume though
it frequently annoys and disgusts me. But it was with mere pain
and no disapprobation that I read a sentence this morning [in
On the Ignorance of the Learned] which goes home to my feeling. "A lounger who is ordinarily seen with a book in his hand,
is (we may be almost sure) equally without the power or inclination to attend to what passes around him or in his own mind."
But having dismissed, though with a struggle, all hopes of reputation, I can read with tranquillity such a damning sentence. I
find other truths equally striking and equally painful in the
course of reading the volume.'

The essays which Hazlitt wrote during this autumn comprise
On a Landscape of Nicolas Poussin, Why Distant Objects Please,
and On Coffee-House Politicians.[1] To wind up the year's ac-

1. The last-named essay informing us that the evening circle at the
Southampton at this date comprised Joseph Hume, William Ayrton, and
Martin Burney – the first and last-named of whom, at least, remained
Hazlitt's fast friends throughout his life.

count – how good a year, no reader of his works will require to be told – he now wrote *The Fight*. The meeting between Neate and Hickman took place, at Hungerford in Berkshire, on 11 December. Hazlitt went to the fight with Joseph Parkes, another of his sporting and social acquaintances of whom we hear little, and he came back from it with Patmore, who dates from this event the beginning of the more than formal acquaintance between them. 'I believe it contributed greatly,' he says, 'to fix and confirm that feeling of regard and interest towards him which all that I had heretofore seen of him had called forth, while all that I had *heard* of him was calculated to persuade me that his character was incapable of exciting any but an opposite impression.'

How narrowly the readers of the *New Monthly Magazine* escaped missing an admirable piece of writing we may gather from a reminiscence of Cyrus Redding, in his book *Past Celebrities* : 'Campbell, chancing to call just as it [the manuscript] reached Colburn's office, the latter put it into his hands, and he took it home. I had engaged to take coffee with the poet, and he produced it. This was contrary to the publisher's arrangement with myself – all was to go through my hands. I imagined he did not suspect that the poet would like it, or that I might keep it back, from the nature of the subject. I said, "Why, it is a very vulgar thing for us! Don't you think so? ... Had we not better return the paper to Hazlitt? We have his series going on besides." "No, no," said the poet, "it is a picture of manners – your (i.e. English) manners. It is a history painting; let us insert it." I said no more, because I feared to talk much about Hazlitt, who had insisted in one of his lectures that Campbell had stolen the line, or the sense of the line,

> *"Like angels' visits, few and far between".*[1]

---

1. The reference is to a footnote to the *Lectures on the English Poets* of 1818 : 'There is the same idea in Blair's Grave –
> *... Its visits,*
> *Like those of angels, short, and far between.*

Mr Campbell in altering the expression has spoiled it. "Few" and "far

Redding, who first met Hazlitt at about the same date as Procter, gives us a portrait which is singularly in confirmation of his: 'I first met Hazlitt at Leigh Hunt's, and scarcely knew what to make of him. He gave one no idea of the man of thought, nor of the sagacity of which he was really the possessor. Except that I heard he had studied painting, and was deeply conversant with art, he would not at the first interview have attracted my attention. Men were present who shone much more in manner and conversation.' Adding that after he had seen him once or twice he did not again fall in with him until he began to work for the *New Monthly,* Redding goes on: 'He concealed nothing. His character was perfectly simple, and he expected to find everybody else the same. He had no concealed thought, for he brought all out, good, bad, or indifferent: it was his nature. It was not wonderful that a man who spoke out all he thought should have been abused and shunned. As to myself, there could be no difference between us. General conversation at long intervals of time made up all our relations with each other.'

It is in relation to the personal background of this year that our concluding letter is of importance:

Hazlitt to Talfourd

Winterslow Hut,

December 1. [1821]

My dear Sir, — I stand exceedingly indebted to you for your kind intentions & exertions in my favour. I am at present driven almost into a corner. What with uneasiness of mind & this failure of Warren's, I hardly know what to do. Could you ask Colburn (with whom I have already communicated) whether he will give me £200 for 20 Essays, advancing one Hundred, that is, the money for the first Ten Essays, which I will engage to complete & deliver in Two months from the

between" are the same thing.' This, we are to understand, Campbell never forgave — a circumstance that was unfortunate when we consider that he was to be Hazlitt's principal editor for the remaining nine years of his life. Hazlitt's relations with the *New Monthly Magazine,* however, as Redding informs us, were always with its publisher, Colburn.

present time, & which he may make use of either for the
Magazine or in a Volume with what title he pleases – only in
the former case I wish to reserve right of copy. I am busy
about Lady Morgan, & will do it *con amore* if I can but get
out of this present hobble. I have about £50 to pay as soon as
I get back to town, which the Review of Lady M. alone would
do, but I am too uncomfortable, I fear, to get through it properly, circumstanced as I am. 50, you will say then, would do.
Be it so; but I should work much better for the other. Also,
propose to him (if you please) the Picturesque Tour in Italy
with an account of the Vatican, at the same price, with one
Hundred for my expenses. The truth is, I seem to have been
hurt in my mind lately, and continual effort to no purpose is
too much for any patience, & mine is nearly exhausted. My
dear Talfourd, if you have a girl that loves you & that you
have a regard for, lose no time in marrying, & think yourself
happy, whatever else may happen. Excuse this from yours
very truly,

W. H.

P.S. – A thought has just struck me, that if Colburn chose
to buy Warren's volume, he might use the Essays for the
Magazine in the first instance (they are all *virgins* but one) &
publish the book afterwards, & in the meantime I will write a
new series; that is, I will sell him 40 Essays or Table-talks for
£400, to do what he pleases with, he advancing me £100
down, & I giving him up half the copy *instanter*. The subjects
are not at all blown upon.

Hazlitt had thus had a financial set-back at a moment which
was peculiarly unfortunate, as we shall understand from the
next chapter. We may note here that Warren's volume passed
to Colburn as suggested, and that, no doubt as a condition of the
arrangement, at the end of this year the *London Magazine* lost
Table Talk, the first to make its appearance in the *New
Monthly,* in January, being *On Going a Journey.*

To bring the year to a close we have one more entry from Crabb Robinson: '19 December: — I went late to Lamb's. A small whist party there. Read to L. some of Wordsworth's MSS. — he hardly seemed to relish them. But Hazlitt was there, and his presence might disturb even L.'s attention.' It might, we imagine, when the diarist was freely mingling poetry with hero-worship. The shade from the next year's events, however, as we have learned, was already across him.

CHAPTER XI

LIBER AMORIS

(1822–3)

*

Men act from passion; and we can only judge of passion
by sympathy.

On Reason and Imagination.

I

'If you have a girl that loves you and that you have a regard
for, lose no time in marrying, and think yourself happy, whatever else may happen.' So we found Hazlitt writing to Talfourd,
and so, in his forty-fourth year, he hoped against hope that it
was to be with himself. The story of his disillusionment is
written in the book whose title is placed at the head of this
chapter.

First of all, of course, it was necessary for him to get rid, in
his own case, of that 'ill-advised connection in marriage' with
which he credits the hero of his only piece of fictional narrative.
His own marriage is not so long ago that we have forgotten its
circumstances, little illumination as it has recently received. He
had been living apart from his wife for some years, certainly
since the end of 1819. In August 1820, as we have seen, he had
removed his town lodging to 9 Southampton Buildings, a few
doors from his own earlier residence. The proprietor of the
house was a tailor named Walker – the tailor, as it happened,
of both Crabb Robinson and Procter – whose elder daughter was
married, at a date before Hazlitt made the acquaintance of the
family, to Robert Roscoe, a solicitor who had lodged in the

house, and a son of that William Roscoe who had been among Hazlitt's early Liverpool patrons. We might have the testimony of Crabb Robinson, if it were called for, that this marriage was an eminently successful one. A second daughter, Sarah, is the heroine of the *Liber Amoris*. The reader of that work may regard its first part as providing the inner history of the past twelve months of our narrative.

Sarah Walker makes her first entry into Hazlitt's extraneous writings in the essay *On Living to One's-Self*, which was written, as we saw, at Winterslow in January 1821 :

He who looks at beauty to admire, to adore it, who reads of its wondrous power in novels, in poems, or in plays, is not unwise : but let no man fall in love, for from that moment he is 'the baby of a girl'. I like very well to repeat such lines as these in the play of Mirandola —

> ' — *With what a waving air she goes*
> *Along the corridor. How like a fawn!*
> *Yet statelier! Hark! No sound, however soft,*
> *Nor gentlest echo telleth when she treads,*
> *But every motion of her shape doth seem*
> *Hallowed by silence* — '

but however beautiful the description, defend me from meeting with the original !

The point of the allusion, of course, was that Hazlitt had already met with the original. Procter's *Mirandola* was produced by Macready at Covent Garden in March 1821, and it was published a little earlier. The same essay contained the reflexion : 'How few out of the infinite number of those that marry and are given in marriage, wed with those they would prefer to all the world : nay, how far the greater proportion are joined together by mere motive of convenience, accident, recommendation of friends, or indeed not infrequently by the

very fear of the event, by repugnance and a sort of fatal fascina-
tion : yet the tie is for life, not to be shaken off with disgrace or
death; a man no longer lives to himself, but is a body (as well
as mind) chained to another, in spite of himself –

· *"Like life and death in disproportion met".'*

Here we have the other side of the Lambs' principle of union
(for other people) 'for the joke's sake'. Of the preliminary
negotiations for the dissolution of the marriage, carried on doubtless through the latter half of the year 1821, we see nothing. At
that date, English law did not place the benefit of divorce within the means of ill-mated members of the professional classes.
In the project which took Hazlitt to Scotland he had the pre-
cedent, if not the guidance, of his colleague John Black of the
Morning Chronicle, who in 1814 had emerged with success from
a similar undertaking.

II

The year 1822[1] opens in a manner sufficiently prosaic, with a
note to Colburn : 'Dear Sir, – Could you favour me with a
proof of the *Fight* this evening, or on Monday? I wish you
would desire the printer to return me the copy. I hope to leave
for Scotland next week, and shall begin the new volume of
Table-Talk as soon as I set out. I am, dear Sir, your much
obliged humble servant, W. HAZLITT.' This is without other
superscription than 'Saturday evening', but the next, from
Hessey, gives us date 23 January : 'My dear Sir, – I have the
pleasure to send you, enclosed, a cheque for twenty pounds. I
have not had time to make out the account; but from a slight
glance at it, I think the paper on the [Elgin] Marbles, just
received, will pretty nearly balance it. Shall I put your signa-

---

1. A reference must be made for this section to the edition of the
Liber Amoris, 'privately printed', of Messrs R. Le Gallienne and W. C.
Hazlitt (1894), which contains, in addition to Mrs Hazlitt's Journal from
April to July, the text of eleven letters to Patmore over the same period.
The legal aspects of the 'Scottish Divorce' are examined with authority
by Mr Birrell in his *English Men of Letters* volume.

ture, W. H. or I., at the foot of the paper? Please to send a line by bearer to answer this question, and to say you have received the cheque – a pleasing journey to you.' Something of the circumstances in which Hazlitt, a few days prior to these notes, had already left Southampton Buildings, will be known to the reader of the *Liber Amoris*. His latest activity, before setting out, was to put his son to school.

He did not proceed direct to Scotland, but was 'detained at Stamford', and there began, dating the manuscript 29 January, 'a book of our conversations (I mean mine and the statue's) which I call *Liber Amoris*'.[1] He did something else, the desire to do which was most probably the cause of his 'detention': he revisited Burleigh, and obtained the materials for the essay on its pictures (and in a greater degree on himself) which came out in the *London Magazine* in April. This done, he resumed his journey. Alighting forty miles short of his destination, at the Renton Inn, Berwickshire, he threw himself, while qualifying by residence for the jurisdiction of the Scottish court, into the second volume of *Table Talk*.

He has been at Renton 'a month yesterday' when, in a letter of early March, the result is reported to Patmore: 'You may tell Colburn, when you see him, that his work is done magnificently, to wit:

    I. On the Knowledge of Character 40
    II. Advice to a Schoolboy 60
    III. Patronage and Puffing 50

1. He was not, of course, at this date contemplating the completion of the published narrative, but was writing the conversations which form its first part to solace himself during his enforced 'probation'. He had undertaken, that is to say, not to return to Southampton Buildings until he was in a position to offer marriage. That the Pygmalion analogy was already in his mind we may know, not only from this reference, but from the *Advice to a Schoolboy* written at Renton: 'We trifle with, make sport of, and despise those who are attached to us, and follow those that fly from us. "We hunt the wind, we worship a statue, cry aloud to the desert." ' The quotation, from Smollett's *Don Quixote,* is one which is much in his mind from this date.

With this burst of work he brought up to more than fifty the
Table Talks which he had written in the space of less than two
years.

The month at Renton was a month of hope, and the work he
did there, as the reader will hardly require to be told, comprised some of the sanest and best of his life. With the report to
Patmore, we may compare the two letters at the end of the first
part of the *Liber Amoris*: 'Feb. 1822 : – You will scold me for
writing, and ask me if this is keeping my promise to mind my
work. One half of it was to think of Sarah : and besides, I do
not neglect my work either, I assure you. I regularly do ten
pages a day, which mounts up to thirty guineas worth a week,
so that you see I should grow rich at this rate, if I could keep
on so.' 'March, 1822 : – You will be glad to learn that I have
done my work – a volume in less than a month. This is one
reason why I am better than when I came. ... I am pleased I
have got through this job, as I was afraid I might lose reputation by it (which I can little afford to lose) – and besides, I am
more anxious to do well now, as I wish you to hear me well
spoken of.' We can have little doubt that these were the actual
words of letters written to Sarah Walker from Renton.

His work finished, he went on to Edinburgh. By 30 March
he has made the personal acquaintance of Jeffrey : 'I have seen
the great little man, and he is very gracious to me – *et sa femme
aussi!* I tell him I am dull and out of spirits, and he says he

cannot perceive it. He is a person of an infinite vivacity. My Sardanapalus is to be in. In my judgement Myrrha is most like S. W., only I am not like Sardanapalus.' The review of Byron's tragedy in the March *Edinburgh Review* is one of the minor mysteries attaching to the editorship of that work. Hazlitt, it is clear, thought that it was going to be his; but the review as it appeared is certainly not his in its integrity, and it was afterwards claimed by Jeffrey. It was, no doubt, like others we have seen (see Appendix), a concerted effort. This letter concludes: 'It is well I had finished Colburn's work, before all this came upon me'.

The month of April, spent by Hazlitt in lodgings at 10 George Street, Edinburgh, was one of the most unfortunate of his life. In ill-health, in uncertainty as to the intentions both of the girl whom he wished to marry and of the wife from whom he hoped to free himself, his nerves played upon daily by the injudicious missives of Patmore, he relapsed from the severe ordinance which he had imposed upon himself for the only time that we know of in the last fifteen years of his life: 'Be it known to you that while I write this I am drinking ale at the Black Bull celebrated in *Blackwood*. It is owing to your letter. Could I think the love "honest", I am proof against Edinburgh ale. She by her silence makes my "dark hour", and you dissipate it for four and twenty hours.' Nevertheless, we can have small doubt that in outward demeanour he struck others as as rational a being as he had struck Jeffrey. On the 16th of a month in which, from his letters to Patmore, we know him to have reached the depths, he forwards a paper on the Edinburgh artist Hugh Williams's *Views in Greece* to Hessey for the *London Magazine*, and says: 'I send the enclosed, but fear it is hardly worth the while. Yet it may oblige a meritorious artist and keep my work unbroken.' His confidants in the business which had brought him to Scotland were Ritchie of the *Scotsman* newspaper, whose acquaintance he had no doubt made in London, and in a less degree Jeffrey, who recommended him to a solicitor. In the last week of April Mrs Hazlitt arrived, and henceforward for three months the curious reader may have the benefit of that lady's published Journal.

We shall content ourselves in these pages with a single quotation:

'Sunday, 28 April, 1822: — Wrote to Mr Hazlitt to inform him I had only between five and six pounds of my quarter's money left, and therefore if he did not send me some immediately, and fulfil his agreement for the rest, I should be obliged to return on Tuesday.

'Tuesday, 30 April: — In the evening, after some hesitation, went to Mr Hazlitt myself for an answer. He told me he expected £30 from Colburn on Thursday, and then he would let me have £5 for present expenses, that he had but £1 in his pocket, but if I wanted it, I should have that. That he was going to give two lectures at Glasgow next week, for which he was to have £100, and he had £80 besides to receive for the Table Talk in a fortnight, out of which sums he pledged himself to fulfil his engagements relative to my expenses, and also to make me a handsome present when all was over (£20), as I seemed to love money; or it would enable me to travel back by land, as I said I should prefer seeing something of the country to going back in the steam-boat, which he proposed. Said he would give the note of hand for £50 to Mr Ritchie for me, payable to whoever I pleased: if he could conveniently at the time, it should be for three months instead of six; but he was not certain of that. Said that Mr Ritchie was a most respectable man, a lawyer, and one of the editors of the *Scotsman*. Enquired if I had taken the oath. I told him I only waited a summons from Mr Gray [Mrs Hazlitt's solicitor] if I could depend upon the money, but I could not live in a strange place without; and I had no friends, or means of earning money here, as he had — though, as I still had £4, I could wait a few days. I asked him how the child's expenses or my draught were to be paid, if he went abroad. And he answered that, if he succeeded in the divorce, he should be easy in his mind, and able to work, and then he should probably be back in three months; but otherwise, he might leave England for ever. He said that as soon as I had got him to sign a paper giving away £150 a year from himself, I talked of going back and leaving everything, as if I meant to bamboozle him. I told him to recollect that it was no advantage for myself that I sought; nor should I get a halfpenny by it; it was only to secure something to *his* child, as well as mine. He said he could do very well for the child himself, and that he was allowed to be a very indulgent kind father; some people thought too much so. I said I did not dispute his fondness for him; but I must observe that, though he got a great deal of money, he never saved, or had any by him, or was likely to make much provision for the child. ... He said I had always despised him and his abilities. I asked if the women with whom he associated were any better judges of them, and told him, that in spite of his assertion, that he did not wish them to know or understand that he had abilities,[1] nobody was more sore on that point; but I added that all recrimination was now useless, as probably all intercourse between us had for ever ended. He said he should be very good friends with me, and acknowledge himself obliged, if I carried through the business; if not, he would never see me again. I told him I should certainly not want to see him in that event. He said that a paper had been brought to him from Mr Gray that day; but that he was only just come in from Lanark, after walking thirty miles, and was getting his tea. Said I had better not come there again; and I told him I did not intend it, without a necessity, and observed to him that I had come in the dusk of the evening, and in a veil.'

In the first days of May we obtain an objective view of Hazlitt which, owing to the circumstances of the moment, is of peculiar interest. We find it in the *Life* of George Combe, the phrenologist and psychologist of Edinburgh, in a letter of date 10 May:

1. Mrs Hazlitt had been reading *On Great and Little Things,* in the February *New Monthly*: 'I do not care a fig for any woman that knows even what *an author* means. If I know that she has read any thing I have written, I cut her acquaintance immediately.' It would appear, however, that on this point Mrs Hazlitt was right.

'I met Hazlitt in Ritchie's at supper. He appears to be about forty. He drank no wine or fermented liquor, but an enormous quantity of tea. He mentioned that he had hurt himself by drinking too freely, and had given up all strong potations. He is short and of a moderate thickness. His head, so far as could be seen, appeared to be as follows: [Here follow the phrenological details, which we shall omit as somewhat overweighting the portrait.] The forehead retreats slightly but is decidedly capacious, and as the face is small it has a fine effect. The expression of the eyes is that of benevolence, veneration, hope, and ideality. The mouth indicates combativeness and destructiveness; lips thin and sharp. When he talks, the manner is bland and destitute of ostentation; clear rather than vehement or sparkling. When he laughs, the features become cuttingly sharp. He is a well-bred man, does not monopolize conversation, listens with attention and interest to any one who speaks, and affects nothing. The sparkling coruscations which gleam in his works are to be traced in his conversation; but they require to be looked for to be discovered, for the manner is so smooth and they flow so much in the current of his ordinary thoughts, that they do not attract attention by their prominence in delivery. If you pause in the conversation and reflect on what has been said during the last five minutes, you perceive that you have been talking with an uncommon man. I left him at half-past one, and he was still sitting.' A day or so later this informant adds: 'Hazlitt is gone to Glasgow, to lecture on the Poets of Queen Elizabeth: he has actually got his published lectures in MS., and means to read them, trusting to the people's ignorance of literature for escaping detection. I had some scruples about lecturing after publishing, but I shall fall far short of this.' Hazlitt went to Glasgow on 4 May, and delivered there, on the 6th and 13th, two lectures, the first on Milton and the second on Thomson and Burns. They were drawn, no doubt, from the *English Poets*.

The lectures over, Hazlitt with Sheridan Knowles, who had been responsible for the arrangements connected with their delivery, started on a walk to the Highlands:

You remember the morning when I said, 'I will go and repose my sorrows at the foot of Ben Lomond' – and when from Dumbarton-bridge its giant shadow, clad in air and sunshine, appeared in view. We had a pleasant day's walk. ... You startled me every now and then from my reverie by the robust voice, in which you asked the country people (by no means prodigal of their answers) – 'If there was any trout-fishing in those streams?' – and our dinner at Luss set us up for the rest of our day's march. The sky now became overcast; but this, I think, added to the effect of the scene. The road to Tarbet is superb. It is on the very verge of the Lake – hard, level rocky, with low stone bridges constantly flung across it, and fringed with birch trees, just then budding into spring, behind which, as through a slight veil, you saw the huge shadowy form of Ben Lomond. It lifts its enormous but graceful bulk direct from the edge of the water without any projecting lowlands, and has in this respect much the advantage of Skiddaw. Loch Lomond comes upon you by degrees as you advance, unfolding and then withdrawing its conscious beauties like an accomplished coquet. You are struck with the point of a rock, the arch of a bridge, the Highland huts (like the first rude habitations of men) dug out of the soil, built of turf, and covered with brown heather, a sheep-cote, some straggling cattle feeding half-way down a precipice; but as you advance farther on, the view expands into the perfection of Lake scenery. It is nothing (or your eye is caught by nothing) but water, earth, and sky. Ben Lomond waves to the right, in its simple majesty, cloud-capt or bare, and descending to a point at the head of the Lake, shews the Trossacs beyond, tumbling about their blue ridges like woods waving; to the left is the Cobler, whose top is like a castle shattered in pieces and nodding to its ruin; and at your side rise the shapes of round pastoral hills, green, fleeced with herds, and retiring into mountainous bays and upland valleys, where solitude and peace might make their lasting home, if peace were to be found in solitude! That it was not always so, I was a sufficient proof; for there was one image that alone haunted me in the midst of all this sublimity and beauty, and turned it to a mockery and a dream!

The snow on the mountain would not let us ascend; and being weary of waiting and of being visited by the guide every few hours to let us know that the weather would not do, we returned, you homewards, and I to London.

So in the *Liber Amoris*; and so, we have no doubt, in fact. Hazlitt took the steamboat to London, returned to Southampton Buildings, and there, on the day following his arrival, enacted the scene which is described in the first letter of the third part of the book. As though for confirmation of every word of it, there survives a note to Hessey, which we are able to date at 18 or 19 May: – 'My Dear Sir, – Will you oblige me by letting me have the following prettily bound: viz., Vicar of Wakefield, Man of Feeling, and Nature and Art? I am here for a day or two, but am going to Salisbury. I have been to New Lanark. – Yours ever truly, W. HAZLITT.' The recipient for whom the books were intended, and the significance of the gift, will not have been forgotten by the reader of the *Liber Amoris*. If the account there given is studied, it will appear certain that Hazlitt changed his mind about going to Winterslow, and instead spent a week at Southampton Buildings, passing for the press the second volume of *Table Talk*.

For his presence in town, Patmore supplies us with one of his rare (and even more rarely accurate) dates: 'May 21 (Tuesday), 1822: – On Sunday, while we (Hazlitt and myself) were with John Hunt, he (Hazlitt) related two or three nice things about Jeffrey.' The nice things have evaporated in Patmore's pages, as they have a way of doing; but we may find the following of interest: 'Returning to my visit to Mr John Hunt, in the Coldbath Fields Prison[1] – after walking and conversing for

1. John Hunt's second term of political imprisonment, of a year from 28 May, 1821, under the Six Acts of 1819. Leigh Hunt's reasons for withdrawing from joint control of the *Examiner* just in time to avoid this

some time in the prison garden, where we found Mr Hunt, he led us to his apartment. Here the first thing that struck me was a picture over the mantelpiece, of an old country-woman in a bonnet, which, it immediately occurred to me, was one I had heard spoken of as Hazlitt's first attempt as an artist. Hazlitt pointed to it with great apparent satisfaction, and asked me if I had ever seen it before, or knew what it was; but he seemed to shrink from distinctly saying *what* it was, and I was left to learn this from inquiry of Mr Hunt himself. The picture, I found, belonged to Hazlitt himself. He kept it as a precious relic, not of his success, but of his *failure,* as a painter – to which art he had at one time intended to devote himself. The reader will probably call to mind some beautiful reminiscences of this picture in his essay, *On the Pleasures* [sic] *of Painting.'*

In the last days of May, Hazlitt left Southampton Buildings (under circumstances which will once more be known to the reader of the *Liber Amoris*) and returned to Edinburgh, where the divorce proceedings were dragging their protracted length, while Mrs Hazlitt was taking extended trips into the Highlands and even to Ireland, on supplemented means which she extracted from her husband under threat of throwing up her part in the affair. He sought out Knowles, but found him 'gone from home'. On 9 June, in a letter to Patmore, we learn : 'Jeffrey (to whom I did a little unfold) came down with a £100 to give me time to recover, and I am going to Renton Inn to see if I can work a little in the three weeks before it will be over, if all goes well. Tell Colburn to send the Table Talk to him, 92 George Street, Edinburgh, unless he is mad, and wants to ruin me and the book.' We know of no work done on this occasion at Renton, and we should very strongly doubt whether the state of his mind (amply illustrated in the published correspondence to Patmore) permitted him to do any. On 20 June he returned to Edinburgh,

second instalment of political martyrdom will be found in a letter to Shelley of 1 March. (*Correspondence,* I. 162.) Whether he wrote the editorial 'libel' on the House of Commons for which his brother suffered does not appear.

to find that Mrs Hazlitt had taken the oath. On the 17th of the following month the proceedings came to their termination, and Hazlitt returned to town to enact the final scenes of the published narrative.

Our first exterior guidance is on 8 September from Haydon to Miss Mitford: 'Hazlitt at present gives me great pain by the folly with which he is conducting himself. He has fallen in love with a lodging-house hussy, who will be his death. He has been to Scotland and divorced his wife [this statement should, of course, be *vice versa*] although he has a fine little boy by her; and after doing this to marry this girl, he comes back and finds she has been making a fool of him in order to get presents, and in reality has been admitting a lover more favoured. Hazlitt's torture is beyond expression; you may imagine it. The girl really excited in him devoted and intense love. His imagination clothed her with that virtue which her affected modesty induced him to believe in, and he is really downright in love with an ideal perfection, which has no existence but in his own head! He talks of nothing else day and night. He has written down all the conversations without colour, literal as they happened; he has preserved all the love-letters, many of which are equal to anything of the sort, and really affecting; and I believe, in order to ease his soul of this burden, means, with certain arrangements, to publish it as a tale of character. He will sink into idiotcy if he does not get rid of it.'

To a date slightly earlier, we should suppose, belongs this reminiscence of Procter's:

Upon one occasion I know that he told the story of his attachment to five different persons in the same day, and at each time entered into minute details of his love story. 'I am a cursed fool,' said he to me. 'I saw J – – going into Will's Coffee-house yesterday morning; he spoke to me. I followed him into the house and whilst he lunched, I told him the whole story. Then' (said he), 'I wandered into the Regent's Park, where I met one of M[ontagu]'s sons. I walked with him some time, and on his using some civil expression, by God! sir, I told him the whole story.' Then he mentioned another instance, which I forget. 'Well sir' (he went on), 'I then went and called on Haydon; but he was out. There was only his man, Sammons, there; but, by God; I could not help myself. It all came out; the whole cursed story! Afterwards I went to look at some lodgings at Pimlico. The landlady at one place after some explanations as to rent, etc, said to me very kindly, "I am afraid you are not well, sir?" – "No, ma'am", said I, "I am not well"; and on inquiring further, the devil take me, if I did not let out the whole story, from beginning to end!'

This has the stamp of authenticity; and receives additional point from the circumstance that Hazlitt told it against himself, as he might have done in an essay. 'To this girl', Procter adds, 'he gave all his valuable time, all his wealthy thoughts, and all the loving frenzy of his heart. For a time, I think that on this point he was substantially insane.'

III

We have seen Hazlitt go down, and we have now to see him get up again. For five months, the longest hiatus in his professional career, he had had no work in the magazines. From November his sketches of the picture galleries, broken off in the spring, were resumed in the *London Magazine* with an article on Fonthill, recently thrown open to the public on its sale by Beckford. From a study of these we are able to say that after the *dénouement* at Southampton Buildings he resorted to Winterslow.[1] He had, for a short time, a new stimulus for his return to work.

1. The first written, although the second to appear in the Magazine (Mr Angerstein's Collection), begins with the apostrophe to Art, 'balm of hurt minds'; the second (Cleveland House) contains the passage; 'And lo! over the clear lone brow of Tudorley and Norman Court, knit into the web and fibres of our heart, the sighing groves wave in the autumnal

At the close of 1821 Leigh Hunt, abandoning all his literary ventures and leaving his brother John in prison, had accepted the invitation of Shelley and departed with his numerous family for Italy. But no sooner had he arrived, than Shelley was drowned (8 July), and the proposed new literary quarterly, the project for which had been one inducement in taking Hunt out, was left to a scarcely compatible partnership between himself and Byron. The situation as Hazlitt found it on his first and second returns from Scotland (John Hunt having been released from his imprisonment at the end of May) he afterwards describes in *On the Jealousy and the Spleen of Party*:

Mr Moore darted backwards and forwards from the Coldbath Fields Prison to the *Examiner* office, from Mr Longman's to Mr Murray's shop, in a state of ridiculous trepidation, to see what was to be done to prevent this degradation of the aristocracy of letters, this indecent encroachment of plebeian pretensions, this undue extension of patronage and compromise of privilege. The Tories were shocked that Lord Byron should grace the popular side by his direct countenance and assistance – the Whigs were shocked that he should share his confidence and counsels with any who did not unite the double recommendations of birth and genius. ... The cabal, the bustle, the confidential rumours were at their height when, after Mr Shelley's death, I was invited to take part in this obnoxious publication.

Hazlitt's part in a publication entitled *The Liberal: Verse and Prose from the South,* is clear enough under the first head, but not very clear under the second. It was, of course, produced and published by John Hunt in London. On 2 October we find air, deserted by Love, by Hope, but forever haunted by Memory!' Hazlitt, no doubt, saw these galleries before leaving town, and visited Fonthill from Winterslow. There is a peculiarly poignant interest in the little volume, *Sketches of the Principal Picture Galleries in England,* that it contains the first evidence of his return to work after his knock-down blow.

Crabb Robinson reading the first number (containing Shelley's 'May Day Night' and Byron's 'Vision of Judgment') and remarking: 'I read the *Liberal*. This worthless work will scarcely reach a second, certainly not a third number.' In this estimate the diarist was just three numbers out: the *Liberal* lasted long enough for Hazlitt, starting with the second number, to make five wholly admirable contributions, including one which we would not willingly be without.

At the conclusion of Mrs Hazlitt's Journal of her Trip to Scotland we may find her entering: 'He said he meant to go to Winterslow and try if he could write, for he had been so distracted the last five months that he could do nothing, and perhaps he would let me know another time what he had suffered. That he might also go to his mother's for a short time, and that he meant to take the child from school at the half quarter, and take him with him.' The second half of this programme I think we may say that he now carried out. After a month's work at Winterslow for the *Liberal* and for the *London Magazine* we find him back in town in time to date his essay on the Dulwich Gallery, and on the boys at the adjacent college, '5 November'. If he then withdrew his own son from school and departed on his visit to Devonshire it would be to a revived impression of 'the country about Nether Stowey' that we owe *My First Acquaintance with Poets*.

Our concluding evidence for the year is given by Crabb Robinson: '3 November: – Read a couple of essays by Hazlitt in bed'. These, no doubt, would be in the second volume of *Table Talk*. 'I afterwards called on Mrs Montagu and had a long chat with her. I was not sorry to find that she views Hazlitt as I do, and I infer from what she said that he no longer visits the house. I hope to hear this confirmed. She intimates that Lamb has broken with him.'

IV

The magazines having been provided for in the manner we have seen, we know of nothing that need have brought Hazlitt back to town until well into the new year. On 8 January Crabb Robinson gives us an entry: 'I read of Lord B. at the Surrey Institution, his Heaven & Earth ... The rest of *Liberal* No. 2 is bad enough – a malignant article or two by Hazlitt have less than his usual talent.' In this the wish was father to the thought, for *On the Scotch Character* and *On the Spirit of Monarchy* are by no means unworthy predecessors of the essay which was next to follow them.

Our first evidence of his return is unfortunate:

Hazlitt to Talfourd

5 Coleman Street Buildings,
Feb. 12.

My Dear Sir, – I have been arrested this morning, and am at a loss what to do. Would you give me a call to talk the matter over, and see if your influence could procure me any terms of accommodation? I am sorry to plague you about my troublesome affairs. Believe me, very truly your obliged friend and servant,

W. HAZLITT.

That the hiatus in the preceding year should have resulted in financial embarrassment is no surprise to us, but we do not know at the instance of what creditor he was proceeded against. The experience was unique in his career, and the impression of it, says his grandson, was never removed from his mind. Talfourd, no doubt, was both able and willing to procure terms of accommodation.

Our next information is contained in a letter of the 25th from John Hunt to Leigh, regarding the affairs of the *Liberal*: 'We have two articles from Mr Hazlitt (*My First Acquaintance with Poets* and a set of *Maxims*) and Mr Hogg is to let us have one soon. Mr Patmore, a friend of Mr Hazlitt's, is also desirous of contributing, but of this you will determine, if the work is to proceed.'[1] The set of maxims did not appear in the *Liberal,* and they formed, no doubt, the volume *Characteristics: in the*

1. Leigh Hunt MSS.

Manner of Rochefoucauld's Maxims, which had been the
occupation of Hazlitt's leisure during his absence from town.
If we wish to know his mind in the interval, it is into this
volume that we glance:

We are not weaned from a misplaced attachment by (at
last) discovering the unworthiness of the object. The character of a woman is one thing; her graces and attractions
another; and these last acquire even an additional charm and
piquancy from the disappointment we feel in other respects.
The truth is, a man in love prefers his passion to every other
consideration, and is fonder of his mistress than he is of
virtue. Should she prove vicious, she makes vice lovely in his
eyes.

It is provoking to hear people at their ease talking reason
to others in a state of violent suffering. If you can remove
their suffering by speaking a word, do so; and then they will
be in a state to hear calm reason.

We may hate and love the same person, nay even at the
same moment.

People try to reconcile you to a disappointment in love, by
asking why you should cherish a passion for an object that
has proved itself worthless. Had you known this before, you
would not have encouraged the passion; but that having been
once formed, knowledge does not destroy it. If we have drank
poison, finding it out does not prevent its being in our veins:
so passion leaves its poison in the mind! It is the nature of all
passion and of all habitual affection; we throw ourselves upon
it at a venture, but we cannot return by choice. If it is a wife
that has proved unworthy, men compassionate the loss, because there is a tie, they say, which we cannot get rid of. But
has the heart no ties? Or if it is a child, they understand it.
But is not true love a child? Or when another has become a
part of ourselves, 'where we must live or have no life at all,'
can we tear them from us in an instant? – No: these bargains
are for life; and that for which our souls have sighed for

years, cannot be forgotten without a breath, and without a pang.

What, on Hazlitt's return, had been his first step?

The answer is contained in a document which Mr W. C. Hazlitt prints in his *Lamb and Hazlitt,* but of which, owing to a misapprehension of the date, he fails to appreciate the significance. It belongs, not to the March of 1822 but to the March of 1823, and it shows Hazlitt to have been still reluctant to issue the work which he had contemplated publishing in the preceding September. Before doing so now, he sent an emissary (a certain 'mild F.', whom we are unable to identify) to lodge at Southampton Buildings, and the document consists of a diary of this friend's reports and of Hazlitt's comments upon them which extends from the fourth to the sixteenth of the month. At the end of it we read: 'Damn'd, treble damn'd idiot, when shall I burn her out of my thoughts?' It was in the hope of doing this, I think we may conclude, that the *Liber Amoris* was now sent to the press. The finishing touches were put to the work by the hand which had in the meantime written *My First Acquaintance with Poets* and *Characteristics*; and as to the 'certain arrangements' of which we found Haydon speaking we have no reason to doubt that the disguise in which Hazlitt now issued the story to the world was deemed by him to be sufficient.

With the book off his hands, he felt able to look round him again. He had come back to new lodgings in the West End. His work for the *London Magazine* was continued, and Table Talk for the *New Monthly* resumed. The *Edinburgh Review* for May contained his admirable survey, *The Periodical Press*. In addition, we are presented with a letter:

Hazlitt to Thomas Cadell
4 Chapel Street West, Curzon Street,
April 17, 1823

Sir, – Unless you agree to give up the publication of *Black-*

wood's Magazine, I shall feel myself compelled to commence an action against you for damages sustained from repeated slanders and false imputations in that work on me.

W. HAZLITT.

Cadell was the bookseller who, at one or two removes, had succeeded Murray in the agency for *Blackwood's.* The student of the refinements of that magazine will find Hazlitt's name beginning to make a reappearance in its columns early in 1822. In March of that year, his review of Scott's *Pirate* in the *London* had been greeted as 'a delightful piece of criticism', and in the same number the Professor of Moral Philosophy had so far relaxed as to remark in the earliest of his 'Noctes': 'O, Hazlitt's a real fellow in his small way'. Hazlitt in Edinburgh, however, seems to have omitted certain measures of prudence which he was expected to take, for in August his *Table Talk* is termed 'pitiable trash', and the Professor concludes a ten-page 'review' with 'merely observing that Hazlitt shewed a great want of trap by not coming to sup with us during his late northern progress'. The process of disillusionment was completed by the essay *On the Scotch Character,* in which Hazlitt had remarked (giving his sufficiently impersonal reasons) that 'of all *blackguards* (I use the term for want of any other) a Scotch blackguard is the worst'. The reprisals with which he was visited for this article were the immediate occasion of his note to Mr Cadell.

Once more a note from Hazlitt is followed by a considerable fluttering in the bookselling dovecotes. Cadell writes to Blackwood, on the 18th: 'Annexed is a copy of a letter I have just received, the contents of which certainly make me feel somewhat uncomfortable. This is the first appeal to me, accompanied with a threat, as publisher of your Magazine, and though Mr H. may be considered deserving of censure upon most occasions, my feelings would not be of the most agreeable nature, were my name brought before the public by him as disseminator of slanderous and false imputations.' Blackwood's reception of the news is not this time extant, but that it caused him anxiety we may probably gather from a letter of May which has survived: 'Cadell's affair is rather more serious. If he be bullied by that vagabond Hazlitt, would it be impossible for you to heal the old wounds between you and Murray? Believe me, it would be worth trying, and Croker[1] is a fine channel. What I principally write to you about is this. As you cannot go soon enough to London yourself to superintend the details of this affair, would it be possible for you to get Cadell to hold over his determination of giving up "Maga" till the end of next month? If so, I offer myself as your plenipotentiary, for, God willing, I shall be in London about the 27th of June. I think I should be able to shew the true state of the case to Cadell, and to palaver him out of sticking to Hazlitt.' The writer of this letter was William Maginn, a subject for a modification of Hazlitt's dictum upon the Scotch character in favour of the Irish, if the *Liberal* had lived long enough. But with its July issue it came to its end, with two contributions from Hazlitt's pen, on *Dr Chalmers and Mr Irving* and on *Arguing in a Circle*.

It is by means of the first of these articles (reporting a sermon of Irving's on 22 June) that we know that he had remained on in town. *Liber Amoris; or The New Pygmalion,* printed by C. H. Reynell, and published by John Hunt,[2] had made its appearance in the first week of May, and was reviewed in the *Examiner* (by Leigh Hunt's successor, Albany Fonblanque) on the 11th. Crabb Robinson was a little slow: '23 June: Finished early Hazlitt's disgusting New Pygmalion. One can tolerate the passion of a St Preux or a Werter as it is set off by the eloquence of Rousseau or Goethe, but such a story as this is nauseous and revolting. It ought to exclude the author from all decent society.

1. John Wilson Croker, Secretary to the Admiralty, and author of a famous review of *Endymion*. We do not know which, if any, of the *Quarterly's* efforts against Hazlitt he may have been responsible for, but regarding the *Table Talk* review of October 1821, he may be found writing to Murray (*Smiles*, II. 44): 'The article on Hazlitt is good'.

2. From the first-named of whom, says Mr W. C. Hazitt, he received £100 for the copyright.

He has been exposed in *John Bull,* and I should think will feel the effects of his exposure of himself in being slighted by many who tolerated him before.'

That this was indeed the effect of the publication of the work we may judge from the letter which follows :

Hazlitt to Thomas Hood

Winterslow Hut,

Saturday, July 19

My dear Hood, – I wish you would tell Taylor that something happened which hurt my mind, and prevented my going to Petworth. I had only the heart to come down here, and see my little boy, who is gone from hence. I will do Blenheim for next month. I used to think she read and perhaps approved these articles. But whatever I can do, implying an idea of taste or elegance, only makes me more odious to myself, and tantalises me with feelings which I can never hope to excite in others – wretch that I am, and am to be, till I am nothing!

Yours truly,

W. HAZLITT.

V

At Winterslow, whither Hazlitt resorted in July, he remained for the rest of this year with but one visit to town which we know of. The period is one in which we see him mainly in his work. For the *London Magazine* he wrote, as he said he would, on Blenheim, and also on Oxford, Wilton House, and Longford Castle – all galleries within his vicinity, which he had known and loved since his earliest period of Winterslow residence. For the *New Monthly,* getting into his Table Talk stride again, he wrote *On the Old Age of Artists, On Sitting for One's Picture,* and *On Application to Study.* In September he was at Fonthill, and here we have a reminiscence of Patmore's, who was also there in the interest of the *New Monthly* : 'Hazlitt particularly piqued himself on his skill in cicerone-ship; and when he was in good health and spirits, there was nothing

pleased him better than to accompany a friend to some celebrated collection of pictures, with which he himself was familiar, but which the party accompanying him had not seen before;
and the first place he proposed that we should go to see was
Sir Richard Colt Hoare's [Stourhead] which is situated a few
miles from Fonthill.

'In going through the various apartments at Sir Richard Colt
Hoare's, and afterwards at Wilton House,[1] I shall never forget
the almost childish delight which Hazlitt exhibited at the sight
of two or three of the chief favourites of his early days, and the
way in which he expressed that delight, not so much to me as
to the attendant who showed us the pictures, and on whom he
seemed to look with a sort of superstitious respect, – as if the
daily looking upon objects which were nothing less than sacred
in Hazlitt's eyes, had transferred something of their sanctity to
him.

'On another day, while at Fonthill, we walked over to Salisbury (a distance of twelve miles) in a broiling sunshine; and I
remember, on this occasion in particular, remarking the extraordinary physical as well as moral effect produced on Hazlitt
by the sight and feel of "the country" ... He spoke on this
occasion of having repeatedly walked from forty to fifty miles
a day in that fashion formerly, and said that he could do so
now with perfect ease and pleasure.' Patmore, of course, in spite
of the unique position in his confidence which he enjoyed for
two or three years, knew Hazlitt with something a good deal
short of intimacy, as he succeeds in revealing nearly always
when he puts pen to paper.

1. Patmore *says* Burleigh House (as he would); but he evidently means
Wilton. I take him to have been the anonymous author of a work entitled
British Galleries of Art, containing articles reprinted from the *New
Monthly*, and published shortly after Hazlitt's book in the following
spring. 'Any merit that may attach to the mere plan of *British Galleries of
Art*,' says the preface, 'belongs entirely to the author of [the *Sketches of
the Principal Picture-Galleries in England*] the separate Papers of which
appeared (also in a periodical work) about the same time with those of
the following which are on the same subjects.'

In September there is a letter from Haydon to Miss Mitford: 'Hazlitt was up last week from Fonthill, where Phillips [the auctioneer who had in hand the sale of Beckford's effects] has fixed him to write up, for fifty guineas, what he wrote down from his conscience last year. He came to town for a night or two, and passed nearly the whole of each in watching Sally's door!' At this date the *Liber Amoris* had been published for more than four months.

He returned to Winterslow, and threw himself once more into his work. The essays written in this autumn are almost more than we can number. He was engaged in this work when the *London Magazine* for October reached him.

We do not know what Lamb thought of the *Liber Amoris*: but we must assume, I think, that he had made no overture to Hazlitt since the spring of 1822. He now repaired the omission, with his 'Letter to Southey'. The Laureate, in writing in the *Quarterly* dated January on 'The Progress of Infidelity', had gone far to suggest that the only thing wrong with the author of the *Essays of Elia* was the company he kept. Lamb's reply is famous. After addressing himself to the vindication of his friendship with Leigh Hunt, he went on:

From the *other gentleman* I neither expect nor desire (as he is well assured) any such concessions as L[eigh] H[unt] made to C[oleridge]. What hath soured him, and made him suspect his friends of infidelity towards him, when there was no such matter, I know not. I stood well with him for fifteen years (the proudest of my life) and have ever spoke my full mind of him to some to whom his panegyric must naturally be least tasteful. I never in thought swerved from him; I never betrayed him; I never slackened in my admiration of him; I was the same to him (neither better nor worse), though he could not see it, as in the days when he thought fit to trust me. At this instant he may be preparing for me some compliment, above my deserts, as he has sprinkled many such among his admirable books, for which I rest his debtor; or, for anything I know or can guess to the contrary, he may be about to read a lecture on my weaknesses. He is welcome to them (as he was to my humble hearth), if they can divert a spleen, or ventilate a fit of sullenness. I wish he would not quarrel with the world at the rate he does: but the reconciliation must be effected by himself, and I despair of living to see that day. But — protesting against much that he has written, and some things which he chooses to do; judging him by his conversation which I enjoyed so long, and relished so deeply, or by his books, in those places where no clouding passion intervenes — I should belie my own conscience, if I said less than that I think W. H. to be, in his natural state, one of the wisest and finest spirits breathing. So far from being ashamed of that intimacy which was betwixt us, it is my boast that I was able for so many years to have preserved it entire; and I think I shall go to my grave without finding, or expecting to find, such another companion.

Reading these words, Hazlitt paused in *On the Pleasure of Hating* to add: 'I think I must be friends with L[amb] again'.

Crabb Robinson, who had been away, returns in October to give us an entry: '26 October: — I met with Talfourd, and heard from him much of the literary gossip of the last quarter. Sutton Sharpe ... lent me the last *London Magazine,* containing Lamb's delightful Letter to Southey which Southey must feel. His remarks on religion are full of deep feeling, and his eulogy on Hazlitt & Leigh Hunt most generous. L. must be aware that he would expose himself to obloquy by such a declaration. It seems that he & Hazlitt are no longer on friendly terms. I do not wish them to be reconciled.'

In the same number of the *London Magazine* in which Hazlitt read Lamb's Letter, he found that the Opium-Eater, presuming a little too confidently upon his temporary eclipse, had been borrowing without acknowledgement from his early work. His letter of reminder, in the Magazine for November, is a model of its kind:

Hazlitt to the Editor of the London Magazine.

Sir, – Will you have the kindness to insert in the LION'S HEAD the two following passages from a work of mine published some time since? They exhibit a rather striking coincidence with the reasoning of the *Opium-Eater* in your late number on the discoveries of Mr Malthus, and as I have been a good deal abused for my scepticism on that subject, I do not feel quite disposed that any one else should run away with the credit of it. I do not wish to bring any charge of plagiarism in this case; I only beg to put in my own claim of priority. The first passage I shall trouble you with relates to the geometrical and arithmetical series. [Here follows the passage from the *Reply to Malthus,* which Hazlitt had reprinted in *Political Essays.*] This passage, allowing for the difference of style, accords pretty nearly with the reasoning in the *Notes from the Pocket-Book of an Opium-Eater.* I should really like to know what answer Mr Malthus has to this objection, if he would deign one – or whether he thinks it best to impose upon the public by his silence? So much for his mathematics: now for his logic, which the *Opium-Eater* has also attacked, and with which I long ago stated my dissatisfaction in manner and form following. [Here comes the second passage.]

This, Mr Editor, is the writer whom 'our full senate call all-in-all sufficient'. There must be a tolerably large *bonus* offered to men's interests and prejudices to make them swallow incongruities such as those here alluded to; and I am glad to find our ingenious and studious friend the *Opium-Eater* agrees with me on this point, too, almost in so many words.

I am, Sir, your obliged friend and servant,

W. HAZLITT.

As to the reply of Hazlitt's 'ingenious and studious friend' in the next number, the reader who is interested in these literary *minutiæ* will do well not to accept Professor Masson's statement that 'it was scrupulously polite to Hazlitt, but with a gleam of menace, as from a rapier half-unsheathed', but to read the correspondence for himself. If it came to rapiers, Hazlitt could at any time make rings round his opium-eating contemporaries in the use of that weapon. De Quincey's reply was lengthy, it expressed considerable contempt for 'a work of Mr Hazlitt's' which he remembered to have 'met with while on a visit to Mr Southey, and read cursorily', but it contained the essential admission : 'I believe that he *has* anticipated me : in the passage relating to the geometric and arithmetic ratios, it is clear that he has'. As Professor Masson says, 'So ended that matter'.

To complete our study of Hazlitt's convalescence, we shall make an extract here from *Whether Genius is Conscious of Its Powers* :

If the reader is not already apprised of it, he will please to take notice that I write this at Winterslow. My style there is apt to be redundant and excursive. At other times it may be cramped, dry, abrupt; but here it flows like a river, and overspreads its banks. ... Here I came fifteen years ago, a willing exile; and as I trod the lengthened greensward by the low wood-side, repeated the old line,

> '*My mind to me a kingdom is.*"

I found it so then, before, and since; and shall I faint, now that I have poured out the spirit of that mind to the world, and treated many subjects with truth, with freedom, and power, because I have been followed with one cry of abuse ever since *for not being a government-tool?* Here I returned a few years after to finish some works I had undertaken, doubtful of the event, but determined to do my best; and wrote that character of Millimant which was once transcribed by fingers fairer than Aurora's,[1] but no notice was taken of

1. The owner of the fingers I am afraid we are not able to identify. Mr W. C. Hazlitt's identification of the subject of this passage (and of a great many other passages, of which Sarah Walker is undoubtedly the subject) with a certain Miss Windham, 'heiress of Norman Court, Winterslow, who married Charles Baring Wall, M.P.', was submitted to a very curious and destructive examination by the late Mr J. Rogers Rees. (*Notes and*

it, because I was not a government-tool, and must be supposed devoid of taste and elegance by all who aspired to these qualities in their own persons. Here I sketched my account of that old honest Signior Orlando Friscobaldo, which with its fine, racy, acrid tone that old crab-apple, G*ff*rd, would have relished or pretended to relish, had I been a government-tool! Here too I have written *Table-Talks* without number, and as yet without a falling-off, till now that they are nearly done, or I should not make this boast. I could swear (were they not mine) the thoughts in many of them are founded as the rock, free as air, the tone like an Italian picture. What then? Had the style been like polished steel, as firm and as bright, it would have availed me nothing, for I am not a government-tool! I had endeavoured to guide the taste of the English people to the best old English writers; but I had said that English kings did not reign by right divine, and that his present majesty was descended from an elector of Hanover in a right line; and no loyal subject would after this look into Webster or Deckar because I had pointed them out. I had done something (more than any one except Schlegel) to vindicate the *Characters of Shakespear's Plays* from the stigma of French criticism; but our anti-Jacobin and anti-Gallican writers soon found out that I had said and written that Frenchmen, Englishmen, men were not slaves by birthright.

Queries, X series, ix. 101.) The results of Mr Rees' researches may here be shortly summarized: (1) No Windham, with an only daughter or heiress, ever possessed Norman Court; (2) Charles Baring Wall not only did not marry a Miss Windham, but lived and died unmarried; (3) instead of acquiring Norman Court by marriage, he inherited it in 1815, his father having acquired the property by purchase in 1807. Hazlitt's son's statement (in the preface to *Winterslow*, 1850): 'One of his [Hazlitt's] chief attractions hither were the noble woods of Tytherleigh or Tudorleigh, round Norman Court, the seat of Mr Baring Wall, M.P., whose proffered kindness to my father, on a critical occasion, was thoroughly appreciated by the very sensitiveness which declined its acceptance', may very well be allowed to stand, but there is nothing here of a sentimental interest. The occasion of the 'proffered kindness', we should have very little doubt, was Hazlitt's illness at Winterslow in 1828.

This was enough to *damn* the work. Such has been the head and front of my offending. ... Mr Blackwood, I am yours – Mr Croker, my service to you – Mr T. Moore, I am alive and well – Really, it is wonderful how little the worse I am for fifteen years' wear and tear!

Little the worse indeed, for in addition to all his essay-writing he had started *The Spirit of the Age,* and the first of these incomparable character-portraits – the Jeremy Bentham – made its appearance in the January *New Monthly.* 'You can hardly suppose', we shall find him telling Landor, 'the depression of body and mind under which some of them were written.'

CHAPTER XII

FRANCE AND ITALY

(1824–5)

*

The rule for travelling abroad is to take our common sense
with us, and leave our prejudices behind.

Notes of a Journey.

I

The year begins with reunion with the Lambs. In the previous
September they had left Covent Garden and begun that outward
flight which took them on this occasion as far as Islington. To
the cottage in Colebrooke Row Hazlitt proceeded on the third
Sunday in January. The date, the 25th, is given us by Crabb
Robinson, who paid a call in the evening, in the company of
Henry Southern, editor of the *Retrospective Review,* shortly to
be the new, and final, proprietor of the *London Magazine.*
'N.B. Hazlitt at Lamb's. We did not speak.' The diarist, we
remember, had been disappointed of a pious expectation.

Hazlitt had come back to new lodgings in the West End, at
10 Down Street, Piccadilly. A first fruit of renewed friendship
with Lamb is supposed to have been that volume of *Select Poets
of Great Britain,* which, with Hazlitt's name on its title-page,
made its appearance in this summer. The work had been begun
earlier as we may know from the note on Shelley, which refers
to him as 'dead since the commencement of this publication';
but it was now brought to completion. Hazlitt's *Poets,* held by so
good a judge as Edward FitzGerald to be 'the finest selection I
have ever seen', was a book which was not without its influence

on the anthologists of the nineteenth century.[1] Its critical notes, in their concision and felicity, take us back to the *Eloquence of the British Senate*. But the compiler, or compilers, proceeded without due regard to the copyright laws, and in 1825, when Hazlitt was abroad, the book was withdrawn from circulation and a second edition without living authors substituted.

What else are we able to say of Hazlitt's activities in this spring? We are able to say that he reviewed for the March *Edinburgh*, with great pleasure, Landor's 'Imaginary Conversations'; that he passed for the press his *Sketches of the Principal Picture Galleries in England*, for Taylor and Hessey; that he finished *The Spirit of the Age*, finding himself half way through the Byron on the death of that poet (19 April); and that, for the second time, he married a wife.

II

We cannot but wish, on Hazlitt's account, that one half of the illumination which has been shed on his parting with his first wife might have been given to his meeting with his second. In as much as 'she fell in love with him on account of his writings,'[2] we feel that she better deserves it. We have, however, to be content with very little. Hazlitt's son says that they met in a stage coach, and that the name of the lady's first husband was Bridgwater. Since he was now of an age to be a credible witness, we feel, not unreasonably, that he might have told us more.

I assume that they were married in April, at Edinburgh.[3]

1. Fitzgerald owned Hazlitt's copy, and may be found in 1876 writing to Charles Eliot Norton (*Letters*, II. 196): 'By way of something better from the old world, I post you Hazlitt's own copy of his English Poets, with a few of his marks for another Edition in it. If you like to keep it, pray do: if you like better to give it to Hazlitt's successor, Mr Lowell, do that from yourself.' This must be numbered as one among the great majority of Hazlitt relics which have gone to America.

2. The authority for this statement will be found reproduced on p. 388.

3. 'I do not remember the maiden name of the lady who was W. H.'s second wife. I did hear that she was Scotch, and that they were married in Scotland.' ... Cowden Clarke to Mr W. C. Hazlitt, 2 November, 1866, Carew Hazlitt MSS.

The place is a guess: the month probably accurate.

Our sole information is derived from the autobiography of the painter William Bewick, published in 1871, to which we have already made reference. Bewick, whom we last met as a pupil of Haydon's, had left London hurriedly in the previous summer in order to escape being involved in that painter's financial embarrassments, and was now executing portraits in Edinburgh. Here he says, 'in 1824, I received an invitation from Mr Hazlitt, who was staying at Melrose, on a marriage tour, to meet Mr Sheridan Knowles, then proprietor of the *Glasgow Free Press*'.

When Knowles had left us, I made the chalk drawing of Hazlitt, size of life, still in my possession. ... Mr Hazlitt, whilst at Melrose, was writing a criticism upon Lady Morgan's Life and Times of Salvator Rosa, for the *Edinburgh Review*, which he laid aside in good-humoured willingness to sit to me. He seemed highly amused and pleased to have the sketch made. During dinner he was gracious and smiling, and asked me to put up the portrait for him to look at. I stuck it up with a fork at each corner into the wainscot over the mantelpiece opposite to him. He frequently laid down his knife and fork to contemplate the likeness, gazing earnestly and long, asking if really his hair was anything like that of the drawing. Mrs Hazlitt exclaimed, "Oh, it is exactly your own hair, my dear."

This portrait, on the authority of the late Mr W. C. Hazlitt, has always been assumed to have been made in 1822, when Hazlitt was in Scotland under different circumstances.[1] The

1. This visit, however, is clearly pointed to by a passage in *On Knowledge of the World* (1827): 'When I told Jeffrey that I had composed a work in which I had in some sort handled about a score of leading characters, he said, "Then you will have one man against you, and the remaining nineteen for you!"' The reference is, of course, to the *Spirit of the Age*, and Hazlitt did not meet Jeffrey again. As to the Bewick portrait, an unpublished letter from Basil Montagu to Hazlitt's son re-

above account, however, which has been curiously overlooked,
I take to be conclusive. Hazlitt's review of Lady Morgan's *Life
of Salvator Rosa* (1823) came out in July, and the two volumes
of that work were awarded, says Bewick, to himself as a souvenir
of the occasion 'with Hazlitt's notes and remarks, made on
reading for his critique'.

If we may follow Bewick further, he invited Hazlitt to accompany him to Abbotsford, where he had some painting business, went alone, informed Scott who was staying at the inn at
his doors; whereupon 'Sir Walter observed, with great apparent
sincerity, that Mr Hazlitt was one of our most eloquent authors,
and a man, as far as he could be allowed to judge, of great
natural and original genius; that it was a pity such great powers
were not concentrated upon some important work, valuable to
his country, to literature, and lasting to his fame'. If this message had been conveyed, we might have pleased ourselves with
its relevance to rival Lives of Napoleon; but when Bewick got
back he found that Hazlitt had 'quitted Melrose for the south',
leaving behind him, with a 'kind letter', the gift above alluded
to. A letter from Scott to Bewick after his return to Edinburgh,
having reference to the picture he had copied on the visit in
question, is of date 18 May, and enables us to place the stay at
Melrose at some two or three weeks earlier.

The month of May is a blank, but we may assume that June
was spent in London, since on the 19th of that month John
Hunt writes to Leigh: 'A volume of Mr Shelley's Posthumous
Poems has just been published. A review of the Poems by Mr
Hazlitt will appear in the next No. of the *Edinburgh Review*'.

garding the *Literary Remains* in which it was reproduced as a frontispiece, is of interest: 'My wife ... particularly desires that it may be
noticed somewhere or other, that Blackwood's Magazine described your
Father as drinking daily, and with a *red spotted face* at the time that
he had abstained for some years from fermented liquor of any kind, and
that he was always remarkable for the marble paleness and clearness of
his complexion. She is also desirous that his neatness, and cleanliness of
apparel, may be noticed – the more so, as the portrait has a slovenly and
reckless air – tho' it has great merits in other respects.' – Leigh Hunt
MSS.

The review appeared in the issue dated July, which also contained the Lady Morgan. On 21 July there is a very charming letter from Hazlitt's mother to her grandson, headed 'My birthday, aged 78', and saying : 'My dear William, — We were all very glad to hear that you were well and happy; and also that your Father and Mrs Hazlitt were comfortable together. ... Tell Father to write to me by you, and now and then besides, and before he goes abroad; I don't like his going; so many die there; such stagnant waters surrounding the towns, and all over the country. We are reading Mrs Piozzi's travels in Italy.' There is no more until 31 August, when John Hunt is once more our and Leigh Hunt's informant : 'Mr Hazlitt and his new Bride have departed for France : he proposes to pass Florence on his way to Rome. *This* Mrs Hazlitt seems a very pleasant and lady-like person. She was the widow of a Barrister, and possesses an independence of nearly £300 a year.'[1] On 15 September Haydon writes to Miss Mitford : 'Hazlitt and his inamorata have now gone to Italy. ... In the *Morning Chronicle* of yesterday is his first letter.' We have one more informant, and one, I think, only. In the previous year Shelley's widow had returned to England, and was now living with her father, Godwin. On 10 October she writes to Mrs Hunt in Florence : 'Hazlitt is abroad; he will be in Italy in the winter; he wrote an article in the *Edin. Rev.* on the volume of poems I published. I do not know whether he meant it to be favourable or not; I do not like it at all; but when I saw him I could not be angry. I was never so shocked in my life, he has become so thin, his hair so scattered, his cheekbones projecting; but for his voice and smile, I should not have known him; his smile brought tears into my eyes, it was like a sunbeam illuminating the most melancholy of ruins, lightning that assured you on a dark night of the

1. Leigh Hunt MSS. The usual account, following Hazlitt's son and grandson, has been 'the widow of a Lieut.-Colonel', but I should be almost disposed to prefer this contemporary evidence of Hazlitt's respected intimate. The amount of Mrs Hazlitt's income is confirmed by J. Payne Collier (letter of 19 February, 1863, Carew Hazlitt MSS.): 'His second wife I never saw, but he one day told me she was "worth £300 a year" '.

identity of a friend's ruined and deserted abode.'

If we wish to realize that Hazlitt had suffered, I think we may do so here.

III

His life from 1 September, 1824, when he left England, to October 1825, when he set foot in it again, is to be followed so easily in his own narrative of his journey that it will not call for extensive portrayal. We shall confine ourselves to annotating that narrative, and adding to it what is possible from exterior sources.

'The first thing I did when I got to Paris was to go to the Louvre.' If Hazlitt had not told us this, we might have known it for ourselves. 'I cast a glance forward, and found that the Poussins were there. At the sight of the first, which I distinctly recollected (a fine green landscape, with stately ruins), the tears came into my eyes, and I passed an hour or two in that state of luxurious enjoyment, which is the highest privilege of the mind of man, and which perhaps makes him amends for many sorrows.' But the Louvre which Hazlitt found was not the Louvre as he had left it twenty-two years before;[1] and on the whole he found it, as he told Landor in Florence, a 'blow'.

What he did not tell Landor — or no doubt he did; but what he did not tell the readers of the *Morning Chronicle* — was that when he got to Paris he found his first wife there.

This pertinacious woman, possessed of some means of her own to which the sum of £150 per annum from Hazlitt was continued under the divorce agreement, was devoting the latter years of her life to seeing the world. Since early July she had been in Paris, and we possess her letters. She also has been to the Louvre, and (as she writes to Margaret Hazlitt) 'was very sorry to find that the Transfiguration, Tancred and Clorinda, and most of those that William copied were gone; it was quite a dis-

---

1. 'I had the good fortune to meet the other day at Paris with my old fellow-student, Dr E[dwards], after a lapse of thirty years; he is older than I by a year or two, and makes it five-and-twenty.' — *Notes of a Journey*. Did Hazlitt's youth seem so very far off from him in these days?

appointment to me'. At the end of July she writes to her son at school : 'Your letter, which I received on Saturday, was not directed properly, though I had given you the address very correctly; it was also very badly and carelessly written. This shows the use of your master's seeing your letters, as he would not have permitted them to have been sent in such an improper way. You say you called on *him* about a fortnight after I went, &c, &c, and leave me to guess who you mean. I am at a loss whether you mean Lamb or Coulson, but I suppose it is one of them.' The text of this letter is imperfect, but it is plain that the lady is anxious for more information than that regarding his father with which her son has supplied her. At the beginning of September there is another letter : 'Write immediately as soon as you hear from your father and tell me. If I understand you right, your father intends remaining abroad for a year or more.' Between this letter and the next (25 September) the encounter in Paris has taken place, and the writer has returned to London: 'When I came away, your father desired his love to you; he intended sending you a letter by me, but did not find himself well enough to write. He is most splendidly situated as to rooms, and gets his food cooked in the English way, which is a very great object to him; but, as may be supposed, it is terribly expensive. He did not agree with Taylor and Hessey about the book at last, so that he will sell it to the best bidder on his return. Meanwhile it is coming out in numbers in the *Morning Chronicle*. I called there yesterday with a message from him to Mr Black, and found the third article was inserted that very day, so I bought it and shall send it to your Grandmother to see, and desire her to forward it to you; and you must keep it carefully to give me, when we meet. ... If you wish to write to your father, his address is A Monsieur, Monsieur Hazlitt, Hotel Des Etrangers, Rue Vivienne, Paris, and he meant to remain there about three weeks longer, and then proceed to Rome.' It was certainly a notable instance of that lack of practical genius which Hazlitt so often deplored in himself, that in marrying with a second wife he should not have made the cut with the first more clean.

The first Mrs Hazlitt being got rid of, the stay made in Paris was not for three weeks but for three months. It was doubtless enjoyable; nor was Hazlitt idle. A number of the essays which compose the *Plain Speaker* were written here, and three of them (*On Old English Writers and Speakers, On Novelty and Familiarity,* and *Madame Pasta and Mademoiselle Mars*) made an immediate appearance in the *New Monthly.* In addition, he wrote thirteen articles for the *Morning Chronicle,* arranged with Galignani to bring out Paris editions of *Table Talk* and *The Spirit of the Age,* and made and enjoyed the acquaintance of Stendhal.

Stendhal, five years younger than Hazlitt, had been in England in 1817, and in his *Correspondence* of the following year we find him showing a knowledge of, and expressing an admiration for, the *Characters of Shakespear's Plays.* It may have been in connection with this book, or with a later one, that he wrote a letter to Hazlitt of which we read in *On Intellectual Superiority* (1823): 'I once showed a person of this over-weening turn (with no small triumph, I confess) a letter of a very flattering description I had received from the celebrated Count [sic] Stendhal, dated Rome.' The two writers now met, and Stendhal's *De l'Amour* formed Hazlitt's travelling companion during his tour, and was brought by this means to the knowledge of readers of the *Morning Chronicle.* Of his visit to Milan we may find him recording: 'I did not see the great picture of the last supper by Leonardo nor the little Luini, two miles out of Milan, which my friend Mr Beyle charged me particularly to see.' Henceforward 'my friend Mr Beyle' may be found figuring more than once in Hazlitt's occasional writings. Stendhal was in Paris during both of Hazlitt's subsequent stays, in 1826–7 and in 1828, and there is nothing unlikely in the surmise that he may have assisted with his advice in the *Life of Napoleon.* With his first novel, *Armance,* Hazlitt shows no acquaintance, and he was dead, of course, before the great novels were published. With Stendhal's own epitaph it is likely that Hazlitt would have been pleased: 'Visse, scrisse, amò'.

On 16 January, the travellers set out for Italy. They journeyed over the Mont Cenis to Turin, and from Turin by way of Parma and Bologna to Florence. Here, so far as we gather, the next stay of any duration was made. At Florence was Leigh Hunt – for no better reason, one thinks, since the death of Shelley and the *Liberal* and his quarrel with Byron, than that he had lacked both the means and the energy to take him home.

From my friend L. H.'s house at Maiano, you see at one view the village of Satiniano, belonging to Michael Angelo's family, the house in which Machiavel lived, and that where Boccacio wrote, two ruined castles, in which the rival families of the Gerardeschi and the Visconti carried on the most deadly strife, and which seem as though they might still rear their mouldering heads against each other; and not far from this the Valley of Ladies (the scene of the Decameron), and Fesole, with the mountains of Perugia beyond. With a view like this, one may think one's sight 'enriched'.

But not, as Leigh Hunt had found, one's pocket. At Florence, also, Hazlitt and Landor met – and liked one another.[1]

Our informant is the artist Thomas Kirkup, writing to Landor's biographer Forster forty years later: 'I perfectly remember Hazlitt's being here. He wished to pay Landor a visit, but was advised not, unless he was introduced. Armitage Brown, who was Landor's greatest friend here, offered him a letter; but Hazlitt said he would beard the lion in his den, and he walked up to his house one winter's morning in nankeen shorts and

1. A 'real conversation' between Landor and Hazlitt may be read in the latter's *The Vatican*, contributed to the *New Monthly Magazine*, for November 1827. In the second edition of *Imaginary Conversations*, Vols. I. and II., published in 1826 (on Hazlitt's recommendation) by Colburn, Landor paid a compliment to *Table Talk* – 'in which publication there are strokes as vivid and vigorous as in any work edited [sic] these hundred years'. An appreciation of the third volume of *Imaginary Conversations* by Hazlitt (14 June, 1828) is one among a number of his contributions to the *London Weekly Review* reprinted by the present writer (*New Writings*).

white stockings; was made much of by the royal animal; and often returned at night; for Landor was much out in the day, in all weathers.' There is not much here, except the suggestion that there was something singular for the time in Hazlitt's dress, which would probably not be an accurate impression. He gave Landor a humorous account of his divorce, which Landor enjoyed; and he advised him upon a change of publisher, which advice Landor took. Forster had other recollections, some of them Landor's own, not all of which he gave to the public; and as a result of them he said: 'Many were the points of agreement, indeed, between Hazlitt and his host; and so heartily did each enjoy the other's wilfulness and caprice, that a strong personal liking characterized their brief acquaintance'. We feel that we should know as much, even if Forster had not said so.

From Florence, at the beginning of April, Hazlitt and his wife moved on to Rome, and from here there is a letter to Landor:

Hazlitt to Landor

Rome, April 9

Dear Sir, – I did not receive your obliging letter till a day or two ago. Mrs H. and myself crossed the mountains pretty well, but had rather a tedious journey. Rome hardly answers your expectations; the ruins do not prevail enough over the modern buildings, which are commonplace things. One or two things are prodigiously fine. I have got pleasant lodgings, but find everything very bad and dear. I have thought of going to spend a month at Albano, but am not quite sure. If I do not, I shall return to Florence next week, and proceed to Venice. I should be glad, if I settle at Albano, if you could manage to come over and stop a little. I have done what I was obliged to write for the Papers, and am now a leisure man, I hope, for the rest of the summer. I am much gratified that you are pleased with the *Spirit of the Age*. Somebody ought to like it, for I am sure there will be plenty to cry out against it. I hope you did not find any sad blunders in the second volume; but you can hardly suppose the depression of body and mind under which I wrote some of these articles. I bought a little Florentine edition of Petrarch and Dante the other day, and have made out one page. Pray remember me to Mrs Landor, and believe me to be, dear Sir, your much obliged friend and servant,

W. HAZLITT.

His address is 33 Via Gregoriana — Salvator Rosa's house. 'I have now lived twice,' wrote Hazlitt, 'in houses occupied by celebrated men, once in a house that had belonged to Milton, and now in this, and find to my mortification that imagination is entirely a *thing imaginary,* and has nothing to do with matter of fact, history, or the senses.' The work which he had done at Rome was the story of his journey from Turin; and he did not resume it until he got to Vevey.

He did not spend the month at Albano, but returned to Florence, and after resumed relations with Landor (to whom he introduced Leigh Hunt), Lord Dillon, Kirkup, and Brown proceeded by way of Bologna to Venice. After a short stay here, the journey was continued, through Padua, Verona, Milan, and the Simplon, into Switzerland. 'In travelling,' Hazlitt says, 'we visit *names* as well as places; and Vevey is the scene of the New Eloise.' They reached it in mid-June.

The day after my arrival, I found a lodging at a farmhouse, a mile out of Vevey, so 'lapped in luxury', so retired, so reasonable, and in every respect convenient, that we remained here for the rest of the summer, and felt no small regret at leaving it. ... Days, weeks, months, and even years might have passed on much in the same manner, with 'but the season's difference'. We breakfasted at the same hour, and the tea-kettle was always boiling (an excellent thing in housewifery) — a lounge in the orchard for an hour or two, and twice a week we could see the steam-boat creeping like a spider over the surface of the lake; a volume of the Scotch novels (to be had in every library on the Continent, in English, French, German, or Italian, as the reader pleases), or M. Galignani's Paris and London *Observer,* amused us till dinner time; then tea and a walk till the moon unveiled itself, 'apparent queen of night', or the brook, swoln with a transient shower, was heard more distinctly in the darkness, mingling with the soft, rustling breeze; and the next morning the song of the peasants broke upon refreshing sleep, as the sun glanced among the clustering vine-leaves, or the shadowy hills, as the mists retired from their summit, looked in at our windows.

The uniformity of this mode of life was only broken during fifteen weeks, says Hazlitt, by the civilities of neighbours. Of these, Captain Thomas Medwin, who had published his *Conversations of Lord Byron* in the previous year, was one.

Medwin, particularly as the biographer of Shelley, does not enjoy a high reputation, and from his *Hazlitt in Switzerland: A Conversation,* purporting to be written down at the time, but not published until fourteen years afterwards, we may content ourselves with a single quotation:

The cottage I found Hazlitt inhabiting is about half a mile from Vevey, and stands on the banks of a small and rapid stream that falls into the lake at the entrance of the town. The house lies very low, so that it possesses no other view from the windows than a green paddock, over-shadowed by some enormous walnut-trees. Behind, and across the rivulet, rises a hill of vines, sufficiently elevated to screen out the western sun. The spot is lovely and secluded.

As is not uncommon with men of talent, his appearance, though not unprepossessing, was by no means striking. He was below the common height; his dress neglected; and his chin garnished with a stubble of some days' standing. The lines of his countenance are regular, but bear evident marks of late and intense application; and there was an habitual melancholy in the expression, as though he had been chewing the cud of past miseries, or brooding on bitter anticipations of the future. His figure was emaciated; and it was evident his mind preyed upon and consumed much of the vital energies of his frame; and this last, as was said of Shelley, seemed only a tenement for spirit.

In the conversation which follows the good things are distributed too equally to carry conviction. It achieves interest only, I think (save for some confirmatory references to the society of Florence), at that point at which Medwin calls for a second time and finds 'on the table the last novel of Sir Walter Scott's'. He mentions the Life of Napoleon which Scott is understood to be writing. 'I, too,' says Hazlitt, 'will write a Life of Napoleon, though it is yet too early.'

'Hazlitt's MSS.', notes Medwin, 'were the most beautiful I ever saw. He told me there was a rivalry between himself and Leigh Hunt on this score; that he would not allow of an erasure or interlineation; nor in running my eye over the MS. of the *Plain Speaker*, did I perceive a single one.' The manuscript referred to is, of course, that of the essays afterwards forming part of that work which we know to have been written at Vevey. The most immediately striking of these perhaps is that *On the Jealousy and the Spleen of Party,* in which some strictures of the poet Moore on Rousseau, which Hazlitt found in the former's *Rhymes on the Road* at the English Library, are answered:

The poet ... falls foul of men of genius, fancy, and sentiment in general, as impostors and mountebanks, who feel the least themselves of what they describe and make others feel. I beg leave to enter my flat and peremptory protest against this view of the matter, as an impossibility. I am not absolutely blind to the weak sides of authors, poets, and philosophers (for "tis my vice to spy into abuses') but that they are not generally in earnest in what they write, that they are not the dupes of their own imaginations and feelings, before they

turn the heads of the world at large, is what I must utterly
deny. So far from the likelihood of any such antipathy
between their sentiments and their professions, from their
being recreants to truth and nature, quite callous and insensible to what they make such a rout about, it is pretty certain
that whatever they make others feel in any marked degree,
they must themselves feel first; and further, they must have
this feeling all their lives. It is not a fashion got up and put
on for the occasion; it is the very condition and ground-work
of their being. ... An author's appearance or his actions may
not square with his theories or his descriptions, but his mind
is seen in his writings, as his face is in the glass. Let me then
conjure the gentle reader, who has ever felt an attachment to
books, not hastily to divorce them from their authors. Whatever love or reverence is due to the one, is equally owing to
the other. To cherish the work and *damn* the author is as if
the traveller who slakes his thirst at the running stream,
should revile the spring head from which it gushes.

In living to vindicate Rousseau on his own soil of the Pays de
Vaud, Hazlitt may not have been unconscious that he was doing
something to vindicate himself.

From Vevey, soon after arrival, he addressed the following
letter to his son at school in Devonshire:

Hazlitt to his Son

Vevey, near Geneva.

Dear Baby, — We are got as far as Vevey in Switzerland on
our way back. I propose returning by Holland in the end of
August, and I shall see you, I hope, the beginning of September.

The journey has answered tolerably well. I was sorry to
hear of poor Miss Emmet's death, and I hope Grandmother
and Peggy are both well. I got your letter at Florence, where
I saw Mr Leigh Hunt and Mr Landor. I have a very bad pen.
The *Table-Talk* and the *Spirit of the Age* have been re-

printed at Paris; but I do not know how they have succeeded. The *Advice to a Schoolboy* is in the first. If you should be in London, remember me to all friends, or give my love to my Mother and Peggy. – I am, dear Baby, your ever affectionate father,

W. HAZLITT.

At the end of August a week's excursion was made to Chamounix and Geneva ('I here saw Rousseau's house,' says Hazlitt, 'and also read the *Edinburgh Review* for May'), and back to Vevey. The return was made down the Rhine through Holland, and home by way of Ghent, Lille, Antwerp, St Omer, and Calais. 'We left Vevey on the 20th of September, and arrived in England on the 16th of October.'

So far we have Hazlitt's own narrative of twelve months of his life, which completed its appearance in the *Morning Chronicle* throughout the month of November. With his return, the curtain once more descends. The only one of his acquaintance to lift it for a moment is Haydon. Writing to Miss Mitford on 10 November he says: 'I have spent three hours with Hazlitt to-day, and spent them with great delight. We talked of Michael Angelo, of Raphael, and – greatest of all is behind – Leigh Hunt, till we roared with laughter, and made more noise with our laughter than all the coaches, wagons, and carts in Piccadilly. ... Hazlitt looks ill; but his jaunt has done him great good, and his present wife a greater. She is a very superior woman, and will make him a decent being in regard to washing his face and hands (et cetera). He was breakfasting to-day as a gentleman should, and seemed to be living "cleanly", as a gentleman ought. I like Hazlitt, in spite of all; everybody must.' While we are not particularly willing to listen to Haydon on the subject of whether Hazlitt washed his hands, this evidence is valuable to us. Its scene is evidently Down Street, and here, we must assume, Hazlitt and his 'present wife' had taken up their abode.

CHAPTER XIII

THE LIFE OF NAPOLEON

(1826–8)

*

> I should be sorry if there were a single word approaching
> to *cant* in this work.
>
> *Life of Napoleon.*

I

THE life of Hazlitt was happy, we sometimes feel, almost in proportion as we hear nothing of it. The eight months which follow his return from abroad form such a period. From the letter of Haydon in November until well into the following year we are almost without information. We need not assume that the whole of this period was spent in London, although we shall find sufficient reason to believe that most of it was. He had written during his stay at Vevey an essay, *Merry England* (appearing in the December *New Monthly*, and signalizing his return) which would serve to remind us, if we stood in need of reminder, of the resources of enjoyment held for him by his own country.

The early part of 1826, the period of the Constable crash, was a season of acute restriction and difficulty in the literary trade, and Hazlitt for the first and last time in his life was 'above the battle'. He was writing to add to an income, instead of writing to lay its foundation. To complete the two volumes of the *Plain Speaker* for publication by Colburn in May, he wrote several essays, and for immediate publication in the *New Monthly* he wrote several more. One of these, *On Persons One Would Wish to Have Seen,* is so certain to have given pleasure to the Lambs that the defective condition of their correspondence in this year is rendered the more regrettable. We are dependent for our information upon Patmore, whose account is as usual not so satisfactory as it might be.

> My first introduction to Charles Lamb [he writes] took place, accidentally, at the lodgings of William Hazlitt, in Down. Street, Piccadilly, in 1824 [*sic*] and under circumstances which have impressed it with peculiar vividness on my memory. Mr Colburn had published anonymously, only two or three days before, a *jeu d'esprit* of mine, which aimed at being, to the prose literature of the day, something like what the Rejected Addresses was to the poetry. ... Scarcely had I been introduced to the newcomers, when Hazlitt pointed to the book which he had laid on the table, and said to Miss Lamb, 'There's something about Charles and you. Have you seen it?' Miss Lamb immediately took up the book, and began to read to herself (evidently with no very good will) the opening paper, which was an imitation of an Essay of Elia.

Unfortunately for the vividness of Patmore's memory, his book *Rejected Articles* was published not in 1824, but in May 1826, and it is to that month that we may suppose his reminiscence to belong.[1] Miss Lamb's lack of goodwill was excusable, for the imitation of the Essay of Elia was a very poor imitation, as, may be added, was the imitation of Table Talk which followed it. The preamble with which Patmore introduced this item is, however, of interest. 'We shall do so', he remarked, 'by saying, that when ever he [Hazlitt] pleases to take the trouble, he may approve himself to all the world, what two of the best judges in it have already pronounced him – the best prose writer of his day, and one of the finest spirits of his age and country.' To

---

1. Patmore has another strange entry: '15 January, 1825: – Tonight (at the Southampton) Hazlitt told some capital things about Dawe the painter'. The date is probably a mistake for 1824; possibly for 1826.

this passage he appended a footnote: 'Hear (if you can), Lord Holland's conversation; and see a letter of Mr Chas. Lamb to Mr Southey, printed some time ago in the *London Magazine*'. This is the only link we appear to possess between Hazlitt and the Holland House circle, which he might, if he had wished, so easily have entered.

Crabb Robinson makes no mention of Hazlitt in this year, and only one during the period of his absence abroad: '29 April, 1825: – I walked to Lamb's. With him I found Knowles, the author of Virginius and of William Tell now coming out. A very Irishman in manners, though of the better kind. Seemingly a warm-hearted man – no marks of talent in his conversation but a bold decisive tone. He spoke of *William* (i.e., Hazlitt) as his friend and this does not speak for his discretion or moral feeling.'

In May *The Plain Speaker: Opinions on Books, Men, and Things* made its appearance in two volumes with Colburn, and in the same month *Notes of a Journey through France and Italy,* with Hazlitt's name on the title-page, came out with Hunt and Clarke. The formation of this firm, succeeding that of John and Henry Leigh Hunt, marked the definite retirement of John Hunt from business, a circumstance which Hazlitt was to be given cause to regret. His seclusion, however, for the moment, from professional anxieties is well suggested by a note which survives from Jeffrey to Procter, in May. Seeking somewhat desperately the latter's literary assistance, Jeffrey adds in a postscript: 'Can you tell me anything of our ancient ally Hazlitt?' If this overture was conveyed, it was not responded to; principally, no doubt, for a reason that will shortly appear.

If we seek Hazlitt during this period we find him at Northcote's studio. Nothing surprises us less than on his return from his tour he should have resumed his attendances on the old artist of whom three years before he had written: 'I know that I can get there what I get nowhere else – a welcome, as if one was expected to drop in just at that moment, a total absence of all respect of persons and of airs of self-consequence, endless topics of discourse, refined thoughts, made more striking by ease and simplicity of manner – the husk, the shell of humanity is left at the door, and the spirit, mellowed by time, resides within! All you have to do is to sit and listen; and it is like hearing one of Titian's faces speak.' His first conversation of Northcote is the dialogue 'On Envy' written for the *Plain Speaker* in this spring. Pleased, presumably, with the result, he wrote six others, and brought them together for the *New Monthly Magazine* under the general title of 'Boswell Redivivus.'

One other intimacy, resumed at Florence in the previous summer, we know to have been continued in London during this winter and spring. This was with Leigh Hunt. Hunt, roused out of his inertia by an offer from Colburn, secured by his brother, that he should contribute to the *New Monthly*, had travelled home from Italy in the preceding autumn, his arrival in England coinciding with Hazlitt's. He went to settle at Highgate, and it is from here, on June 20, that he writes a letter which is important to us. Addressing Hazlitt, he says: 'I know but one thing that would take me to town sooner than the pleasure of passing an evening with your masculine discourse on one side the table and "the calm of pleasant womankind" which you have on the other. Pray forgive my saying this, and let Mrs Hazlitt forgive me, but I am more at ease with you in your own house than anywhere else, and have felt so comfortable there both in Florence and in Down Street, that I trust to please you by saying what I do, and think you should be pleased because it is true. Pray are you not acquainted with an awful fact of the name of Atherstone? active, good humoured robust gentleman who writes poems on earthquakes and fills a dozen pages with the shrieks of women and children. I bethought me of getting an eclipse from Lamb and Coleridge, to surprise him, but though he knows Coleridge, Lamb might not know him.' We do not know whether Hazlitt was acquainted with Edwin Atherstone, author of *The Last Days of Herculaneum,* nor does it matter.

The next news is Leigh Hunt's also. Writing to Procter in

July he says: 'Hazlitt is gone to France, and is to write Buonaparte'.

II

In the preface to the completed *Life of Napoleon*, published in the year of Hazlitt's death, we read: 'Much time was occupied and great expense incurred to obtain ample materials for the present work. Not satisfied with books and written documents, Hazlitt saw and conversed with the persons most likely to afford him information. He resided two years in Paris for this especial purpose.' This estimate (not, of course, Hazlitt's own) we may resolve without difficulty into the thirteen or fourteen months of his residence in Paris in 1826-7, followed by a further visit of three or four months a year later. For the first of these periods he enjoyed the company, the financial assistance, and no doubt the encouragement of the lady who had married him 'on account of his writings'.

Our authority for this statement is the evidence of a certain Mr G. Huntly Gordon of the Stationery Office, who committed it to writing in the year 1866:

If it had not been for his *second* wife, it is very improbable I should have ever known him. The manner was this. One of my earliest recollections, when I was just at the age when one feels the full force of female loveliness, was a day passed in her charming presence, at an uncle's of mine in Scotland, when she was about nineteen, and on her way to some relations in the island of Granada. I believe she was of a very good family, and had not been many weeks in the island before she was snapped up by a planter. No wonder! for I still think she was one of the loveliest girls I ever saw. Her first husband died shortly after the marriage. It is so long ago that I do not remember her maiden name, but she was connected somehow with an aunt of mine, and, having heard that she was in Paris and married to your grandfather, I found her out when I was passing a few weeks there [in 1827], being very desirous of renewing my acquaintance with my former flame of one day, and to see Mr Hazlitt, many of whose works I had read with much delight. She told me she never saw him take such a fancy for any one as he did for me. I suppose this was because he found me a capital listener. ... Once when I dined with them, and he drank three or four basins of Tea, he dissertated most charmingly from six o'clock till two in the morning, and was my cicerone in the Louvre one day from ten till four. His conversation on that day I thought better than any book I had ever read on the art pictorial. He was more striking and eloquent even than his printed pages.

This letter, addressed to the late Mr W. C. Hazlitt during the composition of the *Memoirs* of 1867, was unfortunately taken by him to refer to the stay in Paris of 1824-5. On the publication of the work, Mr Gordon wrote:[1] 'Had I seen the proof-sheets of the Life of your grandfather where you give an extract from my note respecting my having dined with him and the second Mrs Hazlitt at Paris, I should have pointed your attention to a strange discrepancy between your dates and mine. I am *quite certain* that it was in 1827 I had that pleasure – though I can in no way reconcile this with your dates either before or after.' In the long interval that elapsed between the publication of the *Memoirs* and his next work on the subject of his grandfather, we must assume that Mr Hazlitt forgot to make this rectification. Mr Gordon's only other recollection of Hazlitt was of 'a long, eloquent, and enthusiastic dissertation on Salisbury Plain, which I heard from his lips one night he spent at my rooms in London a few years before his death'. He never, he adds, saw Mrs. Hazlitt again.

With this piece of evidence freed from the misconception

1. Letter of 4 June, 1867, in the British Museum (Carew Hazlitt MSS.). The student may be glad to receive the assurance that the 'Mr Leslie of the War Office' to whom he will find a portion of the above recollection attributed in Mr Hazlitt's last work (*The Hazlitts,* pp. 251, 259) is no other than the above-named Mr G. Huntly Gordon of the Stationery Office

which has hitherto attached to it, we shall no longer be in doubt as to the circumstances in which the first two volumes of the *Life of Napoleon* were composed. This book, which was the summit of Hazlitt's ambition as a writer, did not 'get itself written at Winterslow', 'far from authorities', etc., but was conceived and very largely executed in Paris, under circumstances that were the nearest to ease and freedom from anxiety of any in his life. The question has now to be answered, what brought these circumstances to an end.

The account given by Hazlitt's son of his father's last years in the *Literary Remains* of 1836 is a curiously unsatisfactory one. His only mention of his stepmother is as follows: 'In 1824 my father married Isabella, widow of Lieut.-Colonel Bridgwater, a lady of some property, with whom myself and he proceeded on a tour through France and Italy.' That Hazlitt's son did *not* 'proceed on the tour through France and Italy', the letter which we have read on page 379, makes sufficiently clear. He may have gone as far as Paris, to join his father and step-mother there before the tour began. But in 1867, when the *Memoirs* were written, Hazlitt's son was fifty-six years of age and was Registrar in Bankruptcy, and we must suppose him to have authorized the account which his own son then made public. This account was as follows:

Mr Hazlitt and his son returned home [from the tour of 1824–5] alone. Mrs Hazlitt had stopped behind. At the end of a fortnight he wrote to her, asking her when he should come to fetch her; and the answer that he got was that she had proceeded on to Switzerland with her sister, and that they had parted for ever!

It appears that my father was excessively hurt and indignant at the whole affair from the first outset, and considered that his own mother had been ill-used – in which there was a considerable share of truth, no doubt; and when he joined his father and step-mother abroad, he, mere child as he was, seems to have been very pointed and severe in his remarks upon the matter. This probably gave Mrs Hazlitt a foretaste of what she might have to expect on her return to England, and led to the determination referred to.

At any rate, they never met again. Their union had been short enough. It amounted to scarcely more than an episode.

It amounted, perhaps, to scarcely more than an episode; but that episode lasted from the spring of 1824 until the late summer of 1827. On the circumstances which brought it to an end, we have one informant and one only. Charles Armitage Brown, the friend of Keats, had seen much of Hazlitt during his stay in Florence in 1825. It is possible that his second wife returned there. At any rate, in Crabb Robinson's Journal of his Italian residence, under date 7 October, 1830, we read: 'We talked about Hazlitt. Brown spoke highly of Hazlitt's wife as a gentlewoman. She fell in love with him on account of his writings. She parted on account of the ill conduct of the boy.' The ill conduct of the boy we take to have been the earliest effective manifestation of that championship of the claims of his mother, which, carried through with remarkable consistency, has resulted in obscuring until this moment the true part played in his father's life by his second wife.

On 9 August Lamb, newly removed to Enfield, writes to Sir John Stoddart, Chief Justice of Malta: 'Hazlitt is resident at Paris, whence he pours his lampoons[1] in safety at his friends in England. He has his boy with him.' If On Disagreeable People (appearing in the Monthly Magazine for August) is a 'lampoon',

1. Presumably Lamb would extend this phrase to cover the remarkable group of essays — On the Want of Money, On the Feeling of Immortality in Youth, On Reading New Books, On Disagreeable People, On Means and Ends — contributed to the Monthly Magazine from Paris, in the intervals of Hazlitt's labours on the Life of Napoleon. The Monthly, under auspices of which not much seems to be known to us, had recently gone into a new series, and that no old magazine could do this without calling upon the assistance of Hazlitt is one of the commonplaces of his later career.

we may think that Hazlitt himself was the object of a part of it :

So far of friendship : a word, if I durst, of love. Gallantry to women (the sure road to their favour) is nothing but the appearance of extreme devotion to all their wants and wishes – a delight in their satisfaction, and a confidence in yourself, as being able to contribute towards it. The slightest indifference with regard to them, or distrust of yourself, are equally fatal. The amiable is the voluptuous in looks, manners, or words. No face that exhibits this kind of expression – whether lively or serious, obvious or suppressed, will be thought ugly – no address, awkward – no lover who approaches every woman he meets as his mistress, will be unsuccessful. Diffidence and awkwardness are the two antidotes to love.

To please universally, we must be pleased with ourselves and others. There should be a tinge of the coxcomb, an oil of self-complacency, an anticipation of success – there should be no gloom, no moroseness, no shyness – in short, there should be very little of an Englishman, and good deal of a Frenchman. But though, I believe, this is the receipt, we are none the nearer making use of it. It is impossible for those who are naturally disagreeable ever to become otherwise. This is some consolation, as it may save a world of useless pains and anxiety. *'Desire to please, and you will infallibly please,'* is a true maxim; but it does not follow that it is in the power of all to practise it. A vain man who thinks he is endeavouring to please is only endeavouring to shine, and is still farther from the mark. An irritable man, who puts a check upon himself, only grows dull, and loses spirit to be anything. Good temper and happy spirit (which are the indispensable requisites) can no more be commanded than good health or good looks; and though the plain and sickly need not distort their features, and may abstain from success, this is all they can do. The utmost a disagreeable person can do is to hope to be less disagreeable than with care and study he might become, and to pass unnoticed in society. With this negative character he should be contented, and may build his fame and happiness on other things.

Offered the choice between his wife's company and his son's, Hazlitt, we must suppose, chose the latter. Firmly fortified in his own opinion of himself as a disagreeable person, he came back to England.

III

He came back to England,[1] and went down to Winterslow. Here we find him in the essay *On a Sun-Dial,* which made its appearance in the *New Monthly* in October.

> For myself, I have never had a watch nor any other mode of keeping time in my possession, nor ever wish to learn how time goes. It is a sign I have had little to do, few avocations, few engagements. When I am in a town, I can hear the clock; and when I am in the country, I can listen to the silence. What I like best is to lie whole mornings on a sunny bank on Salisbury Plain, without any object before me, neither knowing nor caring how time passes. ...

The man who has recently completed the quarter of a million (not negligible) words of the first two volumes of the *Life of Napoleon,* has earned the right, for a short while, to have no object before him; but not for long, if he is Hazlitt. During this autumn he remained at Winterslow, writing *The Shyness of Scholars, Why the Heroes of Romances are Insipid,* and *The Main Chance* for the *New Monthly, On Personal Identity* for the *Monthly, On Knowledge of the World* and *On Public Opinion* for a new paper, *The London Weekly Review,* and *The Dandy School,* an examination of the earliest novel of that

1. It was now, perhaps, 'at the end of a fortnight', that he wrote to his wife asking when he should come to fetch her; and heard in reply that she had 'proceeded on' to Switzerland. The inapplicability of this phrase to the return from the tour of 1825 is obvious.

smart young man Mr Benjamin D'Israeli, for the *Examiner*. He prepared his major work for the press, and he fell ill. In a letter to his publisher we hear from him:

Hazlitt to Charles Cowden Clarke

December 7.

Dear Sir, — I thought all the world agreed with me at present that Buonaparte was better than the Bourbons, or that a tyrant was better than tyranny. In my opinion, no one of an understanding above the rank of a lady's waiting-maid could ever have doubted this, though I alone said it ten years ago. It might be impolicy then and now for what I know, for the world stick to an opinion in appearance long after they have given it up in reality. I should like to know whether the preface is thought impolitic by some one who agrees with me in the main point, or by some one who differs with me and makes this excuse not to have his opinion contradicted? In Paris (*jubes, regina, renovare dolorem*) the preface was thought a masterpiece, the best and only possible defence of Buonaparte, and quite new *there*! It would be an impertinence in me to write a Life of Buonaparte after Sir W. without some such object as that expressed in the preface. After all, I do not care a *damn* about the preface. It will get me on four pages somewhere else.[1] Shall I retract my opinion altogether, and foreswear my own book? Rayner [the printer] is right to cry out: I think I have tipped him fair and foul copy, a lean rabbit and a fat one. The remainder of vol. ii will be ready to go on with, but not the beginning of the third. The appendixes had better be at the end of the second vol. Pray get them if you can: you have my Siéyes, have you not? One of them is there. I have been nearly in the other world. My regret was 'to die and leave the world rough copy'. Otherwise I had thought of an epitaph and a good end. *Hic*

---

1. This course was adopted, and in the second edition of the work which Hazlitt's son prepared (1852) the preface will be found still disguised as the opening portion of the first chapter of the third volume.

*jacent reliquiæ mortales Gulielmi Hazlitt, auctoris non intelli-
gibilis: natus Maidstoniæ in com[it]atu Cantiæ, Apr. 10,
1778. Obiit Winterslowe, Dec. 1827.* I think of writing an
epistle to C. Lamb, Esq, to say that I have passed near the
shadowy world, and have had new impressions of the vanity
of this, with hopes of a better. Don't you think this would
be a good policy? Don't mention it to the severe author of the
Press, a poem [McCreery] but methinks the idea arridet
Hone. He would give sixpence to see me floating upon a pair
of borrowed wings half way between heaven and earth, and
edifying the good people at my departure whom I shall only
scandalise by remaining. At present my study and contemplation is the leg of a stewed fowl. I have behaved like a saint,
and been obedient to orders.

Non fit pugil, &c., I got a violent spasm by walking fifteen
miles in the mud, and getting into coach with an old lady
who would have the window open. Delicacy, moderation,
complaisance, the *suaviter in modo*, whisper it about, my dear
Clarke, these are my faults and have been my ruin. Yours
ever,

W. H.

I can't go to work before Sunday or Monday. By then the
doctor says he shall have made a new man of me.

IV

While Hazlitt was recovering from his illness at Winterslow,
the *Life of Napoleon* was approaching publication in London.
In the first week of January it was noticed by anticipation (that
is to say, from advance copies, according to the custom of that
day) both in the first number of James Silk Buckingham's and
Henry Colburn's new organ, the *Athenæum,* and in D. L.
Richardson and J. A. St John's *London Weekly Review.* Two
notes from Hazlitt to Henry Hunt and Cowden Clarke respectively, having reference to these and other publishing
arrangements, survive. 'Do not suppose I am vexed', the second

concludes, 'I am only frightened.' He had, indeed, good reason to betray some anxiety over a publication of his own, for the first and last time in his life. He was back on the unaided efforts of his pen again, the *Life of Napoleon* meant much to him, and the greater portion of the second half of it remained to be written.

It is in these circumstances that, in reply to an inquiry, we find him addressing the son of his old publisher as follows:

Hazlitt to David Constable

Winterslow, near Salisbury
Jany. 10th, 1828.

Dear Sir, – I have to thank you for your obliging letter, which I received in due course. It has come into my head that I could make a little volume of outlines or elements of the following subjects. 1. Of Law. 2. Of Morals. 3. Of the Human Mind. 4. Of Taste. 5. Of Political Economy. 6. Of English Grammar. On all of these but the fifth, I have something new to offer. Do you think you could print such a work (I would leave the price to you) or that it might possibly do for the Miscellany? You will perhaps see that the papers have taken to praise me: I suppose they are tired of abusing me. As to Titian, I have no theory; but one of our wiseacres at Rome (seeing a sketch of it in the room of a young artist there) asked if it was not intended for Christ and the woman of Samaria? If you want to see how dry I can be in the way of elementary analysis, Ritchie has a book of mine *On Human Action* which no one can charge with being florid or *ad captandum vulgus*. – I remain, dear Sir, your truly obliged, humble servant,

W. HAZLITT.

How the years slide on! If I should go to Paris in the spring, could you find any use for a series of papers on French plays and players? I am a great admirer of their theatre – as much so as I abominate their style of art.

The chapters forming the 'little volume' here proposed (but not published in Constable's Miscellany or otherwise)[1] were the occupation of his convalescence during January and February. Having failed, as I think we may conclude, to obtain the sum of money which was important to him by the labour of a few weeks at Winterslow, he came up to town to make a short return to dramatic criticism.

Before doing so, however, with the first half of the *Life of Napoleon* behind him and the second immediately before him, he wrote for the *Weekly Review,* dating it 'Winterslow, 20 February', his *Farewell to Essay-Writing*: 'What sometimes surprises me in looking back to the past, is, ... to find myself so little changed in the time. The same images and trains of thought stick by me : I have the same tastes, likings, sentiments, and wishes I had then. One source of this unbendingness (which some may call obstinacy), is that, though living much alone, I have never worshipped the Echo. I see plainly enough that black is not white, that the grass is green, that kings are not their subjects; and, in such self-evident cases, do not think it necessary to collate my opinions with the received prejudices. In subtler questions, and matters that admit of doubt, as I do not impose my opinion on others without a reason, so I will not give up mine to them without a better reason; and a person calling me names, or giving himself airs of authority, does not convince me of his having taken more pains to find out the truth than I have, but the contrary. Mr Gifford once said, that "while I was sitting over my gin and tobacco-pipes, I fancied myself a Leibnitz". He did not so much as know that I had ever read a metaphysi-

---

1. Our evidence that they were written is contained in the *Memoirs* of 1867 (I. xxxii), where the following figure among MSS. at that date in Mr W. C. Hazlitt's possession : *Outlines of Morals; Outlines of the Human Mind; Political Economy; Outlines of Grammar.* One of these papers has since been reprinted (*Political Economy*, 'New Writings : Second Series'). The chapter *On Law* one takes to be identical with the *Project for a New Theory of Civil and Criminal Legislation* published in *Literary Remains* and based on the schoolboy essay which Hazlitt wrote in his fifteenth year.

cal book : — was I, therefore, out of complaisance or deference
to him, to forget whether I had or not? I am rather disappointed, both on my own account and his, that Mr Hunt has
missed the opportunity of explaining the character of a friend,
as clearly as he might have done.[1] He is puzzled to reconcile
the shyness of my pretensions with the inveteracy and sturdiness
of my principles. I should have thought they were nearly the
same thing. Both from disposition and habit, I can *assume*
nothing in word, look, or manner. I cannot steal a march upon
public opinion in any way. My standing upright, speaking loud,
entering a room gracefully, proves nothing; therefore I neglect
these ordinary means of recommending myself to the good
graces and admiration of strangers (and, as it appears, even of
philosophers and friends). Why? Because I have other resources,
or, at least, am absorbed in other studies and pursuits. Suppose
this absorption to be extreme, and even morbid, that I have
brooded over an idea till it has become a kind of substance in
my brain, that I have reasons for a thing which I have found
out with much labour and pains, and to which I can scarcely do
justice without the utmost violence of exertion (and that only to
a few persons) — is this a reason for my playing off my out-of-the-
way notions in all companies, wearing a prim and self-com-
placent air, as if I were "the admired of all observers"? or is it
not rather an argument (together with a want of animal spirits)
why I should retire into myself, and perhaps acquire a nervous
and uneasy look, from a consciousness of the disproportion between the interest and conviction I feel on certain subjects, and
my ability to communicate what weighs upon my own mind to
others? If my ideas, which I do not avouch, but suppose, lie
below the surface, why am I to be always attempting to dazzle

---

1. In his *Lord Byron and His Contemporaries*, published by Hunt &
Clarke simultaneously with the *Life of Napoleon*. A short note, without
date, is printed by Mr W. C. Hazlitt in *Lamb and Hazlitt*: 'Dear
Clarke, — Convey (the wise it call) the enclosed hare & Wiltshire bacon
to the most agreeable of biographers at Highgate; & the other thumper &
the article to the Editor of editors, J. S. Buckingham, Esq.'. I cannot see
that any article by Hazlitt appeared in the *Athenæum*.

superficial people with them, or smiling, delighted, at my own want of success?

'What I have here stated is only the excess of the common and well-known English and scholastic character. I am neither a buffoon, a fop, nor a Frenchman, which Mr Hunt would have me to be. He finds it odd that I am a close reasoner and a loose dresser. I have been (among other follies) a hard liver as well as a hard thinker; and the consequences of that will not allow me to dress as I please. People in real life are not like players on a stage, who put on a certain look or *costume,* merely for effect. I am aware, indeed, that the gay and airy pen of the author does not seriously probe the errors or misfortunes of his friends – he only glances at their seeming peculiarities, so as to make them odd and ridiculous; for which forbearance few of them will thank him. Why does he assert that I was vain of my hair when it was black, and am equally vain of it now it is grey, when this is true in neither case?[1] This transposition of motives makes me almost doubt whether Lord Byron was thinking so much of the rings on his fingers as his biographer was. These sort of criticisms should be left to women. I am made to wear a little hat, stuck on the top of my head the wrong way. Nay, I commonly wear a large slouching hat over my eyebrows; and if ever I had another, I must have twisted it about in any shape to get rid of the annoyance. This probably tickled Mr Hunt's fancy, and retains possession of it, to the exclusion of the

---

1. We compare a pleasant 'Wishing Cap' paper, descriptive of some of the cherished personal souvenirs in his literary collection, which Leigh Hunt contributed to the *Edinburgh Magazine* for January 1833: 'The lock of Mr Hazlitt's hair is a good thick ring, smooth and glossy, and almost black. Those who remember this great writer, during his latter years only, have no conception what a fine head of hair he had at a period a little earlier. It rapidly degenerated, and he cut it off as if in spite, and suddenly appeared with a docked grizzled head, to the great resentment of his friends, and (what he could not easily believe, or pretended not to believe) of the ladies.' This must have been subsequent to the Bewick portrait of 1824, and we have no picture of Hazlitt with the 'iron-grey hair' of his last years (*post,* page 408) noted by the Cowden Clarkes.

obvious truism, that I naturally wear "a melancholy hat".

'I am charged with using strange gestures and contortions of features in argument, in order to "look energetic". One would rather suppose that the heat of the argument produced the extravagance of the gestures, as I am said to be calm at other times. It is like saying that a man in a passion clenches his teeth, not because he is, but in order to seem, angry. Why should everything be construed into air and affectation? With Hamlet, I may say, "I know not *seems*".

'Again, my old friend and pleasant "Companion" remarks it, as an anomaly in my character, that I crawl about the Fives-Court like a cripple till I get the racket in my hand, when I start up as if I was possessed with a devil. I have then a motive for exertion; I lie by for difficulties and extreme cases. *Aut Cæsar aut nullus.* I have no notion of doing nothing with an air of importance, nor should I ever take a liking to the game of battledore and shuttlecock. I have only seen by accident a page of the unpublished Manuscript relating to the present subject, which I dare say is, on the whole, friendly and just, and which has been suppressed as being too favourable, considering certain prejudices against me.

'In matters of taste and feeling, one proof that my conclusions have not been quite shallow or hasty, is the circumstance of their having been lasting. I have the same favourite books, pictures, passages that I ever had – nay, I may indulge a hope that my thoughts will survive me. This continuity of impression is the only thing on which I pride myself. Even L[amb], whose relish of certain things is as keen and earnest as possible, takes a surfeit of admiration, and I should be afraid to ask about his select authors or particular friends, after a lapse of ten years. As to myself, any one knows where to have me. What I have once made up my mind to, I abide by to the end of the chapter.'

While Hazlitt was writing this, and looking out upon the fields in which Charles and Mary Lamb (as he recalled) had strolled eighteen years before, Lamb was reading the *Napoleon*. On the 25th he informs Cowden Clarke, to whom he owed the book: 'Hazlitt's speculative episodes are capital; I skip the Battles'.

V

Hazlitt's return to dramatic criticism was made once more in the service of the *Examiner*. His articles extend from 16 March to 1 June, and they show no falling off. His residence now, to the best of our belief, was at 40 Half-moon Street; but we do not see him here in any reminiscence or correspondence which has survived. His concluding article, on Kean in Paris, was written from that city to make its appearance in the *Examiner* of 15 June.

This second residence in Paris we must assume to have been wholly spent in the labours necessary to the completion of the *Life of Napoleon*. We have no witness of his visit this time, nor do we know the extent of its duration. Before the autumn was long commenced he was once more back at Winterslow. He was living now, not at the Hut, but at a cottage in the village, as the letter which follows makes clear:

Hazlitt to the Postmaster, Salisbury

Winterslow, near Salisbury.
Oct. 6, 1828.

Sir, – I live at this place, the distance of which from Winterslow Hut is a mile and a half, and from Winterslow Hut to Salisbury six miles and a half. Each letter or newspaper I receive (brought out from Salisbury) is charged 4*d*. additional, which I understand is too much. This imposition is accompanied with impertinence and collusion, which make it worse. I sent a man down last night for a newspaper, which I was particularly anxious to see, and it was refused to be given up, because the messenger had not brought the 2*d*., though the landlady has in her possession 2*d*. of mine that had been left as change out of a letter paid for yesterday. This happens whenever the landlady at the Hut (Mrs Hine) is in the humour, and the object is to keep the 2*d*. for the letter-carrier

the next day. Nor is this all. The letters received in so unpleasant a manner do not reach Winterslow till the morning
or middle of the next day after they arrive in Salisbury. They
are brought out by the Guard at night, and sent up to the
village at their leisure the next morning. For the additional
4d. many persons would be glad to fetch them out from
Salisbury the same day, so that they would be received here
two hours after they reach Salisbury, which would be a great
convenience, and in some cases an object of importance.

I am, Sir, your very obedient, humble servant

W. HAZLITT.

With Hazlitt working 'double tides' at Winterslow, the year
comes to an end.

CHAPTER XIV

CONCLUSION

(1829–30)

★

Death cancels everything but truth.
The Spirit of the Age.

I

WITH the *Life of Napoleon* finished he came back to town. It was, no doubt, high time that he should do so. His work was done, but it was not yet paid for. While the concluding volumes of the book were passing through the press, he had no recourse but to throw himself once more into journalism.

He took stock, no doubt, of his position. The *Examiner* had passed virtually out of the hands of the Hunt family, although his publisher (Henry) kept his nominal connexion with it for a few months more. Between Albany Fonblanque, its present editor, and Hazlitt I think we may assume that relations in the preceding spring had been polite rather than cordial. Among the magazines he had the *Monthly* and the *New Monthly* for stand-bys, the latter still under the unsympathetic editorship of Campbell; but a year had passed since he had taken his farewell to Essay Writing, and he knew (no one better) that the productivity in that form which he had maintained for nine years could not be kept up for ever. He therefore turned to something which he could do more easily, and with this end in view revived in the columns of the *London Weekly Review* the conversations with Northcote which had been broken off in the magazine two years before. At the same time, from the first month in the year, he entered into an alliance with a new Sunday journal, the *Atlas,* which remained unbroken until the pen fell from his hand in his penultimate illness.

The paper which had the harvest-home of Hazlitt's mind, and which showed, on the whole, a fairly adequate appreciation of its privilege, is very little known to us. It was started in 1827 by R. S. Rintoul, an eminent journalist of the Scottish Radical school, who a year later left it with his staff and founded the *Spectator*. It is of this first editorial regime that Hazlitt in his essay *On the Causes of Popular Opinion* (January 1828) may be found remarking, in answer to some not very handsome strictures upon the *Plain Speaker*: 'If the Editor of the *Atlas* will do me the favour to look over my Essay on the Principles of Human Action, will dip into any essay I ever wrote ... and will take a sponge and clear the dust from the face of my "Old Woman" (which he can see at a common friend's [John Hunt's]), I hope he will, upon second thoughts, acquit me of an absolute dearth of resources and want of versatility in the direction of my studies.' The successor to Rintoul in the editorial chair of the *Atlas* was one Robert Bell, who made an excellent paper of it.

The hand which wrote in this journal on Hazlitt's death is unknown to us:[1]

All our contemporaries have mistaken, or otherwise failed to appreciate truly, the character of William Hazlitt. His memory is entitled to justice, of which he had but little when living. He was not the sort of man to whom justice could have been done effectually, for there was a waywardness in him that was sure to upset the cup before the wine was emptied. Perhaps it is the nature of genius – and he had an abundant share – to make its own circumstances, and to make them too of the troubled cast. He made a name at little cost, and preserved it indifferently, as if it were to show the greatness of his powers, that could sustain without effort what the toil of

1. I think it very likely, however, that this estimate is Cowden Clarke's.

others could not accomplish. Had he chosen to labour at the improvement of the faculties he had, and the enlargement of their application, there would be little need to enquire into the mysteries of his moral constitution. To those who knew him best he was the greatest marvel. They saw what the world could not see, the strangest combinations and the most perplexing contradictions.

Much has been said of the caustic bitterness of his style, when occasion demanded it, and the public have not hesitated to ascribe it to his natural disposition. The inference was hasty and erroneous. Hazlitt was mild, even to a child's temper; he was self-willed, but who needed to have drawn out the venom? Had he been suffered to pursue his career at his ease, he would not have afforded grounds for charging malignity upon him. The malignity grew up elsewhere, and extracted from him all the gall that was in his heart. For some unaccountable reason, which Hazlitt could never fathom, *Blackwood's Magazine* took an extraordinary pleasure in ridiculing him. They went beyond ridicule – they made him appear all that was base in public and private, until at last his fame became a sort of dangerous notoriety. His political and religious opinions were represented in such odious colours, that even the booksellers – our trading ones – shrunk from the publication of his writings, as if they contained nothing but treason and blasphemy. That impression went abroad, and nearly ruined him. He attributed it solely to the writers in *Blackwood,* who painted him as a Cockney of the worst description, mixing up wickedness with namby-pamby. Even Lady Morgan, smarting under his criticism in the *Edinburgh Review,* followed up the cry in her stupid *Book of the Boudoir*. It was not surprising that a man of Hazlitt's solitary habits should feel and resent this in his brooding moods. He did resent it, and fearfully, and the passion of revenge was instilled into his being, subdued only by the imperious presence of philosophy. He had strong passions and affections; and they swelled the torrent. Those who charge him with evil should pause over the story of his agitated life.

When you were first introduced to Hazlitt, with this previous impression of his bold character in your mind, you were
disappointed or astonished to meet an individual nervous,
low-spoken, and feeble, who lived on tea as a regimen. There
was not a particle of energy about him ordinarily. His face,
when at repose, had none of the marks of extraordinary intellect, or even of animation. The common expression was
that of pain, or rather the traces left by pain. It was languor
and inertion [sic]. But when he kindled, a flush mantled
over his sunken cheeks, his eyes lighted up wildly, his chest
expanded, he looked like one inspired, his motions were eloquent, and his whole form partook of the enthusiasm. This is
commonly the case with men of genius, but it was so in a remarkable degree with him. His conversation, generally, was
ragged in expression, exceedingly careless as to phraseology,
and not always clear in purport. He used the most familiar
words, and, for ease sake, fell into conventional turns of
language to save himself the trouble of explanation. This was
not so, however, when he grew warmed. Then he sometimes
mounted into sublime flights. But his conversational powers
were, at the best, below his literary capacity. ...

The work by which Hazlitt will be remembered, and
through which he desired to transmit his name and his
opinions to posterity, is his *Life of Napoleon Buonaparte*. It
was the greatest undertaking in which he ever engaged. It
exhibits his powerful mind in a position most favourable for
its display; and presents an imperishable record of the strength
and versatility of his genius. As a history, it has the merit of
rendering narrative subservient to instruction, by making
events the keys to thought. Hazlitt was too abstract and
philosophical for the labour of details; hence his work contains so much of fact as is necessary to the ends of truth, and
may be perused from the beginning to the end without inspir-
ing in the reader a single misgiving that a page of matter has
been wasted. That is a merit in an extensive history, not to

speak of its other higher merits, that we have rarely an opportunity of applauding.

The reference to Hazlitt's 'dangerous notoriety' reminds us that
though he had written thirty or forty first-class essays since the
Plain Speaker, no later collection into volume form was issued
during his lifetime, and we can only conclude that he could
not find a publisher for them. As for *Blackwood's Magazine,*
we may find a good deal more of philosophy than of the passion
of revenge in his last reference to it. This was in the essay *On
Public Opinion,* written after his return from Paris in 1827.
'Suppose', he had said, 'an individual of whom it has been repeatedly asserted that he has warts on his nose, were to enter
the reading-room aforesaid in the Rue de la Paix – is there a
single red-faced country squire who would not be surprised at
not finding this part of the story true – would not persuade
himself five minutes after that he could not have seen correctly,
or that some art had been used to conceal the defect, or would
be led to doubt, from this instance, Mr Blackwood's general
candour and veracity? On the contrary, the gentleman would
be obliged to disbelieve his senses rather than give Mr Blackwood the lie, who is read and believed by the whole world. He
would have a host of witnesses against him: there is not a
reader of Blackwood who would not swear to the fact. Seeing
is believing, it is said. Lying is believing, say I.'[1]

1. A short summary may be given here of *Blackwood's* principal references to Hazlitt from the *Liber Amoris* to his death. In October 1823 he
had figured as 'a small, fetid, blear-eyed pug', and in March 1825 as 'an
acknowledged scamp of the lowest order – a scamp by his own confession
steeped in ignorance and malice to his very ribald lips'. In October of the
same year the author of *Noctes* breaks into verse –

> *'Pygmalion is proud o'er his cups to disclose
> Like a gem from Golconda, my Twit at his nose';*

while in November 1826 the Editor of the *New Monthly* is asked: 'Why
is not Hazlitt kicked out of the concern?' In April 1827 one of the Professor's characters is told that he has 'the face of a satyr – absolutely
getting like Hazlitt's'. In March 1828 Wilson, in a review of Hunt's *Lord
Byron and His Contemporaries,* takes advantage of the occasion to inform

On the death of the *Weekly Review* in April, the 'Real Conversations' were transferred to the *Atlas,* where they figured as 'Conversations as Good as Real' until the end of the year. The only third party to these conversations who has left his impressions is, I think, Patmore: 'I have several times been present when Hazlitt has been at Northcote's, and has taken part in those admirable Conversations with the venerable artist, in which he [Hazlitt] professed that he used to take such delight. ... The simple truth on this matter is, that it was the astonishing acuteness and sagacity of Hazlitt's remarks that called into active being, if it did not actually create, much of what was noticeable in Northcote's conversation. Almost everything that he said in the way of critical opinion, on any topic, that might be in question, was at least *suggested* by something which Hazlitt would either drop in furtively as the point arose, with a humble and deprecatory, "But don't you think, sir" – or it was superadded to some inconsequent or questionable observation of Northcote's, with an assenting "Yes, sir; and perhaps – ," adding the true statement of the case, whatever it might be. And with these intellectual promptings, the truth and acuteness of which Northcote perceived and caught up immediately, he would go on talking "like a book" (as Hazlitt used to describe it) for half an hour together; and Hazlitt would sit listening in silent admiration, like a loving pupil, to the precepts of his revered master – he, the pupil, being all the while capable of teaching or confounding the master, on almost every point of

Hazlitt that he is 'excommunicated from all decent society'; while in December he says: '[I] who was not minding the maniac and had not kicked him for years'. The death of Hazlitt, so far as I have been able to observe, was suffered to pass by this magazine without notice. In this connection we may note what George Gilfillan of Edinburgh wrote in his *Third Gallery of Literary Portraits* (1854): 'Wilson and Lockhart bent all their young power against a writer whom both in their hearts admired, and from whom both had learned much. The first twenty-five volumes of *Blackwood's Magazine* are disgraced by incessant, furious, and scurrilous attacks upon the person, private character, talents, and moral and religious principles of Hazlitt, which future ages shall regard with wonder and disgust.'

inquiry that could by possibility come into discussion between them.'[1]

Crabb Robinson proves but a broken reed for the last stage of our journey, but he gives us a couple of entries which fall within this year:

'28 March: – I rode to Brighton in the Bolt and Tun coach. ... Began Hazlitt's *Notes on Tour in France, &c.*'

'13 April: – Rode to London in the Union coach. ... Hazlitt's Tour in France delighted me for the capital sense running through the whole, in spite of prejudice & malignity & ignorance.' The diarist must have been hard put to it to find these qualities in that work. In June he himself went to Italy, where he remained until after the death of Hazlitt.

The remarkably beneficial effects of death upon our appreciation of our contemporaries will be illustrated if we take here the concluding entries of our diarist. They belong to the year 1831, when he was once more at Brighton: '15 December: – I read Hazlitt's *Conversations of Northcote,* which will serve to occupy me while I remain here. A delightful book. I was reading it to-day, before & after dinner.' '16 December: – To-day I finished Hazlitt's *Conversations of Northcote.* I do not believe that Boswell gives so much good talk in an equal quantity of any part of his Life of Johnson. There is much more shrewd-

---

1. Much the same opinion is given by a writer in the *Athenæum* (2 October 1830); and the *Atlas* in its review of the artist's *Life of Titian* (21 December 1830) remarks: 'He is not the same Mr Northcote we meet in Mr Hazlitt's conversations'. In this work, however, we are to understand that Hazlitt gave Northcote his assistance. His son says, in the *Literary Remains*: 'The Life of Titian ... bears the name of Mr Northcote on its title-page, but, in point of fact, all Mr Northcote's share in the work was a mass of extremely unconnected manuscript, of which it was almost impossible to find the beginning, middle, or end. When reduced into something like order, this portion of the material, with the addition of a great many notes, &c., by my father, extended but to a volume and a quarter of the work. The remainder consists of a translation of Ticozzi's celebrated life of the great painter, by my father and myself.' When Northcote died, he was found to have left Hazlitt, who had pre-deceased him, a contingent legacy of one hundred pounds. – (Fletcher, *Conversations of Northcote with James Ward,* 1901.)

ness & originality in both Northcote & Hazlitt himself than in Johnson; yet all elderly people – my friend Amyot, for instance – would think this an outrageous proof of bad taste on my part. I do believe that I am younger in my tastes than most men. I can relish novelty, & am not yet a *laudator temporis acti.*'

Our principal witnesses to Hazlitt in his last years in London are the Cowden Clarkes, in their *Recollections of Writers* (1878). In July 1828, Charles Cowden Clarke married, in her twentieth year, the Mary Novello with whom Hazlitt's son had received instruction in Latin at the hands of Mary Lamb. 'Writing the Fine Arts for the *Atlas* newspaper', we read, 'and the Theatricals for the *Examiner* newspaper, gave us the opportunity of largely enjoying two pleasures peculiarly to our taste'.

After some reminiscences of Godwin and of Horace Smith the Clarkes go on : 'But there was a third whom we frequently encountered on these occasions, who often sat with us during the performance, and compared notes with us on its merits during its course and at its close. This was William Hazlitt, then writing the "Theatricals" for *The Times* newspaper. His companionship was most genial, his critical faculty we all know; it may therefore be readily imagined the gladness with which we two saw him approach the seats where we were and take one beside us of his own accord. ... At one period of the time when we met Hazlitt so frequently at the theatres Miss Mordaunt (afterwards Mrs Nesbitt) was making her appearance at the Haymarket in the first bloom and freshness of her youth and beauty. Hazlitt was "fathoms deep" in love with her.' I have tried to make this passage the ground for establishing that Hazlitt entered at this date upon a second period of association with *The Times*, but have not succeeded. The statement is, I am afraid, only one of those inadvertences to which literary reminiscences are so much subject. Miss Mordaunt's first appearance was on 18 October of this year, but I cannot find that Hazlitt wrote of her either in *The Times* or the *Atlas*. His theatre-going was now most probably done for his own pleasure.

The Clarkes have another reminiscence : 'It was our good

fortune to see a magnificent copy that Hazlitt made of the
Hippolito de Medici, when we called upon him at his lodgings
one evening. The painting – mere stretched canvas without
frame – was standing on an old-fashioned couch in one corner
of the room leaning against the wall, and we remained opposite
to it for some time, while Hazlitt stood by holding the candle
high up so as to throw the light well on to the picture, descant-
ing enthusiastically on the merits of the original. The beam from
the candle falling on his own finely intellectual head, with its
iron-grey hair, its square potential forehead, its massive mouth
and chin, and eyes full of earnest fire, formed a glorious picture
in itself, and remains a luminous vision for ever upon our
memory. ... Under that straightforward, hard-hitting, direct-
telling manner of his, both in writing and speaking, Hazlitt
had a depth of gentleness – even tenderness – of feeling on certain subjects; manly friendship, womanly sympathy, touched
him to the core; and any token of either would bring a sudden
expression into his eyes very beautiful as well as very heart-
stirring to look upon. We have seen this expression more than
once, and can recall its appealing charm, its wonderful irradi-
ation of the strong features and squarely-cut, rugged under
portion of the face.'

We may make one further extract: 'His facility in composition was extreme. We have seen him continue writing (when
we went to see him while he was pressed for time to finish
an article) with wonderful ease and rapidity of pen, going on
as if writing a mere ordinary letter. His usual manuscript was
clear and unblotted, indicating great readiness and sureness
in writing, as though requiring no erasures or interlining. He
was fond of using large pages of rough paper with ruled lines,
such as those of a bought-up blank account book – as they
were. We are so fortunate as to have in our possession Hazlitt's
autograph title-page to his *Life of Napoleon Buonaparte,* and
the proof-sheets of the preface he originally wrote to that work,
with his own correcting marks in the margin. The title-page is
written in fine, bold, legible hand-writing, while the proof cor-

rections evince the care and final polish he bestowed on what he wrote. The preface was suppressed, in deference to advice, when the work was first published.' We should hardly suppose that this was the reminiscence of Hazlitt's publisher, who, by failing at this juncture, involved the concluding volumes of the *Life of Napoleon* in the vortex of bankruptcy, and deprived their author of the reward of his toil.

The reader who is in the habit of thinking of Hazlitt as flying into a rage when the least thing went wrong with him will seek in vain for any break in the flow, or in the temper, of his contributions to the *Atlas*. He was back at the stage of the *Round Table* again, and the columns of this journal are a mine of his established and recognizable opinions.[1] In the last week of June he wrote on *Mr. Jeffrey's Resignation of the Editorship of the Edinburgh Review,* and after giving some reasons for the decline of that journal concluded: 'Those who know Mr Jeffrey at a distance admire him; those who are better acquainted with him love and respect him; all will be glad of a distinction grateful to his feelings, and which has been merited neither by servility nor faction, but by an union of firmness with moderation.'

One of the first steps of Jeffrey's successor was to seek out Hazlitt:

Hazlitt to Macvey Napier

No. 3, Bouverie Street, Fleet Street,
July 13, 1829[2]

Dear Sir, – I was pleased to hear that you had been so good as to make some inquiries after me through Messrs Longman. I need not say that I shall be happy if you will lay your com-

1. A mine which was by no means worked to exhaustion by Messrs Waller and Glover in their Collected Edition. In addition to a number of papers from Hazlitt's pen reprinted by the present writer (*New Writings: First Series*), a weekly feature entitled 'Memoranda on Men and Things' is full of his characteristic stories and opinions. The probability is that Hazlitt spent the last eighteen months of his life not only in writing for the *Atlas*, but in talking for it.

2. This and six following letters, first published by the present writer in the *Athenæum*, 15 August 1919, from the originals in the British Museum.

mands upon me to do any thing that lies in my power. There
are two works lately published that I think I might make
something of, *viz.,* the Life of Mr Locke by Lord King &
Southey's Dialogues of Sir Thomas More. But I only suggest
these for your better consideration. I hope that Mr Jeffrey is
well, & I remain, Dear Sir, very respectfully, your obliged
humble servant,

W. HAZLITT.

The final period of Hazlitt's association with the *Edinburgh
Review,* which was now entered upon, lasted until his death.
On 21 July we find him consenting to write on Dr Channing
(neither of the works for which he had asked being entrusted
to him), and adding: 'In case this and the others should fail, let
me suggest another subject, the forthcoming Life and Writings
of Defoe, in which I should be somewhat *au fait* and could treat
con amore. I should be sorry to do an indifferent article for a
commencement'. On 26 August the Channing is sent and Hazlitt says: 'I have only to add that if you think the article I have
sent will do, I would beg for a small advance upon it. I would
not thus early appear in *formâ pauperis,* but the loss of £200 on
my Life of Napoleon through the failure of Messrs Hunt &
Clarke has driven me to great straits at the present moment.'
Both *American Literature – Dr Channing* and *Flaxman's Lectures on Sculpture* were in the *Review* for October. The number
was the first under the editorship of Macvey Napier, and on
23 November we find Jeffrey writing to his successor: 'Your
American reviewer is not a first-rate man – a clever *writer*
enough – but not deep or judicious – or even very fair. I have no
notion who he is. If he is young, he may come to good – but
he should be trained to a more modest opinion of himself, and
take a little more pains, and go more patiently and thoroughly
into his subjects.' That Jeffrey should fail to recognize the hand
of his 'ancient ally' in a long and thoroughly characteristic
article is quite in the spirit of Hazlitt's relations with the *Edinburgh Review.*

In a letter of 7 November we learn: 'I am about the Defoe, and shall attend to your advice. The only reason why I presume to think that my articles may do for the *Edinburgh* (not in the sense in which some people would pretend) is that they make perhaps a variety. If not so good, they are different from others, and so far, are the better for being worse. There are licences in criticism, as well as in poetry.' The *Life of Defoe* of Walter Wilson, Lamb's colleague of the India House, is the subject of two letters we possess in this month. On the 15th Lamb writes to Wilson: 'Hazlitt is going to make your book a basis for a review of De Foe's Novels in the *Edinbro'*. I wish I had health and spirits to do it. Hone I have not seen, but I doubt not he will be much pleased with your performance.' And Hone, on the 22nd, having been taken by business to Manchester, writes to Mr Hurst of the firm of Longmans: 'At the time of my leaving London, I expected to return within a week, and to do what I could in a needful and kind way for my old friend Mr Walter Wilson's *Life of De Foe* ... The copy of De Foe which I received at the same time with my own, for Mr Hazlitt, I took to him the same day, and left him gratified by receiving it, and in the best disposition to set to work upon it kindly.'

Lamb was at Enfield, and Hazlitt was in Fleet Street, and in this year we receive little evidence that they can have met very much. Lamb's one sojourn in town was in July for ten days, and in the course of it we find him writing to Bernard Barton; 'I have ceased to care almost about any body. The bodies I cared for are in graves, or dispersed.' Hazlitt, however, was not yet in his grave. A letter of 8 December, to the same correspondent, seems to indicate that their *rapprochement* had been recent.[1] Referring to an event which, as we have seen,

---

1. A letter to Moxon is without date, and we do not know to what month to attribute it: 'Young Hazlitt lives, at least his father does, at 3 or 36 (36 I have it down, with the 6 scratch'd out) Bouverie Street, Fleet Street. If not to be found, his mother's address is, Mrs Hazlitt, Mrs Tomlinson's, Potter's Bar. At one or other he must be heard of.'

had happened in the summer, Lamb says: 'Hazlitt has just been defrauded of £100 [*sic*] by his Bookseller-friend's breaking'. Mr Lucas says there is no record of Hazlitt's visiting Enfield, but at the same time he prints the evidence of Lamb's juvenile neighbour, Thomas Westwood, that he remembered him there. I think we may date such a visit at November, and suppose it, once made, to have been more than once repeated.

Of Hone, Patmore tells us something: 'If I were required to name the person among all Hazlitt's intimates in whose society he seemed to take the most unmingled pleasure[1] – or I should perhaps rather say, with whom he felt himself most at ease and "comfortable" – I should say it was the late William Hone, author of the celebrated "Parodies".

'It has been my lot during the last fifteen years to associate more or less familiarly with a large proportion of the most intellectual men of an age which perhaps deserves to be characterized as the most intellectual that the world ever knew; and I confess that no part of such intercourse has connected itself with more perfectly pleasant recollections and associations than do the three or four evenings that I remember to have spent with Hazlitt and Hone, in the little dingy wainscoted coffee-room of the Southampton Arms, in Southampton Buildings, Chancery Lane. There, after having dreamed and lingered at home over his beloved tea from five or six o'clock till ten or so at night, Hazlitt used to go every evening, for years, to take his supper (or dinner, as the case might be) of either cold roast beef or rump-steak and apple tart; for he rarely tasted anything else but these – never by choice, unless it were a roast fowl, a pheasant, or a brace of partridges, when his funds happened to be unusually flourishing. And there you were sure to find him, in his favourite box on the right-hand side of the fire-place, sitting (if alone) upright, motionless, and silent as an effigy,

---

1. Patmore, of course, is a *round about* writer, who does not mean to exclude by this form of expression what he says in numerous other passages as to the paramount place held by Lamb in Hazlitt's esteem and affection.

brooding over his own thoughts, and, at the same time, taking in and turning to intellectual account every word that was uttered by the few persons who used at that time habitually to frequent the house, and to most of whom he was known; at the same time, casting furtive glances at the door every time it gave intimation of opening, partly in the hope, partly in the fear, that the in-comer might be some one of his own particular intimates, who came there, as he knew, solely to seek him.'

To bring the year to a close, we shall make an extract from the last of the *Conversations of Northcote*. The old painter has been indulging (or has been credited with indulging) in a little excursus upon the faults of his visitor; and Hazlitt replies:

I confess all this, but I hardly know how to remedy it; nor do I feel any strong inducement. Taking one thing with another, I have no great cause to complain. If I had been a merchant, a bookseller, or the proprietor of a newspaper, instead of what I am, I might have had more money or possessed a town and country-house, instead of lodging in a first or second floor, as it may happen. But what then? I see how the man of business and fortune passes his time. He is up and in the city by eight, swallows his breakfast in haste, attends a meeting of creditors, must read Lloyd's lists, consult the price of consols, study the markets, look into his accounts, pay his workmen, and superintend his clerks: he has hardly a minute in the day to himself, and perhaps in the four-and-twenty hours does not do a single thing that he would do if he could help it. Surely, this sacrifice of time and inclination requires some compensation, which it meets with. But how am I entitled to make my fortune (which cannot be done without all this anxiety and drudgery) who do hardly any thing at all, and never any thing but what I like to do? I rise when I please, breakfast *at length,* write what comes into my head, and after taking a mutton-chop and a dish of strong tea, go to the play, and thus my time passes. Mr — — has no time to go to the play. It was but the other day that I had to get up a little earlier than usual to go into the city about some money transaction, which appeared to me a prodigious hardship : if so, it was plain that I must lead a tolerably easy life : nor should I object to passing mine over again.[1]

II

We open the last year of Hazlitt's life with a letter :

Hazlitt to Macvey Napier

January 15, 1830

Dear Sir, — I have done as well as I could. I hope it will do. I hope you will let me know soon. If it is inserted, I shall be glad of a remittance for it as soon as convenient : but though I have put some strength & truth into it, I fear there is very little discretion. Your ever obliged servant,

W. HAZLITT.

The subject of this letter is Wilson's 'Life and Times of Defoe', which made its appearance in the *Review* dated January. That he was indeed still capable of strength and truth we may judge not only from this article but from the 'Specimens of a Dictionary of Definitions' with which, to supply the place of Northcote, he opened the year in the *Atlas. The Ideal, The Spirit of Controversy, Envy, An Analysis of Prejudice, Further Thoughts on Prejudice, Party Spirit* — if he had written on these subjects before, he wrote on them now with a mastery that he had not previously excelled.

The next letter, which is the last we possess from his pen, acquaints us with his final change of address :

1. If this passage were not a little long for the purpose, I should propose it as an admirable one to set up over the door of that handsome block of commercial offices which, under the name of Hazlitt House, now occupies a site adjacent to the Southampton Coffee-house and the scene of the *Liber Amoris*.

Hazlitt to Macvey Napier

6 Frith Street, Soho

March 19, 1830

Dear Sir, – I have looked at Cloudesley & think I may make an article of it whether as a failure or successful, if you will give me a certain latitude, I do not mean of space but style. I have a design upon Jefferson's Memoirs, if you please, & promise to do it well. I am not sorry I had not Southey, as it is so ably done.[1] I received your remittance & am thankful for that, & still more for your approbation of my last. Pray tell me if there is any hurry: I hope to send you in a fortnight, if I am not prevented by accidents.

I remain, Dear Sir, ever your truly obliged humble servant,

W. HAZLITT.

In the course of his article, *Mr Godwin*, Hazlitt remarked: 'A writer who gives us *himself*, cannot do this twenty times follow-

1. The reader who supposes that Hazlitt had wished to have a last 'knock' at Southey will correct that impression if he will look again into the *Spirit of the Age*. Procter's phrase with regard to his racket-playing – 'He liked a stout opponent, but he did not bear malice' – comes to mind in this connection. The same, I am afraid, cannot be said of his opponents. The reader of Southey's *Doctor* (1834–9) will find it full of slighting references to Hazlitt's ability. In his 'Recollections' in the *New Monthly Magazine* of November 1830, Procter said regarding Coleridge: 'When that very clever person shall hear of the death of poor Hazlitt, he will, I hope, forget the differences that existed between them, and, in the spirit of that religion of which he once professed himself a minister, forbear even a derogatory hint of the dead'. Coleridge, for some years past a King's Pensioner of the Royal Literary Association, forbore in the manner following:

Obiit Saturday, Sept 18, 1830

W. H. *Eheu!*

Beneath this stone does William Hazlitt lie
    Thankless of all that God or man could give,
He lived like one who never thought to die,
    He died like one who dared not hope to live.

The effect of this epitaph is a little reduced when we find that Coleridge kept it on hand and adapted it to serve a number of obituary purposes.

ing. He gives us the best and most prominent part of himself, and afterwards, "but the lees and dregs remain".' He may have felt the truth of this in his own case; but there is little fault to be found with his last contribution to the *Edinburgh,* which came out in April. The reviewer of Southey's *Dialogues of Sir Thomas More* was Macaulay. The 'accidents' to which Hazlitt referred were the attacks of his constitutional malady, under one of which he had nearly died two years before, and which were now visiting him with increasing frequency.

At the end of April, indeed, his weekly article disappears from the *Atlas.* At the same moment (2 May) the journal reviews the *Life of Napoleon* in four volumes, bearing the imprint of Effingham Wilson.

Hazlitt's work was now done, and he took his relaxation. Our informant is Procter in the paper which he wrote at his death : 'He was fond of the theatres, and frequented them to the last. His earliest admiration rested on Mrs Siddons, his latest on her niece. The last he thought full of promise; the first he held to have touched the summit of perfection. Who is there that has said things so eloquent of *her*? In every paper, and magazine, and review, in which he wrote, the traces of his admiration may be seen. He regarded her as he would a Muse or a Sibyl – as the crowned and ruling spirit of tragedy. "While the stage lasts" (wrote he ten years ago), "there never will be another Mrs Siddons!" And now, Mrs Siddons has survived him, who so long and disinterestedly laboured in her service. With almost twice the weight of years upon her head, she yet lives to value (I hope) the "golden opinions" which he lavished upon her. His criticisms remain. They are worthy still to give her pleasure, and to throw lustre on her retreat. They are a legacy, not the least valuable which critics and poets have bequeathed her, and one that will not be the first to perish. His estimate of Miss Fanny Kemble was different from that of Mr Hunt. He acknowledged the dawn of great qualities in her; he admired (not quite without exceptions) her Juliet, and liked exceedingly to listen to the music of her voice. I met him one evening accidentally at the play, when he spoke very pleasantly of her, and said that he thought she would succeed in Lady Constance – a great compliment from him. His love for the theatres, and his constancy in visiting one of them (Covent Garden), are recorded in a paper called *The Free Admission,* which appeared three or four months ago in the *New Monthly Magazine.*' It appeared in July, and was followed, in August, by *The Sick Chamber.* In these two essays we have the setting for Hazlitt's last summer – his sick-room in Frith Street, and his 'beloved corner' in the second circle at Covent Garden. 'I would,' he says, 'if I could, have it surrounded with a balustrade of gold, for it has been to me a palace of delight.'

I am inclined to think that we get our latest glimpse of him in the pages of Cyrus Redding's *Past Celebrities*: 'I met Hazlitt one day in Dean Street, Soho. After a few words upon some other topic, I said "You have not seen Hunt lately? Have you seen Talfourd?" He replied, to my surprise, that he was then on his way to Hampstead [Highgate], to make all square with Hunt, for he was well aware I knew there was a difference between them. "I have not been at the Temple, but I am going to see Hunt," he said, as if nothing had passed. I told him I had heard of the difference; he replied, "He has forgot, I dare say; if he has not, I have".'

In his essay *On the Fear of Death* in 1822 he had written: 'No man would, I think, exchange his existence with any other man, however fortunate. We had as lief *not be,* as *not be ourselves.* There are some persons of that reach of soul that they would like to live two hundred and fifty years hence, to see to what height of empire America will have grown up in that period, or whether the English constitution will last so long. These are points beyond me. But I confess I should like to live to see the downfall of the Bourbons. That is a vital question with me; and I shall like it the better, the sooner it happens!' It happened in the last days of July, at the Revolution of the Three Days. Hazlitt, in his sickroom, wrote in the following month his last essay, *On Personal Politics.* 'Let him [Charles X] go where he chooses', he concluded, 'with a handsome pension; but let him not be sent back again (as he was once before) at the expense of millions of lives!' To this he added a foot-note, containing probably his last written words: 'Even then I should not despair. The Revolution of the Three Days was like a resurrection from the dead, and showed plainly that liberty too has a spirit of life in it; and that the hatred of oppression is "the unquenchable flame, the worm that dies not".'

The 'spirit of life' in Hazlitt is described for us by Procter: 'I saw him (once only) as he lay, ghastly, shrunk, and helpless, on the bed from which he never afterwards rose. His mind seemed to have weathered all the dangers of extreme sickness, and to be safe and strong as ever. But the physical portion had endured sad decay. He could not lift his hand from the coverlet; and his voice was changed and diminished to a hoarse whisper, resembling the faint scream that I have heard from birds. I never was so sensible of the power of death before.' From the last week of July, Charles and Mary Lamb were close at hand, having a holiday in town at their and Hazlitt's old address, Southampton Buildings. In September *Conversations of James Northcote, Esq., R.A.,* was published by Colburn.

It is Procter who says: 'It has been said that Hazlitt died, forsaken, and in poverty. *This is not the fact.* He was as well off as he generally was; and he had friends who provided all that was necessary for him, and stood by him to the last.' This is confirmed by a writer in the *Athenæum* (who may have been R. H. Horne): 'His death was occasioned by organic disease of the stomach, of many years' standing. He retained the entire possession of his faculties to the last moment of his life; and, almost free from bodily pain, he died with perfect calmness of mind ... The report that he died in a state of destitution is happily incorrect. He had, within two or three months, received considerable sums from a great publishing house, for his *Conversations of James Northcote* and other works, and also various other sums, of consequence in the aggregate, for his writings in the periodical press.' Talfourd tells us: 'In a moment of acute pain, when the needless apprehension for the future rushed upon him, he dictated a brief and peremptory letter to the Editor of the *Edinburgh Review* [*sic*], requiring a considerable remittance, to which he had no claim but that of former remunerated services, which the friend,[1] who obeyed his bidding, feared might excite displeasure; but he mistook Francis Jeffrey; the sum demanded was received by return of post, with the most anxious wishes for his recovery – just too late for him to understand his error.'

On his deathbed, we are told, he asked for his mother, who was in Devonshire, in her eighty-fifth year. To his son, whose part in preserving his father's memory is an equivocal one, we may be grateful for recording his last words: 'Well, I've had a happy life'.

The final entry may belong, as of right, to Sarah Hazlitt, once Stoddart: 'William Hazlitt, senr., died at his lodgings, No. 6, Frith Street, Soho, London, on Saturday, 18th September, 1830, at about half-past four in the afternoon, aged 52 years, five months, and eight days. Mr Lamb, Mr White,[2] Mr Hessey, and his son were with him when he died. He was buried on the following Thursday (23rd) at the burying ground of St. Anne's, Soho, at five o'clock in the afternoon.'

The 'old and warmly attached friend' who erected a tombstone bearing the following inscription is said to have been Charles Wells:

1. This friend, as an article 'Hazlitt's Death-bed' in the *Monthly Magazine* for March 1833 informs us, was his 'faithful companion' Martin Burney. Carlyle, who did not know Hazlitt personally, but was with Jeffrey when the letter was received, says that the amount asked was £10, the amount sent £50. – (*Reminiscences*, II. 38.)

2. Edward White, of the India House, not, of course, the author of *Falstaff's Letters,* who had died in 1820. This is one of the friends of Hazlitt's last years of whom we see almost nothing. He owned, for some years, Hazlitt's portrait of Lamb which is now in the National Portrait Gallery.

Here rests

WILLIAM HAZLITT

Born April 10, 1778. Died 18 September, 1830.

He lived to see his deepest wishes gratified
as he has expressed them in his Essay,
'On the Fear of Death'.

Viz.:
'To see the downfall of the Bourbons,
And some prospect of good to mankind':
(Charles X
was driven from France 29th July, 1830).

'To leave some sterling work to the world':
(He lived to complete his *Life of Napoleon*).

His desire
That some friendly hand should consign
him to the grave was accomplished to a
limited but profound extent; on
these conditions he was ready to depart,
and to have inscribed on his tomb,
'Grateful and Contented'.

He was
The first (unanswered) Metaphysician of the age.
A despiser of the merely Rich and Great:
A lover of the People, Poor or Oppressed:
A hater of the Pride and Power of the Few,
as opposed to the happiness of the Many;
A man of true moral courage,
Who sacrificed Profit and present Fame
To Principle,
And a yearning for the good of Human Nature.
Who was a burning wound to an Aristocracy,
That could not answer him before men,
And who may confront him before their Maker.

He lived and died
The unconquered Champion
of
Truth, Liberty, and Humanity,
'Dubitantes opera legite'.

This stone
is raised by one whose heart is
with him, in his grave.

In 1870 this stone was taken down, and the present less contentious memorial substituted:

ON THE NORTHERN SIDE OF THIS GROUND LIE THE
REMAINS OF
WILLIAM HAZLITT, PAINTER, CRITIC, ESSAYIST.
BORN AT MAIDSTONE, APRIL 10, 1778.
DIED IN SOHO, SEPTEMBER 18, 1830.

III

Hazlitt died and was buried, in the heart of his beloved West End, where the motor-buses now go past him and the theatres have come westwards to stand at his either hand. His death, save for some short-lived controversy over the degree of poverty in which he had died, passed for the greater part unnoticed. In France both he and his work were known;[1] in Germany Heine championed his memory. But in his own country, where there came within eighteen months the logical end of the age through which he lived, he was neglected and forgotten. His life, bounded at one end by the War of Independence and the French Revolution, and at the other by the Reform Bill, was not seen to be possessed of any kind of symbolic value. His

1. The *Spirit of the Age*, under the title of 'Beaux Esprits Contemporains', had appeared serially in the *Revue Britannique* during 1826–7. A paper, 'Des Drames Historiques de Shakespeare', in the same review for May 1829, is announced as by 'le cèlebre et spirituel Hazlitt'. On his death he is described as 'un des écrivains les plus piquans et des penseurs les plus originaux de l'Angleterre moderne'.

steady rise from the oblivion in which he appeared to die may be shortly traced in the concluding pages of this narrative.

In 1836 Bulwer Lytton, introducing the *Literary Remains* brought together by Hazlitt's son, remarked: 'Posterity will do him justice – the first interval of peace and serenity which follows our present political disputes will revive and confirm his name. A complete collection of his works is all the monument he demands.' In 1837 R. H. Horne, in introducing Hazlitt's *Characteristics* (the first of his works to be re-issued after his death) quoted Bacon on the fate that attends 'great wits' as contrasted with 'men of capacity', and said: 'Thus it has hitherto been with the writings of William Hazlitt, though there were strong political and personal causes, in addition, to account for it. Some of his admirers will object that the above remarks hardly apply to him, and that, considering all things, he is already appreciated by as large and "fit" an audience as could have been expected in his time. Perhaps so; but I consider that neither the extent nor the *degree* of appreciation, with very few exceptions, is yet, by comparison, more than a fraction of that which he will eventually obtain. ... If those quarterly and monthly reviews, and other lion-and-unicorn periodicals, in whose pages he has been most traduced and insulted, should be extant fifty years hence, they will all say the same.'

In 1845 De Quincey found the whole work of Hazlitt 'for the present deeper in the world's oblivion' than the essays of John Foster. Three years later Cyrus Redding remarks: 'If a love of literature, properly so called, should revive in England, Hazlitt will be more highly estimated than he has yet been, and more liberally judged'. In 1854 Gilfillan, in his third *Gallery of Literary Portraits,* notes that 'there is no good edition, cheap or dear' of Hazlitt's works, and speaks of it as 'a disgrace to literature'. This disgrace Hazlitt's son and grandson, from about this date, took the first steps to remove. Two years before the *Memoirs* of 1867 we find Procter remarking: 'The decisions of a hostile majority pressed down the reputation of William Hazlitt, and no one has taken the trouble to elevate it to its proper position since'. In the 'seventies Walter Bagehot succeeded to the mantle of Macaulay, and spoke in private of rendering an acknowledgement to their common master which he did not publicly perform. In the 'eighties Stevenson made his discovery that 'though we are mighty fine fellows nowadays, we cannot write like Hazlitt'. Another twenty years pass, and the Collected Edition of his works is achieved, which, as Bulwer Lytton had said, is all the monument he demands. In introducing that edition, Mr W. E. Henley, writing of Lamb's words on Hazlitt, said: 'Thus does one Royalty celebrate the kingship and enrich the immortality of another'. Hazlitt, probably, never expected to be hailed in terms of royalty: his own claim was more simple. 'It is too much', he wrote in *On the Difference between Writing and Speaking,* 'to ask that our good things should be duly appreciated by the first person we meet, or in the next minute after their disclosure; if the world is a little, a very little, the wiser or better for them a century hence, it is full as much as can be modestly expected.'

APPENDICES

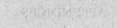

APPENDICES

I

LIST OF PRINCIPAL PRINTED AUTHORITIES FOR THE LIFE OF HAZLITT

BEWICK – *Life and Letters,* edited by Thomas Landseer, 2 vols., 1871.

BLACKWOOD – *Annals of a Publishing House*: *William Blackwood and His Sons,* by Mrs Oliphant, 3 vols., 1897–8.

CLARKE, COWDEN – *Recollections of Writers,* 1878.

COLERIDGE – *Anima Poetæ,* edited by E. H. Coleridge, 1895; *Essays on His Own Times,* 3 vols., 1850; *Letters,* edited by E. H. Coleridge, 2 vols., 1895; *Life,* by J. Gillman, 1838; *Life,* by J. D. Campbell, 1894; *T. Poole and His Friends,* by M. E. Sandford, 1888.

COMBE, GEORGE – *Life,* by C. Gibbon, 1878.

CONSTABLE – *Archibald Constable and His Literary Correspondents,* edited by T. Constable, 3 vols., 1873.

DE QUINCEY – *Works,* edited by D. Masson, vols. IX and XI, 1889–90.

GILFILLAN – *Third Gallery of Literary Portraits,* 1854.

GODWIN – *Life,* by C. Kegan Paul, 1876.

HAYDON – *Life,* edited by Tom Taylor, 3 vols., 1853; *Correspondence and Table-talk,* edited by his son, 1876.

HAZLITT – *Collected Works,* edited by A. R. Waller and Arnold Glover, with an introduction by W. E. Henley, 13 vols., 1902–6; *Life of Napoleon,* 4 vols., 1828–30; *Liber Amoris, or The New Pygmalion,* with additional matter now printed for the first time from the original manuscripts, privately printed, 1894; *Literary Remains,* with a notice of his life, by his son, and thoughts on his genius and writings, by E. L. Bulwer and Mr Sergeant Talfourd, 2 vols., 1836; *Memoirs,* by W. Carew Hazlitt, 2 vols., 1867; *Four Generations of a Literary Family,* by W. Carew Hazlitt, 2 vols., 1897; *Lamb and Hazlitt,* edited by W. Carew

Hazlitt, 1900; *The Hazlitts: an Account of their Origin and Descent*, by W. Carew Hazlitt, privately printed, 1911; *Liste Chronologique des Œuvres de*, par Jules Douady, Paris, 1906; *New Writings, First and Second Series*, collected by P. P. Howe, 1925–7.

HONE – *Life*, by F. W. Hackwood, 1912.

HUNT, LEIGH – *Autobiography*, 1850; *Correspondence*, edited by his son, 1862; *Foliage*, 1817; *Lord Byron and his Contemporaries*, 1828.

JEFFREY – *Life*, by Lord Cockburn, 2 vols., 1852.

KEATS – *Complete Works*, edited by H. Buxton Forman, vols. IV and V, Letters, 1901.

KNOWLES – *Life*, by R. B. Knowles, privately printed, 1872.

LAMB – *Life*, by E. V. Lucas, 1905; *Works of Charles and Mary Lamb*, edited by E. V. Lucas, vols. VI and VII, Letters, 1905.

LANDOR – *Life*, by John Forster, 2 vols., 1869.

LOCKHART – *Life and Letters*, by Andrew Lang, 2 vols., 1897.

MEDWIN – 'Hazlitt in Switzerland: A Conversation,' *Fraser's Magazine*, March 1839.

MILL, JAMES – *Life*, by A. Bain, 1882.

MITFORD – *Life*, by A. G. L'Estrange, 3 vols., 1870.

MOORE – *Memoirs, Journal, and Correspondence*, edited by Lord John Russell, 8 vols., 1853–6.

MURRAY – *A Publisher and His Friends*: *Memoirs and Correspondence of John Murray, 1768–1843*, by Samuel Smiles, 2 vols., 1891.

NAPIER, MACVEY – *Selected Correspondence*, edited by his son, 1879.

PATMORE – *My Friends and Acquaintance*, 3 vols., 1854; *Rejected Articles*, 1826.

PROCTER – 'My Recollections of the late William Hazlitt,' *New Monthly Magazine*, November 1830; *Charles Lamb*, 1866; *An Autobiographical Fragment*, edited by Coventry Patmore, 1877.

REDDING – *Fifty Years' Recollections*, 3 vols., 1858; *Past Celebrities Whom I Have Known*, 2 vols., 1866.

RICKMAN – *Life and Letters*, by Orlo Williams, 1912.

ROGERS – *Life*, by P. W. Clayden, 1887.

SHELLEY – *Life*, by Edward Dowden, 2 vols., 1886.

SOUTHEY – *Life and Correspondence*, edited by C. C.

Southey, 6 vols., 1849–50; *Letters*, edited by J. W. Warter, 4 vols., 1856; *Early Life*, by W. Haller, 1917.

STENDHAL – *Correspondance*, publiée par A. Paupe et P.-A. Cheramy, 3 vols., 1908.

TALFOURD – *Final Memorials of Charles Lamb*, 2 vols., 1848.

WEDGWOOD, THOMAS – *Life*, by R. B. Litchfield, 1903.

WILSON, JOHN ('Christopher North') – *Life*, by Mrs Gordon, 1862.

WORDSWORTH – *Life*, by W. A. Knight, 3 vols., 1889; *Life*, by George M. Harper, 2 vols., 1916; *Letters of the Wordsworth Family*, edited by W. A. Knight, 3 vols., 1907; *Memorials of Coleorton*, edited by W. A. Knight, 1887.

II

SUMMARY OF PAINTINGS KNOWN TO HAVE
BEEN EXECUTED BY HAZLITT, 1800–1812

A LIST of the paintings executed by Hazlitt, which I believe to be complete according to our present knowledge, is as follows:

'An Old Woman', his first picture (in bad preservation), in the Maidstone Museum.

Portrait of his father, Royal Academy, 1802; probably that attributed to John Hazlitt in the Maidstone Museum.

Self-portrait in the Louvre, 1802 (in bad preservation), in the Maidstone Museum.

Five copies made in the Louvre for Mr Railton of Liverpool – Titian's 'Hippolito de' Medici', 'Mistress' and 'Young Man with a Glove', Raphael's 'Holy Family' and 'Transfiguration' (portion). Duplicates of the two first named of these, made 'for his own use', together with his copy of Lana's 'Death of Clorinda' are in the Maidstone Museum.

Portrait of Coleridge, 1803; whereabouts unknown.

Portrait of Hartley Coleridge, 1803; whereabouts unknown.

Portrait of Wordsworth, 1803; destroyed.

Portrait of Dr Shepherd of Gateacre, Liverpool, 1803; whereabouts unknown.

Portrait of Lamb, 1804, in the National Portrait Gallery.

Portraits of Sheridan Knowles and his sister; whereabouts unknown.

Portrait of a Gentleman (? Lamb), Royal Academy, 1805.

Portrait of Mr Howell of London, 1811; whereabouts unknown.

Portrait of Thomas Clarkson of Bury, 1811; whereabouts unknown.

Portrait of Thomas Robinson of Bury, 1812; destroyed.

A good many other portraits must have been painted between 1803 and 1808, of which no record exists. No specimen of Hazlitt's landscape painting (Wem, 1805–7, Winterslow, 1808–11) appears to have survived.

III

HAZLITT'S PATRON

A PASSAGE in the essay *On the Want of Money*, written in Paris in 1827, has proved a stumbling-block to Hazlitt's editors and biographers for more than half a century. The passage is as follows:

I never knew but one man who would lend his money freely and fearlessly in spite of circumstances (if you were likely to pay him, he grew peevish, and would pick a quarrel with you). I can only account for this from a certain sanguine buoyancy and magnificence of spirit, not deterred by distant consequences, or damped by untoward appearances. I have been told by those, who shared of the same bounty, that it was not owing to generosity, but ostentation – if so, he kept his ostentation a secret from me, for I never received a hint or a look from which I could infer that I was not the lender, and he the person obliged. Neither was I expected to keep in the background or play an underpart. On the contrary, I was encouraged to do my best; my dormant faculties roused, the ease of my circumstances was on condition of the freedom and independence of my mind, my lucky hits were applauded, and I was paid to shine. I am not ashamed of such patronage as this, nor do I regret any circumstance relating to it but its termination. People endure existence even in Paris: the rows of chairs on the Boulevards are gay with smiles and dress: the saloons, they say, are brilliant; at the theatre there is Mademoiselle Mars – what is all this to me? After a certain period, we live only in the past. Give me back one single evening at Boxhill, after a stroll in the deep-empurpled woods, before Buonaparte was yet beaten, 'with wine of attic taste', when wit, beauty, friendship, presided at the Board! Oh no! Neither the time nor friends that are fled can be recalled!

The subject of this passage has been variously identified – by the late Mr W. C. Hazlitt with Thomas Wedgwood, who died in 1805, and whose country house was at Tarrant Gunville, near Blandford, Dorset; by Messrs Waller and Glover (tentatively, and as to the early part of the passage) with Francis Jeffrey. There can be no doubt, however, that it is Richard ('Conversation') Sharp who is alluded to, whose hospitality at Fredley Farm, Mickleham, which he occupied from 1797 to his death in 1835, enters at so many points into the social and literary life of the period.

Sharp, having met Hazlitt in the Lakes and 'liked him' (*ante*, p. 96), entered Parliament in 1806, in his forty-seventh year, as a follower of Fox, and throughout the session of 1807 we find him a leading opponent of that Expedition to the Baltic which Hazlitt's political pamphlet of the preceding summer had submitted to criticism. His reputed acuteness in metaphysical discussion was, of course, the occasion of his sobriquet. We know him, in addition, to have been the friend of Horne Tooke, the sharer of the old Radical's philological as well as his political interests until his death in 1812, and an attendant at those Sunday gatherings of the latter at Wimbledon of which Hazlitt has left us a picture in the *Spirit of the Age*. Between Boxhill and Wimbledon, no doubt, we have the background to Hazlitt's thirtieth year which is missing with the Lamb correspondence.

The relations of Coleridge with this patron, and, indeed, the figure of Richard Sharp in general, are singularly little illumined in extant correspondence. One letter from Coleridge to Sharp has been printed (*Letters*, II. 47), of date 15 January 1804, and any one who turns to it with a knowledge of the variations of Coleridge's epistolary style will have little difficulty in concluding that relations between them at this date were not intimate. During February and March they were meeting in London (Southey, *Letters*, I. 279; Knight, *Letters of the Wordsworth Family*, III. 380), and at the end of the latter month Coleridge departed for Malta. On his return in August 1806, his political opinions cannot have commended him much to Sharp, and that Hazlitt owed to him the revival of an acquaintance begun under his auspices in the Lakes does not seem probable. Sharp, we can have little doubt, took Hazlitt up as a consequence of the publication of *Free Thoughts on Public Affairs*, and in the two years which precede that event, as in the circumstances of the publication itself (*ante*, p. 85) we see no sign of a patron.

If the poets can have had little to do with Sharp's patronage of Hazlitt, we cannot, I believe, acquit them quite so easily of a share in its 'termination'. The year 1808 was a critical one in English politics, marking as it did the outbreak of the Peninsular struggle and the considerable further shifting to the right of Liberal opinion which followed upon the death of Fox; and the strength of Wordsworth's political feelings at this juncture may be learned from his *Convention of Cintra* of the following year. His feelings regarding Hazlitt at the same date are, no doubt, sufficiently indicated by the passage reproduced in the text (*ante,* p. 129). During this visit to town, the poet, as we know (Knight, *Life,* I. 377), was seeing much of Sharp, and that he may have availed himself of the occasion to paint the character of Hazlitt in not very favourable colours would not, in view of other evidence we possess, appear altogether improbable to us. In July 1809, we find that Sharp is once more visiting the Lakes (Southey, *Letters,* II. 148), and in August we have a letter from Southey to Rickman (ibid., II. 160) which interests us: 'Walter Scott wrote to me to say that Canning had a great wish to serve me, and that he, Scott, had been commissioned by him to find out in what manner it might be done conformably to my inclinations. Sharp was here at the time. I told him of this, and he advised me to ask for the stewardship of the Derwentwater Estates, which will soon be vacated by death. Upon this I wrote to Scott, and also to [Charles Watkins] Wynn; both agreed that it would be the best thing possible for me, and both advised me, as a *sine qua non*, to make interest for Lord Lonsdale's countenance. Behold me thus place-hunting, in regular form. I got Sir George Beaumont to write to Lord Lonsdale.'

Hazlitt, in the meantime, so far from occupying himself in 'place-hunting', had retired to Winterslow to write his *History of English Philosophy* and *English Grammar* – both, evidently, fruits of his Richard Sharp-Horne Tooke association. The hundred pounds, the loan of which we find him contemplating as an aid in 'setting off' (*ante,* p. 126) was, no doubt, to have come from this patron: at least we know of nowhere else where he could have turned at this date for such a sum. It may or may not have been forthcoming; but what is pretty certain is that between this date and the following February the withdrawal of Sharp's favour had wrecked the *History of English Philosophy*. From this time forward there is no room in his career for a patron.

Crabb Robinson, we may note, was absent from England for the precise period we have regarded as probable for the duration of this relationship, and this circumstance accounts, no doubt, for his nowhere showing any knowledge of it. He did not himself meet Sharp until 1829, on the introduction of Wordsworth.

ON THE AUTHORSHIP OF A REVIEW OF
'CHRISTABEL'

PROCTER says of Hazlitt: 'He did not carry poisoned arrows into civil conflict. He was never dishonest. He never struck down the weak, nor trod on the prostrate. He was never treacherous, never tyrannical, never cruel.' We know of nothing to lead us to a reversal, or to a modification, of this judgement, except a single review which has been the subject of some controversy. Hazlitt, as we have seen, reviewed 'Christabel' for the *Examiner* of 2 June 1816. The question is, did he or did he not write another review of the poem in the form in which it appeared in the *Edinburgh Review* for the following September? Crabb Robinson, reading this review on its appearance (*ante*, p. 220) found it 'a very stupid review', and gave no indication of a belief that it was Hazlitt's until he was told so by Coleridge (*ante*, p. 245). But Coleridge, we do not forget, had found Hazlitt's hand in a review of 'Remorse' in the *Morning Chronicle* eight months before the latter began to contribute dramatic criticism to that journal (*ante*, p. 166).

The attribution of the authorship of this review to Hazlitt has formerly rested on a passage in the *Biographia Literaria*:

> In the *Edinburgh Review* it ['Christabel'] was assailed with a malignity and a spirit of personal hatred that ought to have injured only the work in which such a tirade was suffered to appear; and this review was generally attributed (whether rightly or wrongly I know not) to a man, who both in my presence and my absence has repeatedly pronounced it to be the finest poem in the language.

In conjunction with which we read a passage (p. 276) in Coleridge's *Life* by Gillman:

> The fragment ['Christabel'] had not long been published before he was informed that an individual had been selected (who was in truth a great admirer of his writings, and whose very life had been saved through the exertions of Coleridge and Mr Southey) to 'cut

up.' 'Christabel' in the *Edinburgh Review*. The subject being afterwards mentioned in conversation, the reviewer confessed that he
was the writer of the article, but observed, that as he wrote for the
Edinburgh Review, he was compelled to write in accordance with
the character and tone of that periodical. This confession took
place after he had been extolling the [*sic*] 'Christabel' as the
finest poem in the language, and ridiculing the public for their
want of taste and discrimination in not admiring it.

As Colonel Prideaux has observed, in discussion with Mr Thomas
Hutchinson (*Notes and Queries*, IX series, x, 388, &c.), 'one would
like to know more of this confession'. While Mr Dykes Campbell
(*Coleridge,* p. 226), regarded the attribution of this review as
'probably, though not certainly, correct', Mr Hutchinson, writing as
a 'reverential student' of Coleridge, has found it to bear 'in every
line the impress of William Hazlitt'. M. Jules Douady, on the other
hand, the latest and the best informed of Hazlitt's bibliographers,
has excluded it from the 'Liste Chronologique' of his works on the
ground that he can find in it 'no trace either of his style, his
manner, or his ideas' (p. 16).

A little more light than it has hitherto received will be thrown on
this question, I believe, if we take here some of the evidence which
exists as to Jeffrey's editorship of the *Edinburgh Review*. Lord Cockburn, in his *Life of Jeffrey* (I. 302), after adverting to his subject's
powers of 'direction and control', goes on: 'Inferior to these excellences, but still important, was his dexterity in revising the writings
of others. Without altering the general tone or character of the composition, he had great skill in leaving out defective ideas or words,
and in so aiding the original by lively or graceful touches, that
reasonable authors were surprised and charmed on seeing how much
better they looked than they thought they would.' In Lord
Brougham's *Autobiography* (I. 265) we read: 'As an instance of the
care he (Jeffrey) took in revising and preparing contributions, I remember an article on the memoirs of Prince Eugene was sent to
Jeffrey by Mill. Jeffrey gave it to Dr Ferrier of Manchester to revise;
and when he got it back from Dr Ferrier, he himself corrected it,
and added the moral reflections and the concluding observations.'
James Mill was not, apparently, among the reasonable authors who
submitted willingly to Jeffrey's improvements. His biographer says
(Bain, *Mill,* p. 110): 'Jeffrey's unceremonious hashing of articles was
very trying to his contributors, and lost him several that he was

unable to replace. Mill could not at this date [1810] afford to quarrel with his means of livelihood.' Neither, of course, could Hazlitt at any time. We appear to possess no record of his opinion, of the editorial 'improvement' to which his work was subject, but Forster, summarizing information at his disposal, says (*Landor*, II. 90): 'Jeffrey had inserted a sentence [in Hazlitt's review of *Imaginary Conversations*, March 1824], in which he had the impudence to declare that but for his discipline Wordsworth would never have written the "Loadamia"!' In general it may be asserted that no article of Hazlitt's in the *Edinburgh Review* is safe from these interpolations, and that, with a single exception, no review of poetry can be regarded in any serious sense as his at all.

To come from the general to the particular, Hazlitt's only article of importance on poetry during the fifteen years he worked for the *Edinburgh* is his notice of Shelley's posthumous *Poems* in July 1824. For this he seems to have been allowed a free hand, and, with the exception of a possible touch here and there from Jeffrey, the article is demonstrably his own. Otherwise the reviews of poetry with which his name is associated are limited to three, and not one of these is recognizable as his work by the time it makes its appearance in the magazine. Two out of three, indeed – the 'Rimini' of 1816, and the 'Sardanapalus' of 1822 – are subsequently claimed for Jeffrey, one by himself (*Contributions to the 'Edinburgh Review'*, 1844), the other by Lord Cockburn in the list of his contributions appended to the *Life*. Nevertheless, clear evidence is presented in the course of this book that Hazlitt considered himself to have had some hand in these reviews. (See *ante*, pp. 264, 320; p. 342.) The third review, that of 'Christabel', is not claimed for Jeffrey by Lord Cockburn, but that nothing decisive as to its authorship is to be inferred from this circumstance may be concluded when we find that Hazlitt's review of the *Biographia Literaria* (signed all over with his style) is so claimed. In each of these three cases – 'Rimini', 'Sardanapalus', 'Christabel' – we may perhaps conclude that the authorship is the same; namely, something of Hazlitt and a good deal of Jeffrey. In view of the latter's conception of the editorial function, which has been here illuminated, we should not be inclined, I think, to attach too much weight to his disclaimer at the end of his remarks on 'Christabel' in answer to Coleridge (*ante*, p. 245): 'I did not review it.'

What appears to be plain is that Coleridge *believed* this review to be Hazlitt's, and that the review as printed is not in its entirety, or

even substantially, his. We may read here its concluding passage,
which is the ground of Mr Hutchinson's charge that Hazlitt on this
occasion 'was guilty of the one unpardonable sin (to borrow a phrase
of Coleridge's) *against his own ghost* – against the convictions and
testimony of his own artistic conscience':

> Upon the whole, we look upon this publication ['Christabel:
> Kubla Khan. The Pains of Sleep'] as one of the most notable
> pieces of impertinence of which the press has lately been guilty;
> and one of the boldest experiments that has yet been made on the
> patience or understanding of the public. It is impossible, however,
> to dismiss it without a remark or two. The other productions of
> the Lake School have generally exhibited talents thrown away
> upon subjects so mean that no power of genius could ennoble
> them; or perverted and rendered useless by a false theory of
> poetical composition. But even in the worst of them, if we except
> the White Doe of Mr Wordsworth, and some of the laureate odes,
> there were always some gleams of feeling or of fancy. But the
> thing now before us, is utterly destitute of value. It exhibits from
> beginning to end not a ray of genius; and we defy any man to
> point out a passage of poetical merit in any of the three pieces it
> contains.

The reader who will compare this passage with Jeffrey's reviews of
'The White Doe' (*Contributions to the 'Edinburgh Review,* III.
270), will be left in no doubt, I think, that the views here expressed
are as clearly his as they are not Hazlitt's. The latter's opinion of
'Christabel', we conclude, is to be found in his *Examiner* review, in
the *Lectures on the English Poets,* and *The Spirit of the Age,* and
the course of his public criticism of Coleridge to be traced in the
writings in which in this book we have traced it.

HAZLITT AND LEIGH HUNT

EXIGENCIES of space in the text have excluded reference to an incident which may be read in continuation of that treated at pp. 318–25. In asserting that he was 'not responsible to' Shelley, Hazlitt, of course, was glancing at the somewhat well-known circumstance that Leigh Hunt was so responsible. Trelawny is probably within the facts, although not sympathetically so, when he says (*Records of Shelley, Byron, &c.,* Preface, 1858): 'Leigh Hunt often said that he was the dearest friend Shelley had; I believe he was the most costly. His theory was that between friends everything should be in common; he said you could not do your friend a greater favour than constitute him your brother, and that he could receive no greater pleasure than answering your drafts: as Leigh Hunt had an ailing wife and seven children, those drafts were frequent.' Shelley apparently paid off £1,400 of Hunt's debts in 1816, and made him other grants until his death (*Letters,* II. 531, 942; Dowden, *Life,* II. 62–3, 114). That this monetary side of their relationship contributed something to Hunt's sensitiveness where Shelley was in question I do not think we need doubt.

Hazlitt included Shelley generously in the *Select British Poets,* and he reviewed his posthumous *Poems* in the *Edinburgh Review* (*ante,* p. 370). In the opening instalment of his *Boswell Redivivus* (August 1826), he took what Hunt conceived to be a liberty with his deceased friend's name. The passage is as follows:

I then observed, I had been to the play with G[odwin] and his daughter, from the last of whom I had learnt something about Lord Byron's conversation. ... I asked her if it was true that Lord Byron was so poor a creature as F – – represented him? She at first misunderstood me, and said, nothing could be meaner than he was, and gave some instances of it. I said, that was not what I meant; that I could believe anything of that kind of him; that whatever he took in his head he would carry to extremes, regardless of every thing but the feeling of the moment; but that I could not conceive him to be in conversation, or in any other way, a flat and *common-place* person. 'Oh! no,' she said, 'he was not. F – – was hardly a fair judge. The other had not behaved well to him,

and whenever they met, F – – always began some kind of argument, and as Lord Byron could not argue, they made but a bad
piece of business of it, and it ended unsatisfactorily for all parties.'
I said, F – – was too apt to put people to their trumps, or to force
them upon doing not what *they* could do, but what he thought *he*
could do. He, however, not only gave his own opinion, but said,
Mr S – – could only just endure Lord Byron's company. This
seemed to me odd; for though he might be neither orator nor
philosopher, yet any thing he might say or only stammer out in
broken sentences, must be interesting: a glance, a gesture would
be full of meaning; or he would make one look about one like
the tree in Virgil, that expressed itself by groans. To this she
assented, and observed – 'At least S – – and myself found it so;
for we generally sat with him till morning. He was perhaps a
little moody and reserved at first; but by touching on certain
strings, he began to unbend, and gave the most extraordinary
account of his own feelings and adventures that could be
imagined. Besides, he was very handsome, and it was some satisfaction to look at a head at once so beautiful and expressive!' I
repeated what F – – told me, that when he and Lord Byron met
in Italy, they did not know one another; he himself from having
grown so thin, and Byron from having grown so fat, like a great
chubby school-boy – a circumstance which shocked his lordship
so much that he took to drinking vinegar at a great rate, that he
might recover the figure of the stripling God. I mentioned some
things that F – – had reported of Lord Byron; such as his saying,
'He never cared for any thing above a day', – which might be
merely in a fit of spleen, or from the spirit of contradiction, or to
avoid an imputation of *sentimentality?* 'Oh!' said Northcote, 'that
will never do, to take things literally that are uttered in a moment
of irritation. You do not express your own opinion, but one as
opposite as possible to that of the person that has provoked you.
You get as far from a person you have taken a pique against
as you can, just as you turn off the pavement to get out of the
way of a chimney-sweeper; but it is not to be supposed you prefer
walking in the mud, for all that! ... No; F – – would make Lord
Byron tributary to him, or would make him out to be nothing. I
wonder you admire him as you do, and compare him to the wits
of Charles II. It isn't writing verses or painting a picture – that,
as Sir Joshua used to say, is what every body else can do: but it is
the doing something more than any body else can do that entitles

the poet or the artist to distinction, or makes the work live. But these people shut themselves up in a little circle of their own, and fancy all the world are looking at them.'

We do not possess Hunt's letter of protest on the appearance of this passage in the *New Monthly,* but Thomas Campbell's prompt – and, as it would seem to us, excessive – repudiation of his contributor is preserved (Hunt, *Correspondence,* I. 251): 'Dear Hunt, – For this detestable passage in Hazlitt's paper I am, as I deserve to be, visited with much regret; but in as far as *you* are concerned, I have not the least consciousness of being to blame. There was, I must say, a culpable negligence in my not rejecting what relates to Mr S., although I declare that, to the best of my remembrance, my offence was no more than oversight; for I could not have deliberately admitted anything so against him, so meanly impertinent, if I had been thinking of what I was suffering to go to press. I know not what I was thinking about, but I suppose I was stupefied by the fatigue of looking over a long roll of articles. The oversight, nevertheless, I repeat, was blameable, and I am justly punished for it by finding myself made the cat's-paw of Hazlitt's calumny.

'As to you, my dear Hunt, I am truly indignant at being made the means of annoying you; but I assure you, *upon my honour,* that the initial F. completely blinded me, and that I should not have guessed you the person *impertinented,* unless I had been told so at second-hand from yourself. If I can say or write anything that can make you a shadow of satisfaction, I am willing to do so; but I suppose you will despise this devil's aspersions, even though they have come from the quarter from which they ought least to have come. Resolving to profit by this painful experience, and to keep a better look-out in future, I am, dear Hunt, with great regard, yours truly, T. CAMPBELL.' The result of the better look-out was that, as soon as he conveniently could, Campbell stopped the publication of the *Conversations* in the *New Monthly.* A minor *contretemps,* regarding a Dr Mudge of Plymouth, whose family conceived his memory to have been 'impertinented' in the sixth conversation, need hardly be gone into.

Hazlitt stood up to Hunt, as he always did: and the only concession we find when he reprints the *Conversations of Northcote* is the negative one that the F – – of the Magazine has become H – – in the book. It is in the light of such incidents as this one, no doubt, that their later relations are to be read.

INDEX

INDEX

443

litt at the Lambs, 200; her MS.
copy of 'Christabel', 212 n; with
Hazlitt at Leigh Hunt's, 237; in
Scotland for the divorce, 342 et
seq; on her husband's abilities,
344; on Sarah Walker, 126; John
Hunt on, 370; in Paris in 1824,
371; and her son, 370; and Hazlitt's last years, 411 n; on
Hazlitt's death, 419

Hazlitt, William, biographical summary:

Chap. I. 1778–95.—Birth and
parentage, 28; in Ireland and
America, 28, 29; first studies in
America affect his health, 30;
earliest memories, 30–2; at
Wem, 31; childish ambitions as
a painter, 32; early promise, 32,
36; attractiveness as a child, 33,
37; visit to Liverpool, 37 et seq;
religious and political training,
34, 36; first play, 36; earliest composition, 37; 'nervous disorders',
38, 39, 139; nocturnal rambles,
38, 50; 'First attempt to think'
(Project for a New Theory of
Civil and Criminal Legislation),
38, 40 and n, 42; enters Hackney
College to train for the Ministry,
39; pursues his own studies to
the detriment of the curriculum,
40 et seq; loses his vocation, 43,
46; begins Essay on the Principles
of Human Action, 45; breaks
down through overstudy, 45, 46,
46 n; returns to Wem, 46

Chap. II. 1796–8. — First
reading, 47 et seq; metaphysical
studies in London, 50; friendship
with Joseph Fawcett, 50 et seq;
reading at Wem (1796–8), 52 et
seq; twentieth birthday, 55;
attachment to the principles
of the French Revolution, 54;
meeting with Coleridge, 58 et

seq; visits Coleridge at Nether
Stowey, 64 et seq; meets Wordsworth, 65; accompanies Coleridge on a walk to Lynton, 66
et seq; attempts to complete
Essay on the Principles of
Human Action, 70; fails and
adopts the profession of painting,
70

Chap. III. 1799–1802.—Training under his brother, 72; at
Bury St. Edmunds, 71 et seq;
described by Crabb Robinson, 71;
at Mackintosh's lectures, 74;
abandons his political interests
for painting, 76; sees his first
Raphaels and Titians at the
Orleans Gallery in London, 76;
memories of painting, 77; sees a
Rembrandt at Burleigh House,
79; first picture, 78; patrons at
Liverpool and Manchester, 80;
portrait of his father in the
Royal Academy (1802), 81, 82;
friendship with Sheridan
Knowles, 82; visits the Louvre to
study, 84 et seq; sees Napoleon,
86; studies French and forms an
admiration for the French
Theatre, 86, 87

Chap. IV. 1803–7.—Return
from Paris and renewed acquaintance with Coleridge, 89;
invited to the Lakes, 92; Coleridge promises him assistance
with the Light of Nature Pursued, 91; on Wordsworth in
1802–3, 93; paints Coleridge and
Hartley Coleridge, 92, 98; paints
Wordsworth, 93 n; on Coleridge's fickleness in the company of Sir George Beaumont,
95, 145; described by Coleridge
to Thomas Wedgwood, 96; and
Coleridge's addiction to opium,
97; a dispute with Coleridge, 98;

EARLY
VICTORIAN NOVELISTS

DAVID CECIL

*

PELICAN A190

Lord David Cecil's study of the seven out-
standing novelists of the nineteenth century
is generally regarded not only as a major
work of literary criticism but also as a brilliant piece of English prose. His sympathetic
approach to the men and women whose
books he is considering does not prevent him
from applying his power of critical detach-
ment, and he can analyse their limitations as
well as their merits. So stimulating is this
process of appraisal that, whether one is
familiar with these novelists or out of touch
with them, Lord David Cecil's infectious
interest is likely to send readers back once
more to the spacious story-tellers of early
Victorian times. The opening essay examines
the general outlook and values of these seven
novelists, their range of interest, their creative energy and their significant limitations.
In the remaining seven chapters – on Dickens,
Thackeray, the Brontës, George Eliot, Trol-
lope and Mrs Gaskell – Lord David Cecil
goes on 'to illuminate those aesthetic aspects
of their novels which can still make them a
living delight to readers'.

CHARLES LAMB
AND ELIA

EDITED BY J. E. MORPURGO

*

PENGUIN 677

Charles Lamb was much more than Elia; as
well as being a wonderful humorist he was
a fine critic, a witty companion and a great
man. Coleridge said of him: 'His genius is
talent, and his talent is genius and his heart
is as whole and one as his head'. Thomas
Barnes said of him that he had written about
Shakespeare 'finer than anyone ever did in
the world', and Wordsworth summed up the
feelings of Lamb's many friends when he
wrote, 'Oh, he was good, if e'er a good man
lived'. In *Charles Lamb and Elia* Mr J. E.
Morpurgo has assembled much that is
familiar and much that is unfamiliar from
Lamb's writings; by careful arrangement
he has shown how the works were the off-
spring of the life – the letters and the essays
often the baby and the grown man of the
same idea. For the most part he has allowed Lamb to tell his own story, but with
his Introduction and his interpolated comments he has made this book at once a
selection from the works of one of the most
important writers of the Nineteenth Century and a biography of one of the most interesting of all literary personalities...

WILLIAM COBBETT

W. BARING PEMBERTON

*

PENGUIN 680

From whatever angle William Cobbett is regarded, whether as a reformer, author, polemical writer, Rural Rider, farmer or paterfamilias, a man is revealed for whom it is impossible not to feel genuine affection. If he was the grandest hater of his day and the last consummate master of prose invective, Cobbett was also one of the most sincere, warm-hearted and single-minded men who ever lived and wrote.

Born, as he was never tired of boasting, the son of a farmer and bred at the tail of the plough, Cobbett was every inch an English yeoman, in appearance, in manner, in character – 'the pattern John Bull of his century', was Carlyle's delineation. He hated cant and affectation, he abominated and distrusted cities (which he called 'wens'), bankers, stockjobbers, paper money and political economists; he adored all forms of sport, was perfectly at home in a cattle market or at a farmers' 'ordinary', and for one blow was ready to return half a dozen. Indeed his whole life from ploughboy to Member of Parliament was little more than a series of fights, and controversies, and personalities.

But of all objects worth fighting for, there was none closer to Cobbett's heart than the preservation of the rural England he had known in his boyhood and its bold independent peasantry, with their full bellies and neat Sunday coats. In his evergreen *Rural Rides* Cobbett has left not only an inimitable picture of a vanished countryside but a testament at once literary, economic and agrarian. Today, when agriculture is rightly coming to be recognised as one of Britain's principal industries, the life of this turbulent Peasant Champion and Philosopher acquires especial interest.

Mr Pemberton's new study is one of that growing number of books which has not previously appeared in any other form, but makes its first bow to the world as a *Penguin*.